Fromm

Far & Wide

A Weekly Guide to Canada's Best Travel Experiences

by Lucas Aykroyd,
Pamela Cuthbert, Jillian Dickens,
Chloë Ernst, Patricia Gajo,
EUR pstead, Hélèna Katz,
uin, and Julie Watson

WILEY

John Wiley & Sons Canada, Ltd.

TOP PICKS   ADVENTURE   CULTURE & HISTORY   NATURE'S GRANDEUR

CONTENTS

EVENTS & FESTIVALS   QUIRKY CANADA   REJUVENATE

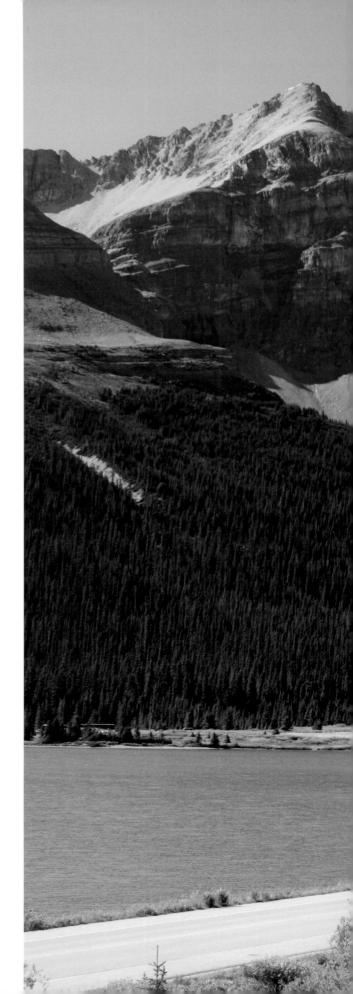

Published by:

John Wiley & Sons Canada, Ltd.
6045 Freemont Blvd.
Mississauga, ON L5R 4J3

Library and Archives Canada Cataloguing in Publication Data

Frommer's far & wide : a weekly guide to Canada's best travel experiences / Andrew Hempstead ... [et al.].

Includes index.
Issued also in an electronic format.
ISBN 978-1-118-09168-5

1. Canada--Guidebooks. I. Hempstead, Andrew II. Title: Far & wide. III. Title: Frommer's far and wide.

FC38.F76 2011   917.104'73   C2011-904244-4

Editor: Gene Shannon

Production Editor: Pamela Vokey

Editorial Assistants: Katie Wolsley, Jeremy Hanson-Finger

Photo Editor: Photo Affairs, Inc.

Cartographer: Lohnes + Wright

Cover and interior text design: Diana Sullada

Printer: Friesens Printing Ltd.

Front cover photo: © Latitudestock/Getty Images

Back cover photo (left): © Robert Postma/All Canada Photos

Back cover photo (middle): © bayoffundytourism.com

Back cover photo (right): © Kathy deWitt/Alamy/All Canada Photos

For information on our other products and services or to obtain technical support, please contact our Customer Care Department within the U.S. at 877/762-2974, outside the U.S. at 317/572-3993 or fax 317/572-4002.

Wiley also publishes its books in a variety of electronic formats. Some content that appears in print may not be available in electronic formats.

Manufactured in Canada

5 4 3 2 1 (FP) 15 14 13 12 11

How to use this book

We've organized this guide so that you can find not only the best that Canada has to offer, but also the best time to try each experience. It's built to fit your schedule—whenever you can get away, we can help you make the best destination choices.

our top picks

For each week, we choose one can't-miss experience and tell you everything you need to know about it—why it's great, how to do it, what to do while you're there, and what your next steps should be.

find your favourite

We've also provided six more top travel experiences for each week to suit the taste of every kind of traveller, from the adrenaline junkie to the person seeking maximum relaxation (and everyone in between). An index of each trip idea appears at the beginning of each month.

find out more

At the end of each entry we provide the best website for you to visit and learn more about each place, so that you can quickly turn your inspiration into reality.

maps

At the end of each chapter we show you where to find each experience, colour-coded by category.

Canadian moments, Canadian voices, and bonus selections

One of the great joys of travelling is learning more about the people and places you visit, and throughout the book we've provided entries that give you insight into Canada's history, its unique culture, and recommendations from some of the country's well-known personalities. Plus, we offer five more great suggestions for things to do that month.

our authors

The writers of this guide are among the premier travel writers in Canada, and bring the unique Frommer's combination of local expertise and independent opinion. Each entry is here because of their insight and experience—they live in these places and know the best that each one has to offer.

about the authors

LUCAS AYKROYD is a Vancouver-based writer whose work has appeared in *National Geographic Traveler*, *Arthur Frommer's Budget Travel*, *Westworld*, *Where Vancouver*, *Western Living*, and *The Georgia Straight*. He serves as a director on the B.C. board of the Travel Media Association of Canada. Above and beyond the travel beat, he covers the Olympic Games, World Hockey Championships, and National Hockey League for IIHF.com. He wrote the majority of the British Columbia entries for this book.

PAMELA CUTHBERT, author of *Frommer's Toronto*, is a food and travel writer and editor. Her work is published in *Maclean's*, *Saveur*, *The Edible City*, *Slow Food Almanac*, and elsewhere. She wrote the Ontario top pick entries for this book.

JILLIAN DICKENS has spent the last six years living, working, and playing in Nunavut. First as a news reporter, then in tourism development, now writing about the territory from her home base in Toronto. A tourism PR specialist moonlighting as a travel writer, Jillian has published her work in the *Globe and Mail*, *Mercedes-Benz Magazine*, and *Up! Magazine*. She is also a contributor to *Frommer's Canada* and wrote the Nunavut entries for this book.

During her Canadian travels **CHLOË ERNST** has skied on the slopes overlooking her Vancouver home, boated on Montréal's Lachine Canal, and learned P.E.I. fiddle tunes. A freelance journalist, she has written guidebooks, articles, and blog posts, including contributions to *Frommer's Best Hiking in British Columbia* and *Frommer's Vancouver & Victoria*. Chloë thanks those who shared their travel tips and vacation memories for this book. Read more about her journeys at www.chloeernst.com. She wrote the My Favourite Places, It Happened This Week, and Canadian Moments sections of this book.

PATRICIA GAJO was born and raised in Toronto, educated in Vancouver (where she majored in linguistics at the University of British Columbia), and now works and plays in Montréal. In between gigs as Montréal editor at *FASHION* magazine, lifestyle writer at Sid Lee (*The Montréal Buzz* for Tourisme Montréal), and content editor of Cadillac Fairview's nationwide the *Experience* eMagazine, Patricia also freelances as a travel writer and media consultant. Things she finds hard to resist include: champagne, foie gras, cashmere, and romantic comedies—preferably all at once. Visit her website at www.patriciagajo.com. She is the author of *Frommer's Montréal & Québec City* and wrote the Québec entries for this book.

ANDREW HEMPSTEAD has been a full-time travel writer for 20 years. He has authored and co-authored more than 60 guidebooks to all regions of Canada, as well as to Australia, New Zealand, and the South Pacific. Hempstead is also  co-owner of Summerthought Publishing, which produces non-fiction books about the Canadian Rockies. He lives in Banff, Alberta, with his wife and children. He is the author of *Frommer's Newfoundland & Labrador* and a contributor to *Frommer's Canada*; for this book he wrote entries covering Newfoundland and Labrador, Manitoba, Saskatchewan, Alberta, and eastern British Columbia.

HÉLÈNA KATZ is an award-winning travel writer and journalist. Her work has appeared in many publications including *Up Here*, *Explore*, the *Globe and Mail*, the *Montreal Gazette*, *Canadian Geographic*, *Homemakers*, and *Above & Beyond*. She is also the  author of four books: *The Mad Trapper*, *Gang Wars*, *Cold Cases*, and *Justice Miscarried: Inside Wrongful Convictions in Canada*. She was raised in Montréal but now calls the North home. She lives in Fort Smith, adjacent to Wood Buffalo National Park, with her partner, their two dogs, a cat, a llama, and the only alpaca herd in the Northwest Territories. Hélèna wrote the Yukon and Northwest Territories entries for this book.

DENIS SEGUIN is an award-winning freelance journalist and filmmaker based in Toronto. His writing has been published in magazines and newspapers around the world and on-line. He wrote many of the Ontario entries for this book.

JULIE V. WATSON is a prolific writer based in Prince Edward Island with 28 books and numerous articles to her credit. Her writing focuses on Canada's Maritime provinces, travel, food, lifestyles, seniors, and entrepreneur-  ship. Julie and her husband travel extensively in the family RV where Julie writes along the way. The award-winning writer shares her passion for writing, POD publishing, and scrapbooking through workshops across Canada, working with her son—Vancouver photographer John Watson. She is the author of *Frommer's Nova Scotia, New Brunswick & Prince Edward Island* and she wrote the entries on those provinces for this book.

advisory & disclaimer

Travel information can change quickly and unexpectedly, and we strongly advise you to confirm important details locally before travelling, including information on visas, health and safety, traffic and transport, accommodation, shopping, and eating out. We also encourage you to stay alert while travelling and to remain aware of your surroundings. Avoid civil disturbances, and keep a close eye on cameras, purses, wallets, and other valuables.

While we have endeavoured to ensure that the information contained within this guide is accurate and up-to-date at the time of publication, we make no representations or warranties with respect to the accuracy or completeness of the contents of this work and specifically disclaim all warranties, including without limitation warranties of fitness for a particular purpose. We accept no responsibility or liability for any inaccuracy or errors or omissions, or for any inconvenience, loss, damage, costs, or expenses of any nature whatsoever incurred or suffered by anyone as a result of any advice or information contained in this guide.

The inclusion of a company, organization, or website in this guide as a service provider and/or potential source of further information does not mean that we endorse them or the information they provide. Be aware that information provided through some websites may be unreliable and can change without notice. Neither the publisher nor author shall be liable for any damages arising herefrom.

how to contact us

In researching this book, we discovered many wonderful places—hotels, restaurants, shops, and more. We're sure you'll find others. Please tell us about them, so we can share the information with your fellow travellers in upcoming editions. If you were disappointed with a recommendation, we'd love to know that, too. Please write to:

Frommer's Far & Wide
John Wiley & Sons Canada, Ltd.
6045 Freemont Blvd.
Mississauga, ON L5R 4J3

travel resources at frommers.com

Frommer's travel resources don't end with this guide. Frommer's website, www.frommers.com, has travel information on more than 4,000 destinations. We update features regularly, giving you access to the most current trip-planning information and the best airfare, lodging, and car-rental bargains. You can also listen to podcasts, connect with other Frommers.com members through our active-reader forums, share your travel photos, read blogs from guidebook editors and fellow travellers, and much more.

JANUARY

Start the New Year Atop Eastern Canada's Highest Peak

The list of activities is endless at Québec's most popular ski resort

Montréalers are spoiled with world-class alpine skiing in their backyard, and they know it. About a two-hour drive northwest of the city, Québec's majestic Laurentian Mountains are blessed, on average, with 380 centimetres (149.6 inches) of snow each year, making the area an absolute mecca for skiers and snowboarders. (And if Mother Nature should hold back, the resort's state-of-the-art snow machines make some of the best fake white stuff around.) Of all the ski towns in the province, Mont-Tremblant is indisputably the biggest, if not the flashiest. And the fun doesn't stop at the end of your ski run—with a host of other outdoor sports, the famous après-ski, a culinary scene, luxurious spas, as well as bars and nightclubs for late-night partying, Mont-Tremblant draws both the stylish and the swift.

Start by hitting the slopes. With the highest peak in the Laurentians at 915 metres (3,002 feet), Mont-Tremblant boasts 95 trails spread out over four mountain faces. Accessible by 14 lifts, including an Express Gondola, once you've reached the summit, the vistas of surrounding villages and lakes will leave you breathless. There are lots of intermediate and advanced runs, and just under a dozen are considered for experts only. Newbies can perfect their skills on more than a dozen trails with a top-notch staff of instructors.

To get yourself acquainted with the area, there are free, daily, guided tours. Enquire at the summit's Grand Manitou for details, or download your "personal concierge" mobile application, available for Android and iPhone. Tremblant tends to be the trendiest of the local resorts, and so can be pricier than smaller hills in the Eastern Townships, or those closer to the city such as Mont Saint-Sauveur or Sainte-Adèle. Expect full-day lift ticket rates in the range of C$75 per adult, with ski rentals about C$45 a day, or snowboards around C$40 a day. Boarders will probably want to pay the extra C$13 for an Adrenalin Park Pass, offering access to 50 rail and jump modules in the South Park. Early risers can take advantage of First Tracks, taking the gondola at 7:45 a.m. to be the first to carve their way through virgin snow beginning at 8:00 a.m. (you'll pay an extra C$21 for the privilege). If you're not in the mood for the slopes, you can try snowshoeing, cross-country skiing, skating, snowmobiling, dogsledding, and even ice-climbing. To get the best deals, always ask about packages when booking your hotel.

And what's a ski trip without some proper après-ski? The same team that updated the British Columbia's world-renowned Whistler resort recently gave

Tremblant a multi-million dollar facelift, giving it cozy, Euro-style ambience. You can stay anywhere from a private condo to a luxury hotel, but the Fairmont Tremblant is the only one that allows you to ski right to the door of the hotel.

When not carving turns, you can roam the pedestrian village popping in and out of familiar retail stores like Burton, Roots, and Columbia, spread out among smaller boutiques. Fortify yourself with a BeaverTails Pastry (*Queues de Castor* in French), the name of the quintessential crepe-like pastry that's fried and loaded with your choice of sweet or savoury toppings. For a lengthier break, warm up to a locally brewed beer at Microbrewery La Diable or unwind at casual The Resto-Bar Le Shack, with its kitschy outdoor-indoor decor. Or, indulge at more upscale restaurant Aux Truffes where the six-course table d'hôte includes foie gras, an appetizer, main, cheese plate, and dessert for C$80. Somewhere in-between is the Bistro de la Forge—at the base of the ski lift—offering a fine view of the mountain and La Place Saint-Bernard.

For a little change of scenery, drive "downtown" to St-Jovite, a strip of restaurants (foodies should look for Le Cheval de Jade), boutiques, antique dealers, and bars. For tired muscles, relax with a little hydrotherapy at Spa Scandinave whose hot and cold waters, Finnish sauna, and massages (Swedish, hot stone, or Thai yoga) in a rustic environment invite you to reconnect with nature. Back at the resort, dance the night away at Le P'tit Caribou or Bar Café d'Époque, or catch a flick at the movie theatre on rue des Remparts.

Feeling lucky? The casino is open seven days a week until midnight, and until 3:00 a.m. on Friday and Saturday nights when there's live entertainment. An express gondola or shuttle from the South Side takes you to 500 slot machines, 16 gaming tables, and Texas hold 'em poker. Keep in mind that the gondola closes at 11:00 p.m. (7:00 p.m. on Sundays), so you may have to take the shuttle bus back depending how long your lucky streak lasts.

If you're not flying in directly to the Tremblant airport (Porter Airlines offers direct flights from Toronto and New York), don't forget that traffic along Highway 15 to and from Montréal can be bumper-to-bumper on Friday evenings and Sunday nights. To avoid weekend lineups (one situation where it's best not to do as the locals do), leave on a Thursday and come back Wednesday. You won't be at a loss for things to do. 🍁

Find out more at:
www.tourismemonttremblant.com/en

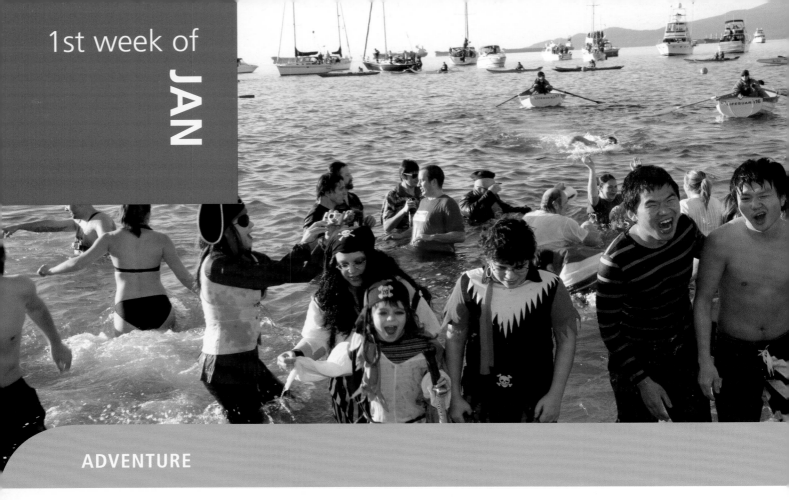

ADVENTURE

▲

Dive into the Polar Bear Swim at English Bay

After partying hearty on New Year's Eve, what better way to herald the new year's arrival than by throwing yourself into the frigid waters of Vancouver's English Bay? Well, it's all a matter of perspective. If you can

The wacky tradition of the Polar Bear Swim at English Bay dates back to 1920.

survive, based on 2011 figures, an air temperature of 2 degrees Celsius (36 degrees Fahrenheit) and a water temperature of 6 degrees Celsius (43 degrees Fahrenheit), buoyed by the whoops of more than 2,000 other friendly fellow crazies—many wearing

costumes ranging from Hawaiian wreathes to firefighters' gear—then . . . take the plunge!

The wacky tradition of the Polar Bear Swim at English Bay dates back to 1920. That's when Polar Bear Club founder Peter Pantages led about 10 swimmers into the ocean near the intersection of Denman and Davie streets. Today, the Pantages family still organizes the fun-filled event, along with sponsors like the Vancouver Board of Parks and Recreation, the *Province* newspaper, and 99.3 The Fox. To become a free club member, register before the 2:30 p.m. start on January 1.

Remember: don't spend too long in the bay, and have someone waiting with hot tea and blankets for you on the beach—surrounded by palm trees and high-rises. Whether you yell "Grrrr!" (bear-style) or "Brrrr!" (human-style) upon exiting the water is entirely up to you. ❦

www.vancouver.ca

Greet the New Year in Traditional Viennese Style

Christmas has *The Nutcracker*. New Year's has *The Waltz King*. The *Salute to Vienna* is a three-hour showcase of light classical pops that will fill your ears and dazzle your eyes with czardas, polkas, operatic outbursts, and of course a complete menu of waltzes from Johann Strauss Jr. and his peers.

Artistic directors Attila and Marion Glatz wanted to bring the Viennese tradition of the Das Neujahrskonzert der Wiener Philharmoniker (you can guess the translation) to North America. Their first concert, held in Toronto in 1995, was sold out. The series has since grown in popularity, expanding to 22 cities (including Montréal, Québec City, Hamilton, Calgary, Edmonton, and Vancouver). No wonder: as light and effervescent

as champagne, the concert puts the blue in the Danube —bringing together a range of outstanding international musical talent, paired with a full symphony orchestra to ring in the new year with aplomb and a bit of oompahpah. Strauss is the patron saint but you'll also hear excerpts from such contemporaries as Lehár, Kálmán, Offenbach, and Stolz. Past collaborators include conductors such as Klaus Arp, Daniel Beyer, and Mika Eichenholz and the Vienna City Ballet and the Hungarian National Ballet. Don't worry: you don't have to stay up late. This is a New Year's Day concert; the show begins at 2:30 p.m. at stately Roy Thomson Hall. Tickets start at C$65.◆
www.salutetovienna.com

Pay Your Respects to the Massive Trees of Cathedral Grove ▶

For some, a trip to Cathedral Grove might evoke images of the high-speed forest chase scene in *Return of the Jedi*. For others, this stand of giant old-growth Douglas firs on Vancouver Island is more like a natural answer to the basilicas of Notre Dame or St. Peter's. Regardless, it's well worth making a stop on Highway 4, just west of Qualicum Beach, in B.C.'s MacMillan Provincial Park.

New Year's Day marks the anniversary of a traumatic event in recent Cathedral Grove history. That day, in 1997, a huge windstorm ripped through the compact area toppling hundreds of trees, some up to 800 years old. However, as you wander along the well-sheltered trails and boardwalks in the park, you'll appreciate that, as nature documentaries say, "the cycle continues." Ferns, fungi, and moss blanket the fallen "nurse logs," which now nurture the ecosystem. And plenty of ancient firs—plus cedar, hemlock, and maple trees—still adorn Cathedral Grove. The tallest fir stands a jaw-dropping

76 metres (250 feet), with a trunk circumference of nine metres (30 feet). There's also an elevated viewing platform on the south side of the park.

Stay on the trails to help preserve the fragile habitat, and watch for wildlife—from woodpeckers to deer.◆
www.env.gov.bc.ca

EVENTS & FESTIVALS	QUIRKY CANADA

Saddle Up for Western Canada's Largest Arts Festival

Not every Alberta rodeo requires horses and steers—sometimes a rabbit is what you need.

The High Performance Rodeo is an arts festival, produced by Calgary's renowned One Yellow Rabbit theatre company, that transforms downtown Calgary with theatre, music, dance, and comedy performed by artists from around the world.

The four-week event is made up of nearly 100 performances that are impressive in their diversity—making it the largest event of its kind in Western Canada. One venue may be hosting a roundtable discussion on the role of arts in society, while across town an audience may be cowering as a troupe of homicidal Russian lesbians take to the stage. Seemingly immune to winter temperatures, spectators line the streets of Chinatown for a parade and converge on Olympic Plaza for an outdoor light and fire display. In the classy confines of Hotel Arts, well-coiffed patrons sample wine during Wine Stage, while homeless Calgarians are encouraged to show their artistic bent during This is My City. The one venue that brings everyone together is Laycraft Lounge, the festival's official watering hole, brimming with performers, audience members, and festival volunteers each night—the perfect venue to end each day's events.❦

www.hprodeo.ca

See What One Red Paper Clip Can Get You

On July 14, 2005, Canadian Kyle MacDonald posted a picture of a red paper clip on an on-line trading site and asked if anyone wanted to swap it for something better. Someone did, and MacDonald was soon the proud owner of a fish-shaped pen. Although it was a simple trade, MacDonald's ensuing transactions had the on-line world riveted.

Although MacDonald used the Internet to initiate trades, he made the deals in person, travelling to Vancouver to swap his paper clip for the pen, journeying all the way to Massachusetts for a camp stove, then back across the United States to trade the stove for a generator. By the end of 2005, he was the proud owner of a snowmobile, which he then traded in January 2006 for a delivery van—which was quickly swapped for a recording contract. The contract was traded to a budding musician for one year's rent on a house in Arizona. As the trades continued—and millions followed on-line—in July 2006, MacDonald traded a movie role for a neat two-story house at 503 Main Street in Kipling, Saskatchewan.

MacDonald has since donated the home to the Town of Kipling, also home to The World's Largest Red Paper Clip—a tourist attraction with a history like no other.❦

http://oneredpaperclip.blogspot.com

◀ Explore and Relax at an Eco-Resort in the Kootenay Mountains

Strap on your cross-country skis and kick off the new year by exploring the winter wonderland surrounding the eco-friendly Nipika Mountain Resort, set in a remote valley near British Columbia's Kootenay National Park.

The lodge itself is a true eco-resort, with power generated by the sun.

Nipika Mountain Resort is contracted by the provincial government to maintain 80 kilometres (50 miles) of cross-country trails, of which 50 kilometres (31 miles) are groomed. Accessible from the lodge grounds, the trail system offers something for visitors of all skill and fitness levels. Trails run along the Kootenay River, to the Natural Bridge formation, and through snow-covered trees. Skating on a cleared pond in front of the main lodge, snowshoeing through the forest, tobogganing on nearby Mount Skedmore, and soaking in the hot tub add to the charm of a winter visit. The lodge itself is a true eco-resort, with power generated by the sun and a small hydro plant, buildings and furniture constructed using lumber from trees killed by mountain pine beetles, and heating provided using dead wood. Sleeping up to eight people each, the resort's seven cabins are extremely spacious and have full en suite bathrooms and kitchens with wood-burning stoves. (Guests bring their own food.) Cabins are modern but were constructed in a very traditional manner—the logs were milled on-site, and construction is done with dovetail notching. ❧
www.nipika.com

It *happened* THIS WEEK:

Sir Sanford Fleming's Standard Time

"Between Halifax and Toronto, [the traveller] finds the railways employing no less than five different standards of time," wrote Sir Sandford Fleming. These varying time zones required that some regular travellers carry watches with up to six faces.

Until the 1880s, locals set their watches to noon when the sun was directly overhead. It meant the clock at Montréal's city hall struck noon 25 minutes before timepieces in Toronto.

As the railway sped up travel, varying local times created confusion for stationmasters and passengers —including Fleming, a chief engineer with the Canadian Pacific Railway. Fleming, whose weighty other achievements include designing the first Canadian postage stamp and founding the Royal Canadian Institute in Toronto, conceived of dividing the world into 24 time zones.

In October 1884, delegates from 25 countries met in Washington D.C. for the International Meridian Conference. Greenwich was voted as the prime meridian, and Fleming's proposal to standardize clocks was backed by U.S. President Chester A. Arthur. Three short months later, on January 1, 1885, the world switched over to standard time.

But not all regions adopted Greenwich as the meridian or smoothly transitioned to the new time zones. While Canada had used standardized time in the railways since 1883 and England since the 1840s, France held out on the meridian issue until 1911.

With standard time, clocks advance an hour for roughly every 15 degrees of longitude. Canada, which covers a quarter-width of the globe, employs six time zones. Four and a half hours separate Cape Spear on the easternmost coast and Boundary Peak on the Alaskan border in the west.

The year 1885 turned out to be a big one for Fleming. Later that year, the last spike of the Canadian Pacific Railway was hammered in at Craigellachie, British Columbia.

Volunteer to Help Pick Icewine Grapes

The unpredictable, nocturnal harvest is your chance to pitch in creating one of Canada's most famous products (and have fun doing it)

You'd better have your bags packed and waiting by the door. If you're planning to join the volunteer pickers who gather to harvest Niagara's precious icewine grapes, ready only when they're kissed with just the right amount of frost, the call usually comes at a moment's notice. And, most often in the middle of the night.

Icewine, one of the top-rated products of the Niagara winemaking region, is recognized as a luxury item the world over. It's made with grapes that are harvested when the temperature dips below −8 degrees Celsius (17.6 degrees Fahrenheit). The water in the fruit freezes, leaving an intensely sweet, concentrated bit of grape juice. It's that honeyed liquid gold that distinguishes the dessert wine and creates its unparalleled floral flavours. The process requires quick action—harvesting must take place before the grapes start to rot. With equal efficiency, the fruit, still frozen, is transported directly for pressing, then left for fermentation.

It's a fickle business. Some years, there's no icewine harvest. In others, such as 2010, the harvest is iffy. After a sodden stretch of rain and temperate weather into early January, the right conditions would seemingly never come. Then, the sun came out—and the temperature plummeted. Which is exactly why pickers take to the vines at the last minute.

Icewine harvesters are culled from neighbouring farms and vineyards, from communities of families and friends—and from willing volunteers who sign up for the privilege of picking all night, as most of the work is generally done in the dark. The best way to get on a list of prospective pickers is to pick a favourite winery, then contact the winery directly by e-mail or phone to offer your services. There are dozens to choose from, plus a wine trail—available on-line—to help with navigation, if the winery's not convenient to visit. Some of the wineries, especially the bigger ones, use mechanical harvesters now, but many still employ the tradition of harvesting by hand. A few that welcome inexperienced harvesters include the notable Henry of Pelham and the younger River Bend. Also, the annual Niagara Wine Festival, which takes place from mid-to-late January, offers a glimpse into the experience with the Discovery Pass, which includes a trial harvest of sorts. Visitors are invited to pick grapes—though just for fun, not to meet any official quotas.

The reality is that picking icewine grapes is bone-chilling work (hand warmers

are often given to volunteer pickers before they set out for the fields). It's also unglamorous. Just think, hours spent bent over vines or working on your knees. But there's something extraordinary about the experience and the conviviality of it all. Some spontaneous pickers recount tales of working under brilliant moonlight, others recall warm and welcome meals served at the end of each shift (shifts generally last about two hours). Relationships and friendships are formed. Food is enjoyed. Fires blaze, both indoors and outdoors. And, naturally, icewine is enjoyed. What's more, the more generous estates regularly send helpers home with a bottle for their efforts.

In Ontario, icewine is an historic creation, an adaptation of the centuries-old tradition of German *eisswein*. First launched in the 1980s by some enterprising vintners looking to make their mark on the world stage, the cool climate conditions and rows of European vinifera (especially the Riesling vines) proved a good match for making icewine—ultimately becoming the region's flagship product. Indeed, icewine helped launch what is now a rich and well-established winemaking region—Canada's biggest—as well as the country's own wine-designation label. The VQA (Vintners' Quality Assurance) guarantees grapes that are 100 per cent locally grown and, in the case of icewine, only naturally frozen.

Today, most wineries in Ontario make icewine. Riesling and Vidal are the most popular varietals, although it's also made using Pinot Gris and Chardonnay grapes—even red-wine grapes, such as Merlot and Cabernet Franc, though the jury's still out on these more recent offerings.

A couple of tips for anyone sampling icewine, which, at about C$50 per half-bottle, is a significant investment: it's best served well-chilled because of the high concentration of sugar. If you pair it with dessert, make sure the dish is less sweet than the wine—otherwise you end up with a sugar competition that can make the wine taste sour. So, pick fruit-based desserts (cobblers or pies are best), or choose creamy cheeses. There's something else: beware of icewine copycats. Made from artificially frozen grapes—think freezer wine, not icewine—these are flooding the market from Asia and elsewhere. A VQA label ensures you're making an authentic purchase.🍁

Find out more at:
www.winesofontario.org

ADVENTURE

CULTURE & HISTORY

Surf Big Winter Waves at Lawrencetown Beach

Word of an incoming January storm lights a fire of anticipation in Nova Scotia's winter surfers. These storms churn up the North Atlantic sending waves crashing towards the coast, as the cold temperatures (anywhere from 0 to 5 degrees Celsius—32 to 41 degrees Fahrenheit—in the water) help create the kind of waves that are the stuff of surfers' dreams. Lawrencetown Beach, on the Eastern Shore, is one of the province's most popular surf spots, attracting enthusiasts from all over the world who come to catch wild winter waves.

Just 30 minutes from Halifax, the beach is often alive with surfers as the morning sun breaks above the ocean horizon. With an ocean-floor topography that provides everything necessary to form sweet breaks and barrels (drumlins from the last Ice Age, long peninsulas, curving bays, and rugged mountains), Nova Scotia's beaches have been rated as high as 3.5 stars (out of four) when conditions are right. Lawrencetown can also experience exceptionally high surf conditions when the remnants of tropical storms and hurricanes make their way up the coast.

Even new surfers can get a rush on Nova Scotia's winter waves. Surf shops offer rental equipment and lessons, and local surfers are always willing to share helpful advice.🍁

www.lawrencetownbeach.com

Discover Bill Reid's Artwork

You probably already carry some of Bill Reid's artwork around with you. The half-Haida, half-American artist—born in Victoria on January 12, 1920—created the two iconic native sculptures depicted on the Canadian $20 bill. You can experience the power of Reid's legacy by viewing both of them in Vancouver.

Admire the late Reid's *The Spirit of Haida Gwaii: The Jade Canoe* in the entrance hall at Vancouver International Airport. (With its overflowing boatload of passengers like the *Bear* and the *Dogfish Woman*, some onlookers joke that the imposing green sculpture should be called *Economy Class*.)

Head to the recently expanded Museum of Anthropology at the University of British Columbia (UBC) to gaze awestruck at *Raven and the First Men*. Showcased in a rotunda, the huge yellow-cedar carving depicts mythological humans emerging from a clamshell under Raven's watchful eye.

Top off this visual feast at downtown Vancouver's Bill Reid Gallery of Northwest Coast Art, where you'll see how his style in gold and silver jewellery evolved. Also be sure to check out various works by contemporary First Nations artists whom Reid inspired. It's no wonder he earned the Order of Canada in 1986.🍁

www.billreidgallery.ca

Skate the Length of Winnipeg's Serpentine River Trail

Beginning in mid-January each year, Winnipeg's frozen Assiniboine River comes alive with fathers shooting pucks with their children, infants skating circles around novices, and couples of all ages holding hands as they glide along what's billed as the world's longest natural skating trail.

> ## Couples of all ages hold hands as they glide along what's billed as the world's longest natural skating trail.

The River Trail is actually two distinct paths—one is groomed for skating while the other is a cleared footpath designated for foot traffic, skiers, and snowshoers. The official length of the trail varies each year, but it's often eight kilometres (five miles) or more in length and—much to the delight of Winnipeggers—nearly always longer than Ottawa's beloved Rideau Canal Skateway (see p. 14). Operation is dependent entirely on the thickness of the river ice (it must be at least 25 centimetres/10 inches thick), but the trail is usually open between mid-January and mid-February. Seven official access points are signposted along the route, including The Forks Marina—the main downtown hub. At this historic attraction, site of the city's original settlement, a snow maze and curling rink add to the festive atmosphere, with weekends full of sleigh rides, face painting, and other wintery games adding to the appeal for families. For those who didn't bring their skates, rentals are available at The Forks Market.❦ **www.rivertrail.ca**

Canadian *moments*

Ice Roads Open

For some residents in Canada's North, it's the difference between paying C$9 or C$5 for a tomato. As rivers, lakes, and muskeg freeze over, locals have access to different stores—and possibly lower prices—hundreds of kilometres away.

In the 1950s, ex-Mountie John Denison started transforming trails into ice roads for motor vehicles.

"The first regular load of freight was mine, and a delegation from the Chamber of Commerce met me," said Denison to journalist Edith Iglauer in her book *Denison's Ice Road*. He spoke of trucking to Yellowknife on the Mackenzie Highway for the first time.

Today, the Northwest Territories has more than 1,400 kilometres (869.9 miles) of ice and winter roads, with Yukon and Nunavut adding more routes to the frozen highway map.

Eight lanes wide, the Tibbitt to Contwoyto Winter Road first opened in 1982. Crossing 600 kilometres (372.8 miles) of lakes and frozen muskeg, it's the world's longest. The mining road stretches into the north from Yellowknife, accessing tundra otherwise only reachable by air.

Each January, Nuna Logistics crews begin work on clearing snow, setting up camps, and measuring ice thickness. The route runs over nothing but water for 87 per cent of its distance. As the ice thickens through March, the mining road will see increasingly larger loads of mining equipment and supplies hauled north.

It's a slow-and-steady job, where trucks travel in convoys. The maximum speed limit is 25 kilometres (15.5 miles) per hour for loaded trucks and 10 kilometres (6 miles) per hour when approaching the portages. Drive too fast and the momentum can generate below-ice waves that break through a surface that's only inches thick.

Ice Road Truckers, a History Channel program, traced the perils on these winter-only ice roads.

"We've got one lake called 'Two-Movie Lake' because it takes two DVDs to cross it," writes ice-trucker Alex Debogorski in his autobiography *King of the Road*.

EVENTS & FESTIVALS

Cheer On Your Favourite Dog Sled Team

Dogsledding is a traditional mode of transportation involving a simple sled and a team of handsome canines. The International Dog Sled Championship of Canada gives you an inside look at all the action—as well as the beauty of Québec's countryside in its magical winter season.

Taking place over two days in January, the competition involves more than 100 teams and 2,500 dogs from five continents, attracting tens of thousands of visitors who come from all over the world—from Argentina to the Philippines.

Races follow the Daaquam River in the quaint village of Saint-Just-de-Bretenières (in the region of Chaudière-

Appalaches) and start at 8:00 a.m., with contestants leaving almost every two minutes. Teams compete in a wide range of different categories: number of dogs (one to ad infinitum); distance covered (from 7.7 to 37.8 kilometres, 4.8 to 23.5 miles); and activity type (from old-school sledding to skijoring, where a person on skis is pulled by one or more dogs). There are also women-only races.

Attendees can get in on the action by partaking in a dogsled ride for about C$8.

Dog owners, take note: you're permitted to bring your own dog onto the grounds, unless your dog is competing.

www.daaquam.org/english/menu.html

◀ Dance in the Snow at Igloofest

From the hipster folk who bring Montréal's Piknic Électronik in the summer (see p. 122) , comes Igloofest —a nine-day outdoor dance party stretched over three weekends in January (Friday, Saturday, and Sunday). Once you're grooving with thousands of your newfound friends, the biting sub-zero temps just might have you hungry for winter all year long.

The main dance floor heats up with both local and international DJs (such as MiniCoolBoyz from Italy or Eskmo from the United States) and mesmerizing lighting effects. On the periphery, there are vodka bars, marshmallow-roasting firepits, mulled wine and beer booths, and hot-dog stands. The high-energy event takes on a kind of wintry Woodstock atmosphere with plenty of space also for lounging around outdoor fireplaces when you need to rest your feet.

A new addition is the Virgin Mobile Igloo that concentrates on local DJ talent and can accommodate a maximum of 150 people. Expect lineups here at busy times, but once inside it can actually get quite steamy.

Last year almost 60,000 partygoers braved the cold along the Quai Jacques-Cartier in the Old Port, showing up in their hottest winter apparel—including ski gear, wacky moon boots, and funky one-piece suits. Tickets can be purchased on-site for about C\$12, but also on the Internet and in select boutiques. Tourism Montréal also offers packages with hotel, restaurant, and other goodies.❦

www.igloofest.ca

Take a Traditional Sleigh Ride at Ross Farms ▼

With the only sounds being a harness creaking, runners gliding through the snow, and the clip-clop of horses' hooves, a sleigh ride through wintry Ross Farm creates a deep appreciation for the slower pace of rural life in New Ross, Nova Scotia. A family or small group gets cozy in the box sleigh as you pass farm buildings, the mill, and duck ponds. Once your tour ends, hot drinks are served up in Rose Bank Cottage.

The teamster at the reins may regale you with history from the 1800s, but don't let his tales distract you from the horses. They're special. The Canadian is Canada's National Horse, an ancient breed whose ancestry is traced back to foundation stock brought to Nova Scotia between 1632 and 1635. The breed almost became extinct and is now an endangered domesticated species.

The horses are an example of one of the crucial roles of this living museum, namely preserving heritage breeds. Berkshire pigs, Cotswold and Southdown sheep, heritage breeds of poultry and cows all love company.

Costumed interpreters make visits to this heritage site enjoyable and informative. You might even get to milk a cow! Many hands-on activities encourage children to get better acquainted with the animals and teach them about farm chores or crafting items used around the farm. Check out the farm's Facebook page to see what's new in the barns, watch videos, and learn about planned activities.❦

museum.gov.ns.ca/rfm/en/home/default.aspx

Skate the Rideau Canal

Embrace winter by exploring the world's largest ice rink

It's one of those incomparable Canadian experiences: lacing up a pair of sharp skates and setting out for a long glide along the picturesque Rideau Canal, which cuts through the heart of downtown Ottawa. Known locally as the Skateway, it's acknowledged by Guinness World Records as the world's largest natural skating rink thanks to its combined width and length. (Winnipeg lays claim to the longest at 8.5 kilometres (5.3 miles), while the Rideau is 7.8 kilometres (4.8 miles) —or the equivalent of 90 Olympic-sized skating rinks.) The Rideau Canal is also a designated UNESCO World Heritage Site.

There are a handful of choice places where you can begin, but it's best for a first-timer to start at the top—meaning the foot of the Parliament Buildings. And to better catch all the sights, from the fairytale Fairmont Chateau Laurier hotel, to galleries and museums, and some of the prettiest parts of the old town, such as Confederation Square. (Though evenings are undeniably romantic, and the canal has been the site of many a marriage proposal, it's advisable to skate in the daylight.) Since the rink generally opens in mid-to-late January, picking a date late in the month means getting in before the crowds descend in February for the nearly month-long annual Winterlude festival.

One of the best things about skating the Rideau is the chance to meander. Far removed from the monotonous circles of most rinks, the Rideau snakes along a wide and pretty path—past residential neighbourhoods and office towers, under snow-covered treetops and historic bridges, ultimately reaching the gathering place at Dows Lake. Here, there's an outdoor art gallery, a pavilion with restaurants, and change rooms.

Getting started is easy, thanks to heated huts— rather grandly called "chalets"—posted at five locales along the route. Nearby skate rentals are convenient, but run to about C$30/day. There are also sleds for rent, a great way to get pre-skating youngsters out on the ice.

To maintain your stamina, tucking into a "beaver tail" is a must. These whimsically named pieces of fried dough-nut earned their moniker for their flat, fan-like shape—much like the iconic animal's rear appendage. The BeaverTails chain, which has a few outlets en route, is about as good as it gets. Cinnamon and maple syrup are favourite toppings. Along with a cup of instant, powdered hot chocolate, it's the perfect quick refuel.

The Rideau draws more than one million skaters each year, many of them locals who use the canal as a wintertime playground or an alternate route to work. While weekdays can be quiet, especially while most people are at work, weekends tend to bring out the whole family.

The rink is routinely patrolled, monitored, and measured for safety concerns. There's a team of teams running the operation: 50 skate patrollers, plus several "ice experts" (think researchers, scientists, and managers) who analyze the ice, assessing its strength and flaws. There's also a drilling team that uses an ice auger to extract core samples for analysis. Then, there are the snow-clearing crews.

Conditions and closures are posted twice daily at www.canadascapital.gc.ca.

The Skateway is part of the historic Rideau Canal, which runs more than 200 kilometres (124 miles) and connects Ottawa (on the Ottawa River) with Kingston (on Lake Ontario). The canal opened in 1832 when Upper Canada needed an independent trade route because conflict in the bordering United States was brewing.

Over the years, the experience of skating the canal has changed. Since it first took form in 1971 as a small stretch of ice cleared in front of the National Arts Centre, there has been a gradual encroachment of theme-park touches. Many parts of the canal are now decorated with music shows, crafts and events, fast food, and other conveniences that can annoy those looking to enjoy the serenity of the experience. Then again, there's always the option of just skating by . . .

When you're finally ready to leave your blades behind, check out some of the many surrounding sites the nation's capital has to offer. A walk around the Canadian War Museum, the extraordinary and controversial museum dedicated to exploring the realities of war, is a sobering stroll. If you're still in the mood for battle, join the public galleries in the House of Commons, if the House is sitting. Our politicians are not afraid of a good verbal scuffle. The National Arts Centre is also nearby. So, too, is the Canadian Museum of Civilization, and the paintings at the National Gallery of Canada. When you're done, strap your blades on again and head homeward.✽

Find out more at:
www.canadascapital.gc.ca

ADVENTURE

▲
Try Winter Scuba Diving in Powell River

Are 1970s horror movies such as *Jaws*, *Orca*, and *Tentacles* guilty pleasures? Lose the guilt and enjoy a thrilling encounter with exotic Pacific Ocean creatures through scuba diving in Powell River, British Columbia. The Sunshine Coast's northernmost city, located 145 kilometres (90 miles) from Vancouver, isn't an obvious vacation spot in mid-January—when the average high temperature only hits 5 degrees Celsius (40 degrees Fahrenheit), also the average water temperature at this time. But chilly weather means less algae bloom, and better water visibility. Just make sure to don a dry suit with thermal protection for warmth.

You can see incredible things with viewing distances of up to 46 metres (150 feet). Try the famous "Emerald Princess" shore dive at Saltery Bay Provincial Park. It features a submerged bronze mermaid statue surrounded by octopi, including the ominous giant pacific octopus, sponges, lingcod, and sea cucumbers. Or, dive around the Malahat, a wrecked World War I-era schooner lying just off the world's biggest floating breakwater next to Powell River's historic townsite. From wolf eels to copper rockfish, more deliciously eerie sights await. And great boat dives abound off nearby Texada Island.

Visit Alpha Dive and Kayak, Powell River's full-service dive shop, to charter a boat, take lessons, or get your scuba gear. It's certified by Scuba Diving International. Jacques Cousteau would approve. ❧
www.divepowellriver.com

CULTURE & HISTORY

Glimpse Prehistoric Hunting Techniques at Head-Smashed-In Buffalo Jump

Buffalo jumps, an exceptionally sophisticated hunting technique employed by indigenous prairie dwellers at least 5,700 years ago, have been discovered across the North American plains. But the largest and best-preserved is Head-Smashed-In, located in the southern foothills of Alberta.

The people of the plains depended almost entirely on bison for their survival and the most successful method for killing these shaggy beasts was to drive entire herds over a cliff face. The topography of this region was ideal for such a jump, with a large basin to the west where bison grazed. They were herded along carefully constructed stone cairns that led to a precipice, where the stampeding bison plunged to their deaths. At Head-Smashed-In Interpretive Centre, disguised in the natural topography of the landscape, visitors can walk out along the top of the jump site, then view interesting and informative exhibits explaining the traditional way of life that existed on the prairies for many thousands of years before the arrival of the Europeans. Round out your visit with a bison burger at the in-house café. ❧
www.head-smashed-in.com

Enjoy Long Nights in Canada's Northernmost Community

Congratulations for making it to Grise Fiord, Canada's northernmost community. You've travelled a long way—3,462 kilometres (2,151 miles) from Ottawa, with an overnight in Resolute Bay. You may have encountered some storms, common in the Arctic during the winter, setting you back another day or more. You've made it through the last leg of the flight, when the Twin Otter heads directly towards the fiord-face before making a 180-degree turn at the last minute, landing safely on the runway. It's a trip relatively few people have made.

You'll finally be able to let go of time, since all hours of the day are basically the same.

The community of 140 people sits on Nunavut's southern Ellesmere Island, 1,544 kilometres (959 miles) from the North Pole. It's January, and you're here to experience life in 24-hour darkness—an ideal platform to watch the eerie green glow of the northern lights dancing through the sky at any time, day or night. You'll finally be able to let go of time, since all hours of the day are basically the same. Looking up at the crisp, star-filled sky at 3:00 p.m. in the middle of the day is a wild, unmatched feeling. Night photography takes on a new meaning too, and you can create stunning images of the frozen landscape, framed with dramatic mountains and rolling tundra. And yes, it's cold. Very cold. Temperatures can dive deeper than –50 degrees Celsius (–58 degrees Fahrenheit), and the average high is –30 degrees Celsius (–22 degrees Fahrenheit) in January. But with a trusty Canada Goose jacket and pants, and the right layers, spending time outside can be quite cozy. Just remember to cover all surfaces, because frostbite sets in quickly.

www.nunavuttourism.com

Loreena McKennitt's *favourite* PLACE

For Celtic singer Loreena McKennitt, it's the journey to Salt Spring Island, B.C., that recalibrates visitors to the island's pace.

"Unless you take one of the little float planes, you work up to the arrival by taking the boat over from Victoria," says McKennitt, who has sold more than 14 million albums worldwide and is a Member of the Order of Canada.

"You're able to approach the whole island as you would a modality of life. It is slower; it is more organic; it's more intimate."

McKennitt's mother lived on the north-of-Victoria island, which she describes as not-too-small and not-too-large.

The Manitoba-born musician also appreciates the diversity of the island's residents.

"Some were born and raised there—they were part of an agricultural base there that was either in apple production or sheep farming. But then you get a professional artistic community of writers, filmmakers, musicians."

Salt Spring (where local debates pit the two-word name against Saltspring) is also home to Canadian artists, including Randy Bachman and Robert Bateman.

Although McKennitt recommends the summer farmers' market and old-fashioned fall fair, she doesn't have a favourite season for visiting the island.

"It's great to go cycling, it's great to go sailing. There are wonderful musical events," she says. The Tree House Cafe, for example, has worthwhile live music on its outdoor patio in Salt Spring's largest town, Ganges.

But more than anything it's the slower pace of life that makes the island so truly special for McKennitt.

"In order to enjoy its riches you need to decompress, to recalibrate before you can get into what that environment so uniquely offers."

EVENTS & FESTIVALS

▲
Get Your Heart Pumping with B.C. Snowshoe-Racing

Although we're still awaiting the first scientifically verified Canadian sighting of the yeti (or even his hairy B.C. cousin, the sasquatch), The Yeti Mountain Snowshoe Series is very real—and very fun. These snowshoe races, currently held on Vancouver's North Shore Mountains and Vancouver Island's Mount Washington, enable cardio athletes to enjoy a challenging workout incorporating different disciplines. The events have become increasingly popular since 2001, when Canada's first mountain snowshoe series took place.

Races are classified as Sport at five kilometres (3.1 miles) or Enduro at 10 kilometres (6.2 miles). Strap on your running-specific snowshoe—bring your own or rent from organizers—and breathe clouds of steam as you crunch your way along hilly, flag-marked trails surrounded by white-crusted pines and firs. To increase the cross-training benefit, try a Winter Duathlon, which includes cross-country skiing. Weekly drop-in clinics are staged at Cypress Mountain so you can build your technique and sweat with fellow snowshoe enthusiasts. Even elite athletes, such as Ironman triathlon champ Peter Reid, are getting in on the action.

The season runs into April, so you can get your yeti on repeatedly. Alternately, it's fun to volunteer (from the sidelines), staffing checkpoints or handing out post-race snacks and drinks to racers. There's nothing abominable about these snowmen.🍁
www.theyeti.ca

Snack on Beaver Tails

Skating Ottawa's Rideau Canal is one of the quintessential Canadian experiences. And one of the quintessential Rideau skating experiences is the "beaver tail" (the name is even trademarked). While you can find them for sale all around Ottawa, it's the kind of thing one should indulge in only after skating a few kilometres. If ordering in French, the term is *queues de castor*.

For those unfamiliar with the beaver, its tail is wide and flat. Hence, the name for what is essentially a flat piece of deep-fried dough topped with butter and slathered with your choice of calorific toppings. Two classics are maple butter and cinnamon and sugar. Be sure to ask for plenty of napkins. These are messy pastries, especially if you opt for the chocolate hazelnut spread, which tends to freeze to the cheeks. Then again, you could try skating at night when the lighted Skateway is at its most romantic, and no one but your companion can see your cheeks. Caution: if you order a hot chocolate to wash down your sweet treat, the sugar rush may be overwhelming.

No wonder U.S. President Barack Obama made this the must-have treat for the First Daughters on his inaugural trip to the nation's capital.❄

www.beavertailsinc.com

Dine Out at a Discount during Montréal's "Happening Gourmand"▾

A post-Christmas feast coma, where you swear off hearty foods and promise to go to the gym, lasts about a week. Come the new year, your appetite should be back. Montréalers then look forward to the Happening Gourmand, happening the last three weeks of January.

Akin to New York City's Restaurant Week, only smaller and wrapped in Old World charm and ambience, a collection of eight restaurants in the picturesque neighbourhood of Old Montréal invite guests in from the cold with tempting set menus, called *prix fixe* or *table d'hôte*. A three-course meal at these fine-dining restaurants will typically be under C$30, generally 30 or 40 per cent less than what you'd normally pay. All owned by the prolific Antonopoulos family (who also own the string of boutique hotels attached to these dining establishments), this food fest allows you to discover each restaurant's different personality, style, and price point. The list includes Galianos, Narcisse Bistro & Bar à Vin, Méchant Boeuf Bar & Brasserie, Modavie Restaurant, Vieux-Port Steakhouse, Suite 701, Aix Cuisine du Terroir, and Verses Restaurant.

Since locals treat the event as a good excuse to beat the post-holiday blues, reservations are highly recommended.❄

www.happeninggourmand.com

Celebrate Chinese New Year in Vancouver and Victoria

Canada's largest Asian community shows its colours

You may or may not believe in the mystical cycles of the Chinese zodiac. But you can always count on a spectacular display of pageantry in Vancouver and Victoria when Chinese New Year arrives, whether it's the Year of the Dragon (2012), Snake (2013), or Horse (2014). Colourful parades, martial arts demonstrations, tea tastings, storytelling sessions, and more add up to the most flamboyant celebration of Asian culture you'll find anywhere in Canada.

The flagship event is the annual Chinese New Year Parade in Vancouver's Chinatown, drawing upwards of 50,000 spectators annually. This is the biggest Chinatown in Canada, dating to the late 19th century.

Choreographed lion dancers and exploding firecrackers deliver excitement along the route, which runs about 1.2 kilometres (0.75 miles), starting at the Millennium Gate on Pender Street. Among the 4,000 parade-marchers, you'll find local merchants and Canadian politicians handing out "lucky money" in traditional red envelopes. Cries of *Gung Hay Fat Choy* ("May you become prosperous" in Cantonese) naturally abound. Also watch for Chinese cultural societies toting banners, the Vancouver Police Department's precision motorcycle team, marching bands pumping out pop, rock, and jazz, and many other performers. It's great fun for the kids—though it can be a little overwhelming for little ones, especially the first time.

Chinatown's delights don't stop at the parade. Head over to the Dr. Sun Yat-Sen Classical Chinese Garden, which hosts a cultural fair for families on parade day. There, calligraphy, drumming, storytelling, and lion-dancing for kids spice up the mix. The elegant Ming Dynasty-style garden, named after the father of modern China, is also worth revisiting at a more tranquil time. Weeping willows and stone lanterns reflect gracefully in jade-green, ornamental pools. It's all meant to represent the balance between yin and yang.

On Keefer and Pender streets, Asian housewares, knick-knacks, and DVDs abound in stores plastered with Chinese signage. You can also peruse the tea shops and food sellers whose offerings include dried scallops, barbecued duck, pig snouts, and innumerable herbs, or grab some dim sum at an authentic Cantonese restaurant. Recently, Vancouver's Chinatown has been revitalized by the addition of some new, hipper eateries, such as Bao Bei, a streamlined "Chinese brasserie" that Air Canada's *enRoute* magazine hailed as one of Canada's 10 best new restaurants in 2010. Try the *shao bing* sandwich (braised pork butt on sesame flatbread) with a side of stir-fried king pea tips in garlic.

Beyond downtown, a visit to the Vancouver suburb of Richmond is another Chinese New Year's must. Just a 20-something minute trip via the Canada Line (the rapid transit line train), Richmond's population is 60 per cent Asian—including many immigrants who came from Hong Kong before the 1997 handover to China—and a more recent wave of Mandarin-speaking arrivals. So the new lunar year means one big party in the Golden Village, a cheerfully chaotic four-block radius adjoining No. 3 Road. Three big Asian-themed malls, all within walking distance of one another, pack in shoppers with special festivities. There, you can watch a huge golden dragon dance at Parker Place organized by local Chinese radio stations. Aberdeen Centre, famed for its indoor Bellagio-style fountain shows and for being home to The Daiso (a Japanese emporium where nearly everything costs just C$2), sells crystals, jade carvings, and "lucky fruit" (such as oranges and tangerines) at its annual Chinese New Year Flower & Gift Fair. At Yaohan Centre, kung fu experts strut their stuff, while lion-dancing and traditional songs enliven the mall. If you're hungry after all this activity, not to worry. Centrally located Alexandra Road, nicknamed "Food Street," features a whopping 200-something Asian restaurants. Taiwanese bubble tea, Thai curry, Vietnamese pho soup . . . just take your pick.

A ferry ride away across the Strait of Georgia,

Victoria's equally worth visiting for Chinese New Year celebrations. Its Chinatown is Canada's oldest, and gained cinematic recognition for a motorcycle chase filmed in Fan Tan Alley—Canada's narrowest street—in 1990's *Bird on a Wire* (with Mel Gibson and Goldie Hawn). The lion dance beneath the Gate of Harmonious Interest at Chinatown's entrance is only slightly more orderly. Two stone lions, donated by Victoria's Chinese sister city of Suzhou, flank the gate. Along Fisgard Street, burgeoning with neon signs and red lanterns, pop into food shops hawking everything from bok choy to pork tongue, and discover how Chinese restaurants tweak their menus for the new year, adding items that portend good luck or wealth. One popular establishment is Don Mee Seafood Restaurant—in business since the 1920s and noted for serving Cantonese and Szechuan seafood dishes amidst a calm green decor. Just around the corner, on Government Street, sample herbal teas with names like "Philosopher's Brew" and "Ruby Pagoda" at Silk Road, a retail store and spa honouring the ancient Chinese tea tradition with striking modern flair.

The way non-Chinese British Columbians embrace new year celebrations reflects how far the Chinese community has come since the first immigrants arrived during the 1858 gold rush. Good fortune, indeed.✺

Find out more at:

www.vancouver-chinatown.com

ADVENTURE

◀ Take Ice-Climbing Lessons in the Canadian Rockies

While most of the focus in late January at Lake Louise is on an ice-carving festival, more adventurous visitors make their way to the "Back of the Lake," a frozen waterfall that's one of the best places in the Canadian Rockies to take your first steps as an ice climber.

For those new to the sport of ice climbing, the sensible approach is to take a course with a local guiding company such as Yamnuska, where the two-day basic ice course is the most popular option. The first day is spent learning about climbing techniques, safety skills, and belaying systems. But it isn't until the second day that the actual thrill of climbing begins, with guides watching students take their first exhilarating steps up a frozen wall of ice. Add a third day of instruction to the adventure and you'll be able to add a multi-pitch climb to your resumé in no time.

Feeling up to more of a challenge? Around one hour's drive north from Lake Louise along the Icefields Parkway is the spectacular Weeping Wall, comprising over 20 named routes up a maze of frozen waterfalls. Even if you're not up to conquering the Weeping Wall, it's worth the drive to watch others grunting up what many regard as Canada's premier ice-climbing destination.❧

www.yamnuska.com

5 faves

Winnipeg's Royal Canadian Mint

Canada's original mint, in Ottawa, now produces only commemorative coins, while the Winnipeg facility, which opened in 1976, produces all of Canada's regular coins, as well as currency for countries worldwide. The process of making money is mind-boggling. The tour offered here will prove it to you.

Celebrate Robbie Burns Day in Halifax

Famous for penning the New Year's classic "Auld Lang Syne," and coining phrases like "The best laid schemes o' Mice an' Men," Scottish bard Robbie Burns still stirs folks to celebrate more than 250 years after his birth in 1759. Few places mark January 25 with as much fervour as Halifax, where two types of Robbie Burns celebrations prevail.

The first, serious about heritage, formally recognizes Scotland's most famous poet with great pomp and adherence to traditional pageantry. The second sees it as reason for a rousing pub crawl to one or more of Halifax's rollicking favourites: The Split Crow Pub, The Loose Cannon Scottish Public House, and Stayner's Wharf are a few of the most popular. No matter which camp you fall into, Nova Scotia (a.k.a. New Scotland) is the place to be. At the more traditional gatherings the haggis is paraded in with bagpipes before Burns's "Address to a Haggis" begins a traditional meal of cock-a-leekie soup, bashed neeps (turnips), and chappit tatties (mashed potatoes). The bard's poems are read, songs are sung, and a wee dram of single-malt Scotch toasts the life, works, and spirit of this son of a peasant farmer. For more authentically Scottish experiences, check out the city's entertainment listings or the Federation of Scottish Clans in Nova Scotia. ❦
www.igc2007.ca

Go Eagle-Watching in Nova Scotia

The largest colony of wintering eagles in eastern North America is cause for celebration in Sheffield Mills, Nova Scotia. For more than 20 years, folks here have invited visitors to come observe and photograph some 500 eagles in their natural habitat. The annual Sheffield Mills Eagle Watch takes place on the last two weekends in January and the first weekend in February, attracting thousands who line the fields around the hamlet—camera and binoculars in hand. What a sight it is to see eagles soaring over snow-covered fields, settled on branches of the leafless trees, or descending to the ground to enjoy a chicken dinner provided by their two-legged admirers. Indeed, the best time to get a close look at both young and mature eagles is in the morning at the feeding site. The regal white-headed birds are the main act, but the community itself rounds out the experience. Hospitable citizens welcome visitors to the Community Hall for pancakes and sausages or a cinnamon bun breakfast, later serving homemade bread and baked beans. They also provide a map showing the best viewing areas and tips for optimal viewing. Live entertainment and educational displays round out a grand winter day. ❦
www.eaglens.ca

Haida Gwaii Cape Fife hike

It's not every day you get to travel to the birthplace of humans (according to Haida mythology). This amazing, multi-day hike travels through old-growth forest, wet-land, and endless beaches of Naikoon Provincial Park, starting and ending at the 109-metre (357.6-foot) basalt columns of Tow Hill.

Québec City's Hôtel du Parlement

Since 1968, what the Québécois call their "National Assembly" has occupied this imposing Second-Empire château constructed in 1886. Twenty-two bronze statues of some of the most prominent figures in the province's history grace the facade. Inside, highlights include the Assembly Chamber and the Legislative Council Chamber.

Camp in a Yurt

Normally only the hardiest of outdoor lovers camp during the icy winter months, but in a yurt—a semi-permanent, canvas-covered shelter mounted on a wooden deck with electric heat and bunk beds—you can suddenly enjoy nature by day and still be cozy at night. Twelve Ontario provincial parks offer this kind of winter camping.

Check out roof-grazing goats

The Old Country Market in Coombs, B.C., has an unorth-odox take on the "green roof" concept. Several goats spend the day calmly munching on the market's sod roof while, below, shoppers browse international foods, baked goods, and ice cream.

EVENTS & FESTIVALS

Embrace the Spirit of the Mountains at the Banff/Lake Louise Winter Festival

For almost 100 years, the Banff/Lake Louise Winter Festival has been setting the standard for winter fun—for both competitors and spectators alike—in these two gorgeous mountain towns.

The highlight of the 10-day festival is Ice Magic at Lake Louise, in which teams of professional ice carvers from around the world must create a themed work of art. By the end of the allotted time, as the finishing touches are made to the icy masterpieces with chisels and hairdryers, the incredible skill and creativity of the carvers become clear. Associated with the main event are a speed-carving exhibition, a Little Chippers Festival for children, and for adults—an outdoor Ice Bar.

One of the more energetic Winter Festival events is the Lake Louise to Banff Loppet & Relay, a cross-country skiing team relay race over a challenging 71-kilometre

The highlight of the festival is Ice Magic.

(44-mile) course that links the two towns. Even if you're not competing, the starting stretch across frozen Lake Louise is a spectacle, while downtown Banff's Central Park makes for a compelling finish. Another longstanding festival event is the Mountain Madness Relay, which combines downhill skiing, cross-country skiing, and skating to create a one-of-a-kind race that begins from the top of Mount Norquay and ends in downtown Banff.🍁
www.banfflakelouise.com

◀ Go Underground in Moose Jaw

The links with Al Capone, America's best known gangster, are cloaked in innuendo. But the Tunnels of Moose Jaw are an interesting and unique attraction—regardless of whether Capone was here or not. Underground tours run year-round, but visiting this Saskatchewan prairie town on the anniversary of Capone's death (January 25) makes it just a little more sinister.

A century ago, many of Moose Jaw's downtown buildings were heated by steam, tunnels linking their basements for ease of access for engineers and workmen. Meanwhile, prohibition ended in Saskatchewan nearly 10 years before most places in the United States, which meant border cities like Moose Jaw were ideal places for bootlegging. (Rumour has it Capone used the tunnels for selling liquor.) The tunnels in themselves are interesting, brought to life through two 50-minute interactive tours, each themed on an aspect of Moose Jaw's history. The guides immerse themselves in character, and are assisted by multimedia presentations, animatronics, and other special effects. The adult-themed Chicago Connection tour has you arriving in Moose Jaw to buy illicit booze from the Capone organization, while the alternate performance (preferred by families with younger children) is Passage to Fortune, focusing on the theme of Chinese immigrants who set up living quarters in the tunnels during the prohibition era.❦
www.tunnelsofmoosejaw.com

Try Specialty Coffees from Victoria's Barista Champ ▶

"For me, tasting a new coffee is incredibly exciting," says Rob Kettner, winner of the 2010 Canadian Barista Championship. Fernwood Coffee Company's savvy java-slinger, who practises his art on a quiet side street near Victoria's Royal Athletic Park outdoor stadium, manages to inject excitement and style into all his savoury brews. Sipping a cup or two in this cozy neighbourhood establishment is a fantastic way to warm up in late January.

It's also an education in specialty coffees. The bespectacled, thirtysomething Kettner roasts his own beans, trading directly with farmers in El Salvador and Brazil whenever possible. He changes Fernwood Coffee Company's seasonal espresso blend two or three times a year and recently hooked up a gleaming La Marzocco Strada EP espresso machine to serve up the tastiest brews. You may also admire the patterned milk textures that adorn Kettner's cappuccinos. Whether the coffee in question brings acidity or sweetness, notes of blackberry or chocolate aftertaste, you'll detect its freshness. Top off

your exquisitely balanced caffeine buzz with yummy baked goods made from scratch daily. The café's coffee brands are also sold at local Thrifty Foods stores.

With all the tasty goodness happening at Fernwood, and his World Barista Championship win, Kettner aims to lift Victoria's mocha profile to new heights. A tasty goal, indeed.❦
www.fernwoodcoffee.com

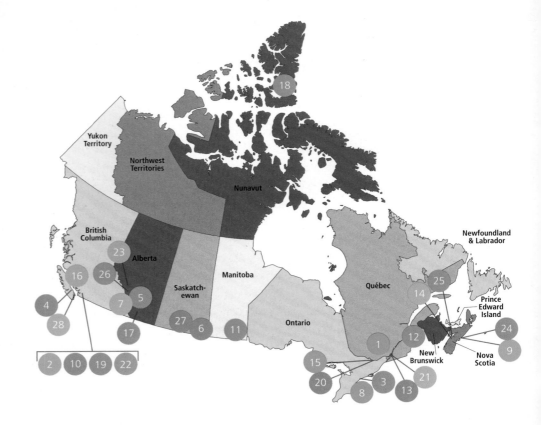

Your next STEP

TOP PICKS

ADVENTURE

CULTURE & HISTORY

NATURE'S GRANDEUR

EVENTS & FESTIVALS

QUIRKY CANADA

REJUVENATE

WEEK 1

1. MT. TREMBLANT, QUE.
Eastern Canada's highest peak
www.tourismemonttremblant.com/en

2. VANCOUVER, B.C.
Polar Bear Swim
www.vancouver.ca

3. TORONTO, ONT.
Viennese New Year's symphony
www.salutetovienna.com

4. CATHEDRAL GROVE, B.C.
Massive ancient trees
www.env.gov.bc.ca

5. CALGARY, ALTA.
High Performance Rodeo
arts festival
www.hprodeo.ca

6. KIPLING, SASK.
One Red Paper Clip house
http://oneredpaperclip.blogspot.com

7. KOOTENAY, B.C.
Kootenays eco-resort
www.nipika.com

WEEK 2

8. NIAGARA-ON-THE-LAKE, ONT.
Icewine grape picking
www.winesofontario.org

9. HALIFAX, N.S.
Winter surfing
www.lawrencetownbeach.com

10. VANCOUVER, B.C.
Bill Reid's artwork
www.billreidgallery.ca

11. WINNIPEG, MAN.
Serpentine River Trail skating
www.rivertrail.ca

12. SAINT-JUST-DE-BRETENIÈRES, QUE.
International Dog Sled
Championship of Canada
www.daaquam.org

13. MONTRÉAL, QUE.
Igloofest dance party
www.igloofest.ca

14. NEW ROSS, N.S.
Sleigh rides
museum.gov.ns.ca/rfm/en/home/default.aspx

WEEK 3

15. OTTAWA, ONT.
Rideau Canal skating
www.canadascapital.gc.ca

16. POWELL RIVER, B.C.
Winter scuba diving
www.divepowellriver.com

17. HEAD-SMASHED-IN BUFFALO
JUMP, ALTA.
Prehistoric hunting techniques
www.head-smashed-in.com

18. GRISE FIORD, NUNAVUT
Canada's northernmost
community
www.nunavuttourism.com

19. NORTH VANCOUVER, B.C.
Snowshoe racing
www.theyeti.ca

20. OTTAWA, ONT.
Beaver tails
www.beavertailsinc.com

21. MONTRÉAL, QUE.
Happening Gourmand
restaurant week
www.happeninggourmand.com

WEEK 4

22. VANCOUVER, B.C.
Chinese New Year
www.vancouver-chinatown.com

23. LAKE LOUISE, ALTA.
Ice climbing
www.yamnuska.com

24. HALIFAX, N.S.
Robbie Burns Day
www.igc2007.ca

25. SHEFFIELD MILLS, N.S.
Eagle-watching
www.eaglens.ca

26. BANFF, ALTA.
Banff/Lake Louise Winter Festival
www.banfflakelouise.com

27. MOOSE JAW, SASK.
Tunnels of Moose Jaw
www.tunnelsofmoosejaw.com

28. VICTORIA, B.C.
Specialty coffees
www.fernwoodcoffee.com

FEBRUARY

Hunt for Bonhomme at Le Carnaval de Québec

A staggering range of activities for young and old await at the world's largest winter carnival

Canada certainly has its hot celebrations, but Québec City's *carnaval* has got to be, hands down, the coolest. The 17-day winter carnival—the largest of its kind in the world, running annually since 1955—is staged in and around Old Québec, the oldest walled city in North America. Millions of revellers come to admire the historic beauty that was once upon a time known as New France (the city feted her 400th anniversary in 2008), as well as engage in dozens of festive outdoor activities.

When you live in Québec City (which is typically one layer of fleece colder than her sister city of Montréal), winter lasts almost half the calendar year, so it's no wonder the city has a solid relationship with this frosty season. The consensus here is: if you can't beat the cold, join it. So don your long johns and parka, then head down to the Plains of Abraham, the historic battlefield where France and England fought the pivotal battle of the Seven Years' War in 1759. On a clear day, the sun's reflection on the snow creates a warm glow and the sprawling open field transforms into Place Desjardins, a gigantic playground where you'll find snow rafting, a 120-metre (393.7-foot) ice slide, dogsled and sleigh rides, human foosball, and sugar shack sampling, or soar above it all via a 152.4-metre (500-foot) zipline.

Young families can let the kiddies loose at the M. Christie/Kraft Village before visiting the Ice Palace (the lights at night are particularly impressive), which is where the Bonhomme Carnaval kicks back when not ice-skating at the mini-rink at Place d'Youville. Not really considered a mascot because he can speak (English and French), he's that tall, white, and handsome snowman with a red toque and multicoloured sash.

Adults can sweat it out in a Jacuzzi or sauna at the Arctic Spas Village, or sip on "Caribou," the signature carnival concoction that blends brandy, vodka, sherry, and port, available at the ice bar outside the SAQ Bistro. On Saturday nights, the Ice Palace becomes party central for live musical entertainment and dancing underneath the stars. If at midnight you still have steam, stroll over to the International Snow Sculpture Event where artists from 50 countries (even some who have never seen snow before) work throughout the night to carve out amazing works of art.

There are also loads of special events on the middle weekend. On Saturday there's a flapjack breakfast, a new tradition of partnering up with the cowboys and girls of the Calgary Stampede. There's also the Night Parade, a uniquely intimate experience of colourful floats brightening up the darkness with music and light—another longtime Québec City favourite. Grab a hot

chocolate and watch the clowns and marching bands go by. The finale float is always the Bonhomme Carnaval. On Sunday, you can watch the finals of the Canoe Race from the Dufferin Terrace. A unique three-kilometre (1.9-mile) competition across the St. Lawrence River, it's a nod to the traditional method of transportation and communication between the mainland and the nearby islands—though these days, high-tech fibreglass canoes have replaced the original ones carved from local trees. They make their way along the river by whatever means necessary: if it's icy, they push the canoe across the slippery surface; if it's slushy, they paddle; and if the river is littered with broken chunks of ice, well, it's a challenging combination of pushing and paddling. Teams take the race very seriously . . . some families have been involved for more than five generations.

Those opting for the full fairy-tale package can hire a horse-drawn carriage for a leisurely tour and overnight at the Fairmont Le Château Frontenac, a castle-like 19th-century building that looms over the river and is said to be the most-photographed hotel in the world. From there, you'll be in a central position to stroll the shops, cafés, nightclubs, and eateries along main drag La Grande Allée or within the city's walls. Just walking

distance away is Aux Anciens Canadiens, a landmark restaurant set in the oldest home in Québec City where the staff dresses in period costume and serves a similarly old-fashioned menu with hearty meat pies, game meat, and other local classics. Adventurous types can brave the Ice Hotel (see p. 59), which is, yes, made completely of ice (don't worry, there are high-tech sleeping bags to keep you from freezing). Last year they moved the location to a more accessible spot only 10 minutes away by car. A little further, but no less interesting, is the Hôtel-Musée Premières Nations, located on a Wendake Native reserve. It takes its inspiration from traditional longhouses and even serves an Amerindian-inspired menu at its restaurant.

In Québec, there's a term of endearment for someone born and raised here; they are called *pur laine*, which means "pure wool." Smart words to think about when packing for Québec City's sub-zero temperatures. Aside from that, take it from Bonhomme Carnaval himself, and don't venture out without a hat. With all the fun you're about to have, there's another Québécois expression to remember: *Attach ta tuque!* Loosely translated, it means, "Hold on to your hat!" ❦

Find out more at: www.carnaval.qc.ca/en

1st week of FEB

ADVENTURE

CULTURE & HISTORY

Glide Along the Bruce Trail on Cross-Country Skis

Sometimes the best sound is no sound at all, save for the shush of cross-country skis gliding along a groomed track in a gentle snowfall. Ontario's Bruce Trail is scenic year-round. But at the height of winter, when the base of snow makes it impassable for boot-wearing hikers, for those on skis the experience is unparalleled.

The Bruce Trail is no walk—or ski—in the park. Stretching 885 kilometres (550 miles) from the Niagara region to Tobermory, with a further 400 kilometres (249 miles) of side trails, it is the oldest and longest continuous footpath in Canada. In February, odds are there will be snow along the trail's entire length. The northernmost section (through Bruce Peninsula National Park) is perhaps the most spectacular, with vistas overlooking Georgian Bay. Guides don't recommend skiing just anywhere, as some parts of the trail are a challenge for hikers—let alone someone on slippery skis. Be sure to dress for the part, with lots of layers you can add and subtract. And, if you're skiing alone, be sure to let your innkeeper know your itinerary and expected return time. Ski rentals are available in most centres along the trail. Expect to pay about C$15 per day for skis, boots, and poles. ❧
www.brucetrail.org

See a Performance by Canada's Largest Opera Company

There's nothing like a diva to warm up a February evening. The largest producer of opera in Canada, and one of the largest in North America, the Canadian Opera Company is internationally renowned for artistic excellence and creative innovation. Recent seasons have featured classic titles like *Rigoletto*, *Tosca*, *The Magic Flute*, and *The Flying Dutchman* evenly mixed with contemporary works that push the form, like *Nixon in China*.

Whether you know your Wagner from your Verdi, or your notion of opera amounts to the notion of "It ain't over till the fat lady sings," the COC's performance space is something to behold. The Four Seasons Centre for the Performing Arts is Canada's first and only purpose-built opera house; tours are available (noon on Sundays, performances permitting) that explain the facility's acoustics and stunning architecture. The true opera buff might want to enhance the experience by visiting the COC's headquarters on Front Street for a peek into the different departments that make the staging possible, from costumes and wigs, to the music library, and props (a private tour is a little under C$100).

Check the website for updates as the COC frequently offers guest recitals by major voices. Rush seats for weekday performances can be surprisingly affordable. ❧
www.coc.ca

◀ Walk the World's Climate Zones at the Montréal Biodôme

Want to globetrot through four major ecosystems in an afternoon? The Montréal Biodôme lets you do it under one roof. Any time of year is a great time to experience this sensorial nature tour and zoo-like showcase, but the tropical rainforest at the biodôme is a particularly welcome respite in winter.

The tropical rainforest at the biodôme is a particularly welcome respite in winter.

The rainforest is actually the largest "corner" of the dome at 2,600 square metres (27,986 square feet). Its temperature is set between 25 and 28 degrees Celsius (77 and 82.4 degrees Fahrenheit) by day, and artificial lighting is used so plants and wildlife feel like they're at home in Costa Rica. Continue your self-guided visit (or rent the audio tour for C$4) along the circular path through to the Laurentian Maple Forest where you can watch beavers, porcupines, and lynxes relaxing "at home" in 9-degree Celsius (48.2-degree Fahrenheit) weather. You'll also see an amazing cross-section of the Gulf of St. Lawrence, where 2.5 million litres (660,430 gallons) of "sea water" create a natural habitat. Finally, it's onto the Labrador coast where it's only between 2 and 5 degrees Celsius (35.6 and 41 degrees Fahrenheit), so time to put the coat back on; here, you'll find the home of the Atlantic puffins, and the sub-Antarctic islands where you can penguin-watch.

A word of advice: plan your day in advance, as the biodôme is a bit of a drive from downtown. There are also combo deals if you also plan on visiting the nearby Insectarium, Botanical Garden, and Olympic tower (legacy of the 1976 Olympic Games). Also, bring your own binoculars or rent them at the biodôme for C$2. ✸
www.ville.montreal.qc.ca/biodome

Michael Kusugak's
favourite PLACE

As a place that has inspired his richly told stories, children's author Michael Kusugak tries to visit Marble Island, Nunavut, every year.

"It's about 30 miles straight out to sea from Rankin Inlet on Hudson Bay," says the storyteller. "The island is all white."

Kusugak's latest book, *The Mean Knight*, investigates the tales of James Knight—an English explorer who was shipwrecked on the island in about 1719.

"He left England and went to look for the Northwest Passage, and he ended up on Marble Island," says Kusugak, who was born in Qatiktalik, now part of Nunavut. "And then he disappeared off the face of the earth."

Seals and all kinds of whales—be it belugas, bowheads, or narwhals—travel through these waters. No one lives on the island, but Kusugak says there are remains of houses, ship ballast from Knight's boats, and the graves of whalers.

"You go out in a boat and you look down into the water and you can see sunken ships."

Knight arrived on the island with a crew of about 40. After two winters, local legends say only five remained and all were starving and suffering from scurvy.

"They would climb a hill where there was a huge pile of wood, waiting for a sign of sails," Kusugak says, while en route to his present home in Qualicum Beach, B.C. "The sails never came."

Visitors to the Hudson Bay island are reminded of this struggle.

"There's a custom about Marble Island that when you go down there for the first time, you have to crawl on your hands and knees, up the beach," says Kusugak. "Just to pay tribute to those dying sailors, I think."

EVENTS & FESTIVALS

Take on the Yukon Quest Race

Harnessed teams of up to 14 excited dogs are behind the starting line in downtown Whitehorse as crowds gather to watch. It's the beginning of the annual Yukon Quest, a 1,600-kilometre (994.2-mile) race between Whitehorse and Fairbanks each February. Dubbed the "toughest sled dog race in the world," the trail travels along frozen rivers, through isolated villages, and over four mountain ranges. It follows historic gold rush and mail delivery routes dog teams once used as northern highways.

The Yukon Quest began in 1984 and the start alternates each year between Whitehorse and Fairbanks. It can take 10 to 16 days for the final team to reach the finish line, depending on weather and trail conditions. Mushers have to successfully complete a 321.9-kilometre (200-mile) and a 482.8-kilometre (300-mile) sled dog race before they can enter the Yukon Quest.

Up to 50 mushers and their teams can participate. In the true northern spirit of self-sufficiency, mushers carry equipment, food, and supplies on their sleds. They aren't allowed to accept any help—except when they reach the race's halfway mark in Dawson City. There are 10 checkpoints along the way and some are more than 200 miles apart. The best places to see the race are from Whitehorse, Dawson City, or Fairbanks, Alaska. ◆

www.yukonquest.com

Look for Signs of an Early Spring in Wiarton ▼

For those looking for ways to speed up the onset of spring, it may be hard to top Groundhog Day in Wiarton, Ontario. For more than half a century, locals have gathered on February 2 to anticipate the predictably unpredictable scurrying of an albino rodent. In other words, what started as an excuse for a party in the dead of winter is still pretty much that.

A bit like Lassie, Wiarton Willie has seen many incarnations. Originally, he was a fur hat thrown into the snow. Standards have improved over the years. Today, Wiarton Willie must be white and be a ground-hog. The secret to this surprisingly tenacious tradition —it's tough to stretch one darting movement of a furry animal into a week-long festival—is that locals have a great deal of fun. The organizers have special titles reflecting the importance of their roles, such as the minister of inter-burrow affairs (which handles the groundhogs) and the minister of hogwash and hot air (who handles the media). Beauty pageants, comedy nights, talent competitions and variety shows, dances, and dinners are all part of the lead up to Prediction Day. Then, in dark morning, everyone gathers for the moment of truth: will Willie see his shadow—thus predicting six more weeks of winter? Prediction Day goes out with a bang . . . and a parade capped with a fireworks display.❦

www.southbrucepeninsula.com

Taste the Ultimate Valentine's Chocolate

Chocolate is one of the culinary world's great gifts to the human palate. But not all chocolate is created equal—the Toronto chocolate maker Soma is in a class all on its own. If early February finds you in the city, there's no better place to procure your Valentine's stash.

Let's get this straight: a chocolatier sources its chocolate from suppliers and then creates confections. A chocolate maker like Soma makes its own chocolate, sourcing raw beans and roasting them on-site. The difference is incredible—and incredibly tasty. Based in Toronto's Distillery District, Soma makes at least seven types of chocolate, allowing its artisans to match cocoa beans to different flavours. For example, its balsamic vinegar truffle is paired with Madagascar chocolate because its acidic fruity notes complement the vinegar, while the nutty notes of the olive oil truffle are complemented by cocoa beans from the Dominican Republic. Taking its name from an ancient Asian elixir that bestowed immortality, Soma aims to keep your taste buds in a state of rapture. At C$2 a truffle, you'll also want to try the Douglas fir. After tasting these chocolates, when it comes to V-day cinnamon hearts probably won't pass muster.❦

www.somachocolate.com

Participate in the World Pond Hockey Championship

The event captures the spirit of how the game was meant to be played

Pure hockey the way the game was meant to be: played outdoors, four-on-four, cheered on by folks who love the game. It's not a thing of the past. You just have to know where to look. You'll find it when you enter the Tobique River Valley at the northern end of New Brunswick's Appalachian Mountain Range—home of the best pond hockey in the world.

Originally the first event of its kind, the World Pond Hockey Championship is held annually in Plaster Rock. Now 10 years old, it's an event that attracts thousands.

Every year, 120 teams of four, and more than 250 volunteers, organizers, and fans, gather in this town of 1,200 for two things: rousing games of pond hockey and good times. It's a winning combination!

Pond hockey is described as the childhood stick-and-puck game: no referees, no goalies, and no boards. Just skates, sticks, gloves, and enough layers to keep your sweat from freezing. Pond hockey is revered for the basics: the symphony of skate blades carving the ice; peals of laughter punctuating the silence of northern woods; vapoury breath and cold, crisp air; the anticipation of 80 teams waiting their turn to compete; and good music, warming food, and camaraderie.

Since its inaugural edition in 2002, the event has caught the imagination and triggered the emotion of hockey enthusiasts worldwide. Teams representing every Canadian province, 35 American states, and 15 countries from around the globe have skated in Plaster Rock. Ordinary folk, celebrities such as Bobby Hull, and even politicians like Canadian Prime Minister Stephen Harper, have travelled to New Brunswick to experience the game in one of its purest forms.

Entering a team requires planning and luck. Each year, organizers invite team entries until mid-to-late May. On June 1st, a lottery is held to select the 120 teams competing in the open division as well as 10 women's teams. While there are hundreds of applications each year, at least 50 new teams are always included—both to inject new blood into the event and to ensure it lives long.

Those attending for the first time will be awestruck when they first see the venue: Roulston Lake and its 24 rinks all laid out in what has been described as "a field of dreams for hockey players." Once on the lake, attendees can experience the sites and sounds associated with 22 games taking place simultaneously. (Two rinks are set aside for the men's and women's championship games.) Fans can walk around the lake and between rinks to watch players from all over the world.

During the day, games take place under the winter sun, at night under lights. A heated pavilion houses a canteen, merchandise sales, and bar area. In the evening this same venue transforms into an entertainment area—complete with East Coast music for all to enjoy. Throughout the weekend, a Welcome Centre hosts an arts and crafts sale.

It takes more than 200 passionate volunteers to make the event a success, and it should come as no surprise that volunteers come from across Canada and around the world. Anyone interested in being part of the action should contact the organizers through the World Pond Hockey Championship website. Many friendships have been forged among non-players who simply wanted to be involved.

Local establishments—such as the Settlers Inn and Motel, Timber Town Lounge, Tobique River Motel & Lounge, Royal Canadian Legion, and Plaster Rock Comfort Grill—are busy providing both food and entertainment. Equally, the nearby communities of Perth–Andover and Grand Falls also see an influx of people swarm their towns at event time. Anyone planning to attend the World Pond Hockey Championship should make room reservations in early June. (Local accommodations generally will not reserve rooms until after the June 1st team lottery.)

While a champion is crowned each year, the event doesn't channel a "win at all costs" vibe. The beauty of the format—120 teams in an "open" division—is that it meets players' needs at different competitive levels. In reality, the event's more about friendships, trading stories, and swapping hockey jerseys. Evening games under the lights with a light snowfall rekindle childhood memories and allow participants to recapture their youth. The weekend fulfills the hopes and expectations of the hockey purist: you hear laughter as much as you do the sounds of skates, sticks, and pucks.

Danny Braun, a founder and organizer of the championship, says what most influenced him to start the event was his lifelong involvement in hockey as a player, coach, and administrator, as well as a childhood filled—hour after hour—playing outside on ponds and rivers, in parking lots and streets.

Today, Braun and championship volunteers receive accolades for their work. Shawn Kallet, a member of the MTV 2-Headed Dogs team from New York City, says they make the event better every year. "Who else could build a new rink and pavilion, run Olympic-style opening ceremonies, bring the Stanley Cup, Bobby Hull, *Hockey Night In Canada*, and the prime minister to Plaster Rock —all while working through the night to resurface the ice so every morning starts with crisp, clean sheets?" ❧

Find out more at:
www.worldpondhockey.com

ADVENTURE

CULTURE & HISTORY

Try a Bevy of Winter Sports at the Top of Mount Royal

Winter's leisurely pursuits are elevated when you're at the top of scenic Mount Royal, Montréal's central landmass (from which the city gets her name) . . . and a nature lover's escape from the city streets below. Rise to the occasion and have some outdoor fun in many different ways, surprising given the convenient inner-city location.

Many a local will be proud to tell you they learned how to skate before walking, and Mount Royal Park's small figure-eight-shaped rink is where many found their ice legs. In optimum weather conditions, skating also takes place on Beaver Lake—a magical experience in itself, even just to watch.

The more cardio-inclined can explore the two square kilometres (0.8 square miles) of space on cross-country skis or snowshoes along three kilometres (1.9 miles) of designated paths. Ask about the guided walks at night, or the educational trek that investigates animal tracks in the snow.

Adrenaline-seekers will gravitate towards the only downhill sport on the mountain. A gentle slope within the clearing has four laneways dedicated to inner-tubing. Rent yours in the cabana at the base of the hill. If you've got your own method of flying, there are another eight lanes free for toboggans, magic carpets, and such.

When it's time to warm up with a hot cup of cocoa, Bistro Le Pavillon (overlooking the skating rink) has a café, restaurant, and public tables if you bring your own snacks. The rental shop has ice skates, ski/boot/pole combos, snowshoes, and helmets. ❦
www.lemontroyal.qc.ca/en

Relive Olympic Fever at the BC Sports Hall of Fame

Most Canadians remember where they were when the opening ceremony for the Vancouver 2010 Olympic Winter Games took place on February 12, 2010. Wherever you were, it's fun to recapture the spirit and hoopla of the Games by visiting the BC Sports Hall of Fame, located in the 55,000-capacity BC Place Stadium, the ceremony's venue.

After extensive renovations, the hall reopened in November 2011. In the new 560-square-metre (6,000 -square-foot) 2010 Olympic and Paralympic celebration gallery, check out spectacular glass cabinets housing artifacts from the XXI Olympic Winter Games and the X Paralympic Winter Games. Among other things, you'll discover a uniform owned by speed skating sensation Denny Morrison (a gold-medal winner), a podium used in a medals ceremony, and the torch used to light the Olympic Cauldron at the opening ceremony autographed by superstar torchbearers Catrina Le May Doan, Nancy Greene, Wayne Gretzky, Rick Hansen, and Steve Nash. Naturally, there are mementos from Canada's golden overtime hockey triumph over the United States on February 28, the final event of the Games.

Don't miss other galleries commemorating the Stanley Cup quests of the NHL's Vancouver Canucks, the Grey Cup titles of the CFL's BC Lions, and the 1980 "Marathon of Hope" of Vancouver's Terry Fox, who heroically attempted to run across Canada to raise funds for cancer research on one leg assisted by a prosthetic leg. ❦
www.bcsportshalloffame.com

Drop a Line In at Canada's Ice-Fishing Capital

Nothing says winter like a frozen lake in February, especially when you're in a warm(ish) hut looking down a fishing line through a hole to the frigid waters of Lake Simcoe. Now's the time to pull on the woollies, bait up that hook, and get primed for the upcoming Canadian Ice-Fishing Championship.

A large inland lake 45 minutes north of Toronto, Lake Simcoe is known as Canada's ice-fishing capital.

A large inland lake 45 minutes north of Toronto, Lake Simcoe is known as Canada's ice-fishing capital. The championship sees a field of two-man teams fishing for 12 hours over two days. The rules are strict and the entry is steep—C$275 per team. But the prizes are rich, with C$20,000 in payouts to teams that score in the top 10. If you want to get in on the experience, or the prize money, ice huts can be rented by the day. Expect to pay C$40 to $50 per person, which should include transportation to and from the hut and—very important—access to a portable toilet. Ice-fishing rods (50.8 centimetres, about 20 inches long) are inexpensive and widely available in the area. If you don't make it for the main event, not to worry. The Winter Perch Attack, a one-day event, is held here in early March. 🍁
www.fishinontario.com

Canadian *moments*

National Flag Day

"We'd like to do a song about nationalism gone astray. It's called 'Flag on Your Knapsack'," Gord Downie said, introducing "Fifty-Mission Cap" during the Tragically Hip's Another Roadside Attraction tour in 1993.

It's a divisive issue for travellers who weigh being identified as tourists against standing out as Canadian.

In 2004, in the wake of George W. Bush's re-election, the Associated Press reported that an American T-shirt company was offering a "Go Canadian" package. Along with the T-shirt, the how-to-be-Canadian kit included a window sticker and pin. Most importantly, it came with a backpack patch displaying the bright, bold colours of the Canadian flag.

While the "Go Canadian" package is no longer available, the tongue-in-cheek blog, HowtoSpotaCanadian.ca offers a term for non-Canadians backpacking with the maple leaf sewn on: "Faux-nucks."

Canadian flag-waving also has an undeniable place at sporting events.

For the 2010 Winter Games in Vancouver, a development company wrapped the Hotel Georgia with the world's largest Canadian flag. The size of the vinyl wrapping? Bigger than an Olympic-sized hockey rink.

Yet despite the international profile of the maple leaf, Canadians barely observe National Flag Day on February 15. The anniversary marks the 1965 inauguration of the current red-and-white maple-leaf design, before which Canada flew and fought under the Red Ensign.

◀ Rub Elbows with Top Designers at Montréal Fashion Week

Montréal is often called the Paris of North America—not only because it's the largest French-speaking city after the City of Light, or because of its long history in textile manufacturing, but also because of its stylish locals. Twice a year, the city celebrates fashion with Semaine de la Mode, where local designers strut their latest collections. Almost all shows have seats available to the public, so it's a unique opportunity to see both veteran and up-and-coming designers up close.

If you've ever been to fashion week in New York, Paris, or Milan, Montréal's version is much smaller in comparison, but it's nevertheless full of energy and, of course, talent. When certain designers with enthusiastic cult followings (such as Philippe Dubuc, Denis Gagnon, Barilà, and Marie Saint-Pierre) present their newest looks, the Marché Bonsecours comes close to bursting at the seams, if you will. And the scene itself becomes a veritable catwalk of fashionistas.

It's a unique opportunity to see both veteran and up-and-coming designers up close.

Individual tickets can cost up to C$30 per person, but this price also gets you into the main waiting room where you can rub elbows with fashion critics, magazine editors, and general fashion lovers, all the while enjoying a drink from the bar. There are also complimentary makeup applications and hair styling while you wait. On one day of the week, the public also has the chance to visit Le Showroom, where you can see the clothing up-close, and in many cases meet the designers of each line.🍁
www.montrealfashionweek.ca

Visit the Romantic Town of Saint-Valentin for Valentine's Day

In Saint-Valentin, Québec, romantics milk Valentine's Day for all its worth in a charming 10-day festival. About one hour south of Montréal, this small rural town is hooked on a feeling and inviting you to join in on the love.

From February 4th to 14th, the Saint-Valentin festival has been giving new energy to its namesake area (population 500) since 1994. Mayor Pierre Chamberland has worked out an itinerary of love-themed activities, including carriage rides, an arts and crafts sale, a dinner and show, a country dancing night, and an annual blood donation drive. Of more local interest, there's also a teen dance, church concerts, and a talent competition.

The Saint-Valentin church is also spreading the word and recently welcomed a new bishop. The festival's Mass for Lovers is one of the busiest days of the year. In it a newly engaged couple is spoiled and celebrated, then treated to a hearty brunch at the Saint-Valentin sugar shack. Everyone else pays C$10.

The town, it seems, brings out the romance in those who visit. Out-of-towners seeking cupid have also been known to drive to Saint-Valentin just to have their Valentine's Day cards stamped at the post office. Others, more impassioned, have even fallen to one knee in marriage proposals. *Ah, l'amour.*❧

www.festivalstvalentin.org

REJUVENATE

Experience Vancouver's Renowned Japanese Culinary Delights ▶

February 11th is the anniversary of Japan's founding. February 14th is Valentine's Day. If you're into combining events, why not grab your sweetie and celebrate by enjoying a hearty serving of Vancouver's celebrated Japanese cuisine?

Tojo's inevitably wins "Best Japanese" in the annual restaurant awards of *Vancouver Magazine* and the local *Georgia Straight* weekly newspaper. Hit up this West Broadway institution and savour the creations of owner-chef Hidekazu Tojo, who has memorized more than 2,000 sushi recipes. The highlight, though admittedly pricey, is the house's *omakase*, allowing maestro Tojo to improvise spectacular new dishes based on your personal tastes. If you prefer menu staples, try the B.C. roll, combining barbecued salmon skin and cucumber slices. (Tojo invented this one in 1974.) Fresh, local ingredients are pervasive—and taste even better washed down with Tojo's premium sake.

Vancouver's romance with Japanese food goes beyond Tojo's. Near the West End intersection of Robson and Denman streets, toast your love with Japanese cocktails and beer while devouring *yakitori* (grilled chicken skewers) and *edamame* (green soy beans) at *izakaya* mainstays like Kingyo and Guu. Or, in the Mount Pleasant neighbourhood, brave the lineup outside Toshi Sushi, and develop a passion for this funky establishment's fresh sashimi and scrumptious miso soups.❧

www.tojos.com, www.guu-izakaya.com

Relive the Olympic Winter Games

2010 is history, but golden memories live on

If it wasn't the most exciting event ever to hit Canada, it sure came close. The 2010 Winter Games held in Vancouver and Whistler electrified the entire nation and a worldwide audience of three billion. Downtown Vancouver transformed into a beacon of red-and-white madness, complete with cowbells, Maple Leaf logos, and high-fives especially when hockey superstar Sidney Crosby scored the winning goal in overtime for Canada in the men's gold medal game against Team U.S.A. The reaction? Picture a Brazilian carnival crossed with an English World Cup soccer victory. Figure skating, downhill skiing, and other sports provided magic moments too.

Now that the Games are long over, can you still find ways to relive the passion of those 17 days? As surely as the Olympic motto is "higher, stronger, faster," the answer is yes.

A great place to start your quest is two hours north of Vancouver, where the world-class ski resort of Whistler still harbours an impressive Olympic legacy.

Downhill daredevils can test their skills at Whistler Creekside, the ski area that hosted both men's and women's races in 2010. Feeling manly? Whiz down the Dave Murray Downhill, where male superstars like America's Bode Miller captured gold. Built for speed, it's the world's second-longest downhill run at 3.1 kilometres (1.9 miles), and you'll feel the rush as you drop more than 1,000 metres (3,300 vertical feet). Catch big-time air going over "Murr's Jump," and savour the rolling terrain and big turns. Whistler Creekside also witnessed thrilling victories by female speed queens like Germany's Maria Riesch. Follow in their turbo-charged ski tracks on a challenging course that combines sections of the Wild Car, Jimmy's Joker, and Franz's runs, finally connecting to Dave Murray. Après-ski, toast the alpine lifestyle with beers at Dusty's Bar & BBQ, next to the Creekside lift.

Want to slide into an even higher gear? Head to The Whistler Sliding Centre, nestled in the Fitzsimmons valley on the southeast slope of Blackcomb Mountain. In 2010, the C$105-million facility hosted bobsleigh, luge, and skeleton events. Check the sporting calendar and attend a 2012 World Cup event or the 2013 World Luge Championship on the 1,450-metre (4,757-foot) track. You can also book individual or group tours. For an experience requiring even more adrenaline, sign up to do your own skeleton run, hitting speeds of up to 100 kilometres (62.1 miles) per hour under the supervision of the Sliding Centre Track Crew (thank goodness!). Listen to the safety briefing, get a helmet and goggles, grab your sled, and let the G-force grab you. This head-first odyssey will last a mere 30 seconds. For C$130, you get two runs and a certificate of completion.

Cross-country buffs, meanwhile, can enjoy hours of skiing on more than 90 kilometres (56 miles) of Nordic trails, emulating Olympic champions like Norway's Petter Northug at the Whistler Olympic Park in the forested Callaghan Valley. If you want to shoot for something more exciting, enroll in the Discover Biathlon program, where you'll learn skate-skiing techniques and blast a rifle at Olympic biathlon targets. And there's much more. Go snowshoeing, view the towering 2010 Olympic ski jumps, or relax at the spacious Day Lodge, which dishes up sandwiches and chili catered by the Bearfoot Bistro.

When you return to Vancouver, recapture Olympic fever with a downtown walking tour. First, check out the Olympic Cauldron that all-time hockey great Wayne Gretzky lit next to the Vancouver Convention Centre, on Vancouver's waterfront, on February 12, 2010. With spectacular floor-to-ceiling windows and an enviro-friendly turf roof, the convention centre was the main media venue during the Games.

Score tickets to a Vancouver Canucks home game at Rogers Arena (known as "Canada Hockey Place" during the Games), and you won't just be gazing at the same ice that hosted the most-watched hockey game in Canadian history. You'll also see some 2010 Olympians showing off their skills, like Canucks goalie Roberto Luongo—who backstopped Canada to gold.

Next door to Rogers Arena is the renovated BC Place Stadium, home to the opening and closing ceremonies in 2010, now featuring a brand-new retractable roof. Inside, visit the new 2010 Olympic and Paralympic celebration gallery at the BC Sports Hall of Fame. The hall owns more than 3,000 Vancouver 2010 items, including medals and torchbearer uniforms.

Just beyond downtown, the Pacific Coliseum (the 2010 figure skating and short track speed skating venue) features the junior Vancouver Giants of the Western Hockey League. Among these 20-and-under kids, you might spot future Olympians in action, such as former Giant Andrej Meszaros, who suited up for Slovakia in 2010.

Another games legacy is the high-speed Canada Line rapid transit light rail line, connecting Richmond and the Vancouver International Airport (YVR) to downtown Vancouver in just over 25 minutes. Travel to Aberdeen Station and take a serene stroll beside the Fraser River to the Richmond Olympic Oval (home to long-track speed skating at games time). While the speed skating track is gone, the C$178-million facility—with a jaw-dropping "wood wave" roof constructed of wood originally damaged by pine beetles, a sustainability success story—has been converted into a multi-purpose fitness facility. Go skating, play basketball, take pilates . . . the heart-pounding options are endless.

Visiting the Vancouver 2010 venues won't likely get many of us on the podium at the 2014 Winter Games in Sochi, Russia. But it's an amazing way to recapture that dreamy international feeling. As David Bowie once sang, "We can be heroes, just for one day." ❧

Find out more at:

www.olympic.org/vancouver-2010-winter-olympics

ADVENTURE

Try "Skijoring" on
Cape Breton Island

The connection between man and dog has long been documented, but at Crown Jewel Resort Ranch near Baddeck, Nova Scotia, that connection is slightly different—it's with a bungee cord. "Skijoring" attaches experienced skiers to a Canadian Eskimo dog's harness via a hip belt. Dogs respond to vocal commands, providing strength and speed as they drag you across the untouched, snowy expanses common in late February. One of only a few Eskimo dog breeders, the folks in Baddeck bring outdoor sport to a new level of authenticity. Skijoring may look easy, but it's more physically demanding than cross-country skiing and the learning curve can be steep.

It all started in Scandinavia with horses, which are easier to control than sled dogs, according to the experts at the ranch who've trained both for the sport. Before you consider tying yourself in, however, you should be both a good cross-country skier and very comfortable around sled dogs. Knowing the dogs' "language" is vital to creating a good team. Otherwise, all you need to bring are your skis (the resort provides everything else you might need). Once you've got the hang of it, many more unusual adventures await at the Crown Jewel, including "scootering"—think dogsledding on wheels—an alternate option for those days when there's no snow.🍁
www.crownjewelresort.com

◀ Voyageur Winter Carnival Festival

Canada was built on the fur trade and Fort William (now Thunder Bay, Ontario) was the centre of that trade in the 19th century. Rebuilt between 1971 and 1984 and returned to its original grandeur, this impressive "living history" experience comes alive in February during the Voyageur Winter Carnival Festival.

In the spirit of the French voyageurs, Aboriginal trappers, and Scottish traders who inhabited this region, you can enjoy dogsled rides, a sugar shack, musket shooting, snowshoe trekking, and lacrosse—Canada's original official sport. Kids will love navigating the giant snow maze and the more contemporary activity of tubing.

While hardy types try to outperform each other in log-sawing, inukshuk-building, and snow-shovelling, families are invited to participate in the relay, the three-legged race, and the create-a-snowman contest. Then there are the more esoteric competitions, such as those for the cutest baby and the prettiest pooch. More sedate participants can enjoy live music and engage in some thoughtful snow sculpturing. When your fingers and toes start to feel numb, head inside and explore the exhibits, guided by costumed characters, representing members of the original colonial and Aboriginal peoples. Period baking, food presentation, and sampling are all part of the package.❦
www.fwhp.ca

Watch Ice Climbers Scale Montmorency Falls ▼

About 12 kilometres (7.5 miles) outside Québec City, it's worth a side trip to Montmorency Falls. In winter the water freezes over, becoming a cascading curtain of ice. You may not want to join those who brave this climb, but the sight alone will give you the shivers.

The dramatic drop is where the Montmorency River reaches a cliff and spills into the St. Lawrence River. The resulting falls are 45.7 metres (150 feet) wide and 83.8 metres (275 feet) high—almost 30.5 metres (100 feet) taller than Niagara Falls.

Some say ice climbing is actually easier than rock climbing, thanks to the spikes you have attached to your shoes. But those who wish to simply observe can linger around the *pain de sucre*—the huge mound of snow and ice that forms at the base of the falls.

Open only on weekends at this time of year, the scenic aerial lift (about C$11) can take you from the base of the falls to the summit—or you can simply drive there. Parking at the bottom or top is C$5 on weekends and free during the week (but remember there's no lift Monday to Friday at this time of year).

Once you're at the summit, there is a (slightly intimidating) suspension bridge from which to view the falls. There's a little café up there too, at Manoir Montmorency, which offers an entire panorama—one that includes Québec City and the St. Lawrence River. The Manoir's Sunday brunches are legendary.❦
www.sepaq.com/ct/pcm

3rd week of

FEB

EVENTS & FESTIVALS

QUIRKY CANADA

Cheer on Future Stars at the World Championships of Pee-Wee Hockey

NHL young guns like Sidney Crosby, Steven Stamkos, and P.K. Subban were smaller (and cuter) once upon a time, but their talents were already starting to shine through at a young age. For emerging young hockey talent, the biggest stage in the world is the Québec International Pee-Wee Hockey Tournament, your first chance to catch a glimpse of the NHL's future stars.

More than 2,300 players aged 11 and 12 travel to Québec City from 16 countries—including as far away as Finland, Russia, and Australia—to compete at the city's Pepsi Coliseum. You may not recognize the names of these pint-sized players now, but hockey icons like Guy Lafleur, Wayne Gretzky, Mario Lemieux, and Eric Lindros have all sharpened their skates for this event. In total, nearly 1,000 players from the half-century-old tournament have gone on to play in the NHL. Prices are considerably lower than your average NHL game (adult tickets are C$6, while entry for kids under 14 is C$2), but the players' hard work and desire to win is just the same—and so is the entertainment value, which is why the 11 days of fierce competition draws more than 200,000 spectators annually.

The tournament overlaps with the city's famous Winter Carnival (see p. 28), so you'll be sure to witness celebrations both on and off the ice all week. ✤
www.tournoipee-wee.qc.ca/EN/index.html

Explore the Government's Former Nuclear Bomb Shelter

Named after John "The Chief" Diefenbaker, Canada's prime minister at the height of the Cold War, this once top-secret installation is a time capsule of doomsday terror and 1960s-era government chic. A short drive southeast of Ottawa, the "Diefenbunker" offers a chance to engage in the Armageddon mindset and envision what life might have been like for the inhabitants of a nuclear winter.

The last defence against an unwinnable nuclear confrontation, the Central Emergency Government Headquarters operated from 1959 to 1994 as a facility to house and protect members of the Canadian government in the event of a nuclear attack. You can explore the four-story, 9,290-square-metre (100,000-square-foot) underground facility yourself, but the two-hour guided tour (call ahead for a reservation) makes the experience that much richer. See the prime minister's suite, the war cabinet room, and the emergency government situation centre, and imagine the bleak task of the technicians in the CBC Radio studio as they broadcast to a nuclear wasteland. There's even a Bank of Canada vault, where gold bullion would have been stored . . . and traded for what? Several of the rooms are devoted to Cold War politics, and the atomic bombing of Hiroshima, Japan. Cold war-themed movies are shown monthly—popcorn included. ✤
www.diefenbunker.ca

◀ Dine at the Stellar Baker Creek Bistro

From the woodsy setting, to the creative menu of regionally inspired cuisine, enjoying a meal at Baker Creek Bistro is the quintessential Canadian Rockies dining experience. Kick off your evening with a cocktail in front of the fireplace at the lounge, and then move on to the charming log dining room, the perfect destination after a day's skiing or snowboarding at Lake Louise.

If you've never tried bison, this is an excellent place to start.

The dinner menu is dominated by creative cooking that uses regional and sustainable ingredients from small suppliers throughout Alberta and British Columbia. If you've never tried bison, this is an excellent place to start. Sourced from a southern Alberta ranch, it's tender and extremely lean—but only slightly gamey. A good way to start dinner is with the elk tartare, which is served with pickled shallots, truffle vinaigrette, and gouda cheese, then move on to bison short ribs braised in locally brewed ale and served with parsnip potato purée. Friendly-yet-professional service and a short but thoughtful wine list round out a world-class dining experience.

The restaurant is associated with the equally appealing Baker Creek Chalets. Each log chalet has an en suite bathroom, log bed, and wood-burning fireplace—the perfect place to curl up in front of after a meal at the restaurant.❧

www.bakercreek.com

It happened
THIS WEEK:

New Two-Dollar Coin

Canada's most famous bear, after Winnie the Pooh, is likely Churchill, the polar bear struck on the two-dollar coin.

Released on February 19, 1996, the "toonie" was designed by Brent Townsend of Campbellford, Ontario. In the town, an 8.2-metre (26.9-foot) high toonie now sits in Old Mill Park honouring the wildlife artist.

Although the Royal Canadian Mint produced more than 375 million toonies in the first year, a decade passed before a name was sought for the bear. In a 2006 poll, "Churchill" won out over Wilbert, Makwa, Sacha, and Plouf.

But unofficially, the polar bear isn't the only animal on the coin. Rotate the tail side of the coin clockwise and the polar bear, with its head down, resembles the head of a Tyrannosaurus Rex. Yet, turn the polar bear upside down and its legs are said to look like four penguins.

The mostly copper centre is locked to the nickel outer ring with a special mechanism. It's so steadfast it would take 10 times the pressure of an average human hand to dislodge. (The mint has patented the technique.) Coins boast a lifespan that's 20 times longer than a paper bill.

Located in Winnipeg, Manitoba, the Royal Canadian Mint also produces foreign coins for countries such as Barbados.

The toonie followed the course of the "loonie," which replaced the dollar bill in 1987. The one-dollar coin features a lone loon, which is how it earned its nickname. The bird's haunting cry, often coming through the morning mist on a lake, is a Canadian symbol. Robert-Ralph Carmichael's design captures that experience in the bronze coin.

Pursue Art and Adventure at La Nuit Blanche

Montréal's all-nighter caps a week of revelry at the city's High Lights Festival

In the thick of winter, Montréal turns up the heat by hosting the Montréal High Lights Festival (*Le Festival Montréal en Lumière*), a culture-packed event that blankets the city, covering all the feel-good things in life like food, drinks, music, art, and sports. The spectacular culmination of this 10-day extravaganza is the ever-popular *La Nuit Blanche*, which closes the show by rocking out from dusk till dawn. Don't expect to sleep, much less stay cooped up inside, when there's so much to see and do.

And does Montréal know how to throw a party! On this particular night, it seems no stone is left unturned. Nearly 200 activities and exhibits are open to the public (many of them free), all of which are spread

out across the island's central core. Carefully divided into different zones—Le Plateau and Mile End to the north, the downtown hub, historic Old Montréal, and the quays in the Old Port, there's also a fourth wing branching out to such sites as Le Stade Olympique, and the Biodôme. Each area boasts its own free shuttle with crossover stops for convenient inter-zone hopping.

The colourful agenda lures vast audiences of all different interests. Why not spend the night (and early morning) deep breathing at a midnight yoga session; deciphering an interactive art installation; ice skating to the tunes of a live DJ; navigating a labyrinth of fir trees; country line-dancing at City Hall (L'hôtel de ville); swimming beneath the stars (the Bonaventure's rooftop pool is heated to 28 degrees Celsius, 82.4 degrees Fahrenheit); observing a glass-blowing demonstration; mingling incognito at a masked ball; taking an after-midnight museum tour via flashlight; attending an intimate movie screening; singing (or merely observing the pros) in opera karaoke (don't you know Puccini's *Si mi chiamano Mimi?*); or all of the above.

Those less inclined to Arctic climes can also opt to discover the *Art Souterrain* ("Underground Art") network of pop-up galleries and quirky performance art in Montréal's famed Underground City—a network of subway stations, universities, museums, shopping centres, and office buildings, all connected beneath the downtown corridor by

a sophisticated web of tunnels. For this special occasion, the Métro (subway) will also run all night long—free of charge. Indeed, sometimes getting to a destination is half the fun.

Paris—the celebrated City of Light—was the first metropolis to start this all-nighter trend in 2002. The adrenalin-fuelled soirée is now enjoyed in Toronto; Brighton and Hove in the UK; Miami, Santa Monica, and New York in the United States; and a host of other international cities, including Singapore, Tel Aviv, and Florence.

Each year since Montréal followed suit in 2003, the number of revellers has increased exponentially—so be prepared for lineups. Main thoroughfares, such as Le Quartier des Spectacles and even Sainte-Catherine Street, become magnets for crowds. And, do note the ending time of each affair as not everything is open until the wee hours of the morning. Places that are 24-hour hangouts throughout the year are—unsurprisingly—busier than usual, such as at La Banquise (a trendy diner specializing in poutine (see p. 311)), the Casino on Île Notre-Dame, and after-hours night clubs in the Village (such as Stereo or Circus).

Due in part to the event's nocturnal timeslot, crowds tend to be more on the adult or young adult side, but there are also many early evening events and activities, such as the 120-metre (394-foot) outdoor ice slide at La Place Jacques-Cartier, that fun-seeking families will still have time to enjoy well before bedtime.

If you have certain activities on a must-do checklist, it's always good to have a backup plan in case something's sold out to avoid disappointment. Better yet, hit the streets with a free festival spirit. If what's on your list is full or busy, there's probably something just as fun around the corner. Being open-minded to the unexpected can sometimes lead you to memorable discoveries.

First-timers should keep in mind that *La Nuit Blanche* is really only one aspect (the glorious end) of a jam-packed 10-day event: the complete Montréal High Lights Festival combines a sophisticated culinary component (each year celebrating a country or theme), a star-studded schedule of song and musical performances, and fine art and dance presentations. So, stay for a while.

Last, but not least: dress warmly. Don't think you'll be the only one in snow pants and moon boots, if that's all you have for sub-zero temperatures. And who says funky toques and big, fluffy mittens are only for kids?🍁

Find out more at:
www.montrealenlumiere.com

ADVENTURE

Race Down the Track at Canada Olympic Park

Dive into an exhilarating adventure by sliding down the bobsleigh run in Calgary, much as the world's best athletes did during the XV Olympic Winter Games, hosted by Alberta's largest city during the last two weeks of February 1988.

Few remember who took home medals at the Games, but anyone old enough will never forget the smiling faces of the Jamaican bobsled team. You'll be smiling too after making the speedy run, driven by a professional driver, when it's not being used as a training facility for the world's best "sliders." (Call ahead to verify when the track's open to the public.) The experience includes an orientation session led by an athlete-in-training, a walk-through of safety guidelines, and then

you're off on the run of your life down a frozen track. During an adrenaline-filled 60 seconds you'll twist down 14 turns, pulling up to 5 Gs and hit a maximum speed of 120 kilometres (75 miles) per hour on a course that develops Olympic champions. At the end you'll get a commemorative certificate and a story you'll tell for years.

As your heart rate slowly returns to normal, relive the glory of the Olympic Games by visiting the adjacent Olympic Hall of Fame and Museum. It's home to Canada's largest collection of Olympic memorabilia, but the interactive displays are the main draw. You'll also get the chance to hold an Olympic torch and shoot a hockey puck. ✦

www.winsportcanada.ca/cop

Visit the Historic Notre-Dame Basilica

The Notre-Dame de Québec basilica-cathedral is a glorious historic structure within the walled city. Recognized as a UNESCO World Heritage Site, its storied past dates back to the time of New France in 1647. Open year-round, the structure is a treat for both history and art lovers—not to mention a welcoming refuge from a harsh Québec winter.

Fires have twice destroyed the Roman Catholic cathedral, the first in 1759 during the Siege of Québec, then again in 1922. Each time, however, this important Christian place of worship was rebuilt, always on the original site. The current Neo-Classic façade is a nod to the Church of Sainte-Geneviève in Paris, and is particularly stunning when blanketed with freshly fallen February snow.

The interior is an impressive display of artwork, showcasing stained-glass windows, a beautifully ornate, gold-plated baldachin, paintings, as well as a chancel lamp—a gift from Louis XIV. There are guided tours of the crypt below, where you can visit the tombs of prominent figures of Québec's past, including four governors of New France and François de Laval, the people's first Roman Catholic bishop. Otherwise the public is free to enter and discover the beauty of the church. Tours are available in both English and French.✹

www.nddq.org

Watch Baby Seals on the Magdalen Islands ▼

The Magdalen Islands make up a small archipelago in the Gulf of St. Lawrence. In summer the area is known for excellent cycling, camping, and water sports, but in winter the landscape freezes over with a captivating display of snow and ice. From here you can embark on a once-in-a-lifetime opportunity to get up-close-and-personal with harp seals and their pups.

Around this time (a very narrow window of two to three weeks), about 250,000 of them migrate here from Greenland where mothers give birth to their babies on the ice floes around the island. The pups, absolutely adorable with their large black eyes, only keep their white coats for about two weeks while they're nursing.

Tourist packages generally include accommodations and a guided helicopter ride (up to three hours long) directly to the ice floes. Once a safe and suitable landing is found, interact with the seals in their natural habitat. Keep in mind, however, that because of the sensitive nature of the animals and the unpredictability of weather (the ice may not be hard enough to land on), tours can be cancelled or seals could be scarce or non-existent.

In such cases, all is not lost, as there are many other unique activities to try, including sea kayaking, ice-fishing, and snowshoeing.✹

www.tourismeilesdelamadeleine.com

4th week of FEB

Celebrate Winter as Early Canadians Did at the Festival du Voyageur

This 10-day winter celebration centres on the traditions of voyageurs, French fur traders who were the earliest Europeans to settle permanently in what is now Canada. Winter conditions were hard on these early immigrants, but the spirit of their joie de vivre comes through in the event that dubs itself "the world's largest kitchen party."

Most events take place in the Winnipeg precinct of Saint Boniface, western Canada's largest francophone community. For the festival, the grounds of Fort Gibraltar are transformed into Voyageur Park. Here you'll find impressive snow sculptures, a snow maze, sleigh rides, toboggan runs, a First Nations village, and a snow bar. Volunteers dressed in voyageur clothing wander through the venue organizing activities and games, encouraging everyone to join the fun. Find your way to the trade fair and you'll find some wonderful arts and crafts—alpaca products, hats made from llama wool, handcrafted wooden toys, gemstone jewellery, and edible delicacies such as bison jerky. Outside the park, venues change yearly for the dozens of concerts that take place, but one of the most intriguing performance sites is the St. Boniface Cathedral. With a long and storied history dating back to the 19th century—including a devastating fire in 1968 which left nothing but limestone ruins—today a smaller church stands, constructed inside the ruins, its outdoor atrium providing the perfect stage for musicians.🍁
www.festivalvoyageur.mb.ca

5 faves

Winter sports at Portneuf wildlife reserve

This nature and wildlife reserve, 130 kilometres (80.8 miles) from Québec City, has all the ingredients for getting the most out of Canadian winter. At 775 square kilometres (299 square miles), the huge park has your choice of snowmobiling, cross-country skiing, snowshoeing, nature walks, and sledding.

◄ Test Your Klondike Skills at the Yukon Sourdough Rendezvous

The Yukon Sourdough Rendezvous is the kind of event where men are men and women are tough. Yukoners take pride in the skills needed to perform such muscular tasks as chopping wood, wielding axes and chainsaws, and racing around with heavy objects. Contestants pit themselves against one another during the Mad(am) Trapper competition to determine who is the ultimate athlete.

Watch or participate to find out who is top dog in the Flour Packing contest, who can walk the furthest with hundreds of pounds of flour on their backs, and who is most skilled in events such as the Axe Throw, Chainsaw Chuck, Swede Saw, and Log Toss. Scores in each discipline are combined to find the Mad Trapper (among the men) and Madam Trapper (among the women). Even dogs get involved in the rendezvous; the Babe Southwick Memorial Dog Sled Races and the Dog Pull give canines a chance to haul their weight.

The Rendezvous began in Whitehorse in 1962. Over the years, the city has hosted such oddball events as the Dog Howling Contest, a competition for the woman with the hairiest legs, and the fellow with the best beard. It's won numerous awards, and television host Rick Mercer taped his show from the site in 2006.♦
www.yukonrendezvous.com

Unwind at Nova Scotia's White Point Beach Lodge

Warmth and the crackle of logs burning in the fireplace. The crash of waves on a beach just outside your window. The perfect pairings for a winter getaway. Served up after the physical joy of a good walk in the crisp sea air, it's the ideal rejuvenating experience.

At White Point Beach Resort, in southeastern Nova Scotia, the Atlantic Ocean is a perfect backdrop to the lodge and cabins. The rustic ambiance is enhanced by a proliferation of bunnies . . . yes, rabbits are permanent greeters here. The Lodge provides a casual retreat, a place to slow down, gaze at the ocean from the indoor hot tub, or float in the heated saltwater swimming pool. You can also visit the Ocean Spa to be pampered to the tune of breaking waves and seabird calls. Perhaps the best aspects of winter visits are the many ways to keep warm. Well-stocked fireplaces or wood stoves in the cottages create an intimate atmosphere. A huge stone fireplace lures guests, inviting them to sit and enjoy the camaraderie of sharing time with others in a lounge (with a water view) designed for lingering. Outdoor temperatures tend to be several degrees milder than inland, warmed by ocean currents. You might even spot surfers riding the waves. Families, including pets, are welcome. The dining room features a "Taste of Nova Scotia" menu focused on local fare . . . with free treats for the bunnies.♦
www.whitepoint.com

Cricket match in Victoria

Cricket has been played in Victoria since the middle of the 19th century. The game continues to flourish here, though English accents are now often replaced with those from the Punjab, the Caribbean, and Down Under. You can see the white-uniformed bowlers and batsmen play at the scenic Beacon Hill Park from May to September.

Nova Scotia Winter Ice Wine Festival

During the first half of February, chefs and winemakers team up to celebrate local food and wine, with numerous tastings and opportunities for hands-on winemaking lessons. Over 10 days, there are more than 40 events celebrating Nova Scotia's award-winning icewines.

Canadian Ski Marathon

This annual, two-day cross-country ski event can be anything from bucolic to gruelling—it's up to you. Divided into 10 sections that span 160 kilometres (99.4 miles)—you can do as many or as few as you like—it attracts 2,200 skiers every year and travels through beautiful wilderness trails.

Cycle Victoria's Galloping Goose Trail

The Goose is mostly graded, relatively level, and passes through some of Victoria's most picture-perfect neighbourhoods and urban wilderness—all the way to Sooke. If you don't want to bike the whole thing, there are numerous places to park along the way.

Your next STEP

TOP PICKS
ADVENTURE
CULTURE & HISTORY
NATURE'S GRANDEUR
EVENTS & FESTIVALS
QUIRKY CANADA
REJUVENATE

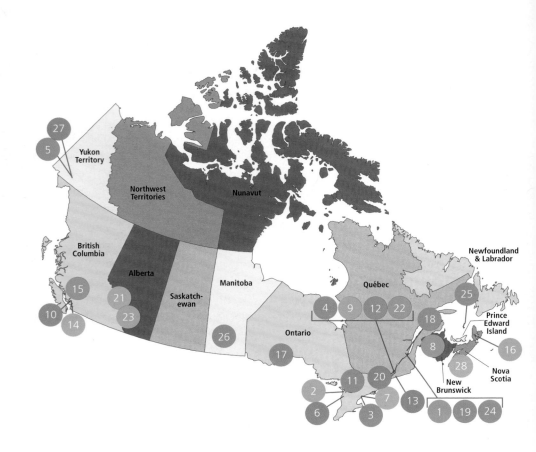

WEEK 1

1 QUÉBEC CITY, QUE.
Carnaval de Québec
www.carnaval.qc.ca/en

2 TOBERMORY, ONT.
Bruce Trail skiing
www.brucetrail.org

3 TORONTO, ONT.
Canadian Opera Company
www.coc.ca

4 MONTRÉAL, QUE.
Montréal Biodôme
www.ville.montreal.qc.ca/biodome

5 WHITEHORSE, Y.T.
Yukon Quest race
www.yukonquest.com

6 WIARTON, ONT.
Groundhog Day in Wiarton
www.southbrucepeninsula.com

7 TORONTO, ONT.
Ultimate Valentine's chocolate
www.somachocolate.com

WEEK 2

8 PLASTER ROCK, N.B.
World Pond Hockey Championship
www.worldpondhockey.com

9 MONTRÉAL, QUE.
Mount Royal winter sports
www.lemontroyal.qc.ca/en

10 VANCOUVER, B.C.
BC Sports Hall of Fame
www.bcsportshalloffame.com

11 LAKE SIMCOE, ONT.
Ice fishing
www.fishinontario.com

12 MONTRÉAL, QUE.
Montréal Fashion Week
www.montrealfashionweek.ca

13 SAINT-VALENTIN, QUE.
Saint-Valentin festival
www.festivalstvalentin.org

14 VANCOUVER, B.C.
Japanese culinary delights
www.tojos.com

WEEK 3

15 WHISTLER, B.C.
Olympic Winter Games sites
www.olympic.org/vancouver-
2010-winter-olympics

16 BADDECK, N.S.
Cape Breton Island skijoring
www.crownjewelresort.com

17 THUNDER BAY, ONT.
Voyageur Winter Carnival Festival
www.fwhp.ca

18 MONTMORENCY FALLS, QUE.
Ice-climber-watching
www.sepaq.com/ct/pcm

19 QUÉBEC CITY, QUE.
International Pee-Wee Hockey
Tournament
www.tournoipee-wee.qc.ca/
EN/index.html

20 OTTAWA, ONT.
Former nuclear bomb shelter
www.diefenbunker.ca

21 BANFF, ALTA.
Baker Creek Bistro
www.bakercreekbistro.com

WEEK 4

22 MONTRÉAL, QUE.
La Nuit Blanche
www.montrealenlumiere.com

23 CALGARY, ALTA.
Canada Olympic Park luge
www.winsportcanada.ca/cop

24 QUÉBEC CITY, QUE.
Notre-Dame Basilica
www.nddq.org

25 MAGDALEN ISLANDS, QUE.
Baby seal–watching
www.tourismeilesdelamadeleine.com

26 WINNIPEG, MAN.
Festival du Voyageur
www.festivalvoyageur.mb.ca

27 WHITEHORSE, Y.T.
Yukon Sourdough Rendezvous
www.yukonrendezvous.com

28 HUNTS POINT, N.S.
White Point Beach Lodge
www.whitepoint.com

MARCH

Drive the Ice Road from Inuvik to Tuktoyaktuk

Be your own "ice road trucker" in this fast-disappearing experience

On the edge of the Arctic Ocean in early March, the days are slowly getting longer. The temperature in Inuvik remains below zero, but it's not the bone-crunching cold of early winter. Cars and trucks ease their way along the 185-kilometre (115-mile) ice road to Tuktoyaktuk—or "Tuk" as it's known to locals. The treeline disappears as you head north, the blue ice is solid beneath your wheels. The road's wide surface looks fragile but is almost as strong and smooth as an Ontario highway.

Once the weather's cold enough winter roads are built over rivers and lakes, providing a lifeline to isolated northern communities such as Tuktoyaktuk that are only accessible by plane the rest of the year. During the few

months of the year the road is open, trucks use them to haul in a year's worth of fuel and other supplies. Meanwhile, residents travel to other communities and visit one another—the roads providing a physical connection to the outside world. It's here and in other parts of the North that people's daily lives and the environment are so inextricably linked.

Ice Road Truckers is a popular reality television series on The History Channel that follows the exploits of truckers who drive heavy loads along ice roads to deliver goods to mines north of Yellowknife and exploration camps north of Inuvik. The show has drawn millions of viewers and makes it look like truckers are risking life and limb. But real life is nowhere near as dramatic. In reality, it's a pretty smooth ride.

Fly from Edmonton to Inuvik on Canadian North or First Air. Inuvik sits two degrees above the Arctic Circle on the scenic Mackenzie River, at the edge of the Beaufort Sea. It's the region's administrative centre and redefines the term "government town." The federal government created the community of about 3,500 Inuvialuit and Gwich'in people in the 1950s to replace Aklavik, a low-lying isolated community nearby sitting in the maze of channels that is the Mackenzie Delta. Aklavik was—and remains—vulnerable to flooding. While some moved to Inuvik, Aklavik's community of nearly 600 remains.

Rent a vehicle from National Car Rental (Norcan Leasing in Inuvik) or Arctic Chalet Car Rentals. The ice road is open from late December to late April, but the best time to drive is in March because the road is still solid but the weather isn't as bone-chillingly cold. For the most up-to-date ice road conditions, check with the Northwest Territories Department of

Transportation before you travel. Prepare cold-weather gear and emergency supplies and ensure your vehicle has a shovel, candles (for emergency heating), extra water, and snacks in case you break down or get stuck. Don't forget to dress warmly and in layers.

The condition of the road depends on the weather. When the road is groomed, it's like driving on pavement. Early in the day, it's often covered with a light dusting of snow, which offers good traction. But, watch your speed. Once the sun starts shining and melting the snow, there's glare ice—which can be slippery. The speed limit is 70 kilometres (43 miles) per hour, but take the time to enjoy this once-in-a-lifetime experience. Drive slowly and stop often to experience walking on the ice, taking pictures, and enjoying the bleak surroundings that seem to go on forever. When will you get another chance to peer through the ice at the Arctic Ocean beneath your wheels? If talk of building an all-weather road to Tuk turns to reality, driving in the tire tracks of ice road truckers may no longer be an option . . . Grab the opportunity while you can!

Once you reach Tuk, be sure to tour Inuvialuit (population 900). Find the marker for the end of the Trans Canada Trail. One of the village's landmarks along the coastline is its *pingos*—unusual mounds of Arctic ice covered with dirt, about 30 to 50 metres (98.4 to 164 feet) high. One pingo is 16 stories high, which lends an interesting visual backdrop to the community. There's so much permafrost here that locals have made good use of it, so be sure to check out the community freezer (carved several metres down into the ice). It gives a whole new meaning to the term "walk-in freezer." Once inside, you can see the layers of ice and sediment that created this fascinating, seemingly barren land. Upon your return to Inuvik, stop by Our Lady of Victory Roman Catholic Church. Nicknamed the Igloo Church, it's round and has a beautifully designed interior.

If you prefer to have your own ice road driver, Up North Travel & Tours (867/587-2480) and Arctic Chalet (www.arcticchalet.com) offer tours. Travel along the Mackenzie River and Beaufort Sea ice following the route of the "Ice Road Truckers."

Find out more at:
www.dot.gov.nt.ca/_live/pages/ wpPages/Winter_and_ice_roads.aspx

ADVENTURE

CULTURE & HISTORY

Ski with the Legendary Nancy Greene at Sun Peaks

Imagine getting to play hockey with Wayne Gretzky or soccer with Pelé—for free. Well, at Sun Peaks Resort, you can do downhill with Nancy Greene, the 1968 Olympic gold medallist in women's giant slalom, at no extra charge. Early March—which typically sees an abundance of fresh powder and sparkling sunshine—is an excellent time to hit the slopes at this popular resort near Kamloops, a four-hour drive from Vancouver.

Greene, named Canada's Female Athlete of the Century in 1999, meets skiers at 1:00 p.m. on Saturdays and Sundays at the top of the Sunburst Express chairlift. "I love Sun Peaks because it's big-mountain skiing, but it's got the more intimate atmosphere of a smaller resort," said Greene. "A lot of people are surprised to see me out on the hill."

She may be near 70 years old, but you'll soon recognize she still brings world-class skill to the slopes. While showing visitors around Canada's third-largest ski area on three mountains—nearly 1,497 hectares (3,700 acres) of skiable terrain with 11 chairlifts and 122 runs—Greene happily answers questions about Sun Peaks while offering tips on improving your form. It's a golden experience. ◆
www.sunpeaksresort.com

Visit Halifax's Historic Pier 21

Pier 21, at the Port of Halifax's south end, began receiving immigrants to Canada on March 8, 1928. Today, the site pays tribute to more than one million people from around the world who chose Canada as their home. From 1928 to 1971 it was Canada's front door for immigrants, refugees, troops, wartime evacuees, and war brides and their children. Arrivals disembarked from trans-Atlantic ships here, where they were interviewed by immigration officials and had their papers checked before boarding trains bound for the rest of Canada. In 1971, Pier 21 closed as an immigration point having admitted large waves of newcomers from places including England, Hungary, Baltic nations, Italy, and Germany. In 1999, Pier 21 opened as a national historic site. Ten years later it became the Canadian Museum of Immigration at Pier 21, only the second national museum to be located outside Ottawa, the nation's capital.

Pier 21's history as an immigration "shed" comes to life through interactive exhibits and displays that allow you to walk around the port and "board" a train heading west. Canada's participation during the desperate days of World War II becomes more real when you realize that 500,000 military personnel boarded ships right here, bound for battle in Europe. For many researching their family's immigration story—by finding names on passengers lists, learning details about the ships and migration procedures, reading the stories of other migrants, and then contributing their own stories—a visit holds significant meaning. ◆
www.pier21.ca

Watch Ice Floes in P.E.I. National Park

As the days get longer and sunnier, Prince Edward Island's outdoor enthusiasts head to the shore to check out the sea ice. Is it moving in or out?

Those with keener powers of observation may spot snowy owls, snow buntin, horned lark, red foxes, or even coyotes.

Ice surrounding Canada's smallest province helps determine spring's arrival by keeping air cool. Prince Edward Island National Park, particularly near North Rustico, is perfect for a walk among ice floes that range in size from a suitcase to a pickup truck—floes stranded on the beach by tides or storms. At this time of year, photographers especially enjoy the contrast between red cliffs, blue skies, and white ice. Those with keener powers of observation may spot snowy owls, snow buntin, horned lark, red foxes, or even coyotes. In some years, free-floating floes look like miniature icebergs. In other years, pack ice—viewed from the cliffs—seems solid enough for a walk to Québec's Magdalen Islands. But, look long enough and the realization comes that the white mass offshore is moving. Before your very eyes, floes constantly grind against one another, rising and falling with every wave and tide action. Know that the ice performs a significant task, protecting cliffs, beaches, and fragile dunes, which winter nor'easters or heavy seas can damage and even sweep away. Don't go beyond the water's edge (the ice is slippery!). And do wear sunglasses. Cross-country skiing, skating at Dalvay, or onshore picnics easily and joyfully fill a winter day at the national park. ❧
www.pc.gc.ca/eng/pn-np/pe/pei-ipe/index.aspx

Canadian moments

RRRoll Up the Rim

Are you a one-thumber or a squeeze-and-roller? Or, perhaps you use a Rimroller—a patented device designed solely to unroll the rim on a Tim Horton's cup.

The annual RRRoll Up the Rim contest, run by nationwide chain Tim Horton's, sees more than 47 million prizes (for 2011) concealed under the rims of its hot-drink cups. That's more than one prize for every Canadian! The coffee and doughnut giant (or "donut" as spelled on Tim's menus) even runs a version of the contest at the Kandahar Airfield in Afghanistan.

In 2006, two Québec families asked the courts to decide the ownership of a found RRRoll Up the Rim cup. While one girl found the cup in a garbage can, she asked another to help her roll up the rim. Under the lip, they found a winning message—for a sport utility vehicle. To add to the bizarre situation, a school employee also claimed the cup was his and wanted a DNA test to prove it.

RRRoll Up the Rim grips many caffeine-loving Canadians with its prizes, ranging from coffee to cars. But all cups are not made equal and chances of winning vary throughout the country.

Jon Lin, an IT auditor, has run the numbers. He analyzes and charts the prize stats each year on his website (www.jonlin.ca). In 2010, British Columbians had the best chance in winning a grand-prize Toyota RAV4, but, calculated Lin, the worst in winning the $10,000 cash prize.

But "Timmy's" as the chain's fondly known, is not popular only at RRRoll Up the Rim time. Canadians reportedly eat the most doughnuts per capita, and the snack even has its own history book—The Donut: A Canadian History by Steve Penfold.

EVENTS & FESTIVALS

Get into the Rhythm of the Vancouver International Dance Festival

Are you in love with the human body's ability to cavort, contort, and create incredible emotions through motion? Then put on your dancing shoes and head for the Vancouver International Dance Festival (VIDF). Established in 2000, this annual multi-week festival showcases local and international contemporary dance artists. With venues ranging from Yaletown's high-ceilinged Roundhouse Community Centre to the park-surrounded Shadbolt Centre for the Arts in Burnaby, you could find yourself enthralled by anything from the dynamic flamenco footwork of Spain's Ana Arroyo to an orchestrally backed performance of butoh (a subversive, evocative Japanese dance with performers in white makeup) by the festival's parent company, Kokoro Dance. Belly dancing, tap dancing, and other disciplines are also on display.

You don't just have to sit and watch. Sign up for one of the festival's contemporary dance workshops at the Harbour Dance Centre on Granville Street, and let master-class instructor Marc Boivin teach you to incorporate ballet principles into your own performance on the dance floor. But it's the interaction with the audience that makes VIDF a unique experience—one that keeps artists from New York to Switzerland coming back year after year to show their support. 🍁

www.vidf.ca

Spend the Night at Québec's Hôtel de Glace —an Ice Hotel ▼

What does an "ice hotel" look like? Picture an artistic feat made from 15,000 tonnes (more than 33 million pounds) of snow and 500 tonnes (approximately 1.1 million pounds) of ice, showcasing a new architectural design each year. This hotel, the only one of its kind in North America, officially opens in January and only lasts until the spring melt—or about three months.

Entrance (about C$20) allows you to tour the property (just outside Québec City) from 10:00 a.m. to 8:00 p.m.; if you arrive after that the price is only C$13 as the sleeping quarters are off limits. And, yes, people really spend the night. There are 21 basic rooms and 15 individually designed suites that offer a themed decor, all with a queen-sized mattress on a block of ice. Guests get a Nordic sleeping bag to keep them warm, up to –40 degrees Celsius (–40 degrees Fahrenheit)—plenty cozy when the interior room temperature averages a balmy –5 degrees Celsius (23 degrees Fahrenheit). A room for two starts at C$400.

Things everybody can enjoy are the exquisite Ice Chandelier, the Ice Chapel (there are 20 weddings in an average year), Ice Slide (for kids of all ages), the Ice Café, and the Ice Bar, where the signature cocktail (ice cider and vodka) is served in a flute chiselled from ice. Stay until midnight if you feel like dancing.

Should there be a naysayer travelling with you who just can't take the cold, there's a heated pavilion, including a restaurant, just next door.🍁
www.icehotel-canada.com

◀ Soak Up the Fresh Air at a Scandinavian-Style Spa

The word spa is actually an acronym for the Latin phrase Sanitas Per Aquam, which means "health through water." An afternoon of hydrotherapy at Scandinave Spa is the perfect way to recharge your batteries before the kiddies get their break in March.

There are two locations in Québec: one in Old Montréal and another in Tremblant, about 90 minutes outside the city. The advantage of the mountain location is that all the pools, saunas, and baths are outdoors— so guests can slow down and rest up deep in Mother Nature's bosom.

Your soak will be accompanied by the sound of birdsong, or the wind caressing the trees as you move between the hot and cold pools. Flip-flops and cover-ups, a worthwhile investment at this time of year, are recommended. You can rent a big robe for C$15, which comes with a free smoothie from the health bar. This wilderness oasis has two hot tubs, a Finnish dry sauna, Norwegian steam bath, three cold baths (get that blood flowing!), and four solariums for supreme relaxation.

Open every day from 10:00 a.m. to 9:00 p.m., it costs C$48 to use the aqua facilities. For those who want to more completely unwind, massage treatments are also available. The grounds are completely co-ed, making them a romantic getaway for couples. But groups of friends also come here to get away and leave the city behind.🍁
www.scandinave.com

Witness the Breathtaking Power of a Pacific Storm

Nature's fury makes for compelling viewing, particularly from inside some of Canada's top hotels

A late winter storm rages at its peak. Amidst tempestuous winds, ocean waves as high as six metres (20 feet) smash the beach, white spray lashing against jagged headlands and huge logs careening into the sand. It's awe-inspiring, a total contrast to the image of serene natural beauty that draws visitors to Tofino the rest of the year. Here, in this laid-back town of 1,600 on the west coast of Vancouver Island, facing the open Pacific Ocean, storm-watching has become a major attraction. In March you can catch the last of the big winter storms, donning a yellow slicker to get outdoors and see some amazingly fierce weather.

Spending a few days storm-watching, surrounded by old-growth cedars and firs in Pacific Rim National Park, comes at a cost. In 2011, Tofino—the last stop on Highway 4—had Canada's highest-priced accommodations on average. Its wintertime popularity is a tribute to the vision of Wickaninnish Inn founder Charles McDiarmid, who opened his luxury resort on the waterfront in 1996, specifically with the newfangled concept of storm-watching in mind. Back then, many locals thought no-

body would come in the off-season, but McDiarmid's big gamble paid off in splashy fashion.

Poetically perched on clifftops, the lavish Relais & Chateaux property offers ocean views from all 75 rooms. And whether you're sipping an espresso in the Driftwood Lounge, dining on fresh-baked halibut and clams at the Pointe Restaurant, or receiving a hot stone massage in the Ancient Cedars Spa, you can always gaze out over the waves pounding Chesterman Beach. Take time to stroll the two separate loops of the Rainforest Trail, full of huge trees and fallen logs encrusted with moss, with banana slugs and ferns everywhere. In 2010, *Travel + Leisure* readers voted the "Wick" Canada's best hotel.

Want a different vantage point? Two more well-regarded resorts await in nearby Cox Bay, only a tad less luxurious. Long Beach Lodge Resort (with its cottages equipped with fireplaces and hot tubs) and Pacific Sands Beach Resort (with its luxury beachfront villas) both offer panoramic ocean views.

There's always something to do in Tofino between storms. Cox Bay is also famed for its superb coldwater surfing, with big waves from the reef at Lennart Island, just offshore. When the weather's not too crazy, watch pro surfers riding the major breaks. Prefer to participate? Get your gear at Live to Surf or Long Beach Surf Shop, and hook up some lessons through Westside Surf School, operated by local pro Sepp Bruhwiler, or Surf Sister—for women only.

In more placid weather, renting a kayak from the Tofino Sea Kayaking Company and paddling around the nearby islands is a perfect introduction to local ecology. In March, more than 10,000 grey whales migrate past Vancouver Island towards the Bering Sea (see p. 75); you might catch sight

of some spouting. Seals swim by occasionally, and blue herons soar overhead.

Back on shore, it's worth doing a little beachcombing. After storms, when blue skies and sunshine often prevail, you can find interesting flotsam and jetsam that's washed up: whale bones, running shoes, downhill skis, or even—if you're extra-lucky—beautiful, coloured Japanese glass fishing floats. Another must-see on Chesterman Beach is the "Carving Shack" where Joe Martin, a member of the Nuu-chah-nulth First Nation, plies his trade. A renowned canoe-maker, Martin has carved nearly 50 of these traditional Native vessels out of red cedar.

Pop into the recently revamped, waterfront Kwisitis Centre (formerly the Wickaninnish Interpretive Centre) at the end of Wick Road. Check out exhibits and films laden with 3D visuals that tell the story of Tofino's Aboriginal people, see cultural artifacts on display, and learn about local marine life and wildlife.

More Aboriginal culture awaits when you head into funky Tofino proper. Notable galleries include Eagle Aerie Gallery, selling original prints with bold red-and-black Native designs and natural scenes by famed artist Roy Henry Vickers. Or there's the House of Himwitsa, a First Nations-owned operation showcasing ceremonial masks, abalone pendants, and moccasins from all along the B.C. coast. Alternately, browse through the hand-blown glass creations of American artist Sol Maya at Spirit of the Fire, Maya's glass studio.

When you're ready for a break, Tuff Beans—an ever-popular organic, fair-trade coffeehouse—dishes up breakfast and lunch all day, plus great chai lattes and hot chocolate. Come dinnertime, critically acclaimed Sobo beckons with its Vancouver Island artisan cheeses, fresh oysters, spot prawns, and woodstone oven pizzas. The creative menu at the tiny Spotted Bear Bistro, which leans on B.C. ingredients, is another magnet serving roasted ling cod with ginger coconut broth and Fraser Valley duck breast with chive parmesan salad.

Whatever the weather brings, Tofino's an ideal place to detox from your busy, urban life. And, when the storms are at their fiercest, there's something pure and true in remembering nature's primal power and beauty. ❧

Find out more at:
www.tourismtofino.com

◀ Go Heli-Skiing in the Powder-Filled Kootenays

If you're an intermediate or advanced skier or snowboarder, bypass the resorts and make reservations to go heli-skiing or heli-boarding in the mind-boggling scenery and deep, untracked powder of the Kootenay region in southeast British Columbia.

The world's original—and now largest—heli-ski operation is CMH, founded in 1965 by Austrian mountain guide Hans Gmoser in the Bugaboos (in the Purcell Mountains of eastern B.C.). Today, the operation has grown to include almost limitless terrain over five mountain ranges accessed from 11 lodges. The routine is simple—CMH guests spend their days skiing and boarding, a helicopter at their beck and call, then retreat to a private CMH lodge to enjoy fine dining and luxuries such as outdoor hot tubs with the best mountain views. Each CMH lodge has its own personality, ranging from road-accessible Kootenay Lodge (perfect for shorter stays), to Galena Lodge (famed for its deep powder and exciting tree skiing). But beware: heli-skiing can become addictive! Around 3,500 guests have skied over one million vertical feet with CMH (earning themselves a distinctive blue ski suit), while a number have skied more than 10 million vertical feet.✤
www.canadianmountainholidays.com

5 faves

North Pacific Cannery Village Museum

British Columbia's oldest working salmon-cannery village reached its apex from 1910 to 1950, when the workforce numbered 400 and the community grew to about 1,200; the cannery has been closed since 1968. Now a national historic site, the complex includes the cannery building, various administration buildings and residences, the company store, a hotel, and a dining hall.

Learn Dene Hand Games at a Northern Festival

Two teams of men are kneeling on gym mats facing each other. One group has their arms crossed against their chests, clenched fists tucked under their armpits. Their opponents stare at them intently as drums beat rhythmically and a crowd surrounds them. A pile of sticks sits in the middle. Welcome to the Canadian Aboriginal Hand Games Championship in Behchoko, near Yellowknife.

Dene hand games are a staple of community festivals and events in the Northwest Territories. These friendly competitions foster cultural and community pride. Members of one team place their hands under a sheet or blanket while they hide an object in one hand. Then they remove their clenched fists.

The captain of the opposing team uses hand signals to try to correctly guess in which hand the object's hidden. Players open their hands to reveal whether or not a guess is correct. Whenever the captain makes an incorrect guess the opposing team receives a stick, marking a point. The person who hid the object that was correctly found is eliminated from the game. Each team typically has four people. The game ends when the captain has correctly guessed (and eliminated) all the players, or the opposing team wins all the sticks.

This is a great sport, if you want to learn more about Dene—and Aboriginal—culture. As you watch from the sidelines, make your own (silent) guesses about where objects are being hidden. How do your skills measure up to the pros?❈
www.denegames.ca

Try Finnish "Kicksledding" in Northern Ontario

Here's an activity for the outdoor winter enthusiast who has done it all. A kicksled is, well, what it sounds like: a scooter for the snow. In other words, two parallel skis joined by vertical shafts and horizontal bars with handgrips. You put a foot on one ski, while the other foot pushes off the ground—propelling you forward. This winter novelty is brought to you courtesy of Mattawa and its four sister counties along the Ontario-Québec border. They've imported a bunch of kicksleds from Finland and rent them by the hour (C$8) or half day (C$12).

It's certainly not a novelty in Scandinavia, where it's more a tool than a toy.

Designed for use on hardpack snow—Scandinavian countries tend to leave their sidewalks unsalted and hard-packed—the standard kicksled looks a bit like a dogsled, with the driver at the back and the cargo up front. A newer version is more akin to a mountain bike, sturdier and lighter. For outdoor recreation, kicksleds offer an excellent form of cardiovascular exercise. And Mattawa features an extensive trail system, with paths specially groomed for the kicksled. (They won't work in deep snow.) The activity was introduced to the area by the owners of Nature's Harmony Ecolodge, who can point you to local trails and rent you a kicksled (about C$12 for a half day).❈
www.naturesharmony.ca/#/winter/winter

National Gallery of Canada
One of the most attractive buildings in Ottawa overlooks the Ottawa River. Inside? More than 800 works regularly on display, with highlights including a comprehensive collection of works by Tom Thomson and the Group of Seven, early Québécois artists, and Montréal *automatistes*.

Fitness and indulgence in Québec's Eastern Townships
The Spa Eastman health and wellness retreat is the only one of its kind. Up your fitness quotient with daily yoga, pilates, Chi-Kung, or kick-boxing, then dine on spa cuisine, or indulge in an extensive list of beauty and relaxation treatments. The resort overlooks the scenic Mount Orford.

Drive the Sea to Sky Highway
Highway 99, from Vancouver to Lillooet, takes you from a dramatic seacoast past glaciers, pine forests, and a waterfall through Whistler's majestic glacial mountains. The four-hour drive winds up a series of switchbacks to the thickly forested Cayoosh Creek valley, and the craggy mountains surrounding the Fraser River Gold Rush town of Lillooet.

Attend a *ceilidh* on Cape Breton Island
Ceilidhs (sort of like musical kitchen parties, or a live gig by local musicians playing Celtic music in a local pub) are one-of-a-kind experiences here. The town of Mabou is a great place to find them, but plenty of ceilidhs take place across the island.

EVENTS & FESTIVALS

▲

Rock Out and Cheer Your Favourite Team at the Brier

If you're Canadian and you're familiar with the terms "skip," "biter," and "hogged stone," you're surely aware of the Brier—the Canadian men's curling championship, held annually in a different Canadian city each year and renowned for its party atmosphere as much as the actual curling.

Each Brier is contested by 12 teams (one from each province—except Ontario, which sends two—and a team from one of the three territories) that have won provincial or territorial championships. The team that wins the Brier then competes as Team Canada at the world curling championships. However, winning the Brier is often considered more difficult, making it curling's ultimate prize.

While teams are competing for the Brier tankard, it's the sell-out crowds of knowledgeable, provincially parochial fans that make the event truly special. Blue Nosers, Herring Chokers, Stubble Jumpers, Moose Men, and Polar Bears are all nicknames fans have given to their home provinces—dressing the part, cheering loudly, and partying into the early hours of the morning at the Patch (as in the brier patch), a drinking-and-dancing space set up by the host city. Western Canada is where the party really takes off; the top-eight attended Briers have all been in Alberta, Manitoba, or Saskatchewan (including two championships in Saskatoon, site of the 2012 Brier). ♣
www.curling.ca

Pay Homage to the Snowking amidst the Houseboats of Yellowknife Bay ▶

The windswept snow crunches underfoot on Yellowknife Bay's icy covering. It's evening and an adult-sized ice castle is alight amidst the most northerly year-round houseboat community in North America. Every year, blocks of snow here are carved into a castle for the Annual Snowking Winter Festival.

Yellowknifer Anthony Foliot, self-appointed Snowking, started the event more than 15 years ago as a fun way for kids to celebrate winter. It's now a month-long festival also enjoyed by adults. Foliot rocks the joint with jam sessions, concerts, a film festival, an art show, snow volleyball, the Snowking Hockey Challenge, the Royal Ball, and other cultural events.

Brightly coloured houseboats have a front-row view of a makeshift hockey rink with wooden boards, two nets, and a hockey stick plunked into a snowbank. During the day, people walk over to the snowy ticket window at the castle's entrance. Then they wander inside for a hot chocolate, climb up to the top for a view of the bay, and watch kids enjoy the slide that has been carved into the snow. Amazingly, even weddings have taken place here in the castle's chapel. ◈

www.snowking.ca

Lounge in the Sublime Columbia Valley Hot Springs

Winter in the Columbia Valley ends earlier than in the adjacent Canadian Rockies, but early March is still too cool for the valley's best-known pursuits such as water sports and golf—making this the perfect time to soak away your cares in one of the region's three hot springs. These pools are particularly stimulating when edged by snow and covered in steam—your head is almost cold in the chill air, but your submerged body melts into oblivion.

Discovered many centuries ago by the Kootenay people who used it as a healing source, the Radium Hot Springs are now diverted into large concrete pools backed by steep cliffs. Nearby hot springs were also used by indigenous people though they wouldn't recognize the place today. Fairmont Hot Springs Resort comprises four-star accommodations, three golf courses, a small ski resort, and resort-style homes. Despite all the commercialism, the hot springs are still the main attraction. Their appeal is simple: unlike most other springs, the water here contains calcium, not sulphur with its attendant smell. More adventurous bathers can find solitude at Lussier Hot Springs, signposted along the unpaved road out to Whiteswan Lake Provincial Park. After scrambling down into a gorge, you find two —usually empty—crudely built pools containing very hot but odourless water. ◈

www.adventurevalley.com

Welcome the First Day of Spring in Stanley Park

Blossoms and totem poles are the jewels of a season in full bloom

It almost qualifies as a miracle. Typically on the first day of spring, while the rest of Canada is still clomping around in boots and mittens complaining about snow-clogged driveways and icy roads, Vancouver's Stanley Park typically offers a blissful blend of cherry blossoms and mild breezes. This is one of the best times of year to experience the 405-hectare (1,000-acre) swath of greenery, just a stone's throw from the glass-towered condos and office buildings of downtown.

So where's the best place to start exploring the urban park that former Governor General of Canada Lord Stanley inaugurated in 1888? At the end of West Georgia Street, where you can begin your park adventure by enjoying a leisurely 1.8-kilometre (1.1-mile) circuit of Lost Lagoon. This tranquil body of fresh water, high-lighted by a soaring fountain and a stone bridge, is named after a 1911 poem by half-Mohawk/half-English author Pauline Johnson. You'll likely spot nesting swans, flocks of ducks, and foraging skunks and raccoons along these shores. (Resist the temptation to feed the raccoons,

which can be persistent.) Pop into the Nature House at the southeast corner of Lost Lagoon to learn more about these critters. Be sure to also check out the nearby biofil-tration wetland where bullfrogs and turtles seek shelter.

Head through the Georgia Street underpass, past Coal Harbour's sailboats and into the park, and you'll soon find the Vancouver Aquarium. Best known for its whimsically beautiful beluga whales, it's a great place to take kids on spring break. They'll thrill to the sight of Pacific dolphins leaping in outdoor shows conducted by trainers, and giggle at sea otters floating on their backs. From Amazon piranhas to translucent jellyfish, the aquarium houses more than 70,000 creatures.

Spring brings innumerable wedding parties and camera-toting tourists to the imposing totem poles at nearby Brockton Point. This showcase of native culture is British Columbia's most-visited attraction. Carved by the Kwakwaka'wakw, Haida, and Nuu-chah-nulth First Nations, the poles colourfully incorporate thunderbird, killer whale, and bear motifs. Purchase Native mementos at the Legends of the Moon Gift Shop, or grab a coffee and snacks at the café.

The totem poles sit within eyeshot of the 8.9-kilometre (5.5-mile) seawall that encircles Stanley Park. The banked concrete pathway is ideal for walking, running, rollerblading, or biking on the first day of spring. But don't rush, or you'll miss some quirky pieces of Vancouver lore.

Near Hallelujah Point, you'll see a 2.7-metre (nine-foot) high bronze statue of Vancouver-born sprinter Harry Jerome. The one-time 100-metre world

record-holder won bronze at the 1964 Olympic Games, but tragically died at age 42. More metallic glory lies ahead. If it's evening, be prepared for the boom of the Nine O'Clock Gun, a cannon fired each night exactly when its name suggests. And on Stanley Park's north side, you'll discover the Girl in a Wetsuit statue on an intertidal boulder. It's Vancouver's graceful answer to Copenhagen's Little Mermaid.

Naturally, much of what makes Stanley Park special in springtime are its gardens. Perennials, annuals, and freshly planted bulbs greet flower lovers at the Stanley Park Rose Garden. Next to the Stanley Park Pitch & Putt, the pink-and-red splendour of the Ted and Mary Greig Rhododendron Garden is another fragrant favourite.

On a clear spring day, the views in Stanley Park show why this corner of Canada is called "Lotusland." Even if you're simply sitting on a log at Second or Third Beach listening to the breeze and gazing out across Burrard Inlet, the vibe—of tranquility and relaxation—is truly palpable.

Take a moment to contemplate Siwash Rock, protruding from the water off the Park's west side. This natural monolith is the subject of a supernatural legend about a Squamish chief who chose to be transformed into stone rather than abandon his wife and child. It's a beautiful counterpoint to the modern skyline serving as its backdrop.

At the Prospect Point Cafe, you can munch on burgers and chowder while relishing a treelined, clifftop view of the Lions Gate Bridge, linking Vancouver to the North Shore. The resemblance to San Francisco's Golden Gate Bridge hits you immediately. Unsurprisingly, the two bridges opened at almost the same time in the late 1930s. The view of the North Shore Mountains—Cypress, Grouse, and Seymour—is even more expansive than it used to be, since a massive windstorm ravaged Prospect Point's old-growth cedars and Douglas firs in 2006. However, new greenery is emerging.

It's the feeling of new life you'll savour at the spring equinox, whether you're bird-watching at the heron sanctuary by the tennis courts near English Bay, taking a romantic horse-drawn carriage ride, or hiking through Stanley Park's twisting, verdant trails. You might even come across lovers in the shade of wooded glens. After all, Lord Stanley (he of Stanley Cup fame) did dedicate the park "to the use and enjoyment of people of all colours, creeds, and customs, for all time."🍁

Find out more at:

www.vancouver.ca/parks/parks/stanley

ADVENTURE

Ski across the Lakes of Quetico

If you're a cross-country skier looking for a challenge in a spectacular setting, consider the Quetico Lakes Tour— an all-day adventure across the frozen lakes of beautiful Quetico Provincial Park, 200 kilometres (124.2 miles) west of Thunder Bay. It's hosted by the Beaten Path Nordic Trails group, but don't be fooled by the name— there's no beaten path to follow. This is all about wide-open spaces.

The conditions are ideal in late March, with milder temperatures but no risk of the lakes thawing. Arrive on the Friday for socializing (and the safety briefing), then get a good night's sleep. The bus leaves early from the town of Atikokan to the trailhead. And the skiing doesn't stop until the day is done. Three routes ranging between 35 and 55 kilometres (21.7 and 34.2 miles) are meant to challenge every skill level, the prerequisite being endurance. Routes are dotted with warming stations staffed by volunteers serving hot drinks and words of encouragement. Some winters offer a smooth-crust surface as uniform as a crisply tucked bedsheet; other years offer bare ice. Seasoned skiers bring their steel-edged skis so they can skate-ski, while skijoring aficionados bring their dogs to help pull them along. Mushers: feel free to bring your sleigh and dog team, so long as they play nicely with other dogs. Heated yurt accommodations are available in the Dawson Campground, but be sure to call ahead. ❧

atikokancanoe.tripod.com/beatenpath

CULTURE & HISTORY

Take in St. Paddy's Day in P.E.I.

For one day every year everyone wants to be Irish . . . and the Olde Dublin Pub in Charlottetown, P.E.I., is the perfect place to fulfill the fantasy. St. Patrick's Day celebrations here begin at 8:00 a.m. and continue straight through until 2:00 a.m. the next morning.

It all starts with breakfast, a rollicking affair with music and step-dancing that is often featured on radio and television across Canada. "We're the first on the go," laughs publican Liam Dolan of the annual fundraiser for the Children's Wish Foundation. And go they do. They even have a special licence to serve Guinness with breakfast, kicking off revelry that continues all day. But expect to line up. At Olde Dublin, the St. Paddy's Day festivities are so popular the pub turns its adjacent restaurant into a pub for the day. "It works," says Dolan, an Irish immigrant himself, "because patrons become Irish. It's fun to see Japanese, Chinese, all nationalities, wearing green, jiggin' to rollicking music, and quaffing green beer. Many have Irish ancestors here in P.E.I., but really it's for everyone."

Olde Dublin is in historic Olde Charlottetown, tucked away on a side street, in a restored warehouse. Other bars "make the party bigger and bigger," perfect for a pub crawl. ❧

www.oldedublinpub.com

◀ Hike to the Top of Mount Royal

As Montréal transitions from winter to spring, immerse yourself in the changing of the seasons on Mount Royal, the highest spot in the city at 234 metres (767.7 feet). A hike to the top not only affords you excellent views of the city, but a welcome breather from everyday urban life.

> Then, there's the leisurely stroll onto the summit loop and, if you like, you can go all the way up to the cross overlooking the city.

Start at the Monument to George-Étienne Cartier, the angel at the base of the eastern slope along Parc Avenue, and follow the path laid out in 1876 by landscape architect Frederick Law Olmsted, who also designed New York City's Central Park. The seven-kilometre (4.3-mile) route winds up a gentle slope to the Chalet lookout, which overlooks downtown, the St. Lawrence River, and, on a clear day, a vista all the way to the Adirondack Mountains. Inside there are vending machines that sell snacks and beverages. Then, there's the leisurely stroll onto the summit loop and, if you like, you can go all the way up to the cross overlooking the city. The trees haven't begun budding yet, so now's as good a time as any to get some great views before the leaves begin to grow—blocking the spectacle below you.

Download an informational podcast for free at the *Les amis de la montagne* website (below), or rent an audiovisual player for C$5 at Smith House (a farmhouse built in 1858). Here you'll also find a café (with liquor licence), as well as a permanent exhibit on the mountain's history, geology, and plant life. ❦
www.emontroyal.qc.ca

FeFe Dobson's *favourite* PLACE

There's no place like home for singer Fefe Dobson.

"Toronto is a happening city," she says. "It's always got live music."

Dobson, who released her third album *Joy* in 2010, appreciates events like Canadian Music Week as well as the great artists who have originated from Toronto. She also sings the city's praises for its fashion, food, and international vibe.

"It's very multicultural. Being biracial, it's great to be able to go to a great Jamaican spot in Toronto . . . and then go for French cuisine, or sushi."

Dobson, who has been nominated for Juno and MuchMusic Video awards, recommends taking in the annual MMVAs—which always take place in Toronto. The street party takes over the music channel's headquarters on Queen Street West, close to some of her favourite places to shop.

"I grew up a lot on punk rock. The further you go west there's a lot of rock-and-roll stores.

"If you want to go shopping for vintage pieces, there's a great place called Kensington Market in Chinatown."

But in a busy city, the Toronto-based singer says there are still opportunities for quiet.

"We still have a lot of parks," she says. "It's always great to go sit at a park, and walk your dog, play music, and sit with an acoustic guitar.

"I still do that—just sit in the park and write in my journal."

As with many Canadians, the welcome of spring strikes an appreciative chord with Dobson.

"I really enjoy spring, because everyone gets really excited," she says. "Everyone knows summer is coming."

EVENTS & FESTIVALS

▲

Cheer on Québec City's Daredevil Skaters

Equal parts boarder cross, downhill skating, and roller derby, the Red Bull Crashed Ice Competition combines agility, speed, and a good dose of chutzpah. The world finals are held every year within the walls of Québec City, attracting more than 100,000 energized spectators to the streets. Even if you come and see this new extreme sport first-hand, you still might not believe it.

It's an amazing event to watch because of its novelty, but also because of its tight turns, deep vertical drops, and daring speed. The athletes who participate are mainly hockey players, and dressed as such, minus the sticks, of course. The track—wide enough to accommodate four players at a time—is a 540-metre (1,771.7-foot) ice path that starts at the foot of the Fairmont Le Château Frontenac hotel and snakes its way down a natural slope.

Hardcore fans tend to arrive early to secure front-row viewing (standing-room only). Otherwise, there are massive screens near the finish line. To get back to the top of the hill, the only (quick) way up is to take

Even if you come and see this new extreme sport first-hand, you still might not believe it.

le funiculaire, an inclined elevator connecting the upper and lower towns. With the athletes riding alongside members of the public, it's a great place to try and meet a skater face to face.🍁
www.redbullcrashedice.com

Listen to "Cowboy Poetry" in Taber

Each year on the third Saturday in March, a rural gathering at a community hall in southern Alberta continues a tradition dating back hundreds of years— a celebration of cowboy poetry.

It's thought that the art of cowboy poetry began hundreds of years ago during cattle drives, when wranglers would talk to resting cattle through the night to keep them calm. This tradition has morphed into cowboy poetry. It is a form of entertainment far removed from country music; it's not about drinking and divorce or girls and gambling, but rather the simple western way of life, with themes centred on ranching and farming, history and horses, and broken-down trucks. The audience is as western as the words, with the small but enthusiastic audience dressed to the nines in faded cowboy hats and Wrangler jeans with oversized belt buckles. Showing a genuine love for the rural lifestyle and an unfettered admiration for the poets, they help make the cowboy poetry experience what it is. But the stars of the show are the poets. They come from all walks of life—working cowboys, school-aged children, or maybe a singer performing Patsy Cline songs. The rhyming poetry started as a way to better remember stories told around the campfire, and you'll still hear the rhythm of a horse's canter in recounting their cowboy tales.🍁

www.albertacowboypoetry.com

Celebrate St. Patrick's Day at the Halifax Brewery Market ▶

Haligonians, particularly the pub crawlers, go all out to celebrate Saint Patrick and all things Irish. Noshing down Irish food such as boiled dinner (corned beef, cabbage, and potatoes being the main ingredients) and green-coloured beer kicks off celebrations often lasting into the wee hours. Rollicking Irish music keeps toes tapping with crowds decked out in green and an amazing array of shamrock accessories.

An excellent way to start off St. Patrick's Day, or any other blustery day on the waterfront, is a visit to Alexander Keith's Brewery in the Brewery Market in Halifax, one of the oldest breweries in Canada. Begin by stepping back to 1863 and raising a glass or two at The Red Stag Tavern. The recreated Victorian taproom is the finale of the Alexander Keith's Brewery Tour. Characters in period costume use music, stories, games, smells, and tastes to give participants a glimpse of a working brewhouse. Escorting folks to the tavern to experience "Alexander Keith's hospitality first hand," actors turn guests over to bar keeps to sample various ales at wooden tables and benches of days past. A good deal for less than C$18.

The Red Stag Tavern is at tour's end, in the skylight-lit centre courtyard of the massive ironstone and granite heritage building. They do St. Paddy proud. Stay the evening or continue to "crawl" the nearby pubs of the historic waterfront. The Brewery Market hosts several excellent eateries, a bakery, and gift shops. Do try a cinnamon roll from Mary's Bread Basket—folks line up for them.🍁

www.keiths.ca

Get a Taste of Spring at a Countryside Sugar Shack

Québec's *cabane à sucres* pour on the hospitality, thick and sweet

Spring is a joyful excuse for city folk to jump in their cars and drive out to the Québec countryside. There, amidst the maple tree forests, they seek out the celebrated *cabane à sucres*, or sugar shacks. When temperatures begin to rise, the sap in these trees begins to stir. A little spout tapped into the bark allows the coveted liquid to drip out into a pail, from which it's collected and boiled down to a delightful goo—Québec's most beloved export, if not its most saccharine. "Sugaring off," as

the process is called, is a French-Canadian tradition dating back to the 18th century. The season reaches full swing in March and lasts through April, bringing sweet relief to Québecers after a long Canadian winter.

While maple syrup is surely the *raison d'être* of cabane à sucre festivities, it's only the beginning of this not-to-be missed experience. A hearty country meal—and the gastronomic coma that ensues—is comparable to a Thanksgiving feast, though with much less formality (did someone say toe-tapping fiddlers?) and a much longer celebration period. Why limit yourself to one day when the season lasts for months?

Typical sugar shacks have rustic, ski-chalet coziness with tables set up, party style, in long rows. Not for the faint of heart, the all-you-can-eat spread includes pea soup, maple-smoked back bacon, baked beans, country-style sausages, meatball ragout, mashed potatoes, *tourtière* (meat pie), devilled eggs, omelette soufflés, *oreilles de crisses* (curly pork rinds fried to a crisp), as well as homemade pickles, breads, and ketchups.

And don't think maple syrup is a hidden ingredient or sauce for discrete dipping. It's used much more like a condiment, poured generously over everything, such that one-litre bottles are known to flow like wine. For dessert, two popular finales are *le pouding chômeur*, an island of cake flooded in maple syrup, and *tarte au sucre* (sugar pie) whose main ingredients are maple syrup (mais oui!), brown sugar, and butter.

About three quarters of the planet's *sirop d'érable* is produced in Québec, so it's only natural that it is part of the culture and discerning local palette. It's a little thinner in texture and lighter in taste than what you might expect, especially if you're used to more corn syrup-based varieties. *Tire sur la neige* (there's no common translation, but literally it means "sap on snow") is the quintessential sugaring off thing-to-do. What is it? Essentially, it's hot sap that has been boiled down to about one-fortieth of its

original state—a golden liquid that's poured over packed snow in long strips and then rolled onto a stick. The end result? A maple-flavoured "lollipop" of sorts.

While there are hundreds of sugar shacks across the province, Sucrerie de la Montagne, a 45-minute drive west of Montréal on Mont Rigaud, is a popular choice if you're aiming for an "authentic" experience. Designated an official Québec Heritage site (read: bring your camera), Sucrerie de la Montagne still uses metallic buckets (almost 3,000!) as they did when Québec was still Nouvelle France. (Some modern versions use plastic hoses to drain the sap from trees.) Adding to the festive spirit, Sucrerie owner Pierre Faucher's musical troupe plays lively rigodon imported from southeastern France that involves wooden spoons, violins, harmonica—and kick-up-your-heels dancing. Afterwards, take a tour of the land on a horse-drawn wagon or, if there's still snow, a sleigh. Prices for adults (13 years and older) are around C$30, and slightly higher from 3:00 p.m. on Saturday to 3:00 p.m. on Sunday, peak festive time. Founder Pierre Faucher has a jovial lumberjack Santa look thanks to his white fluffy beard and plaid wool shirts. Faucher's land is extraordinary because it's open year-round, with optional overnight accommodation (in rustic "maisonettes") and cross-country skiing, nestled in a 48.6-hectare (120-acre) forest that includes a general store for maple syrup in all its forms, butter, taffy, bonbons, and more.

A little more on the haute side, in 2009 Chef Martin Picard (of the legendary Montréal restaurant Au Pied de Cochon) opened his own version of a cabane à sucre in St-Benoît de Mirabel, about an hour's drive from the city. Picard is, yes, that chef who experimented with feeding maple syrup to geese on his food show *The Wild Chef*. If you don't already have a reservation, try booking now for next year. In 2011, the menu was C$54 per person, but C$20 for kids under 12.

Another option with a relaxing twist awaits at Auberge des Gallant. Besides a traditional cabane à sucre, the property boasts a quaint inn with a fine-dining room that, in-season, offers a "Maple Discovery Menu" (from C$60 per person), as well as a spa where you can treat yourself to a body scrub and maple butter massage (C$125 for 80 minutes).

Maple syrup has become a bit pricey as of late, so buying it direct from the source has its advantages. Grocery stores often have the best deals. If you're travelling, opt for syrup in cans over glass bottles (which can be kept for long periods in your cupboard). That way, come spring, even when you're not in Québec you can have your maple syrup—and eat it too!

Find out more at:
www.sucreriedelamontagne.com,
www.cabaneasucreaupieddecochon.com,
www.gallant.qc.ca

ADVENTURE

Fly with an N.W.T. Ice Pilot ▶

Passengers fill the waiting room at the Buffalo Airways hangar in Yellowknife, a short distance from the airport's main terminal. They're about to board a bulky-looking, green-and-white plane that looks like it has emerged from another era—and it has.

The first Douglas DC-3 aircraft flew in 1935. Although production ended in 1945, the rugged DC-3 continues to be a staple of the Buffalo Airways fleet, making it one of the rare airlines to fly these sturdy vintage aircraft. The planes ferry passengers and cargo across the frozen North under the watchful eye of owner "Buffalo Joe" McBryan and thousands of viewers of the popular television show *Ice Pilots NWT*. The reality show follows Buffalo Air employees and flight crews as they load up

and deliver food and other cargo to isolated communities across the North, particularly in the dead of winter.

Although the fuselage may look old, this is one sturdy bird. The plane tilts a bit while it's sitting on the tarmac. Walk uphill to your seat: it's relatively comfortable, but the noise of the engines is louder than more modern aircraft. The company's only scheduled passenger flights leave Hay River at 7:30 a.m. and fly over Great Slave Lake for this one-hour commercial flight before landing at the Buffalo Airways hangar in Yellowknife. It's C$200, one way. At the end of the day, McBryan climbs into the cockpit and flies home at 5:00 p.m. ❧

**www.buffaloairways.com,
www.icepilots.com**

◀ Refresh Your Soul at Victoria's Butchart Gardens

The Butchart Gardens was designated a National Historic Site in 2004. Victoria's most-visited tourist attraction offers a delightful living legacy, especially in the first week of spring. Inhale the fresh breeze from nearby Tod Inlet as you admire daffodils, crocuses, and cherry blossoms. It's hard to imagine that this 22-hectare (55-acre) Eden began as a worked-out limestone quarry back in 1904—the vision of a cement industrialist's wife, Jennie Butchart.

Start at the Sunken Garden, one of Victoria's most-photographed vistas. Wander along curving pathways amidst hyacinths and heather. Gaze into deep ponds below the central Mound, and listen to splashing water, from trickling waterfalls to the multi-jetted Ross Fountain, colourfully illuminated at night. Here with kids? Visit the menagerie-style Rose Carousel, where gaily chiming tunes accompany rides astride giraffes and ostriches in a skylit pavilion.

Coast Salish totem poles gaze towards the Japanese Garden, where a red torii gate leads to exquisitely crafted stone lanterns, tiny bridges, and a wooden, water-powered "boar-scarer." Then, funnily, you can rub the bronze snout of a Florentine boar statue (for luck) near the Italian Garden's Star Pond. Finally, take tea at the visitor centre—but also buy seeds from the gift store to grow your own living legacy. It's two hours refreshingly spent. ❧

www.butchartgardens.com

Get Up Close to the Sea Giants at the Pacific Rim Whale Festival

If your impression of whales comes mostly from the fearsome monster in Disney's *Pinocchio*, you owe yourself a trip to the Pacific Rim Whale Festival. Co-hosted annually by the communities of Tofino and Ucluelet on Vancouver Island's west coast, the week-long event celebrates the northbound migration of some 20,000 grey whales in an atmosphere of peace, education, and fun. This journey from Mexican waters towards summer feeding grounds in the Bering Sea is the longest mammalian migration on the planet.

Head out in open-air Zodiac boats or heated cabin cruisers to view grey whales at a safe distance, getting insights from naturalists on board. It's stunning to realize these cetaceans weigh up to 36,000 kilograms (80,000 pounds) while living mostly on a diet of plankton. You may also spot orcas, humpbacks, and the odd minke whale, spouting, tail-slapping, and breaching.

After some awe-inspiring encounters, head to shore to attend a whale-themed crafts fair, or participate in a sandcastle-building competition. Take kayaking or scuba-diving classes. Enjoy a gala dinner at Tofino's luxurious Wickaninnish Inn, or load up at the Chowder Chowdown at the Ucluelet Community Centre. Educational talks, marine photography seminars, rainforest walks, live music, whale-themed movie nights . . . it all adds up to a whale of a time. ❧

www.pacificrimwhalefestival.com

EVENTS & FESTIVALS

QUIRKY CANADA

Indulge in a Week of Tasting at Vancouver's Premier Wine Festival

At the end of March, Vancouver hockey fans are bubbling with excitement about the imminent NHL playoffs, but local wine connoisseurs find the Vancouver International Playhouse Wine Festival even more intoxicating. It's one of the city's true institutions, running since 1979, and ranks among North America's top wine festivals. In 2011, nearly 180 wineries from 15 countries poured their vintages for 25,000 guests.

There are an almost overwhelming number of dinners, tastings, and other events you can enjoy in one week. Sip Napa Valley Cabernet Sauvignon and devour prime rib steak at downtown's Joe Fortes Seafood & Chop House, sample Italian food and wine pairings at Yaletown's Lupo restaurant, or check out top bottles from South Africa at Burnaby's Hart House Restaurant. Cultural venues abound, too, like the Museum of Vancouver and the Vancouver Art Gallery. Most events, however, take place at the white-sailed Vancouver Convention Centre, on Vancouver's waterfront, including the International Festival Tasting. There you can (theoretically) try all the festival wines in a huge ballroom. The swanky Bacchanalia Gala Dinner and Auction at the Fairmont Hotel Vancouver lives up to its name.

Want to volunteer? Fill out a form on the festival website and commit to two five-hour shifts. (No imbibing on the job, but you'll get free tasting tickets for another night, plus other perks.) ❦
www.playhousewinefest.com

Visit the "Two-Starbucks Corner" in Vancouver

The first Starbucks coffee shop opened on March 30, 1971, in Seattle. Yet if you want to mark that anniversary by truly delving deep into mocha madness, get your java jolt at the unique "two-Starbucks corner" in downtown Vancouver. At the intersection of Robson and Thurlow streets, in the midst of prime shopping real estate, you'll discover a Starbucks with huge glass windows on the southwest corner—and another one with a cozier feel on the northeast corner. Hey . . . your caffeine cravings might kick in all over again while you're crossing the street!

It just goes to show that while the world's largest coffeehouse company was closing hundreds of outlets in the United States during the economic downturn that began circa 2008, Vancouver's thirst for coffee remained incredibly insatiable. (There are nearly 200 Starbucks in Metro Vancouver.)

The intersection's also infamous for other reasons, namely as the starting place for the 1994 Stanley Cup riot—when hockey hooligans ran wild, smashing storefront windows after the Vancouver Canucks lost game seven to the New York Rangers. But that was then, and this is now. Get your java fix here—at either of these two Starbucks locations—then hit the streets and do some shopping on Robson, called "Vancouver's most famous shopping street." ❦
www.starbucks.com

Shop for Vintage Fashions in the Plateau

Many a Montréal *modeuse* (French for "fashionista") attributes her (or his) unique style to vintage shopping. Unlike some of the bigger cities like Toronto or New York City, used clothing here is still quite reasonably priced. With the sidewalks finally free of snow and ice, it's time to hit the pavement for some first-class, second-hand deals.

A good starting point in the Plateau is the four boutiques in a row on Saint-Laurent Boulevard just below Duluth. There's a fun mishmash of old, new, and recycled in-house designs at CUL-DE-SAC. Kitsch'n'Swell has a '50s clothing twist, while sister store Rokokonut offers a selection of goods from the '40s to the '80s—including kitchen and decor items you wish you didn't sell at last year's garage sale. Friperie Saint-Laurent has a nice selection of leather coats and hipster shoes.

With the sidewalks finally free of snow and ice, it's time to hit the pavement for some first-class, second-hand deals.

One block north, take a little detour on Rachel Street to Leora, then head to Maskarad and Les Folles Alliées on Mont-Royal Avenue.

Dedicated shoppers who do their research will likely find themselves in the Mile End, a trendy neighbourhood a short walk north of the Plateau. Two good streets for vintage shopping are Bernard (for Local 23 and Arterie), and Saint-Viateur (General 54 and Bohème Friperie). Don't forget to eat a famous Montréal bagel (see p. 253) while you're in the area. 🍁
**www.myspace.com/culdesacmtl,
www.kitschnswell.ca**

It *happened*
THIS WEEK:

Bluenose Launched

*In the town of Lunenburg down Nova Scotia way,
In 1921 on a windy day,
A sailing ship was born, "Bluenose" was her name,
Will we ever see her kind again?*

The first verse of an ocean-spilling song about the Bluenose, written by David Martin, still evokes the Bluenose's weighty place in Atlantic Canadian history.

Halifax architect William J. Roué designed the ship while Lunenburg's Smith & Rhuland (known for building schooners) built the vessel for C\$35,000. The ship had the world's largest working mainsail and, from the outset, Captain Angus Walters aimed to contest the International Fishermen's Series—the focus of a long-time rivalry between Canada and America. The Bluenose would go on to win the race four times between 1921 and 1938.

During the Great Depression of the 1930s, the Bluenose acted as a tour boat. Now, the replica Bluenose II also welcomes passengers aboard for sailing charters. And, when not touring internationally, the schooner still calls Lunenburg its home harbour.

The first Bluenose had a rather quiet end, given her racing honours. She was sold to the West Indian Trading Company, transporting freight until January 28, 1946. As Martin's song points out:

*Then on the Caribbean, one dark and stormy night,
She ran into a reef and died.*

The schooner's curious name is shared with Nova Scotia residents. Although the term's true origins aren't confirmed, a few theories circle about fishermen wiping their cold noses with blue-dyed mittens.

"Bluenoses are all a-stirrin' in winter," says the character Sam Slick, who often takes an unfavourable view of Nova Scotians in *The Clockmaker*. Born in Windsor, Nova Scotia, Thomas Chandler Haliburton published the bestseller in 1836.

As for the most famous Bluenose, the sleek wooden schooner now graces Canada's 10-cent coin, and Nova Scotia licence plates.

Your next STEP

TOP PICKS

ADVENTURE

CULTURE & HISTORY

NATURE'S GRANDEUR

EVENTS & FESTIVALS

QUIRKY CANADA

REJUVENATE

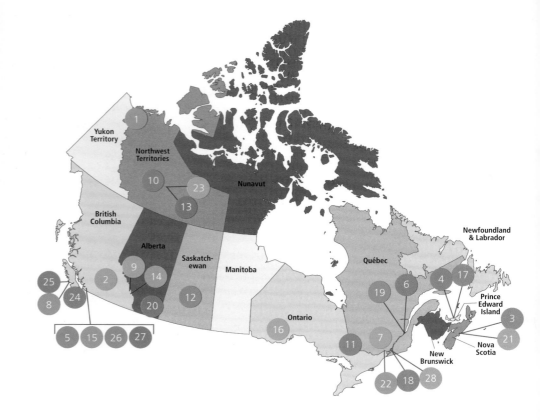

WEEK 1

1 INUVIK, N.W.T.
Ice road driving
www.dot.gov.nt.ca

2 KAMLOOPS, B.C.
Skiing with Nancy Greene
www.sunpeaksresort.com

3 HALIFAX, N.S.
Pier 21
www.pier21.ca

4 P.E.I. NATIONAL PARK, P.E.I.
Ice floe–watching
www.pc.gc.ca

5 VANCOUVER, B.C.
Vancouver International
Dance Festival
www.vidf.ca

6 QUÉBEC CITY, QUE.
Hôtel de Glace
www.icehotel-canada.com

7 MONT-TREMBLANT, QUE.
Scandinave Spa
www.scandinave.com

WEEK 2

8 TOFINO, B.C.
Pacific storm–watching
www.tourismtofino.com

9 KOOTENAY NATIONAL PARK, B.C.
Heli-skiing
www.canadianmountainholidays
.com

10 BEHCHOKO, N.W.T.
Aboriginal Hand Games
Championship
www.denegames.ca

11 MATTAWA, ONT.
Northern Ontario kicksledding
www.naturesharmony.ca/#/winter/
winter

12 SASKATOON, SASK.
The Brier curling championship
www.curling.ca

13 YELLOWKNIFE, N.W.T.
Snowking Winter Festival
www.snowking.ca

14 RADIUM HOT SPRINGS, B.C.
Columbia Valley Hot Springs
www.adventurevalley.com

WEEK 3

15 VANCOUVER, B.C.
Stanley Park
www.vancouver.ca/parks/parks
/stanley

16 QUETICO, ONT.
Frozen lake cross-country skiing
atikokancanoe.tripod.com
/beatenpath

17 CHARLOTTETOWN, P.E.I.
P.E.I. St. Patrick's Day
www.oldedublinpub.com

18 MONTRÉAL, QUE.
Mount Royal hiking
www.lemontroyal.qc.ca

19 QUÉBEC CITY, QUE.
Red Bull Crashed Ice skating
competition
www.redbullcrashedice.com

20 TABER, ALTA.
Cowboy poetry
www.albertacowboypoetry.com

21 HALIFAX, N.S.
Alexander Keith's Brewery
www.keiths.ca

WEEK 4

22 MONT RIGAUD, QUE.
Countryside sugar shacks
www.sucreriedelamontagne.com

23 YELLOWKNIFE, N.W.T.
Flying with a northern ice pilot
www.buffaloairways.com

24 BRENTWOOD BAY, B.C.
Butchart Gardens
www.butchartgardens.com

25 TOFINO, B.C.
Pacific Rim Whale Festival
www.pacificrimwhalefestival.com

26 VANCOUVER, B.C.
Playhouse Wine Festival
www.playhousewinefest.com

27 VANCOUVER, B.C.
Two-Starbucks corner
www.starbucks.com

28 MONTRÉAL, QUE.
Vintage fashion shopping
www.kitschnswell.ca

APRIL

Catch a Cirque du Soleil World Premiere

Be among the first to see the troupe's latest offering at its hometown debut

There's a reason why Cirque du Soleil may very well be the best—if not the grandest—circus on the planet. The highly acclaimed "Circus of the Sun" is like nothing you've ever seen before. If you're not already hooked, it's never too late—or too early—to discover this creative and inspiring universe.

As an omnipresent brand that boasts 22 different shows spanning more than 250 cities in each of the four corners of the globe, it's hardly a stretch to imagine the Cirque phenomenon is happening at any given moment somewhere in the world. However, proud Montréalers are the first to point out that all the magic starts right here in their own backyard. The Cirque du Soleil headquarters, creative think tank, and high-tech professional training facilities are all here in Montréal, the place CEO and original clown Guy Laliberté calls home. Locals (and tourists, of course) are usually the first to enjoy the latest and greatest offerings in the constantly evolving repertoire.

The excitement blossoms in spring when, after a long winter, the city emerges from hibernation with budding tulips and chirping birds—the ideal setting for the return of Cirque du Soleil's "grand chapiteau," the iconic blue-and-yellow tent that's erected along the quays of the historic Old Port.

If you're one of the rare few who are still in the dark Cirque-wise, the two-and-a-half-hour spectacle (with 30-minute intermission) forgoes the traditional circus ring and animals, opting instead for a more story-based performance. Visual poetry is epitomized in a tapestry of artistic staging, dazzling costumes, and signature live music combined with awesome acrobatics, modern dance, and comedy. It's entertainment for all, from wide-eyed toddlers, to teens with short attention spans, to even the most blasé of cosmopolites.

Montréal premieres typically occur every other year during the month of April, alternating with existing shows that return in June by popular demand. What this means for lucky viewers is that one can see the show before it officially hits the road—and the world at large. Details—including the name and theme—are typically kept under wraps until the actual debut, so it's always a special feeling to be among the first to comment on what will eventually hit the international stage.

For example, while the rest of humanity waited for *Kooza* (it opened in Montréal in 2007) or *Ovo* (in 2009), most Montréalers had already experienced them. Montréalers got a similar preview of the 2010 launch of *Totem*,

Robert Lepage's visually poetic exploration of the evolution of man—a show that went on to globetrot across Canada, the United States, and the United Kingdom. Do note, however, that non-touring shows open in their resident cities; this was the case with *O* and *Zumanity*, just two of seven permanent productions in Las Vegas, as well as *La Nouba* in Orlando, *Zed* in Tokyo, *Zaia* in Macau, and *Banana Shpeel* and *Wintuk* in New York.

But nobody, it seems, can outshine Montréal in terms of circus-mania. In 2010, the unofficial City of Circuses created its own International Festival of Circus Arts—an 18-day event in July welcoming more than 100 circus performers from visiting countries. The colourful celebration, which unfolds in the Old Port, Latin Quarter, and other select venues downtown, also embraces smaller circus offshoots such as Cirque Éloize and Les 7 doigts de la main.

Cirque de Soleil is an essential ingredient in the quintessential Montréal experience, so if you're Cirque-curious, best to plan your accommodations ahead of time. Also worth noting is that circus enthusiasts seize on limited VIP tickets that allow them special seating and backstage access to the performers. There are only about 2,600 spots in all, so, needless to say, prime seating inside the cozy Montréal venue sells out fast.

Many hotels offer circus packages, so be sure to ask when making reservations. Parking near the big top (you can't miss it) is available, but can get crowded. If your accommodations aren't within walking distance, better to hire a taxi or take public transit. In any case, you'll likely want to walk about the bustling Old Port or Old Montréal—before or after the show.

Cirque du Soleil was founded in 1984 by a duo of street performers, Guy Laliberté and Daniel Gauthier, from Baie-Saint-Paul, a small town just east of Québec City. It originally launched in conjunction with the province of Québec's 450th anniversary celebrations. While Gauthier is no longer a partner, having sold his part of the company in 2000, Laliberté alone is a Montréal icon. Besides winning a multitude of awards and having a star on Hollywood's Walk of Fame, you may also recall his much-media-hyped tour into outer space—which he did sporting a red clown's nose. One can't get more "out-of-this-world" than that.🍁

Find out more at:
www.cirquedusoleil.com

ADVENTURE

CULTURE & HISTORY

Hike Haida Gwaii's Spectacular Cape Fife Loop

It's not every day you get to travel to the birthplace of humans. This amazing, multi-day hike travels through old-growth forest, wetland, and the endless beaches of Naikoon Provincial Park on Haida Gwaii, formerly the Queen Charlotte Islands. From the moment you get to the trail-head, you'll feel like you're headed into a magical world.

You can think of the 35-kilometre (21.7-mile) hike in three separate legs: the forested walk from near the Tow Hill kiosk out of Cape Fife; the East Beach stretch to Rose Spit Ecological Reserve; and the sunset stretch, from Rose Spit back to the Tow Hill Ecological Reserve. The Cape Fife leg is where, in Haida mythology, Raven coaxed the first humans to life, and most of the islands' ecosystems are represented on this route. During the second leg, the pre-vailing wind is behind you, and there are always fascinating shells and myriad rock colours; the beach goes on and on, and you're not likely to see a soul. On the return section of the loop, you'll find Dungeness crab, or scallops after a big storm, and clams after the ebb tide. Eagles, ravens, and seagulls soar overhead.

There is a cozy ranger cabin where you can stay for free during your first night, and a campground after the second leg that costs C$20 during high season (May to September only). There's no cost for wilderness camping en route. 🍁
www.britishcolumbia.com/parks/?id=200

Visit the Legislative Assembly of Nunavut

The seats are lined with seal skin, the mace is an engraved, jewel-encrusted, narwhal tusk, traditional museum-quality art lines the walls, and the official language is Inuktitut. The Legislative Assembly in Iqaluit is decidedly Nunavut-centric, and a trip to the capital would not be complete without a visit. The building is impressive —even more so when you learn it's technically a prefab.

The best times to visit are when the assembly is in session, which is three times a year, usually in fall, winter, and summer. Check the assembly's website in advance for the schedule. Perhaps the best time to visit is on April 1— the anniversary of Nunavut's creation, Canada's newest and only Inuit-governed territory. A visit to the assembly also gives you a chance to witness Canada's only example of consensus-style government in action. Those who linger after a session can also witness a Nunavut-style press scrum. Think rubber boots, lots of plaid, and reporters addressing politicians by first name. You'll also get to meet members of the Legislative Assembly and the premier, and might even be able to ask your own burning questions.

Note that although free tours are available through-out the year, they're not offered while the assembly is in session. However, visitors are still welcome to take self-guided tours and encouraged to observe proceedings. 🍁
www.assembly.nu.ca

Go "Rock Hounding" in Nova Scotia

Legend has it that the mythical Mi'kmaq deity, Glooscap, was first to discover amethyst in the cliffs of the Minas Basin and Bay of Fundy in southwestern Nova Scotia. People continue to roam the beaches seeking the beautiful transparent quartz crystal shaded from mauve to rich purple. April showers clear away old snow and mud, but encourage rain gear and good footwear. Try your luck walking the beach at Cape Blomidon near Wolfville, or get the lowdown on the best places to search by visiting Rob's Rock Shop in Kentville for expert advice and maps. They stress the importance of planning around tide times, which, around the cliffs, can literally and figuratively be the difference between life and death. Folks at the shop

People roam the beaches seeking the beautiful transparent quartz crystal shaded from mauve to rich purple.

go rock hounding almost every day and allow people to follow along, so call ahead before visiting. Nova Scotia's amazing geological history and constant tidal action make it a fantastic place to hunt for agates, jasper, quartz, and other precious and semi-precious stones. Best of all, rock hounding is free and requires a hammer, a bag to carry your bounty—and a few tips from the locals. ✤

www.nstravelguide.com/what/ rockhounding

It *happened*
THIS WEEK:

Bell Island Explosion

Bell Island sits in the cup of Conception Bay, New-foundland. The island was once a prosperous mining community, but extracting iron ore from underwater mine shafts eventually became too costly and in 1966 the last mine closed. While Bell Island saw the only German attack on North American soil during World War II, it experienced a very different explosion on April 2, 1978.

On a Sunday morning, when most Bell Islanders were readying for church, a hum followed by a boom startled everyone as a terrific explosion melted telephone wires, blew up television sets, and killed animals in a Lance Cove barn. It blasted craters into the ground and was heard as far away as Cape Broyle, about 56 kilometres (34.8 miles) away.

A History Channel-aired documentary investigated the blast, interviewing eyewitnesses such as Barbara McKim.

"We looked out in time to see an oval-shaped object that was moving very, very quickly," said McKim, recalling what she experienced that morning in 1978. "It was quite loud, quite deafening."

Satellites measured light emissions equalling a 10-megatonne blast, reports the documentary, and the boom brought investigations from Canadian, American, and Russian officials.

With few official records available on the causes of the mysterious blast, conspiracy theories have included everything from Cold War–era weapons testing to ball lightning—a rare electrical current with an unpredictable pattern and a bluish glow.

EVENTS & FESTIVALS

Cheer for the Blue Jays on Opening Day

There are many signs of spring in Toronto, but one of the most reliable is the crack of a bat and the cry of "Play Ball!" on the opening day of baseball season. It's a ritual witnessed by 50,000 people at downtown's Rogers Centre each April, as they spend a few hours fantasizing about the summer to come and a winning season.

Tickets for the Toronto Blue Jays home opener can be hard to come by on game day (unless you heed the scalpers' siren call), but can be found easily later in the week or with a little advance planning. The good news is that, compared to the city's other professional sports teams, tickets are affordable, ranging from C$75 for a seat behind home plate to C$15 for a spot in the outfield

bleachers. Once you're seated, you can start enjoying all the rites of summer—a beer, a hot dog, and heckling the opposing team. The Jays, despite being nearly 20 years removed from their back-to-back World Series victories, usually field a competitive team, and opening day often brings a hated divisional rival to town.

Cheer on the home team's new players, join in on the seventh-inning stretch, and hope a foul ball flies your way. If you're lucky, the stadium's retractable roof will be open for an early heat wave . . . and a hint of summer will appear like a mirage on the horizon. ✤
www.torontobluejays.com

See the World's Biggest Hockey Stick ▼

For many Canadians, the start of the NHL hockey playoffs is the biggest time of the year. Get into the puck-loving spirit by heading to Vancouver Island and viewing the world's biggest hockey stick, officially recognized by Guinness World Records. Other cultures may construct huge tributes to dead pharaohs (the pyramids) or presidents (Mount Rushmore). But this is Canada.

The humongous icon is hard to miss as you drive along the Trans-Canada Highway through Duncan, B.C., about 60 kilometres (37 miles) north of Victoria. The city of 5,000 is dubbed the "City of Totems" for its abundance of carved, wooden native poles. However, the 62-metre (205-foot), 27,670-kilogram (61,000-pound) hunk of hockey lumber mounted on the side of the Cowichan Community Centre wins the Stanley Cup for sheer size. Made of Douglas fir and reinforced with steel beams, it's displayed with a matching one-metre (3.2-foot) black puck. Pull over and take some "they'll-never-believe-this-back-home" photos.

The mother of all hockey sticks was originally created for EXPO '86, the 1986 World's Fair in Vancouver. Duncan edged out 34 other communities for the right to display the stick. Locals see it as their answer to Paris's Eiffel Tower. Don't even mention that other stick in Eveleth, Minnesota—them's fightin' words!✿
www.vancouverisland.com

◀ Take a Train Ride into History in Tatamagouche

Ever dreamed of sleeping in a caboose or baggage car? Head for the Train Station Inn in Tatamagouche, Nova Scotia. The folks here like trains so much they collected them, along with a century-old brick station, to create a unique place that belongs on everyone's must-do list.

To train lovers, it's like time stood still. Luggage is piled on the station platform. Breakfast is served in what was once the men's waiting room—now lined with lanterns and memorabilia. A gift shop is located in what used to be the ladies' waiting room. Guest rooms are upstairs. Outside, The Dining Car serves lunch and dinner. Refurbished cabooses and boxcars provide more spacious accommodations, with private bathrooms and living area. The railbed where it all lies is part of The Trans Canada Trail.

The village has just enough shops and eateries to entice lingering. It may also seem familiar. Tatamagouche, and Train Station Inn owner James LeFresne (who's known to appear wearing a full conductor's outfit) were featured on the second season of the CBC television program *The Week the Women Went*. LeFresne's an encyclopedia of history and information.✿
www.trainstation.ca

Head North for Toonik Tyme

Iqaluit knows how to celebrate the sun after a long, cold winter

After a long, cold, and dark winter in the Far North, the sun is something to celebrate. You know it's spring in Iqaluit by the raccoon-eyed locals who return from a day out on their snowmobiles, rosy-cheeked and beaming. Thick slabs of ice covering the rivers, lakes, and bays are thawing, and nature's accessible once again. The excitement is contagious . . . it seems the whole territory is itching to get outside and play.

This is why there's Toonik Tyme—a six-day community celebration of organized joy. Families from around Nunavut descend upon Iqaluit, offices close, and visitors stare wide-eyed at the wild events scattered throughout the capital. Events range from the traditional, to the modern, to the bizarre.

The name Toonik Tyme comes from the Tuniit people, who lived in the vast Arctic region before the Inuit. (The singular form of Tuniit is Toonik, and the singular form of Inuit is Inuk.) Each year, the community chooses an honourary Toonik—usually an outstanding member of the community—be it for their hunting or sewing skills, or ability to care for others. A host of famous figures have also held the title, including Prince Charles.

While there's not a main feature to the festival, Inuit cultural events are indeed the highlight. Seal-skin kamiiks strapped to your feet, snuggled inside a cozy Inuit-made parka (the mercury's risen, but temperatures are still most likely between –10 and 5 degrees Celsius—14 and 41 degrees Fahrenheit), you'll stroll to the central grounds and up to a circular crowd that's forming. This is the igloo-making contest, where men race to build traditional ice-houses as rapidly as possible —without sacrificing quality. Men kneel on the ice, carving square blocks from the ice's compact surface, placing them atop one another as it has been done for centuries. While the atmosphere's relaxed, the work isn't . . . contestants wipe their brows, steam rising from their foreheads, while assessing their opponents. For the past eight years Solomon Awa has taken home top prize— usually cash, and maybe a barrel of fuel, or even a bag of flour.

Contests are big in Inuit culture, and biggest during Toonik Tyme. It seems for every task, there's a contest. Contests in both tea- and bannock-making take place over an open fire, which the contestants build from scratch. The seal-skinning contest, while perhaps too vivid for some, is fascinating to watch. The skill and ease the women use to prepare the pelt and remove all the meat and fat (while taking care not to puncture the skin) is truly mesmerizing.

That all said, Toonik Tyme is not strictly traditional. Throughout the event, visitors

will hear the high-pitched buzz of snow machines zipping around the city, either for transportation or sport purposes, or most commonly as part of an event. Perhaps the most fear-inducing is the Uphill Climb, where diehards take their custom-made, Frankenstein-like machines to the edge, racing them directly up the steep incline on the tundra (which forms the backdrop of most views from the city). In this case, safety does take a holiday as flips and rollbacks happen—but everyone wears a helmet.

As mentioned, some events do tend towards the bizarre. Fear Factor is by far the most wild and most popular of all events. As in the television show, contestants must eat a selection of strange foods—in this case country–specialties, the term used for traditional Inuit grub. Audience members watch, eyes wide shut, as their peers scarf down mixtures of fish blood, live worms, and caribou guts.

While Iqaluit is Nunavut's capital, it is still a frontier town. Visitors shouldn't expect the same quality standards with food or service as in more southern locales. The best advice is to come with an open mind and no solid plans. Once you let go of expectations, the fun begins.

Remember to bring a packed wallet. All goods are either flown or shipped in from the south, so prices are double what they might be in any other Canadian city. Thirty dollars for a simple lunch, including soup, sandwich, and drink combo, is normal. Hotels average C$200 per night, per person.

The good news is that most of Toonik Tyme's events are free, or cost very little, including the entertaining opening and closing ceremonies which cost about C$2 a ticket. However, Big Band Night will set you back about C$40. (Tickets are tough to find, so contact festival organizers early for those.)

The only other advice needed is to take any opportunity to chat up the locals. The stories that come from a people with such a rich history—living a double life of ancient traditions and modern sensibilities, as the Inuit do—are some of the most fascinating accounts on the planet. But don't be offended if people are quiet. Shyness is common for people from the Far North. Just know that if someone raises their eyebrows it means "yes," and if they squinch their nose, it means "no!" 🍁

Find out more at:

www.tooniktyme.com

ADVENTURE

CULTURE & HISTORY

Hang Ten in Tofino

In 2010, *Outside* magazine hailed Tofino as "the best surf town in North America." While this laid-back rainforest community on Vancouver Island's west coast doesn't boast the bronzed bodies of, say, California's Huntington Beach, it gets amazingly consistent big waves facing the open Pacific Ocean. Water temperatures hold steady year-round at 10 degrees Celsius (50 degrees Fahrenheit) along Tofino's 35 kilometres (22 miles) of coastline. Surfing in April on spacious Long Beach, or underrated Cox Beach, lets you beat the high-season tourists.

Before you start carving waves and pulling adrenalized tricks—like the more than the 100 pros that come to town for October's annual O'Neill Cold Water Classic—you'll want some coldwater gear. Visit stores like Long Beach Surf Shop and Storm Surf Shop. Neoprene wetsuits, booties, and gloves will make your surfing experience way more copacetic. And, get lessons from Tofino's certified instructors, such as Tofino Surf School and Pacific Surf School, where technique, safety, and etiquette are on the menu. Craving extra personal attention? Guests at Long Beach Resort can book customized 2.5-hour lessons, while Surf Sister caters exclusively to female wave catchers.

When you're ready, the epic Pacific winds will blow you and your board across some of Canada's finest breaks. ❦
www.tourismtofino.com

Hunt for Fossils in Nova Scotia

Spring is the perfect time to visit Nova Scotia's Joggins Fossil Cliffs—the crowds are smaller and the erosion of the cliffs is high, exposing new fossils with every tide and weather event. Winter storms, ice floes, and 15-metre (50-foot) Fundy tides mean constantly changing discoveries for tenacious fossil seekers (remember that finders are forbidden from being keepers here). This World Heritage Site is described by UNESCO as the "coal age Galapagos" due to the wealth of fossils dating from 354 to 290 million years ago—in fact, the world's oldest reptile fossil (about 312 million years old) was found here more than a century ago. It's the only place on earth where visitors can view these rare fossils of plants and animals preserved in the place where they lived. Coal–era trees stand where they grew; footprints of creatures are frozen where they walked; dens of amphibians are preserved with remnants of their last meal; and remains of the earliest reptiles are entombed within once-hollow trees. Discoveries include species found nowhere else on earth.

Joggins Fossil Centre helps visitors understand what to look for and reveals what discoveries have already been made here. Dress warmly as it may be cool on the beach. In early April you need to phone ahead to visit the centre and schedule a guided tour of the cliffs. Then, venture out on your own to step back in time. ❦
www.jogginsfossilcliffs.net

Spend the Morning amidst Fernie's Diverse Wildlife

While Fernie continues to attract skiers to the Rocky Mountains well into April, this small southeast B.C. town is also a wildlife-watching mecca. Hook up with interpretive naturalist Lee-Ann Walker, who has guided area tours since 1983, and you'll discover a pristine environment teeming with extraordinary variety at this time of year—from dry, open grasslands with blooming crocuses to cedar forests laden with snow.

Both bald and golden eagles can be sighted migrating north towards Alaska along the Rocky Mountain Trench.

At 8:00 a.m., heading into the wilderness in Walker's minivan, you'll soon spot bachelor herds of bighorn rams congregating in the Elk Valley, while whitetail deer and mule deer nibble on shrubs. Hop out for a little snowshoeing, and watch for beavers happily building a dam on Lizard Creek. Both bald and golden eagles can be sighted migrating north towards Alaska along the Rocky Mountain Trench. Birders will also rejoice in the abundance of varied thrushes, American dippers, and mountain bluebirds. Walker supplies binoculars, spotting scopes, and nature guidebooks—not to mention her homemade biscotti and blueberry muffins. When noon arrives, you'll scarcely believe you've been out there for four hours. It's a great change of pace from carving powder.❀
www.fernienature.com

Canadian moments

Hockey Playoffs Begin

Come April, Saturday's Hockey Night in Canada morphs into an even more consuming event: playoff season.

Hockey is said to be a religion in Montréal, owing in part to the Montréal Canadiens and the team's 24 Stanley Cup wins. But it's not only Québecers who love the game: Edmonton stops flushing when a hockey game is on.

The city's utility company, EPCOR, released data on water usage during the men's hockey final at the Vancouver 2010 Olympic Winter Games. It showed an unreal pattern: water consumption spiked hugely at the end of every period. The presumed cause? Hockey fans using the bathroom during the break.

The spikes and drops were even more pronounced for Oilers games during their 2006 bid for the Stanley Cup.

Beyond the millions who tune in to hockey (10 million watched the Canada-U.S. men's Olympic hockey final in 2002), Canadians put other parts of life on hold for the good ol' game.

Should a game be tied when the buzzer sounds at the end of the third period, the match-up goes into overtime and displaces other scheduled programs. In the 1998–99 television season, for example, CBC's The National delayed more than 25 per cent of its nightly 10:00 p.m. newscasts.

At the University of Saskatchewan, Professor Michael P.J. Kennedy teaches a course on Canadian literature and hockey. Canadian writers ranging from Alice Munro to Mordecai Richler and Roch Carrier have written about hockey. Adding to the list, even Prime Minister Stephen Harper is penning a book about the nation's favourite sport.

2nd week of APR

Catch Runway Mania at Vancouver Fashion Week ▶

For more than a decade, Vancouver Fashion Week (VFW) has spotlighted this city's underrated fashion scene. The brainchild of local promoter Jamal Abdourahman, it's outlasted its imitators, and has distinguished itself by showcasing Asian and Indian designers as well as brand names like Versace. The venues change yearly, ranging from the Vancouver Convention Centre to Granville Street's glitziest nightclubs. But the flair for fun and frivolity remains the same.

Vancouver talent always shines. On the catwalk, you might see extravagant corsets by Lace Embrace Atelier's Melanie Talkington, whose creations appeared in the 2011 fantasy film *Sucker Punch*. Or the latest incarnation of Patricia Fieldwalker's Adagio silk lingerie collection,

which has graced magazines like *ELLE* and *Glamour*. Chloe Angus, who makes eco-friendly wraps and skirts, and Cheri Milaney, whose Italian-influenced blouses incorporate high-end fabrics, are two Vancouver designers who have used VFW to springboard to international success. Cameos by TV personalities, from *Fashion TV* host Jeanne Beker to *Project Runway* contestant Gordana Gehlhausen, are frequent.

Want a break from the fabulous after-parties and cocktail chatter? Head east of downtown for unique boutique shopping on South Main Street (also known as the SoMa neighbourhood). Bodacious (catering to curvy women) and Smoking Lily (known for its silk scarves with prints of insects and antique chairs) are among the highlights. ❧
www.vanfashionweek.com

◀ Cross the World's Longest Covered Bridge

With a reputation for granting wishes and encouraging kisses, the longest covered bridge in the world in Hartland, New Brunswick, is more than a treasured National Historic Site. The kissing legend began when young men stopped their horses halfway across the bridge to share a kiss with their young ladies. When the bridge was subsequently covered, much debate resulted—townsfolk worried that hiding the young folks from view was invitation to inflaming loose morals.

The horses are gone, but the bridge still inspires romance. Another legend says wishes made as you enter the bridge—with eyes closed, fingers crossed, and holding your breath until you exit—will come true. Drivers, of course, cannot participate. Though some say simply holding your breath brings good luck!

In early April, when spring is in the air, visitors to Hartland may well witness an impressive movement of ice in the St. John River. In 1920, two spans were swept away by ice, nearly destroying the bridge. Today, vigilant townsfolk take steps such as breaking up ice jams to protect the aging structure, built in 1901. You can drive across the bridge at Hartland, the smallest incorporated town in New Brunswick (population 902), but there are some vehicle restrictions. If you don't meet them you can cross using an adjacent walkway, added in 1945.❧

www.town.hartland.nb.ca/html/bridge.htm

Taste the Best of Canada's Up-and-Coming Chefs (or Become One Yourself)

Great chefs do not spring to life fully formed. Some go to Le Cordon Bleu Ottawa Culinary Arts Institute first. (The school's in-house restaurant is a training ground for these chefs-in-progress.) Should spring find you in the nation's capital, you'll have an opportunity to experience fantastic food for a reasonable price.

Of course, if you wish to pay full price you can. In the evenings, executive chef Yannick Anton holds court and the theme is French cuisine with a modern twist. But two days of the week, Thursdays and Fridays, school is on in the kitchens and front-of-house. It's a win-win situation: patrons enjoy a three-course lunch for under C$30 and students perfect their techniques. If the results prove inspirational, you can put on the whites yourself. Every second Saturday, Le Cordon Bleu offers one-day gourmet sessions with themes that vary with the available seasonal ingredients. One session might focus on the tastes of southern France, another on pastries. For those with more time and greater inclination, four-day courses are offered. "Boulangerie" is devoted to the art of breadmaking, from *boules* to *baguettes*. It may be a bit early to enjoy a drink on the wraparound terrace, but one never knows. The restaurant's open Wednesday to Saturday for lunch and dinner.❧

www.lcbottawa.com

Take In the Vancouver Sun Run

Fitness meets fun in Canada's largest road race

Every spring, the Vancouver Sun Run explodes the myth of the loneliness of the long-distance runner. How? By attracting upwards of 50,000 participants for the scenic 10-kilometre (6.2-mile) circuit—an event that saw a record 59,179 registered participants in 2008. (That's more people than the entire population of Charlottetown, capital of Prince Edward Island.) Since its humble beginnings in 1985, the Sun Run has become Canada's largest road race, and the second-largest 10-kilometre event of its kind in North America. Thousands of kids aged 12 and under also take part, though as part of the Mini Sun Run—a 2.5-kilometre (1.5-mile) event.

Now, forget about the numbers for a minute and focus on the fun. You don't need to be an Olympic gold medal contender to do the Sun Run. In fact, you don't even need to get sweaty. Many registrants sign up as part of a team, representing their workplace, school, church, political party, or other cause of their choice, and simply walk the distance together, chatting and laughing. (If truth be told, some might even stop en route for coffee at the ubiquitous Starbucks or Blenz stores.)

It doesn't matter if you can't challenge the 1996 course record of 27:31 set by Kenya's Joseph Kimani. Or the women's record of 30:58 set by another Kenyan, Isabella Ochichi, in 2006. You can still enjoy the course views of the mountains, ocean, and glass-towered skyline amidst cherry blossoms and tulips. Not to mention the gorgeous guys and luscious lasses in their form-fitting, locally designed Lululemon running shorts. Welcome to one of Canada's fittest cities!

So, what actually happens on Race Day?

A buzz of optimism and excitement pervades West Georgia Street, where crowds stretch between the venerable Fairmont Hotel Vancouver and the Corinthian columns of the downtown location of the Bay, Canada's venerable department store. Manoeuvring your way through enthusiastic runners warming up, plus family, friends, and other supporters, you follow the signs to your designated, colour-coded start zone—somewhere between blue (elite) and red (walkers). Just make sure your bib number is firmly pinned to your Sun Run T-shirt and your electronic timing chip is attached to one of your sneakers. And, it's always a good idea to hit one of the portable toilets before the start gun sounds.

Music is everywhere. The Neurotics, a '60s pop-rock cover band, crank out Van Morrison and Beatles tunes, along with corny quips, atop an elevated platform. They're the first of some 20 live bands you'll encounter along the course. After an aerobics-themed stretching session led by local fitness instructors

and a mass singalong of "O Canada," the race finally gets underway at about 9:00 a.m., with wheelchair and elite athletes getting first dibs. No worries if it takes you a while to get going: the clock only starts ticking when you cross the official start line.

Relish the long slope down towards Stanley Park, which can give you a great pace through the first kilometre, even if you're elbow-to-elbow with other runners. The course swings left on to funky Denman Street, before looping right on Lagoon Drive, overlooking Lost Lagoon—whose romantic, swan-laden waters fringe Stanley Park. You'll cut throughs the edge of the park before curling left towards English Bay with its palm trees and clapping spectators. Grab a cup of water from a volunteer and keep going.

Eventually, you reach the art-deco style Burrard Street Bridge—the halfway point, where the angled climb to the crest of the bridge can really get your thighs burning if you're pushing it. (Then again, the looming sight of the Molson brewery might remind you of one possible post-race reward.) The course wends its way through the Kitsilano and Fairview neighbourhoods, including the side streets looking down on False Creek, before settling into West 6th Avenue. At last, with everything from Bob Marley to Deep Purple echoing in your ears, you turn left onto the Cambie Street Bridge—forging ahead to the finish line on the other side of False Creek.

Be sure to take in the post-race party, with water, food, giveaways, massages, live music, and more in the vicinity. Savour the sense of accomplishment as you stretch out those tired-but-happy muscles. You're right next to where the Olympic opening and closing ceremonies were held, where Canada took hockey gold . . . having just turned in your own medal-worthy performance—at least in your own mind.

Should you prefer to taste some Sun Run excitement as a volunteer rather than as a participant, you can sign up in advance for a minimum six-hour shift. You might find yourself providing directions, dispensing bananas and bagels, or staffing a first-aid station. Otherwise, what's arguably best about the Sun Run is that partial proceeds benefit the Raise-A-Reader literacy campaign.

Now, run along folks . . . 🍁

Find out more at:

www.sunrun.com

ADVENTURE

Spend a Week Traversing the Rockies on Skis ▶

By late April, many people's thoughts have turned to spring, but high in the Rockies the snow cover is still deep and the chill of winter has passed—making this the best time of year to venture out on a week-long, hut-to-hut ski tour. Travelling with expert guides, you're free to soak up the breathtaking views and pristine powder of the backcountry wilderness.

Unless you're experienced in backcountry winter travel, the best way to tour the Canadian Rockies on skis is by using an experienced outfitter like Icefall Lodge. Aside from the luxuries of the accommodations they offer, they offer well-trained guides and logistical support—meaning all you need to carry as you ski is a daypack. The adventure begins with a helicopter ride from Golden, British Columbia, to the remote Mons Hut—only accessible on a guided tour. Two days are spent at the hut—skiing nearby landmarks such as Mons Glacier and the North Glacier on Mount Forbes (the highest mountain in Banff National Park). The third day is spent skiing to Lyell Hut for a two-night stay, after which a one-day,

You're free to soak up the breathtaking views and pristine powder of the back-country wilderness.

mostly downhill, push is made for Icefall Lodge. Though far from the nearest road and 1,900 metres (6,300 feet) above sea level, skiers arriving here enjoy excellent cooking, a sauna, and comfortable beds. Leaving the lodge on the final day, it's a short but steep ascent to Ice Pass. Then it's downhill all the way along the Rostrum Valley, to Icefall Brook—and back to civilization. ❦
www.icefall.ca

◄ Catch Cherry Blossom Fever on the West Coast

Although Canadians east of the Rockies sometimes call British Columbia "Lotus Land" due to the laid-back, comfortable lifestyle of its inhabitants, it could more accurately be dubbed "Cherry Blossom Land." Each April, mild climates in Vancouver and Victoria enable millions of pink and white blossoms to flourish.

Cherry blossoms achieve true cultural status at Vancouver's Nitobe Memorial Garden on the University of British Columbia campus. Named after a Japanese diplomat, the traditional garden's abundant blossoms are reflected in ornamental pools, evoking life's beauty and transience. Surrounding stone lanterns and bridges imply Shinto and Buddhist values.

Want more? Stroll through Stanley Park, the 405-hectare (1,000-acre) stretch of greenery that adjoins downtown Vancouver, and you'll discover cherry blossoms from the shores of Lost Lagoon to the park's glorious Rose Garden. Boasting some 37,000 cherry trees citywide, Vancouver has a four-week Cherry Blossom Festival, including a haiku competition, and blossom-painting classes at VanDusen Botanical Garden.

Of course, more pink-and-white petals await in Victoria, the "Garden City." Admire them at the world-famous Butchart Gardens, the 60.7 hectare (150-acre) Beacon Hill Park, or the University of Victoria campus.❧
www.nitobe.org, www.vcbf.ca

Take a "Sea Safari" Out of Horseshoe Bay

Usually the word "safari" connotes lions and elephants in East Africa. But when you visit West Vancouver's Horseshoe Bay, about 30 minutes from downtown Vancouver, it's quite a different story. The family-operated Sewell's Marina offers exciting, two-hour "sea safari" eco-tours of local ocean waters. If you want to imagine you're in a high-speed, James Bond–style boat chase (minus the gunfire), you've come to the right place.

Don your orange lifejacket, board the 9.1-metre (30-foot) Zodiac, and prepare for wildlife sightings. As the boat zooms north up Howe Sound (powered by twin outboard engines) leaving a magnificent frothy wake, you may spot bald eagles soaring overhead. After looping past Anvil Island, odds are good that a group of cute—if also somnolent and fishy-smelling—harbour seals will greet you at Pam Rocks, reclining as your pilot cuts the motor for a photo-op. Also be on the lookout for deer, otters, cormorants, and herons en route.

After zipping past the greenery of Gambier and Bowen islands, you'll finish up with great views of the towers and beaches at Vancouver's English Bay and West Van's luxury homes. Packages that include dinner at Horseshoe Bay's Boathouse Restaurant, a round at the Furry Creek golf course, or a seaplane flight are also available.❧
www.sewellsmarina.com

EVENTS & FESTIVALS

QUIRKY CANADA

Party Slopeside at the TELUS World Ski & Snowboard Festival

Seeking to relive the heady blend of sports, culture, and partying that swept Whistler during the 2010 Winter Games? Your best bet might be the TELUS World Ski & Snowboard Festival. Despite its name, this 10-day extravaganza—the largest annual snowfest in North America—caters to more than just hardcore two-plankers and boarders.

Naturally, you can watch top pro freeskiers pulling tricks and shredding on the Degree Superpipe and Big Air jump, or gape at skillful boarders carving their way through the Mogul Mash. Whistler is the final stop on the Association of Freeskiing Professionals world tour.

Also check out free afternoon concerts at Skier's Plaza, featuring modern pop-rock acts like Tokyo Police Club, Broken Social Scene, and Gogol Bordello. Attend an activewear fashion show or the gala screening of the 72-Hour Filmmaker Showdown contest at the Whistler Conference Centre. View winter sports photography exhibits, or watch short plays by Whistler's Chairlift Revue ensemble. There's even a dog parade. And to live up to the festival motto of "Party in April. Sleep in May," dancing and drinking at Whistler Village nightclubs such as Buffalo Bill's and Garfinkel's is always encouraged.❦
www.wssf.com

Tour Some of the World's Largest Roadside Attractions

Late April is the perfect time for scenic drives, like a road trip hunting for a bevy of items laying claim to a "world's-largest" title, all contained in a single river valley.

In the St. John River Valley, they like things big. So, searching for the world's largest fiddleheads is an appropriate first mission. Harvested after snows melt along the riverbanks, fiddleheads are the official symbol for this picturesque New Brunswick drive, and the first fresh, local greens of spring. At Plaster Rock, fiddlehead woodcarvings stand 7.3 metres (24 feet) high—and are definitely worth checking out.

There's also The Coleman Frog at Fredericton's York Sunbury Museum. Maybe not the world's largest but, at 19.1 kilograms (42 pounds), big enough! Not far away, in Maugerville, a giant potato (5.8 metres, about 19 feet high) graces the roadside. The town of Nackawic has an axe worth grinding—at 15 metres (50 feet) high, making it the world largest. It's also a reminder of the importance of the forest industry, and a scene for some fun photos. Upriver, in Hartland, cross the world's longest covered bridge (see p. 91).

You may not actually see Grand Falls' claim to impressiveness. It, like the site of the nearby world's largest pond hockey tourney (see p. 34), might have already melted away by mid-April. Folks here used 2,500 ice blocks to create a massive dome igloo 9.3 metres (30 feet) in diameter and 5.4 metres (17.5 feet) tall, setting a new world record in 2011. They stuffed about 300 people inside and will be happy to show you the photos to prove it.❦
www.sjrvta.com

Take an Ice Cider Tasting Tour of Rural Québec

In spring, it's a lovely fragrant time to visit Frelighsburg in the Québec countryside to see where the magic of ice cider brews—and where it began.

What started out as an oddity is today a specialty liqueur. Located in the Eastern Townships (about a 90-minute scenic drive from Montréal), the Clos Saragnat vineyard and orchard is where ice cider creator Christian Barthomeuf still operates the good old-fashioned way; that is, with manual labour and love, working the soil with his horses. Barthomeuf made his first ice cider in 1989 and has since won several awards. He has a small boutique open from 10:00 a.m. to 5:00 p.m. on weekends starting in mid-April, then daily about a month later.

What started out as an oddity is today a specialty liqueur.

Barthomeuf has also collaborated with Domaine Pinnacle, an orchard and cidery virtually across the street. It's definitely worth the quick jaunt over by car to see the newer, bigger, and more modern facilities. They also have a selection of different ice cider products, including a sparkling version.

Time permitting, another well-known cider house is La Face Cachée de la Pomme ("The hidden side of the apple"), close to the U.S. border in Hemmingford. Most of these *cidreries* ("cider houses") offer tastings, some free, some not. In Montréal, you can also buy most of these brands at the provincial liquor store chain (La SAQ) and Clos Saragnat is also available at Le Marché des Saveurs du Québec at the Jean Talon market. 🍁

www.saragnat.com

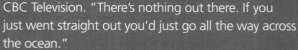

Rick Mercer's *favourite* PLACE

Rick Mercer considers himself blessed to have travelled to so many remote Canadian towns. But nowhere trumps home—Middle Cove, Newfoundland—where the beach is always the first place he visits.

"You always stop at the top of the cliff because the road goes from the top of the cliff, which is a couple hundred feet high, and then goes right down to the beach," says the Canadian satirist and host of the *Rick Mercer Report* on CBC Television. "There's nothing out there. If you just went straight out you'd just go all the way across the ocean."

But it's not a sandy beach. About 20 minutes north of St. John's, Middle Cove is rugged and stunning.

"You can have a bonfire there in the evening. Although you have to be careful about the odd rough wave," says the Newfoundland-born, Toronto-based comedian.

A friend had an after-wedding reception on the beach one summer, complete with torches and bonfires.

"They had barbecues and the whole thing set up. Then a wave came in and whoosh . . . all the lights, everything instantly black because the fires were put out. And a couple of the guests ended up in the drink."

Everyone was safe, "But that's the reality of the ocean in Newfoundland. It's not to be trifled with."

There aren't any must-go places in town, which Mercer calls more, "a community of houses."

"But you can drop into Mum and Dad's," he says. "They're always happy to have visitors."

Enjoy Spring Skiing at Sunshine Village

The famed Rockies resort is renowned for powdery panoramas and wonderful warmth

As the promise of spring approaches in the Canadian Rockies and the summer season of hiking and golfing gears up, you can still be carving through virgin powder at Sunshine Village, where skiing and snowboarding extends well into May. In fact, with more than 10 metres (33 feet) of snow recorded each year, the only reason the resort actually closes for the summer is typically because of waning interest, not lack of snow.

Cradled in a snow-filled bowl high atop the continental divide, accessible only by gondola, Sunshine Village is an alpine resort famed around the world for its deep powder and stunning mountain scenery. By late April, the weather has warmed, days have lengthened and mid-winter crowds at Sunshine are a distant memory. For beginners, there's a wealth of groomed runs—perfect for effortless cruising—while for serious skiers and boarders, snow coverage remains excellent on the steep and challenging terrain for which the resort is legendary. But there's something else about springtime at Sunshine—a joie de vivre that permeates the resort. You can see it on the faces of young lift operators

working on early-season tans, in the smiles of vacationing families, and in the relaxed actions of grizzled locals swapping yarns on the outdoor tables at Trapper's Pub.

The first people to ski what is now known as Sunshine were two local men, Cliff White and Cyril Paris, who returned from a backcountry trip in the spring of 1929 with stories of deep snow and ideal slopes for skiing. (Subsequently, a rustic log cabin was used as a base for overnight ski trips.) By 1942, a lift was constructed. The White family, synonymous with the Sunshine area for many years, ran the lodge and ski area while buses negotiated the steep, narrow road that led to the base area. Today, Sunshine Village has grown into one of the world's most modern resorts. A high-speed gondola whisks people six kilometres (3.7 miles) from the valley floor to the village, where there's a lodge, restaurants, and ski school. Chairlifts provide access to trails on three mountains as well as a sprawling terrain park. Beginners spend their time enjoying the mellow slopes, served by the Strawberry and Wawa chairs, and experienced skiers and boarders head to

the powder-filled runs of Goat's Eye Mountain. Looking for a real challenge? Take the narrow plunge down Delirium Dive, one of the steepest lift-accessed runs in North America.

The best way to experience the resort is by making reservations at Sunshine Mountain Lodge, the only ski-in, ski-out accommodation in the national parks of the Canadian Rockies. Accessible only by gondola after the daytime crowds have retreated to other Banff accommodations, you and a lucky few can retreat to slopeside rooms—then be first on the slopes the following morning. Extensively revamped in recent years, guest rooms feature floor-to-ceiling windows with sweeping views across the resort. Each is decorated in a woodsy yet stylish theme, with flat-screen TVs, jetted tubs, and iPod docking stations as bonuses. The outdoor, 30-person, hot tub is a popular place to soothe weary muscles after a day on the slopes, followed by dinner at one of two dining choices. Chimney Corner is a casual lounge with a wood-burning fireplace, while the Eagle's Nest Restaurant will surprise you with modern presentations of Canadian specialties.

As a self-contained resort, it's possible to spend your entire vacation at Sunshine Village, but there's plenty to see and do elsewhere in Banff National Park. The resort town of Banff, population 8,000, is where most park visitors base themselves. Staying in town lacks the convenience of being up at Sunshine Village, but allows visitors more options for daytime activities and dining. Banff has evolved far beyond its roots as a resort village centred on hot springs—but remains at its most appealing when blanketed by snow. Overlooking the town of Banff are the steep slopes of Banff's Mount Norquay resort, while farther up the Bow Valley, Lake Louise is yet another world-class alpine resort. In spring, however, Banff National Park is about much more than skiing and snowboarding. At higher elevations, such as the road to Moraine Lake, you can cross-country ski or snowshoe through forests of snow-covered trees. By early April, larger wildlife moves to lower valleys, making a drive along the scenic Bow Valley Parkway a great opportunity to view bears, deer, elk, and wolves. 🍁

Find out more at:
www.skibanff.com

◀ Tackle Rock Climbing Lessons in Squamish

If you saw the 2002 Al Pacino thriller *Insomnia*, filmed in Squamish, you may have spotted the Stawamus Chief looming in the background. Standing 700 metres (2,300 feet) tall, it's North America's second-largest granite monolith, located along the Sea-to-Sky Highway between Vancouver and Whistler. "The Chief" has enticed rock-climbing enthusiasts for more than 50 years. But that's just a starting point. There are 1,500-odd routes around Squamish you might explore as Squamish is considered one of the world's top climbing and mountaineering areas. Adrenalin, meet discipline!

"The Chief" has enticed rock-climbing enthusiasts for more than 50 years.

Get your gear at local rock-climbing stores, such as Climb On and Valhalla Pure Squamish. Companies like Squamish Rock Guides, Slipstream Rock & Ice, or WestCoast Mountain Guides will gladly school you in technique in April, when the year's peak-climbing starts getting underway. Feel your heart pound as you re-enact the historic 1961 ascent of the Grand Wall of the Stawamus Chief by Jim Cooper and Ed Baldwin. Single-pitch rock-climbing routes abound at Smoke Bluffs Park. Throughout Squamish, explore a wide range of rock faces, from beginner climbs to challenging 5.14 pitches that require expert scrambling, rappelling, and dexterity with rope and crampons. Are you ready to rock?🍁

www.squamishclimbing.com

Visit Historic Expo '67 Sites ▼

From April to October, Expo '67 (the World's Fair) welcomed some 50 million visitors to Montréal, including Queen Elizabeth II, Grace Kelly, and General Charles de Gaulle. Of the 850 pavilions and buildings that were created—many by architects and engineers from the 62 participating countries—several remain. Spring is prime time to visit these design gems, all nestled in a lovely outdoor setting.

All the sites are located on Parc Jean-Drapeau, which encompasses both Île Sainte-Hélène and Île Notre-Dame. La Ronde amusement park has rides, games, and a petting zoo; American corporation Six Flags purchased it in 2001. The original France and Québec pavilions became one, and now make up the Casino de Montréal. What's known as the Biosphère used to be the American pavilion created by futurist Buckminster Fuller. The cage-like geodesic dome now houses an eco-museum where you can learn about environmental issues in an interactive and entertaining setting. If it looks familiar, you may be thinking of Spaceship Earth at Walt Disney World Resort.

Visitors are free to discover the park by foot, bike, in-line skates, or picnic in designated areas. Separated from the city by a dividing body of water, the Montréal skyline is a postcard panorama in the distance. Île Sainte-Hélène is also a veritable open-air gallery of beautiful sculptures originally commissioned for Expo '67. ❧

www.collectionscanada.gc.ca/expo

Fish for Rainbow Trout off the World's Largest Freshwater Island

Manitoulin Island, the world's largest freshwater island, is considered one of the premier fishing regions in Canada. The island is so big it has sizeable lakes of its own—including Lake Manitou, noted for its walleye, northern pike, smallmouth bass, perch, and salmon. But Manitoulin's bays, inland lakes, and streams are most famous for their rainbow trout. The season opens the fourth week of April. Bait those hooks: it's not uncommon to land a nine-kilogram (20-pound) monster.

Rainbow trout are coldwater fish and Manitoulin was tailor-made for them. The depth of the water and the abundance of bays and inlets make it ideal for rainbow trout to spawn in big numbers. Locals say Manitowaning Bay is the prime location along the 180-kilometre (111.8-mile) island, not least because the cages of a local trout farm recently burst— releasing tens of thousands of captives. The spring rainbow run sees many anglers wading into the flows of the Mindemoya, Manitou, and Kagawong lakes. When you're not out fishing, visit the Ontario Ministry of Natural Resources orientation centre at Blue Jay Creek. A self-guided tour features an underwater diorama and outdoor trail along with explanations of the ministry's sustainability programs, including its spawning beds for rainbow trout. ❧

www.manitoulinislandfishing.com

Spend a Week with the World's Best Documentary Films

If you're an aficionado of documentary film, you'll be hard-pressed to find a better festival on the planet than Toronto's Hot Docs. All the qualities that make documentaries such a satisfying cinematic experience are magnified in this compact, rigorously programmed event.

While the city's premier cinema scene, the Toronto International Film Festival (see p. 210), gets most of the ink, Hot Docs is considered the more user-friendly experience. Screening venues are situated nearby one another, audiences are sophisticated, and the films—many of them world or North American premieres—are consistently strong. That's the beauty of documentary—there are no celebrities, meaning you won't find yourself in a lacklustre movie selected only because its star has agreed to attend the festival. Instead, many Hot Docs screenings are attended by the director and often the subjects of the films. The downside is that after a week of screening the best of the world's documentary crop, you may feel compelled to change the planet.

For a life-changing experience, the price is certainly right. At about C$100, the Hot Docs Festival Pass provides 10 single tickets to any screening, making it an ideal choice for an individual, couple, or even a group. Tickets and passes are available on-line and at the box office generally in about mid-March and there are often early-bird specials offering additional tickets, good for any screening. ❦

www.hotdocs.ca

5 faves

Richler neighbourhood tour

Fans of the late CanLit icon Mordecai Richler will find a wealth of familiar sights from his books while walking through the Plateau and Mile End neighbourhoods. Make sure to hit such Richler landmarks as the St-Viateur Bagel shop, rue St-Urbain (Saint Urbain Street), Schwartz's Montréal Hebrew Delicatessen, and the author's final resting place at Mount Royal Cemetery.

Pay Homage to the World's Biggest Pyrogy

Glendon, population 470, is a long way from anywhere (actually, it's a three-hour drive north of Edmonton), but it gets a steady stream of visitors searching out the world's biggest pyrogy, an eastern European staple similar to a dumpling. Those looking for a filling meal have come to the right place.

Canada is home to the world's third-largest Ukrainian population (behind only Ukraine itself and Russia), with the heritage and traditions particularly strong across northern Alberta, where eastern European settlers arrived in the 1890s. A century later, Glendon helped promote its heritage—while also adding to the world of giant-sized, small-town attractions—by unveiling the nine-metre (27-foot) high pyrogy speared by an oversized fork in downtown Pyrogy Park. (Pyrogy is the preferred local spelling for what's known as a pierogi or perogi in other parts of the country.) This dining staple is built of fibreglass and steel, and weighs 2,700 kilograms (6,000 pounds). For the full Glendon pyrogy experience, head across the road from Pyrogy Park for a meal at the Pyrogy Park Cafe (pyrogies are served, of course, boiled or fried and filled with mashed potato, cheese, sauerkraut, or fruit), then reserve a room at the Pyrogy Motel. Need directions? Just look for Pyrogy Drive as you enter town. If the pyrogy has whet your appetite for weird Ukrainian roadside attractions, head two hours south of Glendon to Vegreville, which boasts the world's largest Ukrainian Easter Egg. ❧

www.md.bonnyville.ab.ca/visitors/ md-communities/village-of-glendon

◀ Spend an Afternoon Café-Hopping on Saint-Denis

After a long hibernation wrapped in layers of wool and fleece, spring brings out the flirty side of Montréal, with locals baring a little skin and flocking to outdoor cafés to enjoy the scent of spring.

Saint-Denis Street is a colourful, mainly French-speaking area filled with quaint walk-up buildings that have been transformed into chic boutiques and cafés, many with umbrella-covered patios where locals pack it in elbow-to-elbow and take in lunch, *cinq-à-sept* (happy hour), or simply a coffee.

The French word for patio is *terrasse*, and it's not so much a place, but a state of mind—or a reward for having survived winter. And everybody knows the east side of Saint-Denis gets the best sunshine. Places with prime terrasse seating include: Le Café Cherrier or Bistro Fruits Folie for brunch, Auprès de ma Blonde (named after a French folk song) for their mussels and fries, Aux Deux Marie café or Brûlerie St.-Denis for coffee, and Rockaberry for pie enthusiasts.

Oenophiles can exercise their palates at Les Cavistes, likely the très chicest terrasse along the strip, with its special outdoor menu—perfect for afternoon grazing. A little further north, but worth the stroll, is L'emporte-pièce, if only for their gourmet grilled-cheese sandwiches. Think blue cheese with caramelized onions on raisin bread, or apple with old cheddar. Just don't forget your sunscreen as you may want to linger awhile! ❧

www.la-rue-st-denis.com

The Giant Moose of Moose Jaw

Sometimes a place really does live up to its name. Along the Trans-Canada Highway near Moose Jaw, Saskatchewan, you'll find Mac the Moose—reputedly the world's largest moose statue. Erected in 1984, it stands 10 metres (32 feet) tall and weighs about 9,000 kilograms (10 tons).

Écomusée du miel

This one-of-a-kind museum, about 30 kilometres (19 miles) from downtown Québec City, is all about honey. Take a "bee safari" to see how it's made, watch the bees at work in the museum's giant glass-walled hives . . . then taste the freshest honey.

Thompson Toronto rooftop pool

One of the swankiest new hotels in downtown Toronto is the Thompson Toronto, and one of its focal points is its rooftop infinity swimming pool with its breathtaking views and cozy fireplace lounge. A place to see-and-be-seen . . . while feeling fabulous.

Moncton's Magnetic Hill

A quirk of geography makes it appear that a car stopped at the bottom of a short downhill stretch will start to roll back uphill. In fact, it's an optical illusion—but that hasn't stopped this from becoming a popular tourist spot, also the site of the largest gift shop in the Maritimes.

Your next STEP

TOP PICKS
ADVENTURE
CULTURE & HISTORY
NATURE'S GRANDEUR
EVENTS & FESTIVALS
QUIRKY CANADA
REJUVENATE

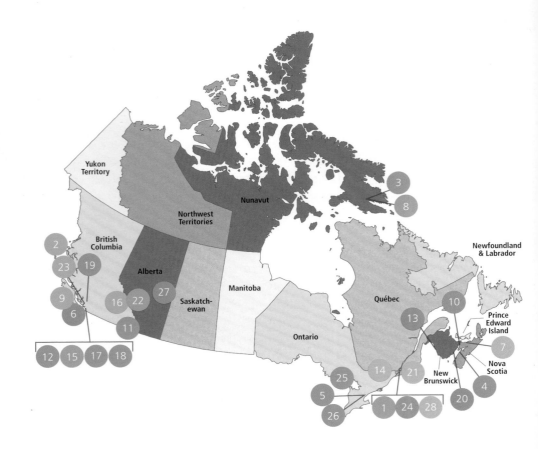

WEEK 1

1 MONTRÉAL, QUE.
Cirque du Soleil Premiere
www.cirquedusoleil.com

2 HAIDA GWAII, B.C.
Cape Fife Loop hiking
www.britishcolumbia.com/
parks/?id=200

3 IQALUIT, NANUVAT
Legislative Assembly of Nanuvat
www.assembly.nu.ca

4 KENTVILLE, N.S.
Rockhounding
www.nstravelguide.com/what/
rockhounding

5 TORONTO, ONT.
Toronto Blue Jays home opener
www.torontobluejays.com

6 DUNCAN, B.C.
World's biggest hockey stick
www.vancouverisland.com

7 TATAMAGOUCHE, N.S.
Train Station Inn
www.trainstation.ca

WEEK 2

8 IQALUIT, NUNAVUT
Toonik Tyme celebration
www.tooniktyme.com

9 TOFINO, B.C.
Tofino surfing
www.tourismtofino.com

10 JOGGINS, N.S.
Joggins Fossil Centre
www.jogginsfossilcliffs.net

11 FERNIE, B.C.
Fernie wildlife-watching
www.fernienature.com

12 VANCOUVER, B.C.
Vancouver Fashion Week
www.vanfashionweek.com

13 HARTLAND, N.B.
World's longest covered bridge
www.town.hartland.nb.ca/
html/bridge.htm

14 OTTAWA, ONT.
Le Cordon Bleu Ottawa Culinary
Arts Institute
www.lcbottawa.com

WEEK 3

15 VANCOUVER, B.C.
Vancouver Sun Run
www.sunrun.com

16 GOLDEN, B.C.
Rockies ski touring
www.icefall.ca

17 VANCOUVER, B.C.
Cherry blossoms
www.nitobe.org

18 VANCOUVER, B.C.
Sea safaris
www.sewellsmarina.com

19 WHISTLER, B.C.
World Ski & Snowboard Festival
www.wssf.com

20 GRAND BAY, N.B.
World's largest roadside attractions
www.sjrvta.com

21 FRELIGHSBURG, QUE.
Ice cider tasting
www.saragnat.com

WEEK 4

22 BANFF, ALTA.
Sunshine Village spring skiing
www.skibanff.com

23 SQUAMISH, B.C.
Rock climbing
www.squamishclimbing.com

24 MONTRÉAL, QUE.
Expo '67 sites
www.collectionscanada.gc.ca/expo

25 MANITOULIN ISLAND, ONT.
Rainbow trout fishing
www.manitoulinislandfishing.com

26 TORONTO, ONT.
Hot Docs film festival
www.hotdocs.ca

27 GLENDON, ALTA.
World's biggest pyrogy
www.md.bonnyville.ab.ca/visitors/
md-communities/village-of-glendon

28 MONTRÉAL, QUE.
Saint-Denis café-hopping
www.la-rue-st-denis.com

MAY

Raise Your Glass High on an Okanagan Wine Tour

Spas, golf, and boating augment this mouth-watering experience

While California's Napa and Sonoma valleys usually claim the spotlight among western North America's wine-producing regions, British Columbia's Okanagan Valley has emerged as a major wine region since the 1990s. Today, you'll discover more than 100 top-flight wineries in this fertile, laid-back area centred on the 135-kilometre (84-mile) long Okanagan Lake, just a four-hour drive northeast of Vancouver. Since production isn't generally on a large scale, you'll find choice bottles that you just can't buy at home. The surrounding amenities and activities—spas, golf, horseback riding, boating, and fishing—are as welcoming as the tasting rooms. Early May is a superb time to visit, with warm weather awakening the vines and the release of the spring wines. The latter is celebrated during the annual Spring Okanagan Wine Festival, where dozens of gourmet lunches and dinners, food pairings, wine education seminars, and live performances at different wineries take things to a truly toast-worthy level. There are so many ways to indulge yourself.

Where to start? The 1996-founded BC VQA (Vintners Quality Alliance) Wine Information Centre in Penticton, at the south end of the lake, will get you pointed in the right direction. Inside the clocktower-adorned building with vine murals, you can taste and purchase more than 600 VQA wines from 80-something wineries, plus cookbooks, corkscrews, and Okanagan cheeses, crackers, and chutneys. Get winery route maps, or get picked up for a winery tour. Bikes, shuttle buses, chauffeured classic convertibles, and even kayaks are among the alternatives to driving.

Reminiscent of Tuscany, the rolling hills of the adjacent Naramata Bench—on the east side of Okanagan Lake—offer some of the region's finest wineries. You can admire the rich-soiled vineyards from out on the cerulean water, taking a wine-tasting cruise aboard the Casabella Princess paddle wheeler featuring local *cuisine du terroir* ("food of the earth") pairings. Or party hard at Bacchanalia, the inevitably sold-out, one-day wine-tasting fiesta with more than 50 Okanagan producers at the Penticton Lakeside Resort.

If you prefer to visit individual Penticton-area wineries, options abound. During the spring wine festival, you could have a catered three-course dinner at the 160-seat bistro at Hillside Estate, savouring newly released Merlot and Muscat. Alternately, though many Okanagan orchards have been converted into vineyards in recent years, fruit remains a major crop—reflected in the selection of vintages at Elephant Island. Next to a tinkling court-yard fountain, sip apricot dessert wine, or try the Pink Elephant sparkling wine made with Granny Smith apples and currants. Or, head 15 minutes south to See Ya Later Ranch, up on Hawthorne Mountain, and sample some award-nominated Rieslings and rosés.

Up the lake near Kelowna, the Okanagan's largest city with 120,000 inhabitants, both Mission Hill Family Estate and Quails Gate are among the "brand name" wineries worth visiting. The massive, Italian-style Mission Hill goes all out for the spring wine festival, inviting top Vancouver chefs to partner with its culinary maestro, Matthew Batey, on a multi-course feast in the Chagall Room—featuring a rare tapestry by famed artist Marc Chagall. Be sure to savour the rich Oculus red wine, one of the signature brands at this two-time Canadian Winery of the Year. In 2008, *Travel + Leisure* hailed Mission Hill's outdoor Terrace Restaurant as one of the world's top-five winery restaurants. Meanwhile, next door, Quails Gate provides an agri-tourism experience with its award-winning wine tours, thoroughly explaining the processes of planting, fermentation, and bottling. It's famed for its Pinot Noir and Chardonnay.

If all this fervent tippling and noshing is taking a toll, change up your pace. Okanagan Lake beckons. Whiz around on a Jet Ski, or fish for large rainbow trout. You can also tee off at one of the award-winning area golf courses, like Vernon's Predator Ridge, which earned Best New Course honours from *SCOREGolf* Magazine in 2010 and hosted the prestigious TELUS World Skins Game. Another option: enjoy a hot stone massage at the on-site Aveda spa.

Wine, spa treatments, and Aboriginal culture come together in a South Okanagan desert setting (Canada's only desert) at Spirit Ridge Vineyard Resort & Spa. This Osoyoos mainstay is part of the Nk'Mip Cellars (see p. 195), the first Aboriginal-owned and operated winery in North America. Under winemaker Randy Picton, it has turned out award-winning Pinot Blancs and Chardonnays. During the festival season, do a "Wake Up With Wine" morning tasting, or watch Aboriginal dance performances while nibbling at food stations throughout the Nk'Mip facility. Then, at the Sonora Spa, zone out with a Sun Dance Massage or a Luxury Lavender Body Treatment, utilizing natural ingredients.

In the big picture, it doesn't matter whether you're imbibing at the spacious Tasting Gallery at Oliver's Jackson-Triggs Okanagan Estate (the brand that produced the official Vancouver 2010 wines) or relishing the Mediterranean-flavoured wine country cuisine at Tinhorn Creek's new Miradoro restaurant. Your Okanagan wine tour will be a genuinely vintage experience. Watch out, California!🍁

Find out more at:
www.thewinefestivals.com

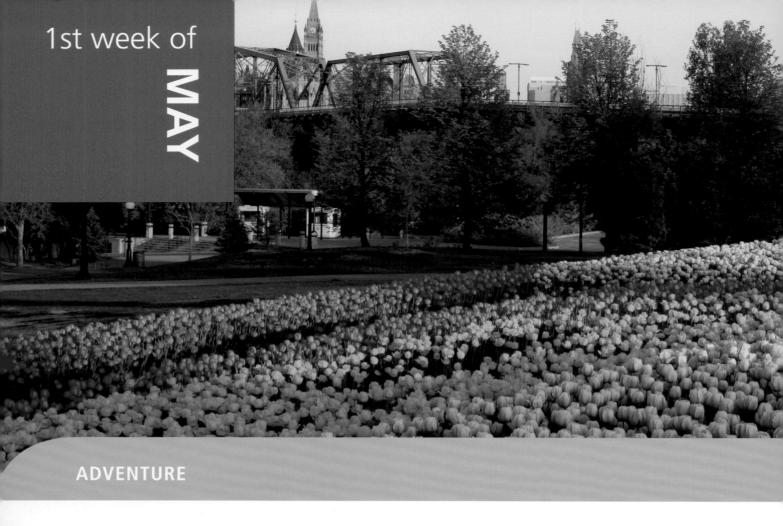

ADVENTURE

Go Sturgeon Fishing on the Mighty Fraser River

Do your favourite novels include Hemingway's *The Old Man and the Sea* or Melville's *Moby Dick*? If you've always wanted to catch a really big fish, set your course for Mission, British Columbia, located one hour's drive east of Vancouver on the Lougheed Highway. The rural, hillside community overlooking the Fraser River has been dubbed the "Sturgeon Capital of the World," and May is a beautiful time of year to see if you can reel in a majestic white sturgeon.

Guided fishing tours are available from reputable local companies like Silversides Fishing Adventures and STS Guiding Service. You'll need the help when you head out on B.C.'s largest river in a customized jet boat. Sturgeon, to say the least, are not to be messed with. These bony-plated monsters can weigh up to 600 kilograms (1,320 pounds), and can be as long as six metres (20 feet). So assistance with selecting the right bait, hook size, and tackle is invaluable. If you prefer

If you've always wanted to catch a really big fish, set your course for Mission, British Columbia.

shore fishing, one sturgeon hotspot is the dyke on the Fraser River between Harbour Park and Dewdney Slough. Surrounded by snow-capped coastal mountains, you'll feel like a true outdoor adventurer if you manage to hook one of these legendary creatures. ❧
**www.silversidesfishing.ca,
www.guidebc.com**

◀ Tiptoe to Ottawa's Tulip Festival

If you love tulips, there are a million reasons to visit the nation's capital in May. Rank after rank, bed after bed, slender green stems are the only things you'll find in common amidst 50 different varieties. There's no more vivid celebration of spring in Canada.

Talk about the gift that keeps on giving. In 1945, the Dutch royal family sent 100,000 bulbs to the Canadian government as thanks for sheltering Princess Juliana and her daughters during the war. One of Juliana's daughters, Margaret, was born in Ottawa. (The hospital room was declared international territory so the little princess could retain her royal Dutchness.) The main floral event takes place at Commissioners Park—where one-third of the now one million bulbs are planted, stretching from Dows Lake along the Rideau Canal to the Garden of the Provinces and Territories on Parliament Hill. The festival's activity hub is Major's Hill Park, where tulips are treated with as much love but a little less reverence. The theme of international friendship is reflected through cultural exhibits and culinary presentations at locations around the city centre. While looking at flowers is free, the festival passport (around C$20) is an option for families with restless children. Craft-making exhibits allow kids to create their own souvenirs.✿

www.tulipfestival.ca

NATURE'S GRANDEUR

Check Out Kootenay National Park's Abundant Wildlife ▶

Early spring is the best time of year for viewing wildlife in Kootenay National Park, the least-known of the four contiguous national parks in the Canadian Rockies. In fact, your chances of seeing large mammals are better here than in adjacent Banff National Park.

Kootenay protects two important wildlife corridors, the Kootenay and Vermilion valleys, both bisected by the Kootenay Parkway. This section of the park is snow-free much earlier than higher elevations, attracting an abundance of large mammals. If you're driving along the Kootenay Parkway in spring and spot a bear feasting on dandelions, chances are it's a black bear, which is widespread throughout the park but not always black (a black bear may be brown). Grizzly bears are present, but much less likely to be spotted by casual observers. (Look for them around Vermilion Pass.) Reliable places to see mountain goats and moose in the Canadian

Rockies are few and far between, but one of the better opportunities is presented by roadside salt licks along the Kootenay Parkway. Elk are more common than both moose and mountain goats; they graze on fresh spring growth where the highway passes through lower elevations, such as along the Kootenay Valley. Kootenay's most famous residents are bighorn sheep, which use the Kootenay Parkway as their own trail through the eastern end of the park, striding confidently through the village of Radium Hot Springs, British Columbia.✿

www.pc.gc.ca/kootenay

EVENTS & FESTIVALS

QUIRKY CANADA

Learn Some New Dance Moves at the City of Bhangra

When *Slumdog Millionaire* swept the 2009 Academy Awards, a new craze for Bollywood-style boogie invaded gym classes and dance studios. Got a thing for northern Indian folk dancing? Head to the annual, multi-day City of Bhangra. Also called the Vancouver International Bhangra Celebration, it's North America's largest festival dedicated to this art form—replete with extravagant hand movements, leaps, brightly coloured turbans, jewellery, and dresses. Vancouver is home to thousands of Punjabi families, and the festival brings out the appeal of multi-faceted bhangra for everyone.

Feel the rhythm of the dhol drum at a free concert outside the Vancouver Art Gallery, where hip-hop beats, funk bass lines, and other influences intermingle with bhangra to create a unique dance party featuring international artists. Check out a fascinating multimedia exhibit—including posters, instruments, and films—on the local history of bhangra at the Museum of Vancouver. Watch Indian and North American teams strut their stuff and compete for cash prizes at the grand finale at the Queen Elizabeth Theatre. Whether you end up learning all the lyrics to the bouncy mega-hit "Dupatta Tera Sat Rang Da," or just relish dabbling in another world beat style, you'll come away energized and smiling.❧
www.vibc.org

Pamper Yourself at Canada's Soap Economuseum

In the days leading up to Mother's Day, when a little pampering and taking care of loved ones is in order, a visit to Savonnerie Olivier Soapery in Ste-Anne-de-Kent, New Brunswick, has just what you need to make mom happy. This soapery teaches a fun approach to skin care, practising a philosophy of kindness and respect for both people and the planet. Here, beauty products are produced from natural ingredients using time-honoured techniques—the soapery is also a living museum, dedicated to safeguarding the traditional soap-making craft of the early 19th century. Indeed, Canada's Soap Economuseum is the only establishment of its kind in North America recognized by UNESCO.

Olivier makes visits special by taking time to share their passion for soap and skin care. Guided tours delve into the history, art, and evolution of skin care through the ages. Live demonstrations of modern-day soap crafting serve as an introduction to the Olivier philosophy of living purely. The soapery comes honestly by its way of thinking: its first batch of pure-plant soaps was produced as Christmas gifts in founder Isabel Gagné's kitchen. They were so well received that she and her husband Pierre opened the soapery and still make products the same way as when they started: by hand. Visitors often get to try this hands-on approach, and the community-based soapery also hand-crafts olive, cocoa, and coconut oils into skin care products.❧
www.oliviersoaps.com

Dine at a Lobster Supper for Mother's Day

As the calendar turns to May, Prince Edward Islanders watch the north shore with great anxiety . . . will the ice be gone so lobster boats can set traps? Do fishermen have time to bring in a harvest of succulent lobster before the first Sunday in May? The fact that Mother's Day coincides with the first haul of lobster is a coincidence—but a very happy one for seafood lovers. They'll readily tell you that at no time of year is lobster as succulent, tasty, or full as it is in those first hauls. Everyone is eager for a good "feed," a chance to enjoy the harvest of the sea.

Everyone is eager for a good "feed," a chance to enjoy the harvest of the sea.

When community lobster suppers first opened their doors, Mother's Day was seen as a good opportunity to sit down with family, friends, and neighbours before summer visitors arrived. Today, those suppers have evolved into full-fledged operations, such as the New Glasgow Lobster Suppers. Started in 1958, the tradition of opening for one day in early May—Mother's Day—has been maintained. It's a day when the traditional whole lobster, freshly baked rolls, salads, and dessert are all still served. (Unlimited tubs of mussels are a newer addition.) Everyone hopes for an Island lobster on their plate, for no lobster's as good to an Islander as that first catch of the season from the north shore.✤
www.peilobstersuppers.com

It happened THIS WEEK:

The Bloody Caesar Invented

Clam juice seems an unlikely ingredient for Canada's unofficial cocktail, but that's what bartender Walter Chell added to tomato juice, vodka, and spices to create a signature drink for the opening of a Calgary Italian restaurant, Marco's.

Spaghetti vongole—clams with spaghetti—inspired the bartender, who called the creation a Caesar. The legend goes that when an Englishman tried the mix, he declared that is was "a good bloody Caesar."

The drink made its debut in May 1969, and Mott's put a bottled tomato and clam juice (Clamato) on the market later that same year. Today, millions of Bloody Caesars are served with brunch and at bars every year. The mix is even available in Mexico.

To make a classic Bloody Caesar, rim a glass with celery salt. Mix one part vodka with four parts Clamato juice over ice. Stir in a few dashes of hot sauce, Worcestershire sauce, and salt and pepper, then garnish with a classic celery rib and wedge of lime. Variations range from adding giant shrimp to pickled green beans.

Staying true to its history, the downtown Westin Calgary still serves Bloody Caesars at the drink's birthplace, now called the Liquid Lounge.

Take In World-Class Theatre in a Postcard-Perfect Town

Whether you prefer Shakespeare or Andrew Lloyd Webber, the Stratford Festival supplies the perfect setting

Each spring, the sleepy town of Stratford blossoms like the surrounding fields of orchards—but instead of yielding bushels of fruit, what blooms is a wealth of absolutely spectacular theatre. Stratford is home to the largest classical repertory theatre in North America, renowned both in Canada and abroad.

The Stratford Shakespeare Festival hits its stride in mid-May, when the season begins in earnest. (The curtain rises on the opening production, generally in mid-April, but there's only one show on offer at this time of year.) While performances continue through mid-October, there's an excitement in the air in early spring as locals and visitors alike clamber to be the first to catch the best of the new offerings.

Stratford has long been associated with the repertoire of its namesake stage, the works of William Shakespeare, and it does excel at classical theatre. This century, especially, the artistic team has updated the festival's profile to make it a destination for new and modern plays, as well as popular entertainment such as Broadway musicals. So, you can choose according to taste and experience: is the main draw an ambitious production of *Jesus Christ Superstar* or a traditional staging of *King Lear*? Does *Camelot* better fit the bill, or an inventive production of *Richard III* starring a woman in the lead role? The ever-impressive lineup is designed to suit tastes from the contemporary to the historic, the comedic to the tragic. In fact, there's so much to choose from, it's often advisable to take in two shows and turn your stay into an overnight or two.

Across the board, Stratford remains a prestigious venue rich with talent, including legends from Canada and elsewhere, and young and emerging artists.

The list is long enough to fill volumes, but a few great names that have been associated with Stratford include: Alec Guinness, John Hirsch, Robin Phillips, Timothy Findley, Alan Bates, Brian Bedford, Len Cariou, Brent Carver, Hume Cronyn, Brian Dennehy, Colm Feore, Megan Follows, Lorne Greene, Julie Harris, Martha Henry, William Hutt, James Mason, Loreena McKennitt, Richard Monette, John Neville, Christopher Plummer, Sarah Polley, Jason Robards, Paul Scofield, Maggie Smith, Jessica Tandy, Peter Ustinov, and Cynthia Dale. There are always visiting directors, surprise cameos, new writers, ambitious artistic directors, and more on show.

The festival's official opening was July 13, 1953, with *Richard III* starring Sir Alec Guinness and staged in a huge tent. The thrust stage of the Festival Theatre—a stage that would prove to be a pioneer in theatre festivals around the world—was still under construction.

Today, Stratford has four theatres. The Festival Theatre has a dynamic thrust stage (a modern recreation of an Elizabethan stage), while The Avon Theatre is a classic proscenium. The Tom Patterson Theatre is an intimate 500-seat theatre and The Studio Theatre is a 278-seat space used for new and experimental works.

The season continues through late October. In May, performances run Monday through Saturday, while later in the season the weekly schedule changes from one month to the next. Ticket prices range from C$25 to C$140, with special deals for students and seniors (for tickets visit www.stratfordfestival.ca). Tickets are also available throughout Canada and the United States at Ticketmaster outlets. The box office for the new season opens in January, though the festival does offer early bookings for American Express cardholders. There are many ways to save, including half-price rush seats, family packages, and discount seats. Balcony seat deals at C$29 are limited to on-line booking and offer 60 tickets for each play (with some exceptions) at this low rate. If you're 16 to 29 years of age, you're eligible to join the Play On program, which offers tickets for C$25. (There are also deals on local dining, shopping, and hotels.)

Stratford has long set its sights on engaging younger generations in the discovery of live theatre. The Family Experience Program offers reduced ticket prices for children 18 years and younger (accompanied by an adult). There are additional attractions too, such as the backstage tour Behind the Festival Curtain, which includes a chance to explore the festival's Costume and Props Warehouse—one of North America's largest. There are also free Meet the Festival events, with members of the acting company and a series of special lectures about the major plays of the season.

Beyond the festival, there's Stratford's pretty down-town with its riverside parks, boutiques, and galleries to explore—all within walking distance. Stratford is also an excellent destination for fine dining. The haute The Church Restaurant is often regarded as one of the city's best: it's a dramatic transformation of an old church into a fine-dining room where the cathedral ceilings are as impressive as the classic menu. For something more casual, Bentley's is a popular watering hole where many of the festival's thespians can be spotted unwinding over a pint with fellow performers. Upstairs from the pub is the Lofts at 99, a modern, comfortable inn offering suites with kitchenettes.

One more thing, for Stratford's younger visitors: this is the hometown of Justin Bieber. And, yes, Bieber tours are available . . .🍁

Find out more at: www.stratfordfestival.ca

ADVENTURE

CULTURE & HISTORY

Scuba Dive under Arctic Ice

Strap on your dry suit and diving gear and take the plunge into the electric blue, big-ice world of the Arctic Ocean. The ultimate adventure? Exploring the underside of icebergs, drifting pack ice, ice floe cracks, and even seal holes one day, and wildlife colonies or the sea floor the next. You may even catch a glimpse of the elusive Narwhal—unicorn of the sea.

Late May is the ideal time to go. Summer's on the horizon and the ice has receded enough to dive, but plenty of ice remains to be explored. Your base is along the sea ice between northern Baffin Island and Bylot Island in Sirmilik National Park, an area framed by stunning fiords. Between dives and at night you'll relax at base camp—a cozy tent village specifically designed for warmth in the most frigid conditions set up right on the sea ice. After a day swimming underneath million-year-old ice, you might spend the evening sipping a cocktail cooled with ice from an iceberg (where else?), enjoying the warm, 24-hour sun on your face as a seal pops up from the same crack in the ice that you saw only a short while earlier from that very same vantage point. Now that's perspective!

There is only one operator offering under-ice dives in Nunavut, the reputable and well-respected Arctic Kingdom.❦
www.arctickingdom.com

Immerse Yourself in Richmond's Amazing Asian Shopping

In Vancouver, you can shop in Asia without going to Asia. Celebrate Canada's Asian Heritage Month by boarding the Canada Line train downtown and taking a 25-minute ride out to Richmond. Disembark at Aberdeen Station, and you'll find three big Asian shopping centres within walking distance. Their gloriously exotic wares reflect this community's diversity: Richmond's population is 60 per cent Asian.

Start at Aberdeen Centre, unmissable with its Bing Thom–designed glass facade. Browse through Daiso, a Japanese chain that opened its first North American location here, selling more than 50,000 high-quality items, from housewares to clothing, for as little as C$2 apiece. Shop at some 160 other stores hawking everything from Asian herbal remedies to heated toilet seats. Watch a Bellagio-style fountain show or stage performances like Japanese Taiko drumming or Thai fruit carving.

Neighbouring Yaohan Centre dazzles with its Osaka Supermarket, selling live seafood, Japanese candies, and egg tarts. Parker Place, Richmond's oldest Asian mall, offers current Hong Kong clothing styles and Cantonese DVDs, plus Vietnamese and Singaporean meals at 20-odd food court outlets.

Don't overlook the Summer Night Market, east on Bridgeport Road. Opening annually in May, it has up to 400 vendors pushing Hello Kitty products, cellphone cases, and outrageously tasty Asian street food on weekends.❦
**www.aberdeencentre.com,
www.yaohancentre.com, www.parkerplace.com,
www.summernightmarket.com**

Enjoy World-Famous Fly-Fishing on the Miramichi

Years ago, salmon fishing on New Brunswick's Miramichi River was the privilege of the rich, famous, and locals. The rich and famous had the wherewithal to get into backcountry fishing camps by horse or canoe; the locals lived there. Unusual in the salmon world, in the spring the Miramichi has an early season for "black salmon" (also known as kelt fishing, the salmon that return to the sea after spawning).

Today, fly-fishing on what is one of the most prolific salmon rivers on earth is accessible to all—but strictly regulated. Visitors to the Miramichi are required by law to be accompanied by a qualified local guide. Fishing camps provide everything needed for a no-fuss experience and they know the nitty-gritty, for example, that unlike most large salmon rivers, the Miramichi is easily tackled with a single-handed rod, the ideal choice for dry fly and bug fishing. Fly-fishing for spring salmon is usually done from a boat, stopping to fish where the fast-moving spring current slows.

> # Royalty (including Prince Charles), prime ministers, presidents, rock stars, and Hollywood icons have cast a line into these legendary waters.

As you drift along, know that in fishing the Miramichi you're in good company. Royalty (including Prince Charles), prime ministers, presidents, rock stars, and Hollywood icons have cast a line into these legendary waters, bringing a whole other element to the camp experience—tall tales. Storytelling is deeply ingrained in the region's roots, just like the tradition of musical kitchen parties, the perfect way to wind down after a day on the river. ✦
www.flyfishingatlanticsalmon.com

Hayley Wickenheiser's
favourite PLACE

In the hockey off-season, you're likely to find four-time Olympic medalist Hayley Wickenheiser out in the Alberta wilderness.

She likes "just being out in the open trails in Kananaskis country," she says. "Whether it's on my mountain bike, or I also ride a dirt bike."

Saskatchewan-born, Alberta-based Wickenheiser loves the challenge of travelling on her own steam. She is a strong advocate for women's hockey, organizing a women's hockey festival in Burnaby, B.C., in 2010.

"Riding is a physical test and a mental test," she says. "It helps me with training, but as well it's like a moving meditation."

Kananaskis Country is a recreation area to the southwest of Calgary. In winter, visitors take to the wilderness for cross-country skiing, snowmobiling, and ice fishing. Thousands of kilometres of trails are used for hiking, backpacking, and camping in summer, while the lakes and streams are open to canoers, kayakers, and anglers. May through October is a great time to explore, says Wickenheiser.

"It's all pretty untapped," she says. Expect to encounter bear, moose, deer, and coyotes.

Though she has only recently started riding dirt bikes on the trails, she has been mountain biking for years. The hockey player loves to reach isolated places, where preparation and self-sufficiency is important.

"You get to get out and into places that you couldn't reach by bike or on foot," Wickenheiser says. "You'll come across hikers, but you don't really see people out there because it's so vast."

EVENTS & FESTIVALS

Sample the Best of Rocky Mountain Cuisine

For connoisseurs of fine wine and lovers of gourmet cooking, the relatively inexpensive and entirely unpretentious Rocky Mountain Wine and Food Festival is an excellent reason to visit Banff.

The main events take place at the aptly named Grand Tasting Hall at The Fairmont Banff Springs Hotel, with three-hour tasting sessions hosted three times over the weekend. Many of the best local restaurants are represented, with chefs cooking up their specialties and serving tapas-size plates for sampling. The chefs are joined by representatives from more than 100 wineries from around the world, each providing samples and tasting tips. A number of local restaurants also host dinners over the weekend. These provide a more intimate setting than the Grand Tasting Hall, but are equally social. You could indulge in an evening of classical French cooking and taste a thoughtful selection of very French wines at classy Le Beaujolais; enjoy a multi-course meal highlighting western Canadian game and produce at the stylish Maple Leaf Grill and Lounge; or help judge which local restaurant cooks up the best ribs at the rowdy Elk and Oarsman Pub. Round out each night with the very latest cocktail concoctions at private parties hosted by local nightclubs.

Once you're done sampling, there aren't many better settings to walk off your meal and create room for the next one.🍁
www.rockymountainwine.com

Visit the Land of 10,000 Snakes ▼

For a spring spectacle like no other in Canada, plan a mid-May visit to the Narcisse Wildlife Management Area—just over one hour's drive from Winnipeg—to view more snakes at one time than it's possible to see anywhere else worldwide.

Five species of snakes are present in Manitoba, but red garter snakes are the only ones that hibernate through winter in communal dens. Dens are found throughout southern Manitoba and can be in burrows, tree roots, or rocky outcrops, but none contain the volume of snakes found at Narcisse—where more than 10,000 snakes occupy a single den in the limestone bedrock. Males emerge from the ground first, in early May—tens of thousands of them, slithering to the surface to await the arrival of females. Up to 100 males then form what's known as a "mating ball," completely surrounding each female. After mating, the snakes disperse throughout the surrounding wetlands, before returning to their dens in the fall. Narcisse Wildlife Management Area protects four snake dens. The dens are linked by an interpretive trail that winds over rocky areas and through open grassland, with observation platforms allowing visitors unobstructed views of the phenomena (don't worry, the snakes are too preoccupied to worry about onlookers). The site has limited services, so bring comfortable shoes, drinks, and snacks. ❦
www.naturenorth.com/spring/creature/ garter/Fgarter.html

◀ See Spectacular Mountain Scenery on One of the World's Best Train Journeys

In mid-May, as the landscape of western Canada emerges from its wintery cover of snow, the world-renowned Rocky Mountaineer train begins operating for the season, running along three captivating routes between Vancouver and the Canadian Rockies.

Considered one of the world's best train journeys, travel aboard the Rocky Mountaineer is during daylight hours only, allowing passengers to fully appreciate the mountains, lakes, and rivers of western Canada from the warmth and comfort of luxuriously appointed trains. While two classes of Rocky Mountaineer service offer the same memorable scenery, GoldLeaf offers upgraded *everything*. For most travellers, the highlight of GoldLeaf is the two-story glass-domed car allowing unparalleled views of the ever-changing landscape, with luxurious and memorable meals—enjoyed in a dedicated dining car outfitted with white linens and freshly cut flowers. In GoldLeaf, meals are prepared by world-class chefs who source the very best ingredients from local suppliers, while wines are supplied by the Okanagan Valley's premier vintners.

The Rocky Mountaineer runs between Vancouver and Banff or Jasper, and from Whistler to Jasper via Prince George. Each trip takes two days, with an overnight stop at a regional hotel (GoldLeaf offers upgraded accommodations). ❦
www.rockymountaineer.com

Tour the Bucolic Gulf Islands

From top-notch wine and cheese producers to outstanding hiking and camping, it's easy to find your "fragment of paradise"

When a BC Ferries vessel sails through Active Pass on the Vancouver–Victoria run, it sounds its horn loudly. Of course, this is to alert other boats as it navigates the narrow gap between Galiano and Mayne islands, two Gulf Islands separating Vancouver Island from the B.C. mainland. But you could also take it as a wake-up call to passengers: "Hey! Remember to check out the Gulf Islands!" Many just pass by these bucolic, green havens without registering them as more than eye candy. However, they offer amazing options for relaxation and outdoor recreation—a strong selling point for the artists, hippies, and retirees who populate them. May is an optimal time to tour this pastoral archipelago, with the rains that mark winter and early spring yielding to sunshine. You can get around by float plane, private boat, or water taxi, or—like most visitors—via BC Ferries.

Galiano Island, named after an 18th-century Spanish explorer, is among the most peaceful and scenic of the Gulf Islands. Inhabited for centuries by the Coast Salish Native peoples, the 30-kilometre (18.6-mile) long island abounds with arbutus and Garry oak trees, sandstone cliffs, and sheltered coves. Springtime brings wild flowers and migrating birds. Hiking is popular, like the trek to the 335-metre (1,099-foot) summit of Mount Galiano. Rent a kayak in Montague Harbour to explore local waters, watching for herons, otters, and sea lions by day, or admiring glorious pink-orange sunsets as evening falls. Galiano, like other major Gulf Islands, has just enough modern amenities such that it doesn't compromise its idyllic charm. Shop for richly textured pottery and glassware, enjoy a blueberry body wrap at the Madrona del Mar Spa, or feast on halibut and chips at the Hummingbird Pub. For your overnight stay, choose from about 10 cozy B&Bs, inns, and cabins.

On Mayne Island, the main attraction is history. Check out the 1885-built, still-in-use Active Pass Lighthouse in Georgina Point Heritage Park—you might see a wedding party there on a nice weekend. The nearby, contemporaneous St. Mary Magdalene Anglican Church has a large sandstone baptismal font, and is surrounded by the graves of pioneers. Mayne is peppered with quaint-looking, eco-friendly cob houses (made out of dirt and straw), which you'll spot while biking the winding roads. In central Miners Bay, sample vegetarian dishes at the café or browse through the bookstore.

North and South Pender Island (joined by a small bridge) are both laden with picturesque bays and harbours, so it's easy to find a private stretch of sandy beach. Not to be missed is Bedwell Harbour, where the luxurious Poets

Cove Resort & Spa offers lodge, villa, and cottage accommodations, plus organic cuisine at the on-site Syrens Bistro. Recreational opportunities abound here, from scuba diving to the nine-hole Pender Island Golf & Country Club. Pick up a bottle of Merlot from the award-winning Morning Bay Vineyard & Estate Winery, Pender Island's first winery.

Another up-and-coming winery, Saturna Island Family Estate Winery, attracts tasting room aficionados to the remote Gulf Island it's named after, drawing kudos recently for its Chardonnay and Pinot Noir. However, since about 40 per cent of Saturna Island has been designated a National Park Reserve, the ideal activity here is roaming the numerous forests, beaches, and wetlands that surround Mount Warburton Pike, the island's tallest lookout at 397 metres (1,303 feet). Wildlife is everywhere, including seals, goats, deer, and nearly 200 different bird species.

Gabriola Island is known for its flourishing artistic community. Check out local galleries and studios, from the bold nature paintings of Paul Grignon at Moonfire Studio, to the wooden shrine chests of Vern Smith at Stones-Throw Studio & Gallery. Ancient petroglyphs created by First Nations—anywhere between 100 and 2,000 years old—are carved into sandstone, and well worth viewing at Petroglyph Park (home to more than 50 such etchings) and Sandwell Park. The Malaspina Galleries, surreal natural limestone formations, are just off the beach at Gabriola Sands Provincial Park. For accommodations, choose from close to 30 B&Bs, or enjoy oceanfront camping at Descanso Bay Regional Park, near the ferry terminal. It's a 20-minute ferry ride to Nanaimo, Vancouver Island's "Hub City."

With more than 10,000 inhabitants, Salt Spring Island is both the largest and most-visited Gulf Island. Sheep, lavender fields, and holistic healers happily coexist here. Absorb the community's funky vibe by attending the Farmers' Market in the village of Ganges on Saturday, shopping for organic goat's cheese, fresh-baked bread, and local artwork. Naturalist-painter Robert Bateman is probably the most famous visual artist who resides on Salt Spring. You can visit more than 30 home-based studios on the island (pick up a studio tour map from the Ganges visitor centre). A host of coffee shops and West Coast and ethnic eateries spice up Ganges, and there are two wineries. Whether camping at Ruckles Provincial Park, cycling, or kayaking around the island, or attending concerts by Salt Spring residents like Randy Bachman (The Guess Who) or Tom Hooper (The Grapes of Wrath), you'll understand why *The Washington Post* once dubbed Salt Spring "the coolest island in Canada."

Find out more at:
www.gulfislandstourism.com,
www.bcferries.com

ADVENTURE

▲
Hang Ten at the Lachine Rapids

Surfing may be unthinkable in a northern city such as Montréal, but diehard dudes know better. Just behind the Habitat 67 building, there's a little stretch of the St. Lawrence River to catch a gnarly wave—a boon for city dwellers who miss the beach but don't have time to hop on a plane to Miami.

Unlike traditional surfing in the ocean, river-surfing takes place on a static wave. What this really means is that you stay in one area (standing or on your belly), while the stream runs beneath you.

During the hottest summer months of July and August, there can be lineups for this relatively small patch of water between the Jacques-Cartier and Victoria bridges. Springtime is less busy, but you'll need to don a full-body wetsuit (rentals are about C$30 a day), as well as neoprene booties and gloves to shield you from rocks. You'll need to bring your own palm tree . . .

You can rent all equipment at Kayak Sans Frontières, where lessons are also available for C$100 a day; they include a life jacket, helmet, and board. If you already know what you're doing, entrance to the river is free, as is the adjacent Parc de la Cité-du-Havre where you can eat a packed lunch, observe, and chill out. You'll have a prime view of Nuns' Island, the Old Port, and the Casino de Montréal. To get there, drive past Habitat 67 and enter the small parking lot, which will lead you straight to the river.🍁
www.ksf.ca

Take in a Billion Years of History at the Royal Alberta Museum

Explore one billion years of natural and human history at the Royal Alberta Museum, which received its Royal designation from Her Majesty Queen Elizabeth II when she visited Edmonton to commemorate the province's centennial on May 24, 2005.

The museum's highlight is the Wild Alberta Gallery, where the province's four natural regions—mountain, prairie, parkland, and boreal forest—are recreated with incredible accuracy. But lifelike dioramas are only part of the appeal. Much of the exhibit encourages visitor interaction, be it solving the mystery of Alberta's most dangerous mammal (hint: it's not a bear); seeing the variety of freshwater fish swimming in local rivers and lakes; touching a grizzly bear's teeth; or hearing the grunting of a bull moose. Elsewhere in the museum, the Natural History Gallery explains the forces that have shaped Alberta's land, describes the dinosaurs that once roamed the province, and displays a large collection of locally collected rocks and gems. Another section, the Syncrude Gallery of Aboriginal Culture, details Alberta's indigenous peoples from their arrival 11,000 years earlier through their modern-day traditions. It's also worth strolling the museum grounds, passing an imposing sandstone structure built in 1913 for Alberta's lieutenant governor en route to a viewpoint with sweeping vistas of the North Saskatchewan River Valley.❧
www.royalalbertamuseum.ca

Cruise the Picturesque Inside Passage ▼

For more than 50 years, the busiest BC Ferries run has been between Tsawwassen (Vancouver) and Swartz Bay (Victoria). Yet the most epic, scenic route is arguably the 15-hour voyage between Port Hardy on the northern tip of Vancouver Island and Prince Rupert, just off British Columbia's central coast. Late spring is an ideal time to cruise the Inside Passage, wedged between green coastal mountains and islands. It's before the height of the tourist season, and frequently affords clear weather with superb wildlife-viewing opportunities.

Heading through Queen Charlotte Sound, you may spot a pod of orca whales breaching and spouting, or see dolphins leaping above the waves alongside your sleek, modern vessel. The 638-capacity, 150-metre (492-foot) Northern Expedition, built in 2009, offers many great vantage points. You'll likely sight bald eagles soaring over firs and pines while feasting on wild salmon in the Vista Restaurant. Throughout the trip, watch for natural and man-made landmarks: the tall peaks that flank narrow Grenville Channel, the Boat Bluff lighthouse, or the eagle head–topped native cultural centre in Bella Bella. There's one journey daily, alternating between northbound and southbound. At this time of year, the entire trip takes place in daylight, allowing it to be firmly etched in your memory.❧
www.bcferries.com

EVENTS & FESTIVALS

QUIRKY CANADA

Dance and Dine Outdoors at Piknic Électronik

Piknic Électronik is an outdoor dance party held every Sunday starting in May that lasts all summer, until September. If you're looking for a sunny place to have a picnic, enjoy some smooth electronic music, and dance, look no further.

This family-friendly hipster rave lasts from 2:00 p.m. to 10 p.m. (It's closed in the event of rain.) And it's cheap, about C$10 per person, with entry for kids under 12 free. As the name suggests, you can bring your own picnic. If you do, you can also pack your own alcohol (or buy it on-site). That said, organizers want to keep the event in the city's good books so they keep an eye out for those who might lose control. Each person can bring one bottle of wine or three cans (355-millilitre, 12-ounce) of beer. Hard liquor is not permitted.

Held in Parc Jean-Drapeau on Île Sainte-Hélène, dancers convene under and around the massive *L'Homme* statue, a nod to Expo '67. Conceived by four friends with a Rolodex of internationally renowned DJs, Piknic is put together by the same group that heads up Igloofest in winter (see p. 13). When it's time to kick up your feet, chill out on one of the scattered mats (or bring your own). Otherwise, there's always the nearby waterfront if you want to escape and take a breather. ❧
www.piknicelectronik.com

Marvel at the Bottle Houses of P.E.I.

What do you do if you have a surplus of bottles? You could emulate Édouard T. Arsenault of Cap-Egmont, Prince Edward Island. He gathered up 12,000, spent the winter cleaning them, then built himself a bottle house. He so enjoyed the result of his labours—a six-gabled house—that he couldn't stop building.

Careful selection of colours and sizes made the house truly unique, whetting Édouard's appetite for building with bottles and mortar. Next came a hexagonal tavern, which now houses unusual bottles with special features (they're displayed rather than used as construction material). A chapel, complete with pews and an altar, was the final building completed by Édouard. It brought the bottle count to 25,000.

Today, Arsenault's daughter and family open the houses to the public each summer. Gardens and the natural beauty of the clifftop location (overlooking the beautiful Northumberland Strait) add to a sense of tranquility. Sunlight turns the buildings into inspiring works of light and colour, enhanced at sunset when vibrant colour streams in from behind the altar in the little church.

As you drive Route 11, keep watch for the giant bottle marking what has become a favourite destination in Acadian P.E.I. ❧
www.bottlehouses.com

Greet the Arrival of Goose Tongue Greens at the Moncton Market

The arrival of Goose Tongues, an edible tidal marsh green, is a special moment at the Marché Moncton Market. Known as *Passe-Pierre* to Acadians, Goose Tongues are actually a seaside plantain. A subsistence food for early Acadians, their spicy saltiness now intrigues chefs dedicated to local flavours—resulting in some friendly competition, as chefs jockey for first place in line to ensure they get some before local vendors sell out. An excellent addition to a salad, or steamed as a side dish, these greens are often pickled in brine for winter use.

This is where you'll find the new and unusual, right next to traditional standbys.

The greens demonstrate the place of farmers' markets in today's Maritime culinary scene. This is where you'll find the new and unusual, right next to traditional standbys. Passions about good food run high with individuals who care about freshness and practise the buy-local movement. Located in the heart of the city centre, Marché Moncton Market attracts vendors and customers from throughout the region, including the many smaller, outlying communities surrounding Greater Moncton. The Festival Hall and adjoining building are filled to the rafters with more than 130 vendors and artisans.

Open only on Saturdays (7:00 a.m. to 2:00 p.m.), an amazing variety of goods is available, including bakery items, local produce, fresh meats and seafood, cheese and eggs, and arts and crafts. Wild harvests, like the Goose Tongue greens, or nosegays of May flowers, help maintain links to the region's heritage. Most of what you'll find is made by the vendors with their own hands. Several eateries are also open for lunch during the week, as well as Saturday, and have become local favourites. ❧
www.marchemonctonmarket.ca

Canadian *moments*

May Long Weekend

Known affectionately as the May "two-four" weekend—coined in homage to a popular Canadian term for a case of 24 beers—this is the time of year when parks open, families visit the cottage, and gardeners dig into the soil.

Officially known as Victoria Day, the holiday recognizes the birthdays of both the reigning monarch and Queen Victoria—the day's namesake—born on May 24, 1819. The holiday always falls on a Monday, on or before May 24.

Unofficially, the weekend marks the promise of warmer weather ahead.

In many parts of Canada, the last frost has usually passed by this weekend—but not everywhere in this vast country. While Vancouver typically sees its last frost in late March, in Moose Jaw it sweeps through until about May 20, while in Thunder Bay it might be early June. So the May long weekend is, generally, good reason to celebrate!

Variation aside, gardening over the May Long is considered a must by many green thumbs. While some will be planting tropical plants like tomatoes, others seed hardier vegetables.

Opening the cottage and camping are also annual rites that celebrate the outdoor spirit. Alberta's Sunshine Village is open for the last ski and snowboard runs of the season, while Calgary's Bowness Park starts renting boats in the Bow River lagoons.

As Victoria Day is a statutory holiday, it generally means a three-day weekend for all but the unlucky folks in Atlantic Canada (though New Brunswick observes Victoria Day as a day of rest). Québec strikes out on its own for the May holiday. The day is celebrated as National Patriots' Day—honouring the anti-British rebellion in 1837.

Most provincial capitals fire a 21-gun salute, and in Victoria—which shares its name with the day—a parade takes over downtown Douglas Street for more than three hours.

Drive the Spectacular Icefields Parkway

Towering peaks and abundant wildlife provide the backdrop for one of Canada's greatest road trips

Snaking through the Canadian Rockies between Lake Louise and Jasper, the 230-kilometre (143-mile) Icefields Parkway is one of the world's most inspiring mountain highways. In late May, before the summer crowds arrive, inspiration is easily found—wildlife is abundant, waterfalls are at their peak, mountaintops are still capped with snow, and the valleys explode in a delicate spring green palette.

Once you leave the frantic pace of the twinned Trans-Canada Highway behind, the impressive scenery of the Icefields Parkway begins almost immediately. Herbert Lake, usually ice-free by May, is a perfect place for early morning or evening photography, when the Waputik Range and distinctively shaped Mount Temple are reflected in its waters. Next up for northbound travellers is Crowfoot Glacier. Clearly visible from a roadside viewpoint, the glacial "claws" have melted in

recent years, but it's an impressive sight nonetheless. Peyto Lake remains frozen well into spring, but it's worth the short walk to a viewpoint overlooking this famously scenic body of water. The turquoise waters of Lower Waterfowl Lake, the roar of spring runoff passing through Mistaya Canyon, and the panorama of new growth across the North Saskatchewan River Valley are all worthwhile stops before beginning the long climb up the "Big Bend" to the Columbia Icefield. A remnant of the last major glaciation that covered most of Canada 20,000 years ago, the icefield has survived due to its high elevation and heavy snowfalls—two elements that also make a springtime visit less exciting than in summer, when the melting snow reveals the actual glacier. Regardless, the surrounding peaks are impressive and the experience of riding an Ice Explorer bus out onto the glacier is unique. The Sunwapta River begins at the

icefield and flows northward towards the town of Jasper—the same route followed by the Icefields Parkway. More glaciers, the tumbling waters of photogenic Tangle Falls, and the power of Athabasca Falls—all framed by snow-capped peaks—ensure visitors don't tire of the scenery. Due to its lower elevation, the northern end of the parkway is snow-free earlier than elsewhere, making this an ideal place for an early-season hike. By the last week of May, the trail to the Valley of the Five Lakes has come alive with greenery, and migrating birds can be seen and heard throughout the valley floor.

The scenery alone qualifies the Icefields Parkway as one of the world's great mountain drives, but in spring

wildlife-viewing opportunities are an added bonus. Beginning in April, black bears and grizzly bears begin coming out of hibernation and larger mammals, such as bighorn sheep, mountain goats, elk, moose, and woodland caribou, move to lower elevations in search of snow-free vegetation. Late May, with dandelions blooming along the roadside, is the best time of year for viewing black bears. And, though dandelions are one of their favourite springtime foods, opportunities for viewing these and other larger mammals are unpredictable. Increase your wildlife-sighting chances by driving in the hours immediately after dawn and before dusk, and searching the landscape at known hangouts, such as Goat Lookout, south of Athabasca Falls, where mountain goats congregate around a salt lick.

It is possible to drive the length of the Icefields Parkway in less than four hours. But to fully appreciate the beauty of the drive, don't. Instead, plan on spending at least one full day—preferably longer—soaking up the scenery of one of the world's great mountain roads. Those equipped for camping will appreciate the numerous campgrounds along the way, while a string

of hostels provide basic accommodation for budget travellers. For unequalled historic ambience, make reservations at Num-ti-jah Lodge. Built by a legendary Banff guide in the 1940s, its distinctive, steeply pitched red roof rises above the trees along the shore of Bow Lake. Upstairs rooms are simple but adequate while, downstairs, guests soak up the warmth of a roaring log fire while mingling in a comfortable library and eating in a dining room lined with historic memorabilia. North of Bow Lake, other accommodation options include motel-style rooms at The Crossing Resort, views of the Columbia Icefield from Glacier View Inn, and cabins and motel rooms at family-friendly Sunwapta Falls Resort.

Although the Icefields Parkway is well travelled in spring, you should not approach the journey lightly. Gas up beforehand, make sure you have a spare tire, check weather forecasts, and don't exceed signed speed limits. If you spot wildlife, pull completely off the road— for both your own safety and that of other travellers.🍁

Find out more at:
www.icefieldsparkway.ca

ADVENTURE

Run the Cabot Trail Relay Race

Up hill and down dale . . . the idea of running a 298-kilometre (185-mile) race up and over steep mountains is a daunting one, but more manageable when broken into 17 relay stages. At the end of May each year, the Cabot Trail Relay Race challenges runners to tackle some of the most arduous and spectacular terrain in North America. Beginning in Baddeck, the course passes through Cape Breton Highlands National Park; beside coast, woodlands, and barrens; and through small communities as it follows the famous scenic drive to the gently rolling Margaree Valley. Race legs vary from 12 to 20 kilometres (7.5 to 12.4 miles) and can cross anything from steep grades to gently rolling terrain. Competitive and recreational runners 16 and older are welcome, but must maintain a minimum pace of 10 minutes per mile. Since 1988, when the race was first conceptualized, thousands have travelled to Nova Scotia to push their limits. Today 70 teams of 17 people (selected by lottery) from across Canada and the United States compete, at a cost of $1,000 per team. That's a lot of runners sharing team spirit and camaraderie, encouraging each other for the 24+ hours it takes to complete the race. Spectator appeal is high as this is one of the largest and most popular running events in eastern Canada. Most begin cheering for their teams at Baddeck, following the race as it progresses.

Inspired? Local accommodations start taking reservations as soon as selected teams are announced, usually by mid-March.❧

www.cabottrailrelay.com

◀ Go British with Afternoon Tea at the Empress Hotel

There's no better city in Canada to celebrate the Victoria Day holiday than ever-so-British Victoria. And what's the most fitting place to mark the birth of Britain's longest-reigning queen? Go to the Inner Harbour and enter the grand lobby of Victoria's Fairmont Empress hotel, where the iconic tradition of afternoon tea dates back to 1908.

At this ivy-covered former Canadian Pacific Railway hotel, it's as much about the ritual as the tea itself. It's a throwback to the glory days of the British Empire. Pink-topped Corinthian columns, huge fireplaces adorned with portraits of George V and Queen Mary, richly patterned carpets, and soothing live piano music convey an ambience of majesty and graciousness. As you sip a steaming cup of the Empress's signature tea, blending organic leaves from Asia and Africa, gaze out over the harbour's sailboats and seaplanes. Nibble on finger sandwiches, such as smoked salmon pinwheels and egg salad croissants, and fresh-baked raisin scones with Jersey cream and strawberry jam, all served on Royal Doulton china by solicitous waiters. You'll wind up describing this relaxing—if pricey (C$50-ish)—experience as "jolly good." The room can fill up quickly, especially in high season, so book in advance.🍁

www.fairmont.com/empress

Get Up Close to Niagara Falls ▼

Niagara Falls is a spectacular sight in every season. But no Falls experience quite captures the roaring foaming fury like the Maid of The Mist tour during the spring. With this much water plunging down so close to you, be prepared to get wet—so bring a waterproof camera.

You'll want to have a look at your watercraft first: those bobbing boats you see in the Niagara Gorge are highly manoeuvrable, 600-passenger, diesel-engine vessels that push as close as possible to the Horseshoe Falls cascade, twisting against powerful currents. For good reason this is one of North America's oldest tourist attractions. Teddy Roosevelt, Marilyn Monroe, and Princess Diana and her sons are among the celebrities soaked by the experience since boat tours began in 1846. A river rushing over a 762-metre (2,500-foot) wide brink—at a rate of 10.2 *billion* litres (or 2.7 billion gallons) per hour—and falling 51.8 metres (170 feet) makes for a deafening roar, a roiling watercourse, and a lot of mist. Have no fear: the Mist supplies recyclable rain slickers. Departures are every 15 minutes from 9:00 a.m. to 7:45 p.m. Adult fares are around C$16 and children (six to 12 years) around C$10. There's no charge for children under five.🍁

www.maidofthemist.com

◄ Peer into Private Places at Doors Open

Whether you seek to peek behind the curtain at the levers of power, relieve a burning curiosity, or briefly enjoy someone else's room with a view, Doors Open is a worldwide phenomenon that assuages the inner snoop. While many cities in Canada have embraced this prying phenomenon (it started in France), its largest incarnation is in the nation's largest city, Toronto, which launched its Doors Open in 2000.

Each year, Doors Open Toronto is based on a theme (in 2011 it was Photography & Architecture) with some 150 buildings of architectural, historical, and cultural interest participating and open for inspection. The city does not lack for hidden recesses and other nooks and crannies . . . even most Torontonians don't know about the unused subway platform hiding beneath Bay Station. Doors Open is by no means all indoors. In some years, the itinerary includes walking tours around larger-scale properties—such as the curved towers and plaza of the Viljo Revell–designed City Hall—and entire neighbour-hoods, including the Beach and the Distillery District. And best of all, admission is free. Be prepared to line up as the locals are every bit as nosy. In 2010, some 250,000 took the opportunity to look behind the velvet curtain.🍁
www.toronto.ca/doorsopen

5 faves

Fort Whoop-Up

This is the original name for the town of Lethbridge, Alberta, and the site of the Fort Whoop-Up Interpretative Centre. Today, there's a replica of the original fort that stood here, and a notorious trading post that traded whiskey to the Plains Indians in return for buffalo hides and horses in the 1870s.

Garter Snake Mating Balls in Wood Buffalo National Park

A rope cordons off a patch of boreal forest near the beginning of the Karstland Interpretive Trail in Wood Buffalo National Park. Behind it, red-sided garter snakes appear woven together in tangled knots as one female is surrounded by as many as 29 males competing for her affection. On the other side of the rope, gawking visitors can't tell where one snake ends and another begins.

Wood Buffalo, which straddles the Alberta–Northwest Territories border, is the most northerly winter home of red-sided garter snakes. They hibernate in small limestone caves and crevices to snooze away the winter, enjoying temperatures that hover just above freezing (0 degrees Celsius, 32 degrees Fahrenheit). Then, they emerge in May for their annual courtship ritual. For the next two weekends, curious eyes from the nearby community of Fort Smith will scour the ground looking for reptilian mating balls that sometimes blend in with the scenery.

After a female has mated, she heads off to her summer feeding grounds in a swampy area just outside the park. The males, meanwhile, hang around the Karstland trail waiting for other females to emerge. Eventually, they too slither away, heading for nearby swamplands where they'll dine on small minnows, mice, and frogs for the summer.❧
www.pc.gc.ca/woodbuffalo

Savour the Views from Canada's Highest Restaurant

By early June, winter is a distant memory and mountain bikers have taken over the slopes that skiers and boarders once ruled at Kicking Horse Mountain Resort, where the crowning glory is the Eagle's Eye Restaurant. At an elevation of 2,347 metres (7,700 feet) above sea level, this is Canada's highest restaurant.

Access to the restaurant is aboard the resort's high-speed, eight-person detachable gondola, which takes just 18 minutes to reach the summit. From the top of the gondola, the stunning 360-degree panorama is equal to any other accessible point in the Canadian Rockies, with the Purcell Mountains immediately to the west and the Columbia Valley laid out below to the east. Perched on the summit ridge, sweeping views from the impressive timber frame restaurant are set off by a stylish timber and stonework interior—including a floor-to-ceiling fireplace and a wide wraparound deck protected from the wind by glass panelling. The wide-ranging menu offers something for all tastes, with an emphasis on Canadian ingredients and simple cooking styles. Eagle's Eye is open daily for lunch and on weekends for dinner, with the evening setting more romantic and the food more adventurous (think salmon baked in a saffron-vanilla cream and served with strawberry salsa).❧
www.kickinghorseresort.com

The Alberta Badlands
The name comes from plains that stretch out in every direction but drop off completely—and without warning—into deep, eerie canyons too deep to descend into, forcing huge detours for those trying to cross in the days long before highways. The area is also starkly beautiful; hiking in Horsethief Canyon, near Drumheller, transports you back thousands of years.

Whale-watching in Victoria
You don't have to travel to remote areas of B.C. to see ocean wildlife—tours leaving from the capital will often find orcas, grey whales, sea lions, porpoises, and harbour seals during the course of a 3.5-hour tour.

Bromont Chocolate Festival
Québec's Eastern Townships are known for being easy on the eyes, but it's your taste buds that will be really excited at this two-weekend celebration of all things chocolate. The town of Bromont's Old Village is taken over by tastings, chocolate-inspired sculptures, and even a dance.

Spend a day at the Toronto Islands
Toronto is blessed with a chain of leafy islands just a brief ferry ride away. Pack a picnic, paddle a canoe, go bare if you dare at the sandy nudist beach, or take in the amusement park for a vacation within your vacation.

Your next STEP

TOP PICKS
ADVENTURE
CULTURE & HISTORY
NATURE'S GRANDEUR
EVENTS & FESTIVALS
QUIRKY CANADA
REJUVENATE

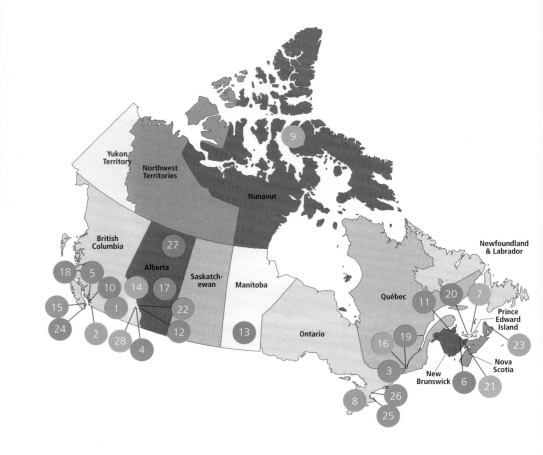

WEEK 1

1 KELOWNA, B.C.
Okanagan wine touring
www.thewinefestivals.com

2 MISSION, B.C.
Sturgeon fishing
www.silversidesfishing.ca

3 OTTAWA, ONT.
Tulip Festival
www.tulipfestival.ca

4 KOOTENAY NATIONAL PARK, B.C.
Kootenay wildlife
www.pc.gc.ca/kootenay

5 VANCOUVER, B.C.
City of Bhangra festival
www.vibc.org

6 STE-ANNE-DE-KENT, N.B.
Soap Economuseum
www.oliviersoaps.com

7 NEW GLASGOW, P.E.I.
Mother's Day lobster supper
www.peilobstersuppers.com

WEEK 2

8 STRATFORD, ONT.
Stratford Shakespeare Festival
www.stratfordfestival.ca

9 SIRMILIK NATIONAL PARK, NUNAVUT
Arctic scuba diving
www.arctickingdom.com

10 RICHMOND, B.C.
Asian shopping bonanza
www.aberdeencentre.com

11 MIRAMICHI, N.B.
Salmon fly-fishing
www.flyfishingatlanticsalmon.com

12 BANFF, ALTA.
Rocky Mountain Wine and Food Festival
www.rockymountainwine.com

13 NARCISSE, MAN.
Snake-watching
www.naturenorth.com/spring/creature/garter/Fgarter.html

14 JASPER, ALTA.
Rocky Mountain train tour
www.rockymountaineer.com

WEEK 3

15 SALT SPRING ISLAND, B.C.
The Gulf Islands
www.gulfislandstourism.com

16 MONTRÉAL, QUE.
Lachine Rapids surfing
www.ksf.ca

17 EDMONTON, ALTA.
Royal Alberta Museum
www.royalalbertamuseum.ca

18 PORT HARDY, B.C.
The Inside Passage
www.bcferries.com

19 MONTRÉAL, QUE.
Piknic Électronik
www.piknicelectronik.com

20 CAP-EGMONT, P.E.I.
Bottle houses of P.E.I.
www.bottlehouses.com

21 MONCTON, N.B.
Goose Tongue greens
www.marchemonctonmarket.ca

WEEK 4

22 LAKE LOUISE, ALTA.
Icefields Parkway
www.icefieldsparkway.ca

23 CAPE BRETON HIGHLANDS NATIONAL PARK, N.S.
Cabot Trail Relay Race
www.cabottrailrelay.com

24 VICTORIA, B.C.
Afternoon Tea at the Empress
www.fairmont.com/empress

25 NIAGARA FALLS, ONT.
Maid of the Mist boat tour
www.maidofthemist.com

26 TORONTO, ONT.
Doors Open Toronto
www.toronto.ca/doorsopen

27 WOOD BUFFALO NATIONAL PARK, ALTA.
Garter snake mating balls
www.pc.gc.ca/woodbuffalo

28 GOLDEN, B.C.
Canada's highest restaurant
www.kickinghorseresort.com

JUNE

Watch the Abundant Wildlife of Prince Albert National Park

See elk, moose, buffalo, and even white pelicans in their natural habitat

Heading north from Saskatoon, Saskatchewan's largest city, rolling prairie farmland gives way to boreal forest, and—come the warmth of spring—the promise of nature-oriented adventures in Prince Albert National Park. The park buzzes at this time of year, not just with long warm days but with the spectacle of fresh spring growth and larger mammals emerging from the long, cold winter.

Everybody travelling to 3,875-square-kilometre (1,496-square-mile) Prince Albert National Park does so by choice—it's not near a major highway, nor is it on the way to anywhere else. As noted naturalist Grey Owl wrote in the 1930s about his Prince Albert National Park cabin, it was "Far enough away to gain seclusion, yet within reach of those whose genuine interest prompts them to make the trip." It's a description that perfectly sums up the park itself. Wildlife is abundant in this forested wilderness, and one of the major attractions—especially in spring

before summer crowds lead larger mammals, such as elk, moose, and black bears, to seek out the solitude of the park's remote reaches. Also present but less frequently seen are lynx, wolves, and woodland caribou. One of Prince Albert's most beloved residents are bison, which once numbered in the millions and roamed freely across North America. Today, the park's herd of 400 are Canada's only herd of free-ranging bison living in their historic range (sightings are most reliable near the park's western edge). Spring is also marked by the return of thousands of migratory birds, with the first arrivals being bald eagles and Canada geese. In early June, up to 15,000 white pelicans descend on the park, nesting and breeding on a remote island, far from human disturbances. The best chance of seeing wildlife is to lace up your hiking boots and take to the trails, which criss-cross the eastern half of the park. Ranging from short interpretive hikes to overnight expeditions, well-formed trails traverse all the best scenery, leading through emerald forests to lakeside viewpoints and along fast-flowing streams to bird-filled marshes. Although the lakes covering 30 per cent of the park remain too cold for swimming until July, by early June they're ice-free, providing the perfect opportunity for canoeing and kayaking.

Although the focus is most definitely on nature at Prince Albert, there's also some fascinating human history to discover. One of the most intriguing people associated with the park is Grey Owl, the world-renowned naturalist and author. Born Archibald Belaney in 1888, he left his English homeland as a young man and spent most of his adult life in the Canadian wilderness. Employed by the government to teach park visitors about the environment, he lived at a remote log cabin in the north of the park through the 1930s. Each summer, he would be visited at

his cabin by hundreds of visitors eager to learn about the plants and animals of the boreal forest. Using his alter ego as an indigenous Canadian and the park as inspiration, his fame as a naturalist and author extended to Europe and beyond. Reaching his cabin requires a degree of backcountry experience, as it's 20 kilometres (12 miles) from the nearest road. But for nature lovers with an interest in Canadian history, the trip—by canoe or on foot—is still a pilgrimage of sorts.

Like its more famous Rocky Mountain neighbours of Banff and Jasper, Prince Albert National Park is home to a bustling tourist centre. The village of Waskesiu, just inside the park's boundaries, buzzes all summer long. Its main street is lined with boutiques, gift shops, and cafés, while trim cottages line shaded residential streets— all within walking distance of a long stretch of sandy beach lapped by the calm water of Waskesiu Lake. Also

like Banff and Jasper, the park's home to an acclaimed Stanley Thompson–designed golf course, though here in central Saskatchewan rates are a fraction of those paid in the mountains.

The majority of park visitors are equipped for camping, with options ranging from full-service, road-accessible campgrounds to primitive sites reachable only by canoe or kayak. Red Deer Campground, for example, has full hookups and hot showers, all within walking distance of a beach and the village of Waskesiu. As one of the most popular destinations in all of the prairies, even in June you should plan ahead by making campsite reservations through Parks Canada before arriving. The village of Waskesiu offers a range of other accommodations, including motels and vacation homes, but again, reservations should be made well in advance.❧

Find out more at: www.pc.gc.ca/princealbert

ADVENTURE

▲

Try Whitewater Rafting on the Ferocious Chilliwack and Thompson Rivers

Washington State's Mount Baker, the tallest peak in the North Cascades range, gets more snow on average than any other ski resort in the world. And that's good news for whitewater rafters. Why? During early June's warmth, Baker's snowpack is still melting, feeding the wild currents in the Chilliwack River, just an hour's drive from Vancouver in the Fraser Valley. And another thrilling day trip—the Thompson River—lies three hours northeast, starting from the village of Lytton.

Licensed rafting companies like Hyak Wilderness Adventures are your gateway to splash-tastic adventure. Clamber into your wetsuit, grab a paddle, and absorb the safety instructions before boarding one of the self-bailing inflatable orange rafts. Follow your guide's paddling instructions and manoeuvre past jutting rocks

and treacherous holes while you breathe in the scent of sunscreen and pine trees—plus snootfuls of water.

Be sure to refuel at lunch, guzzling gourmet roast beef and tuna sandwiches, veggie sticks, and lemonade. You'll need it. The Chilliwack River features the extra-challenging Tamahi Rapids, used for training by Canada's national kayak team. Meanwhile, seemingly every rapid on the cliff-lined Thompson is nicknamed "Devil's Kitchen" or "Jaws of Death," which is self-explanatory. Yes, your muscles may ache on the drive home—but the adrenaline buzz will keep you happy indefinitely.❧
www.hyak.com

Visit the Site of the John and Yoko Bed-In

Late at night on one May day in 1969, newlyweds John Lennon and Yoko Ono arrived at Montréal's Queen Elizabeth Hotel, where they staged their highly publicized bed-in, a peaceful protest against the Vietnam War. On June 1, Lennon wrote and recorded the song "Give Peace a Chance." While there are no organized tours of the famous suite 1742, it's a popular room for fans of both Lennon and the Beatles to book—not to mention a romantic option for honeymooning couples.

While some claim a vibe or spirit remains, others expecting a glittery shrine may be a little disappointed. Besides a small plaque on the door bearing the words "John Lennon Suite" (plus a watchful security camera, as the sign has been "lifted" more than once) and a selection of black-and-white photos inside, the otherwise-legendary room looks like any other. The bed has since been moved (it was originally up against the window) and the rest of the furniture updated.

The year 2009 marked the bed-in's 40th anniversary, a sentimental date that was complimented by an exhibit (*Imagine: The Peace Ballad of John & Yoko*) at the Montréal Museum of Fine Arts. The City of Montréal also commemorated the peace initiative with an outdoor installation along a pathway in Mount Royal Park where *Give Peace a Chance* has been translated into 40 languages.❧
www.fairmont.com/EN_FA/Property/QEH/ AboutUs/HotelHistory.htm

Cast a Line during Fish New Brunswick Days ▶

Get your rod ready! Fish New Brunswick Days are an excellent opportunity for both resident and non-resident anglers to try fishing *without* purchasing a licence. This fishing paradise has over 60,000 kilometres of rivers, streams, and lakes, home to 53 species of fish. Daunting? New Brunswick Natural Resources suggests anglers check with local fishing-tackle retailers or an experienced angler to find a prime fishing hole. Get the skinny on rules and regulations before casting that rod. If you want to keep Atlantic salmon, for instance, you must have a licence, otherwise it's catch-and-release. Though non-residents don't need to hire a guide during Fish New Brunswick Days, going with an expert will ensure a fulfilling experience. Outfitters are experts at fishing for Atlantic salmon, brook trout, landlocked salmon, and white or yellow perch (all of which are in season at this time of year). They also know the best fishing holes. The only thing left for you to figure out is where to start pan-frying your catch over a campfire.❧
www.tourismnewbrunswick.ca/Home/ Activities/SportRecreation/Fishing.aspx

EVENTS & FESTIVALS

QUIRKY CANADA

▲ Tour Montréal on Two Wheels at Bike Fest

Montréal is North America's bicycle capital. Held at the beginning of June, Bike Fest celebrates this passion with tens of thousands of participants pedalling their bliss in a long weekend of outdoor fun. It's a great way to explore the city (often traffic-free) and meet other cyclists.

The citywide festival gets bigger and bigger every year with many activities for the whole family to enjoy, from four-wheelers to pro-enthusiasts. The first is Tour la Nuit, an easy-breezy nocturnal run covering 20 kilometres (12.4 miles) of car-free riding around the city. The longer, bigger Tour de l'Île maps out 52 kilometres (32.3 miles) of leisurely cycling, with several rest stations along the way offering cyclists free snacks and drinks. The event starts at 9:00 a.m. and is a go—rain or shine. After you've reached the finish line, the party keeps going with live entertainment, amusement park food, and rides for the kiddies. There are also more intense choose-your-own trips planned, ranging from 75 to 150 kilometres (46.6 to 93.2 miles) outside the city in scenic areas like Tremblant and the Eastern Townships.

Rates are relatively low, and start at about C$20 for Tour la Nuit and can be combined as part of a package for better deals. Do be mindful, however, that prices get progressively more expensive the closer you get to the peddling date.❦

www.velo.qc.ca/english/index.php

Wait for Alien Visitors

On June 3, 1967, Paul Hellyer, a federal government minister, flew into the small northern Alberta town of St. Paul to open a new tourist attraction. It was an expensive and grandiose project that garnered much publicity, and was expanded in 1992—but has yet to receive a single official visitor.

St. Paul is home to the world's only UFO landing pad. The raised platform is supported by concrete pylons. And to ensure extraterrestrial visitors understand what it's all about, there's an adjacent building shaped like a UFO. The pad also holds a time capsule—to be opened in 2067—and a plaque that reads, in part, "That future travel in space will be safe for all intergalactic beings, all visitors from earth or otherwise are welcome to this territory and to the Town of St. Paul." Each provincial flag flies high above, while a chunk of rock from each province is embedded in the pad itself. The adjacent UFO-shaped building has photos from around the world of UFO sightings, crop circles, and the like, as well as explanations of memorable hoaxes. The local tourism board even has a dedicated phone line for alien encounters. Simply call 888-SEE-UFOS.❦

www.stpaulchamber.ca/ufolanding.html

Cycle P.E.I.'s Meandering Confederation Trail

On a warm day when spring is in the air, cycling the Confederation Trail is the perfect way to see the bucolic countryside of Canada's smallest province. Most sections of this linear parkway for cyclists and hikers are rated as easy-to-moderate, and there are dozens of access points in cities, towns, and villages along the way. A fine gravel surface generally means smooth cycling.

Keep your eyes peeled for eagles, especially near Mount Stewart.

P.E.I.'s section of the Trans Canada Trail (formerly a CN railbed) takes cyclists through some of the most beautiful countryside in the province. Nature lovers appreciate transitions from wetlands to hardwood groves, farmlands to villages, streams and rivers to bays and waterfronts. Keep your eyes peeled for eagles, especially near Mount Stewart where they celebrate an early June Eagle Watch at the Hillsborough River Eco-Centre beside the trail. Many former railway stations along the way have found new lives: Elmira, the end of the line in the railway era, now houses a railway museum, while station stops such as Georgetown and Kensington now offer restaurants, facilities, and accommodations nearby.

For avid riders, meeting the Tip-to-Tip Challenge is the ultimate goal. The 273.4-kilometre (169.9-mile) tip-to-tip portion of the traffic-free trail goes from the western end of the island to the east. Branch trails to Borden–Carleton (Confederation Bridge), Charlottetown, eastern communities, and an unconnected section at Wood Island bring the length to 400 kilometres (248.5 miles). A "Cycle Welcome" program provides information about accommodations, which range from hotels and motels in cities, to country inns and B&Bs in villages. Tour companies will also rent bicycles, arrange transportation, and book accommodation for you. ❧

www.gentleisland.com/confedtrail

Canadian *moments*

North Bay Shad Flies

For North Bay residents, the arrival of summer presents a unique hazard: it's the slick dead shad flies on the town's roads in June and July.

As soon as the shad flies—one of the oldest still-living insect species on earth (with a family history dating back about 300 million years)—start emerging from Lake Nipissing in late June, the critters blanket walls and vehicles. Also known as mayflies, the adults never eat. They breed in flight above the lake and the females lay eggs in the water.

During the infestation, hoteliers hose them from the exterior walls while city residents have been known to end baseball games early for the sheer number of insects. It's a common sight to see shad flies buzzing en masse around lampposts. North Bay is one of the few places where the winged insects congregate in such swarms.

Shad flies live only a few days before they die. And it's then that the roads grow slick in places and shopkeepers sweep the four-winged insects into heaps on North Bay sidewalks.

The resilient local residents count it as a blessing that the ancient species has an ill-developed lower jaw and therefore doesn't bite.

Healthy numbers of shad flies bode well for the fishing season, say anglers. Lake Nipissing is renowned for its walleye and giant sturgeon. As the sturgeon can live for more than 100 years and reach 90 kilograms (200 pounds), it's not surprising they developed a taste for mayflies, which they snack on in abundance.

Search for Icebergs in Newfoundland and Labrador

Go on an icy adventure in Canada's easternmost province

A century after an iceberg put a tragic end to the maiden voyage of the Titanic off the coast of Newfoundland, viewing these ancient wonders is a major springtime attraction in Canada's easternmost province. Although Newfoundland's Iceberg Alley, along the island's northern coast, is one of the most reliable and accessible places in the world to view icebergs, there are no guarantees as to where and when you'll find them. If your trip to Newfoundland is all about icebergs, set the second week of June as a target date. They appear along the Newfoundland coast as early as May, but often get caught up in sea ice, while by late June through July, numbers taper off as temperatures warm.

Icebergs sighted off the coast of Newfoundland and Labrador mostly originate from Greenland (only around 10 per cent are from the Canadian High Arctic). They are formed when an advancing glacier slowly inches forward into an ocean, until massive pieces of ice break off and are carried south by ocean currents. Each year it's estimated that more than 40,000 icebergs are produced by glaciers flowing into the ocean from Greenland's west coast. Of these, many float off into the Atlantic Ocean or get hung up in bays along the coast of northern Labrador, slowly melting into oblivion. Numbers vary wildly, but each year, travelling at around 0.7 kilometres per hour (0.4 miles per hour), anywhere from 500 to 1,000 float alongside Labrador's coast and reach Newfoundland's north coast. Ranging from the size of a compact car (these smaller icebergs are known as "growlers") to as big as a multi-story high-rise, "bergs" come in every shape and size, with colours ranging from the whitest of white to deep blue.

Word travels quickly when a berg is spotted floating by the city of St. John's, as locals and visitors alike scramble to the top of Signal Hill for the best views. Reached by road from the provincial capital of St. John's in five or six hours, the village of Twillingate promotes itself as the "iceberg capital of the world," and is indeed the best-known destination for viewing icebergs. This historic fishing village of 3,500 is well prepared for the springtime onslaught of visitors, with boat tours leaving regularly from the town dock, and even an art gallery devoted to the bergs. One of the most experienced captains, Cecil Stockley of Twillingate Island Boat Tours, has been taking visitors out into Iceberg Alley for more than 25 years.

The joys of visiting Newfoundland and Labrador extend well beyond viewing floating chunks of ice. Overlooking scenic Notre Dame Bay, Twillingate itself has much to offer. Perched on a rocky island linked to the

mainland by a series of causeways, the village boasts an interesting museum filled with Inuit and pioneer artefacts, an art gallery (featuring iceberg artwork, of course), and whale- and bird-watching boat tours. It's a long drive up the Northern Peninsula to St. Anthony, the other iceberg-viewing hotspot, so plan on extra days at L'Anse aux Meadows, a national historic site protecting the site of a thousand-year-old Viking village, and in the mountainous wilderness of Gros Morne National Park.

While no one can predict exactly when and where an iceberg will appear, modern technology provides a helping hand. Satellite imagery helps shipping and the offshore oil and gas industry predict the paths of icebergs, but is also used on the website www.icebergfinder.com. A joint initiative between government and private enterprise, this is the one-stop spot for planning the course of your iceberg-viewing trip to Newfoundland, with a regularly updated map plotting the location of icebergs as they move slowly through Iceberg Alley.

Both Twillingate and St. Anthony, the two most popular iceberg-viewing destinations, have a range of accommodations, with the former offering a wonderful selection of character-filled bed and breakfasts such as the Harbour Lights Inn, which has ocean views. And, though St. Anthony is more remote than Twillingate, if you're serious about your icebergs a visit here allows the flexibility of catching a ferry between nearby St. Barbe and Labrador, then driving up the Labrador Straits, where shore-based viewing is usually more productive than from the island of Newfoundland. On a remote island north of St. Anthony, Quirpon Lighthouse Inn may be the ultimate destination for iceberg viewers. This 10-room inn is a restored light-keeper's home overlooking Iceberg Alley. Guests arrive by boat from the mainland and spend their days viewing ice-bergs by boat or kayak, while enjoying complete solitude and wildlife such as whales and birds. Home-cooked meals and gracious Newfoundland hospitality add to the charm.🍁

Find out more at:
www.newfoundlandlabrador.com

2nd week of

JUN

ADVENTURE

◀ Canoe the Bowron Lakes

In the 1860s, eager gold prospectors rushed to the Cariboo region in British Columbia's Interior. Today, canoeing the Bowron Lakes circuit remains a golden experience, particularly on the cusp of summer when wild flowers flourish and there's limited traffic of the human variety. Soft, muddy canoe portages are eased by the "canoe carts" most visitors use.

The 116-kilometre (72-mile) loop, which starts near the Gold Rush town of Barkerville, offers many advantages—as veteran guide Dave Jorgenson of Whitegold Adventures notes. "The opportunity to paddle amid the Cariboo Mountains every day is incredibly unique. You get to start somewhere and end up in the same place. And the terrain is always changing."

Indeed. Paddling through a wilderness landscape laden with tall cedars, thunderous waterfalls, and secluded marshes, you may often find yourself gazing towards Mount Ishpa, the park's tallest peak at 2,530 metres (8,300 feet). Yet that reverie could easily be interrupted by a mighty moose crashing out of the underbrush, shaking his growing antlers as he stands in a nearby creek. Bears, beavers, bald eagles, muskrats, and deer are also likely sightings.

It's so beautiful that when you complete your week-long circuit, you may feel a little blue—like the glacial silt-tinted waters of the Cariboo River.✤
www.env.gov.bc.ca/bcparks/explore/ parkpgs/bowron_lk

5 faves

Get outdoors at Jacques-Cartier National Park

Raw natural terrain with flowing river rapids and deep canyons make this an ideal spot for adventure. In summer, there's hiking, mountain biking, canoeing, kayaking, and fishing, while nature specialists offer educational tours and talks.

140

Walk amidst Prehistoric Fossils at Dinosaur Provincial Park

When prehistoric animals roamed what is now Alberta, the climate was hot and humid. Today in summer it's simply just hot, which makes the cooler temperatures experienced in June an ideal time for hiking through the badlands of fossil-filled Dinosaur Provincial Park—a two-hour drive east of Calgary.

Paleontologists digging in the park have uncovered 35 species of dinosaurs, along with the skeletal remains of crocodiles, turtles, fish, lizards, frogs, and flying reptiles. Not only is the diversity of specimens great, but so is the sheer volume—more than 300 museum-quality specimens have been removed and are exhibited in museums around the world, including at the nearby Royal Tyrrell Museum (also worth a visit). A road through the park leads past two dinosaur digs, but the best way to fully appreciate the importance of the site and its dinosaurs is by joining a guided walk into an area of the park where public access is restricted. Although the park was established to protect the dinosaur bone beds, stands of cottonwoods and a variety of animal life add to the appeal and were instrumental to UNESCO's designation of the park as a World Heritage Site in 1979.

Within the park is a field station, primarily a research facility, but which also has a number of dinosaur displays. Park services are limited to camping and a convenience store. For motels and restaurants, base yourself in the nearby town of Brooks.

www.tpr.alberta.ca/parks/dinosaur

Chase Big Game at Elk Island National Park

By the second week of June, spring has taken hold in Elk Island National Park—the weather has begun to warm, animals are emerging from slumber, and the aspen forests are turning a delightful spring green. Opportunities for sightings abound as the park is home to more than 3,000 large mammals—one of the highest concentrations of big game in the world.

The park, less than an hour's drive east of Edmonton, preserves a remnant of the aspen parkland that once covered the entire northern flank of the Canadian prairies. It may seem a little unusual, but the park is fenced, thereby ensuring its resident elk, moose, bison, and white-tailed and mule deer don't stray onto surrounding farmland. Within its 194-square-kilometre (75-square-mile) boundary there are also coyotes, beavers, muskrats, mink, porcupines, and more than 200 species of birds. Two species of bison—wood and plains—inhabit the park but are separated to prevent interbreeding. Once thought to be extinct, the wood bison are descended from a herd discovered in the north of the province more than 50 years ago—and are the purest herd in the world (the bison can easily be viewed from the roadway). A large day-use area in the heart of the park is the start of many trails, which also has canoe rentals, a golf course, and a beach.

www.pc.gc.ca/elkisland

Squamish Test of Metal mountain bike race

The event bills itself as "a Canadian epic" and for good reason—it covers a 67-kilometre (42-mile) course with over 1,200 metres (3,937 feet) of climbing. Whether you're one of the 1,000 riders or thousands of spectators, the sights are spectacular.

The Montréal Grand Prix

This Formula 1 event is the city's single biggest tourist event of the year, attracting more than 100,000 spectators to Circuit Gilles Villeneuve. With all these people descending on the city for the racing, the restaurants and nightclubs are at their peak.

Tour the Kingsbrae Garden

A horticultural garden, rather than a botanical one, this gem in Saint Andrews, New Brunswick, is compared to an enormous and beautiful coffee-table book. A sculpture garden, labyrinth, ponds, woodland walking trails, and secluded spots to simply absorb the surroundings add to the sheer pleasure.

Visit the Alberta oil sands

Visitors from around the world come to check out the world's second-largest oil reserve, and you can take a weekend tour of Fort McMurray that includes a tour of the Suncor facility and entrance to the Oil Sands Discovery Centre.

EVENTS & FESTIVALS

Immerse Yourself in One of Canada's Largest Arts Festivals ▶

LuminaTO is one of Toronto's signature events, a 10-day feast of street-crawling immersion in arts, culture, and creativity. High quality theatre, dance, music, literature, food, visual arts, fashion, film—it's all on display and nearly 80 per cent of events are free.

With its mix of international, national, and local artists—a recent edition featured 320 artists from 30 countries and 800 artists from Canada—the festival offers a mind-bending diversity of experiences from around the world and around the corner. The biggest of big names have contributed to LuminaTO's reputation: composer Philip Glass performed the world premiere of his adaptation of Leonard Cohen's *Book of Longing*, while artist Max Dean displayed his kinetic installation

The Robotic Chair. Major international theatrical works have been commissioned for the festival—2008 saw a production of *A Midsummer Night's Dream* with a company of South Asian dancers, acrobats, and martial artists—but programming input also comes from the National Ballet of Canada, the Young Centre for the Performing Arts and its Soulpepper Academy, Harbourfront Centre, Tapestry, Theatre Direct, the Art Gallery of Ontario, and the Toronto International Film Festival's newly opened Bell Lightbox. With more than 150 events in 36 venues, and a focus on accidental encounters with art, there's a good chance you too will be illuminated.❧
www.luminato.com

Beam Yourself to Vulcan for "Spock Days"

Each June, hundreds of "Trekkies" beam themselves into the southern Alberta town of Vulcan for an annual convention officially known as VulCON: Spock Days/Galaxyfest. If you're a fan of any of the *Star Trek* series, this may be your kind of town.

Vulcan was named by a railway surveyor many decades before the creation of the original *Star Trek*, but the town has been playing up its relationship with Mr. Spock's fictitious home planet since 1993, when the first convention took place. The gathering is an opportunity for fans to meet *Star Trek* celebrities, buy and sell memorabilia, and enjoy all the usual small-town fair events—think pancake breakfasts, parades, and fireworks. The centre of attention throughout the gathering is the spacecraft-shaped Vulcan Tourism and Trek Station, where intergalactic visitors not in character can dress up in Starfleet uniforms then pose under Star Ship FX6-1995-A, or head out on a walking tour where interpretive panels are presented in both English and Klingon.

Even if you're not a Trekkie, the town deserves kudos for its cosmic marketing strategy. The convention attracts a who's who of actors linked to the franchise, and the town even petitioned strongly for the right to screen the worldwide premiere of the most recent *Star Trek* movie (the lack of a movie theatre in Vulcan was a problem).❋
www.vulcantourism.com

◀ Get Pampered at Clayoquot Wilderness Resort

If your image of camping involves grungy tents, baked beans, and pit toilets, a visit to Clayoquot Wilderness Resort will reveal how much more luxurious it can be in the 21st century. Even a three-night stay here starts at close to $5,000 (all-inclusive) per adult, but the memories are priceless. Board a Seair float plane at Vancouver International Airport's South Terminal, and in 50 minutes you'll arrive at the Condé Nast–touted resort on Vancouver Island, north of Tofino at the mouth of the Bedwell River. Mid-June weather is frequently gorgeous in this rainforest zone.

Wake up in your king-sized bed in a luxury tent with an en suite bathroom, antique furnishings, and Wi-Fi Internet. After your gourmet breakfast, endless activities await. Enjoy a therapeutic massage in the Healing Grounds spa. Go kayaking or horseback riding. Embark on a bear-watching or whale-watching adventure. Try river fishing for cutthroat trout, or ocean fishing for salmon in a 25-foot open-air boat. Take a day trip to the geo-thermal pools of Hot Springs Cove, or discover West Coast native history on Flores Island. Shooting, archery, mountain biking, and ziplining are also available. By dinnertime, you'll be ready to devour the signature oyster chowder or prosciutto-wrapped halibut.❋
www.wildretreat.com

Spend National Aboriginal Day Delving into First Nations Culture

In B.C., First Nations people across the province show off their heritage

For most people, June 21st is simply the first day of summer. But in Canada, that date takes on larger significance with National Aboriginal Day. From coast to coast to coast, Canada's Aboriginal people—the First Nations, Inuit, and Métis—use words like "celebration," "unity," "culture," and "pride" to describe what they cherish about this day, originally instituted in 1996 by Governor General Roméo LeBlanc. For Aboriginal Canadians and non-Aboriginal Canadians alike, Aboriginal culture becomes ever more vivid—

another reason to delve further into First Nations art, music, and cuisine. The range of ways to participate and learn, particularly in British Columbia, will let your imagination take wing . . . like the legendary thunderbird.

Around Metro Vancouver, opportunities to learn about Aboriginal culture abound—varying yearly. The Vancouver Aboriginal Friendship Centre Society organizes Aboriginal prayers at its Hastings Street headquarters, a colour-splashed parade on Commercial Drive, and traditional canoes and teepees at nearby Trout Lake. In Richmond, you can watch Métis, Haida, and Tsimshian dancers, check out Aboriginal-themed films, and attend a mask-making workshop at the Minoru Cultural Centre. Head out to Fort Langley, the former trading post where British Columbia was proclaimed a Crown colony in 1858, and enjoy traditional Kwantlen dancing and a salmon barbecue. Another Fraser Valley destination is Mission's Xa:ytem Longhouse Interpretive Centre, where you can mark the occasion by viewing Sto:lo cultural performances, weaving bark bracelets, and feasting on Native bannock. In addition, see the cedar longhouse, two pit houses, and sacred transformer stone that grace this site of a 9,000-year-old Aboriginal village.

Of course, some famous year-round attractions closer to downtown Vancouver are also worth exploring on National Aboriginal Day. In the heart of iconic Stanley Park, you'll discover Klahowya Village, which demonstrates several Aboriginal traditions. (Entrance is free.) Shop for sweetgrass baskets and bent wood boxes, ride the "Spirit Catcher" miniature train on a trip through Aboriginal history, and learn about the role of the raven, wolf, and whale in First Nations culture. And don't miss the superb, photogenic totem poles at Brockton Point. Just down from the Fairmont Hotel Vancouver lies the Bill Reid Gallery of Northwest Coast Art, where you can savour the legacy of one of Canada's greatest contemporary Native artists. Gaze at his mesmerizing

Mythic Messengers bronze frieze, depicting characters from the Bear Family to the Eagle Prince. Reid's exquisite gold-and-silver jewellery with Aboriginal motifs is also on display, along with pieces by other artists Reid has inspired. The half-Haida product of Victoria gets even more recognition at UBC's Museum of Anthropology, where his huge cedar sculpture, *The Raven and the First Men*, is displayed. Also, admire huge totem poles—both in the glass-walled Great Hall and outside, next to two Haida houses.

Two hours north, in Whistler, visit the 2008-built Squamish Lil'wat Cultural Centre; named after the two nations whose joint territory it occupies, the centre hosts storytellers and offers bannock-baking lessons to mark National Aboriginal Day. The dynamic, three-story, cedar-and-glass building also features an 80-seat theatre with a film on local Aboriginal culture, striking dugout canoes, and many other artifacts within its 2,824 square metres (30,400 square feet). Purchase moccasins and masks at the inviting gift shop, and view the longhouse and pit house next to the forest outside.

Over on Vancouver Island, National Aboriginal Day takes centre stage at Ship Point in Victoria's Inner Harbour. Kids can learn how to draw First Nations art in chalk on the sidewalk and make their own spirit stones. Expect live dance performances and an artisan market with native keepsakes and food. A must-see in the provincial capital is the nearby Royal BC Museum, graced by totem poles in adjacent Thunderbird Park. Among the museum's main displays are the First Peoples Gallery, showcasing ceremonial masks, stone carvings, and a Kwakwaka'wakw longhouse where firelight flickers and chants reverberate in the background.

Even smaller Vancouver Island communities find ways to beat the National Aboriginal Day drum with pride. On the west coast, near Tofino, head to Wickaninnish Beach in Pacific Rim National Park. Here, take a rainforest tour of the Nuu-chah-nulth Trail, featuring cultural signs and a 2005-erected totem pole from the Ucluelet First Nation. Amidst singing and dancing, artisans sell traditional Native crafts, and there's a salmon beach barbecue. Not to be outdone, on the east coast of Vancouver Island, Comox's I-Hos Gallery—operated by the Comox First Nation—offers cedar basket–weaving classes to mark the day. In this venue overlooking the Comox Glacier, you can buy prints and wood carvings that reflect local myths about whales and double-headed sea serpents. A welcome-dance ceremony occurs at the Comox Band Hall (also known as K'ómoks Band Hall).

Ultimately, it's the spirit of sharing that lingers with you when National Aboriginal Day comes to a close. It's as if a giant, carved welcome figure has come to life and put its arms around you. All in all, it's a good feeling—one truly experienced in Canada.🍁

Find out more at:
www.ainc-inac.gc.ca

Rappel Down Cliffs in New Brunswick

As you approach the cliff edge at Cape Enrage, take a good look at what many describe as the most beautiful view in Canada, the Bay of Fundy. Listen to the waves rolling onto the fossil-strewn beach below. Then commit the image to memory—once you harness up for rappelling and start your descent, your concentration must be fully on the rock face.

Standing poised on top of the 42.7-metre (140-foot) cliff edge is a heart-stopping moment, especially for first-timers. With your back to open space, it takes courage to step into mid-air with only a rope as a lifeline. But then, each time you kick off the rock for another downward plunge, a sense of freedom—almost of free flight—replaces the fear. It's absolutely thrilling!

With your back to open space, it takes courage to step into mid-air with only a rope as a lifeline.

The staff at the Cape Enrage Interpretive Centre provide gear, training, and advice on the rock face—important because 15-metre (50-foot) tides can cause erosion where you don't expect it (appointments are needed to descend, because of the changing tides). Cape Enrage got its name from the turbulent waters that pass over a reef that's one kilometre (0.6 miles) and the pounding surf caused by currents and wind that are in opposition. The many shipwrecks here are proof: this is one of the most hazardous areas for mariners in the upper bay.

Once you tire of heart-pounding views, make your way over to the historic 1840 lighthouse, where an interpretive centre offers rock climbing, initiative games, an obstacle course, hiking, and walks along the fossil-rich ocean floor and saltwater marshes. 🍁

www.capenrage.ca

◄ Enjoy Classic Theatre in Picturesque Niagara-on-the-Lake

Stratford has Shakespeare, Niagara-on-the-Lake has George Bernard Shaw. The Shaw Festival has moved from strength to strength in its more than 50 years, developing an internationally renowned repertory company and a reputation for innovation.

Which is to say, the Shaw is more than Shaw. While the playwright left a vast body of work that's still being performed, the festival also celebrates the art of playwrights active during his long life (1856 to 1950) such as Noël Coward, Lillian Hellman, and Somerset Maugham, as well as new works that explore the period: 2005 saw the world premiere of Ann-Marie MacDonald's *Belle Moral: A Natural History*. One year may see a revival of Lerner and Loewe's *My Fair Lady*, a production of Tennessee William's *Cat on a Hot Tin Roof*, or the debut of a play developed in the festival's workshop. Artistic director Jackie Maxwell has committed to mounting at least four plays by female playwrights each year. With four festival stages, there's always a choice of productions to see.

A wide range of deals packaging tickets with dinners or hotels are available. Those seeking a more hands-on experience can book immersive packages that include backstage tours, encounters with festival actors, even singalongs on musical productions.❦
www.shawfest.com

Go Horseback Riding amidst the Canadian Rockies ▼

Horses were used for transportation in the Canadian Rockies by the earliest explorers, but ever since the railway was completed in the 1880s they've remained a practical and enjoyable way to travel in wilderness areas. Options range from regular trail rides to overnight pack trips, but all have one constant—mild springtime temperatures and a lack of bugs that make early June an excellent time of year to saddle up for the adventure through some spectacular mountain scenery.

Nestled on a wide bench on the edge of Canmore, the experienced wranglers at Cross Zee Ranch have been leading city slickers through the Bow Valley since the 1950s. From expansive stables, one-hour rides pass through thickly wooded areas along open meadows and to high lookouts. Southeast of town, in Kananaskis Country, things get more serious at Boundary Ranch, where traditions of early outfitters such as Tom Wilson, the Brewster Brothers, and "Wild" Bill Peyto live on through pack trips consisting of up to six hours of riding per day, with nights spent at a remote tent camp established in a high alpine meadow. Meals are cooked and served cowboy-style—no frills and no complainin'—but it's all part of the experience. The region is very remote, with an abundance of wildlife and excellent fishing in high mountain lakes.❦
www.boundaryranch.com

EVENTS & FESTIVALS

QUIRKY CANADA

Golf under the Midnight Sun

It's midnight on June 21 and the sun is shining. Golfers at the annual Yellowknife Golf Club are lined up and ready to tee off at the Canadian North Midnight Classic tournament. But they aren't the only ones! Foxes and ravens (the size of turkeys) wait in the shadows, creating hazards of their own at Yellowknife's 18-hole golf course. Stealing balls isn't in the playbook, but these tiny competitors have plenty of practice.

The club was established as a nine-hole golf course in 1948, with the fuselage of a crashed Royal Air Force DC-3 serving as the first clubhouse. Today, it's a scenic course with sand fairways and artificial greens. Prepare to carry around a piece of turf (to tee off with) and watch for thieving ravens. The first local rule is that no penalty will be assessed when a raven or other animal takes off with the ball.

The club has been hosting the Midnight Classic golf tournament since 1968. Such Canada Golf Hall of Fame members as Gary Cowan, Bob Panisuk, Doug Roxburgh, and Cathy Sherk have participated in the event.❧
www.yellowknifegolf.com

Walk through a Forest of Signs

A homesick United States Army GI was helping build the Alaska Highway in 1942 when he installed a sign pointing towards his hometown of Danville, Illinois, and how many miles away it was located. Since then others from around the world have added signs at the spot in Watson Lake to represent their hometowns, including Aachen, Germany, and Sudan, Texas.

The Watson Lake Sign Post Forest now has more than 65,000 signs. They look as different as the places they name. Some signs are several metres long and wide, others are the size of a wafer-shaped street sign. Every year, 2,500 to 4,000 signs are added to the forest. The Town of Watson Lake looks after the site and adds more posts for the signs as needed. Visitors walk through the forest, spread over several acres. Look for your hometown amidst the signs.

In 1992, a time capsule and cairn were added to the site—to be opened in 2042. After admiring the signs, step inside the Watson Lake Visitor Information Centre to see a display detailing how the Alaska Highway was built.❧
www.yukoninfo.com/watson/ signpostforest.htm

Go Houseboating on the Rideau Canal

The oldest continuously operated canal system in North America, the Rideau Canal is one of the jewels of Ontario—not to mention a houseboater's dream! The views are unlike any you can experience from a wheeled vehicle. The pace is so relaxed, the traffic literally floats around you. And when's the last time you caught a fish from your car?

The oldest continuously operated canal system in North America, the Rideau Canal is one of the jewels of Ontario.

Okay, the journey isn't all canal. The 202-kilometre (126-mile) system uses sections of major rivers and some lakes. It was a vital trade link in Upper Canada when it opened in 1832, connecting the cities of Kingston and Ottawa and ensuring a line of communication in the event of war with the United States. Nowadays, it's a recreational waterway par excellence, although history is not far away: most of the 45 locks in the 23 stations in the system have hand-operated lock mechanisms. (Don't worry: Parks Canada staff do all the work.) The vessels themselves are simple to operate. An 11.6-metre (38-foot) houseboat that sleeps six can be rented for approximately C$1,400 a week, while bigger boats will cost more than C$2,000. Some rental operators offer weekend rates, though two nights is typically the minimum rental period. Along the way, there are plenty of stores catering to house-boaters. Veteran canal-users recommend beginning your journey at Kingston Mills, travelling all the way to the eight-lock steps beneath Ottawa's Parliament Hill. ❧
www.rideau-info.com

Bret "the Hitman" Hart's

favourite PLACE

The food and the nightlife keep drawing retired pro-wrestler Bret "the Hitman" Hart back to Montréal, Québec.

"I love Montréal, I can't wait to go back," says Hart. "To me it's better than going to Europe."

He recalls the days that the World Wrestling Federation (now World Wrestling Entertainment) would roll into town for a sold-out event at the old Montréal Forum.

"We'd be looking forward to getting off the plane, getting downtown to Montréal, and grabbing a smoked meat sandwich or a corned beef sandwich," he says. "You can stop at a truck stop, a little café or whatever, and you're still going to get the best breakfast, the best lunch. There's no such thing as bad food in Québec."

He speaks warmly of the friendly locals, great seafood, and loyal wrestling fans.

"I always found the French people that I ran into, whether it was at a gas station or a 7–Eleven . . . I thought they were really accommodating and went out of their way to be as helpful as possible."

To see the province at its best, Hart suggests making a trip to Québec City in winter or visiting for Saint-Jean-Baptiste Day on June 24.

But Montréal also offers year-round entertainment.

"I'd always go to a hockey game," he says, and "the burlesque clubs are a novelty."

"The nightlife in Montréal is as good as anywhere in the country."

Soak Up the Sounds of the World's Biggest Jazz Festival

You're guaranteed to find an incredible range of music and talent . . . much of it for free

I f all the world's a stage, the spotlight certainly shines on Montréal during her most glorious days of summer. Set during the last week of June and the first few days of July, the Festival International de Jazz de Montréal shuts down traffic in a small corner of the downtown corridor, transforming the city for 12 magical days into a festive epicentre, and possibly the largest jam session on the planet.

It all started with the late great Ray Charles, who inaugurated the festival back in 1980. Over the years the stellar list of talent has showcased musical icons including Miles Davis, Wynton Marsalis, Ella Fitzgerald, Sara Vaughan, Tony Bennett, James Brown, Sting, Cesaria Evora, Norah Jones, Diana Krall, Paul Simon, and Bob Dylan, just to whet your palate. Dubbed the World's Largest Jazz Festival according to Guinness World Records in 2004, it's also the most important one in every music lover's calendar, embracing a spectrum of musical influences, including blues, world beat, Brazilian, Cuban, African, reggae, electro, and pop.

Artists typically perform at ticketed indoor venues like the grand Salle Wilfrid-Pelletier, or more casual spots like Metropolis and Club Soda. But what jacks up the cool factor of this hot and hazy summer celebration are the hundreds of outdoor concerts—all of them free. Spread out over 10 al fresco stages from noon to midnight, the largest of the lot is the Scene General Motors planted at the foot of Place des Arts. Thanks to its esplanade of cascading steps, a makeshift amphitheatre is created that accommodates up to 200,000 spectators who gather here rain or shine. (Shows are never cancelled, though sometimes delayed due to weather.) Certainly, as in 2009, when the artist is someone like Stevie Wonder, a little drizzle's not going to dampen spirits.

Even if you're not a jazz lover, the grounds are entertaining for folks of all ages. Street performers abound. And because cars are banned, the whole area

is a safe place for kids. Temperatures at this time of year can get hot and hazy (more than 30 degrees Celsius, 86 degrees Fahrenheit), so slather on the sunscreen, wear a hat, and hydrate sufficiently. For more immediate relief, you can splash yourself at the fountains atop the Place des Arts steps, or the water jets in the new Quartier des spectacles. If you're feeling hungry, there's no lack of fast food options: hot dogs, ice cream bars, and cold beverages are all available in a fairground-like ambience. Otherwise, two hipster bistros have recently opened nearby: Brasserie t! (by star chef Normand Laprise) and F Bar (owned by Carlos Ferreira, whose eponymous seafood restaurant is a Montréal landmark).

While you're breaking bread, don't be surprised when you're suddenly rubbing elbows with someone famous, since there are more than 3,000 artists from more than 30 countries there to enjoy the festival themselves.

In all, more than two million people typically attend. Get organized by downloading the free app on your iPhone, iPod Touch, iPad, or BlackBerry. A good central meeting point is the Maison du Festival Rio Tinto Alcan, the building on the corner of Sainte-Catherine Street (just west of Jeanne Mance) where the east-facing windows are filled with black-and-white portraits paying tribute to such jazz legends as Antonio Carlos Jobim, Aretha Franklin, B.B. King, Chick Corea, Herbie Hancock, Leonard Cohen, Miles Davis, Paco De Lucia, and Pat Metheny, to name a few. Located in this historic Blumenthal Building, this Jazz Fest headquarters houses an intimate concert hall, L'Astral, Le Balmoral bistro terrace, and, of special interest to jazzophiles, La Médi-athèque on the third floor where you'll find jazz-related archives, concert footage, publications, and some 30,000 CDs and albums (no entrance fee).

Tickets go on sale around the second week of March, so plan ahead if there's a certain act you'd like to see. Or play it by ear: jazz acts stream out beyond the grounds, so adventurous travellers can also check out more intimate hangouts like Diese Onze and Bily Kun in the Plateau, Lion d'Or in the Village, or Modavie and Narcisse in Old Montréal. Downtown institutions to note are Upstairs Jazz Bar & Grill, and the House of Jazz (formerly known as Biddle's), the latter being a slick art deco lounge where both Oscar Peterson and Oliver Jones, both from Montréal, have graced the stage.

Your best bets for getting around are walking and BIXI (Montréal's public bike-sharing system) and, if you still have a way's to go, taxi or metro. As far as accommodation, for extreme convenience the Hyatt's in the middle of the action (and seemingly overflowing with celebrities). It also offers great patios with bird's-eye views of Sainte-Catherine Street below. Other choice hotels nearby include Loews Hôtel Vogue (the first boutique hotel in Montréal) and French chic Hôtel Le Germain Montréal. Guaranteed, no matter where you stay, you'll be sure to catch jazz fever!✸

Find out more at:
www.montrealjazzfest.com

ADVENTURE

Paddle the Gruelling Yukon River Quest

The Yukon River Quest is a punishing marathon that retraces the route of Klondike gold seekers. Now, at the end of June, paddlers from more than a half-dozen countries make the 740-kilometre (459.8-mile) trek to test their endurance amidst rugged wilderness during the race from Whitehorse to Dawson City.

The "Race to the Midnight Sun" starts at Whitehorse's Rotary Peace Park and can take 40 to 55 hours to complete. Up to 100 canoe and kayak solo competitors and teams churn through Class I rapids most of the way, although some spots have Class II and Class III. Participants race around the clock, save for two mandatory rest stops. Challenges include crossing the windy and unpredictable Lake Laberge, navigating the tricky Five Finger Rapids, battling sleep deprivation, hypothermia, and sore muscles, and trying to stay awake through the night (while still paddling). Days may be warm but the nights are cold, wet, and windy.

By the third day, racers sometimes experience exhaustion-induced hallucinations. About a quarter of them quit, suffering from hypothermia, fatigue, and huge blisters.

Teams can (and probably should) bring a support crew. You'll be sure to see some extraordinary sights during the race—such as the soaring cliffs and historic buildings at Fort Selkirk—but none will likely be as exciting as the finish line. ❀

www.yukonriverquest.com

CULTURE & HISTORY

Join Québec's Biggest Party on Saint-Jean-Baptiste Day

The entire province of Québec fetes Saint-Jean Baptiste, the patron saint of French Canadians, every June 24. Not so much a religious holiday as a day of cultural pride, it's a party akin to the Fourth of July in the United States, or even Canada Day on July 1. And let's not forget: it's a paid day off for pretty much everyone in the province. Even if you're not French, or even Canadian, you're still invited.

Expect fireworks, BBQ picnics, face painting, and of course the ubiquitous blue-and-white *fleur-de-lis* flag. In Montréal, there's the traditional Parade of Giants, which takes on massive proportions with larger-than-life characters marching through the streets. The lineup includes prominent Québecers such as former premier and famed separatist Réne Lévesque, hockey hero Maurice Richard, and singer-songwriter Félix Leclerc. Similarly, the party continues in Québec City; the Plains of Abraham turns into a massive outdoor dance party with local celebrities performing—or just partying— with the rest of the province.

The holiday is on the same day every year, so most rejoice when it falls on a Friday or Monday . . . making for a nice long weekend. ❀

www.fetenationale.qc.ca

◀ See Rare Wildlife at Grasslands National Park

On the Prairies, spring is a time of growth and movement; a surprisingly diverse flora bursts with life while animals emerge from long winter slumbers. It's an ideal time of year to explore Canada's only national park that protects what scientists call a "mixed-grass prairie ecosystem."

It's an ideal time of year to explore Canada's only national park that protects what scientists call a "mixed-grass prairie ecosystem."

Grasslands National Park is comprised of two separate tracts of land. The main focus for visitors is on the more accessible West Block. Begin your prairie adventure by stopping by the Visitor Reception Centre in the town of Val Marie; from there, a road loops through the West Block, crossing the wide and shallow Frenchman River. If you take off on just one hike, make it the Two Trees Interpretive Trail—an easy stroll that traverses a coulee and rises to a ridge for river views. Access to the East Block is by a rough unpaved road from the north, but visitors are rewarded with stunning views of the area's extensive badlands (a unique and memorable landscape created through erosion). One of the park's most interesting residents is the black-footed ferret, once thought to be extinct. Even smaller is the black-tailed prairie dog, also known as the "barking squirrel" for its response to those it perceives as intruders; look (and listen) for them throughout the park. 🍁

www.pc.gc.ca/grasslands

It happened
THIS WEEK:

St. Lawrence Seaway Opens

It raises ships longer than two (Canadian) football fields to the height of a 60-story building. The St. Lawrence Seaway opened officially on June 26, 1959, with high-profile guests such as Queen Elizabeth II, U.S. President Dwight Eisenhower, and Canadian Prime Minister John Diefenbaker in attendance.

Often called an "engineering marvel," the network of rivers, lakes, canals, and locks connects Lake Superior to the Atlantic Ocean—a distance of 3,700 kilometres (2,299 miles). But this is not the impressive distance: Lake Superior sits at 183 metres (600.4 feet) above the Atlantic Ocean and sea level. The rapids are like a staircase in-between, with the first step being the Lachine Rapids in Montréal.

Prior to the Seaway's opening, vessels bypassed the river through the original seven locks of the Lachine Canal: a narrow waterway first used in 1825.

Industry clustered around the Canadian transportation lifeline and source of hydro-electrical power. Factories—including the Five Roses flour warehouse and the Redpath sugar refinery—set up operations along the canal.

Despite being widened over the following decades, the Lachine could not handle the increasingly large ships that routinely travelled the St. Lawrence River. When the Seaway opened in 1959, it quickly replaced the canal as the main route to the Great Lakes. By the 1960s, efforts had begun to refill the Lachine Canal, concrete refineries were beginning to crumble, and towers were beginning to rust.

Fifty years on and the decay is still present, but the canal's also seeing revitalization. It is protected as a national historic site, with a government-run boat tour and bike paths along the shore banks. Even the old shot tower, where molten lead was dripped into water to form perfect spheres for ammunition, adjoins renovated canal-view condominiums.

EVENTS & FESTIVALS

Bring the Kids to Manitoba's Largest Annual Fair

The country comes to the city for two weeks in late June during Winnipeg's Red River Exhibition. What began in 1952 as a simple agricultural exhibition has now grown into Manitoba's largest annual fair.

Usually simply known as "The Ex," it's held at the sprawling 36-hectare (90-acre) Red River Exhibition Park, on the west side of Manitoba's capital. The overriding theme is family fun, with children drawn to Prairie Town Adventures, where they can get down and dirty learning the finer points of farming, digging for dinosaur bones, and pretending to be firefighters. Music is also a large part of the fair, with well-known pop and country musicians performing on the Main Stage, and a wide variety of acts—think magicians, comedy, and music—entertaining visitors from the Red Barn Stage. The Trade Show is an important part of the event, but like other aspects it's made kid-friendly with attractions like the Fishing Pond, where kids can learn how to cast a line—and even reel in fish. A midway, talent show, photography show, and food fair with many different options including—surprise, surprise—a number of healthy eating options, bring out more than 175,000 people each year to this spot in the heart of Canada.❦

www.redriverexhibitionpark.com

Camp on the Amazing Lake Athabasca Sand Dunes ▼

They may never make the cover of *Islands* magazine, but the magnificent Athabasca Sand Dunes of northern Saskatchewan are a natural wonder nevertheless. Although the dunes are very remote, if you do make the effort, plan your visit for late June when temperatures have warmed but the notorious "bug season" has yet to begin.

Sand dunes are usually associated with beaches or arid landscapes, but the 100-kilometre (62-mile) Athabasca dunes are linked geologically to the ice ages. Many millions of years ago, layers of silt that washed down an ancient river were compressed by successive sheets of ice into sandstone. Later, the sandstone was eroded by glaciers, wind, and water to create the dunes. The indigenous Dene people tell a different story; they say the dunes were created by a giant beaver that ground the sandstone with his tail after being speared by a giant man. The fragile sand dunes ecosystem is very different from the surrounding boreal forest, with endemic plant species like field chickweed and felt-leaved willow found nowhere else in the world.

Visiting the remote Athabasca Sand Dunes Provincial Park is an adventure like no other. With no roads penetrating this far north, the only access is by float plane. Upon arrival, visitors must be completely self-sufficient—simply pitch your tent and enjoy the sandy solitude.🍁
www.tpcs.gov.sk.ca/AthabascaSandDunes

Pull Up a Stool at One of Vancouver's Favourite Brewpubs

June 28, 1984, was a date in Vancouver history worth toasting, marking the opening of Granville Island Brewing (GIB)—Canada's oldest operational microbrewery. Celebrate that anniversary by quaffing a few pints as you explore Vancouver's favourite brewpubs, which have helped transform the Pacific Northwest into a beer-lover's paradise.

At GIB, nestled under the Granville Street Bridge in a high-ceilinged building, a behind-the-scenes brewery tour is always a highlight. For C$9.75 per adult you'll drink deeply of the mysteries of boiling, fermentation, and aging, amidst the rich scent of malted barley and glistening conditioning tanks. Tours conclude in the taproom with three sample beers, including the likes of Cypress Honey Lager and Kitsilano Maple Cream Ale.

The Dockside Brewing Company, another Granville Island institution that overlooks False Creek, lures people with its clean, bitter Johnston Pilsner and hibiscus-infused Jamaican Lager.

Head into downtown Vancouver for people-watching on the Yaletown Brewing Company patio, where a Hill's Special Wheat Hefeweizen makes the gorgeous scenery look even better. At the 1,394-square-metre (15,000-square-foot) wood-panelled Steamworks, located harbourside near Gastown's cobblestone streets, sip a Signature Pale Ale with its spicy hop finish. Or, mix it up and try something different: a seasonal Raspberry Frambozen.🍁
www.gib.ca, www.docksidebrewing.com, www.drinkfreshbeer.com, www.steamworks.com

Your next STEP

TOP PICKS

ADVENTURE

CULTURE & HISTORY

NATURE'S GRANDEUR

EVENTS & FESTIVALS

QUIRKY CANADA

REJUVENATE

WEEK 1

1 PRINCE ALBERT NATIONAL PARK, SASK.
Wildlife-watching
www.pc.gc.ca/princealbert

2 LYTTON, B.C.
Whitewater rafting
www.hyak.com

3 MONTRÉAL, QUE.
John and Yoko's bed-in site
www.fairmont.com/EN_FA/Property/
QEH/AboutUs/HotelHistory.htm

4 MIRAMICHI RIVER, N.B.
Fish New Brunswick Days
www.tourismnewbrunswick.ca/
Home/Activities/SportRecreation/
Fishing.aspx

5 MONTRÉAL, QUE.
Bike Fest
www.velo.qc.ca/english/index.php

6 ST. PAUL, ALTA.
UFO landing pad
www.stpaulchamber.ca/
ufolanding.html

7 CHARLOTTETOWN, P.E.I.
Confederation Trail cycling
www.gentleisland.com/confedtrail

WEEK 2

8 TWILLINGATE, NFLD.
Iceberg Alley
www.newfoundlandlabrador.com

9 BOWRON LAKE PROVINCIAL PARK, B.C.
Bowron Lakes canoeing
www.env.gov.bc.ca/bcparks/
explore/parkpgs/bowron_lk

10 DINOSAUR PROVINCIAL PARK, ALTA.
Hiking among prehistoric fossils
www.tpr.alberta.ca/parks/dinosaur

11 ELK ISLAND NATIONAL PARK, ALTA.
Big game—watching
www.pc.gc.ca/elkisland

12 TORONTO, ONT.
LuminaTO arts festival
www.luminato.com

13 VULCAN, ALTA.
Spock Days
www.vulcantourism.com

14 TOFINO, B.C.
Clayoquot Wilderness Resort
www.wildretreat.com

WEEK 3

15 FORT LANGLEY, B.C.
National Aboriginal Day
www.ainc-inac.gc.ca

16 CAPE ENRAGE, N.B.
Cliff rappelling
www.capenrage.ca

17 NIAGARA-ON-THE-LAKE, ONT.
Classic theatre
www.shawfest.com

18 CANMORE, ALTA.
Rockies horseback riding
www.boundaryranch.com

19 YELLOWKNIFE, N.W.T.
Midnight sun golfing
www.yellowknifegolf.com

20 WATSON LAKE, Y.T.
Sign Post Forest
www.yukoninfo.com/watson/
signpostforest.htm

21 RIDEAU CANAL, ONT.
Rideau Canal houseboating
www.rideau-info.com

WEEK 4

22 MONTRÉAL, QUE.
Montréal Jazz Fest
www.montrealjazzfest.com

23 WHITEHORSE, Y.T.
Yukon River Quest paddling race
www.yukonriverquest.com

24 QUÉBEC CITY, QUE.
Saint-Jean-Baptiste Day
www.fetenationale.qc.ca

25 GRASSLANDS NATIONAL PARK, SASK.
See rare wildlife
www.pc.gc.ca/grasslands

26 WINNIPEG, MAN.
Red River Exhibition
www.redriverexhibitionpark.com

27 ATHABASCA SAND DUNES PROVINCIAL PARK, SASK.
Sand-dune camping
www.tpcs.gov.sk.ca/Athabasca
SandDunes

28 VANCOUVER, B.C.
Vancouver brewpubs
www.gib.ca

MALIGNE TOURS
BOAT HOUSE

Celebrate Canada Day in the Nation's Capital

From morning to midnight, Ottawa throws the country's biggest party

The Maple Leaf is everywhere in Canada's capital as the country celebrates its birthday. From the tree-lined streets of pretty, downtown Ottawa, to the canopies of green that shade Parliament Hill in the peak of midsummer, the iconic leaf is most commonly found in its red-and-white form: on thousands of furiously waving Canadian flags.

It's a day to celebrate all that is Canada: that means music, fireworks, fine food and drink, dancing in the streets, parades, marching bands, and Mounties. (Okay, there are politicians' speeches too, but they can be skipped for the real fun.) Sometimes, even royalty drops by: the big news for 2011 was that newlyweds William and Kate, just two months after their Westminster Abbey nuptial spectacle, joined the party in Ottawa on Canada Day.

The official ceremonies begin at 9:30 a.m. with the raising of the flag and a moment to honour the country's military and naval forces.

Atten--tion! At 10:00 a.m. sharp there's the colourful Changing of the Guard. This entails marching bands, pomp and pageantry, military drills, and the main ceremony performed by the Governor General's Foot Guards. At 10:30 a.m., the RCMP (Royal Canadian Mounted Police, otherwise known as the Mounties) stage a military-style equestrian show with music. Everyone loves the traditional red serge uniforms.

At the core of Ottawa's festivities is the midday live concert featuring the country's top musicians—rock, pop, hip-hop, world, country, jazz, and classical music are on the bill—as well as masters of dance and stage. Expect top Canadian artists like Sarah McLachlan, Diana Krall, or Blue Rodeo. Tens of thousands gather on the Hill to sing, dance, and party for the 90-minute bash and all ages are welcome. It's a great way to catch top Canadian talent and get a sense of what's *au courant* in the performing arts. There's an air show, too: the famous Snowbirds, along with CF-18 fighter jets, soar overhead with their breathtaking, synchronized stunts.

There are dozens more events and happenings, many of them free.

Music rings out all over town: the Ottawa Jazz Festival stages a series of free concerts at Confederation Park from 11:00 a.m. to 7:00 p.m. On Canada Day, the National Arts Centre's (NAC) musical program is one of the city's most ambitious—and it's all free. A typical July 1 begins at 10:00 a.m. with the 400-voice Unisong Massed Choir, then moves onto a series of hourly kids' concerts, a series of standout performances by the NAC Orchestra, the NAC Young Artists Programme, and African Drummers. As well, there are backstage tours to view the theatre's workings.

July 1 is also a good time to check out the city's top sites —so long as you don't mind lineups, as most offer free admission for the day—particularly Parliament Hill. The Canadian Museum of Civilization, the National Gallery of Canada, the Canadian Museum of Nature, and the Canadian War Museum, to name a few, all open their doors *gratis*, with many featuring special exhibits around the day's theme.

There's also an assortment of off-beat options. If your inner farmer is eager to join in the fun, visit the Canadian Agricultural Museum (this country was built on agriculture) and enjoy free ice cream (which you can make on-site) and other family friendly activities, plus exhibits that tell the story of one of Canada's most important industries. Or, check out the modest and historic Bytown Museum to discover Ottawa's history. The Canadian Aviation and Space Museum also gets in on the fun with patriotic exhibits, including mighty flying machines (past and present) from Cessnas to Spitfires (think World War II and the Red Baron). The museum is particularly strong on warplanes.

The day closes with a spectacular fireworks show over the Ottawa River.

Rideau Street keeps a street party humming all day with sports demonstrations, skateboard competitions, crowded patios, street food (including the Annual Great Canadian Chicken BBQ), and live music.

As nightfall descends, evening concerts begin. Again, event organizers manage to attract top names like Alex Cuba, the Barenaked Ladies, and Céline Dion to regale the crowds as the party continues on Parliament Hill. There are performers in both official languages, as well as traditional and contemporary Aboriginal singing and dancing.

The day closes with a spectacular fireworks show over the Ottawa River (starting at about 10:00 p.m.). The best views are from across the river in Gatineau at the Canadian Museum of Civilization or Jacques Cartier Park. The unofficial partying continues into the night on both sides of the river, in open parks, on restaurant patios, and in crowded clubs. July 2 is a good day to plan on sleeping in. 🍁

Find out more at:
www.canadascapital.gc.ca

1st week of
JUL

ADVENTURE

Hike into Skoki Lodge

Skoki Lodge is one of the Canadian Rockies' best-kept secrets, especially in early July when newly melted winter snow reveals a wonderland of alpine meadows. Tucked away in a remote valley northeast of Lake Louise in Banff National Park and accessible only on foot, it's a must-stay for anyone looking for the quintessential backcountry mountain experience without having to pitch a tent.

Dating to 1931 and now a national historic site, the lodge is rustic but comfortable and extremely welcoming. Guests stay in cabins, while at the main lodge a wood-burning fire is at the heart of both the dining room and lounge, where everyone comes together each evening to swap tales from the trail and mingle with the convivial hosts. Access to the lodge is along a well-travelled, 11-kilometre (6.8-mile) hiking trail that climbs gradually into the valley via a pass high above the treeline. Plan on staying two or more nights and you can spend your days exploring the most remote and inviting valley features. Trails radiate from the lodge like spokes, leading to tiny Merlin Lake, which is framed by the colourfully named Wall of Jericho, to the thundering waterfall passing through the Natural Bridge, and around Fossil Mountain to Ptarmigan Lake, where marmots and pikas find a home in extensive rockslides.❦
www.skoki.com

◄ Check Out the Best of Newfoundland Theatre in Gorgeous Trinity

Early July is the beginning of the annual Seasons in the Bight Theatre Festival, hosted by the historic Newfoundland fishing village of Trinity. But the festival offers much more than performing arts—it perfectly links the past to the present, encouraging visitors to immerse themselves in the celebrated culture of Canada's easternmost province while enjoying an historic fishing village.

The main venue is a recreated fishing shed on Green's Point, at the eastern side of the village. Musical and dramatic productions written and performed by some of Newfoundland's best writers and actors are scheduled two or three times weekly. But the most dramatic performances take place on the streets of Trinity. The New Founde Lande Trinity Pageant is a walking, talking, and singing routine presented by costumed performers. Following the actors along narrow streets lined with white picket fences and well-tended gardens, you'll be regaled with colourful stories, meet local characters, and be invited to sing along to the words of "Ode to Newfoundland."

Extend your time in Trinity by making reservations at the character-filled Artisan Inn (choose the Gover Suite for its stunningly private oceanfront deck), then dining at the in-house restaurant on perfectly presented cod followed by delicious rhubarb pie.✤
www.risingtidetheatre.com

Unwind at Jasper's Spectacular Maligne Lake ▼

With its breathtaking mountain setting, an abundance of wildlife, and a wealth of opportunities for outdoor recreation, Maligne Lake ranks among the great natural wonders of Canada. Located high in the heart of Alberta's Jasper National Park, the summer season is short, with early July being prime season for wildflowers and clear skies.

The most popular activity is to glide across turquoise waters on a scenic lake cruise bound for Spirit Island, where time is spent on the remote shoreline admiring one of Canada's most photographed lake-and-mountain panoramas. More adventurous visitors set out in canoes and kayaks for secluded coves to spread out a picnic lunch or cast for fighting rainbow trout. Landlubbers are also spoiled, as far as choice. Hiking trails suited for all levels of fitness lead from the lakeshore, through pristine forest, to secluded lakes, rising above the treeline for sweeping lake views and the chance to get up close and personal with local inhabitants such as pikas and marmots. Or, you can do nothing at all—and simply admire the stunning scenery while breathing in some intoxicatingly fresh mountain air. Who could ask for more?✤
www.malignelake.com

EVENTS & FESTIVALS

QUIRKY CANADA

Get In Touch with Your Scottish Roots

Don y'r kilt, laddie, it's time to muscle up! For about 150 years, powerful athletes have been tossing cabers, hammers, stones, and sheaves as they compete in traditional events at the Antigonish Highland Games in Nova Scotia. First held in 1863, the oldest annual highland games outside Scotland are fantastic to watch. "Heavy Events" are contests of strength and athleticism that reflect farming traditions and keep spectators spellbound. The Sheaf Toss determines who could toss a sheaf of wheat the highest. Farmer's Walk participants strive for the fastest time carrying 91.6-kilogram (202-pound) weights in each hand. Tug O' Wars take brute strength and teamwork.

Pipers piping, kilts swirling, and drums drumming put the beat of the highlands in the air. The atmosphere is electric for the International Gathering of the Clans, which brings together family and social groups with roots in Scotland. Those with Scottish heritage can trace their roots, walk Clan Alley, hear Gaelic spoken, celebrate the Clan of the Year and participate in the Kirkin' O' the Tartan (a traditional blessing ceremony)! The festival is also a family affair. *Tir Nan Og*, Gaelic for "Land of Eternal Youth," features fun for children —including a haggis toss, mini caber toss, jumps, and races. There are endless ways for young or old to get involved: dine at special dinners, dance at ceilidhs, take in arts displays, and soak in the music at square dances and concerts.♦
www.antigonishhighlandgames.ca

Drink an Orange Julep at the Big Orange

If you're driving to downtown Montréal from the airport along boulevard Décarie, chances are you'll notice the Gibeau Orange Julep. On a hot and hazy summer day, join the lineup at this giant citrus sphere, then sit at one of the picnic tables or in your car and sip their legendary orange creamsicle–tasting drink.

The Big Orange, as it's called, was built in 1945, expanding from two stories to three in 1966. The nostalgic joint and its adjacent parking lot hold many memories for Montréalers—those who recall a time when the waiters and waitresses worked on roller skates. Speakers at either end of the corner lot play non-stop tunes.

If you're wondering what's inside the monstrous ball, there are offices and locker rooms, but you can tell the kiddies it's the biggest vat of sweet nectar in the world. When you get to the cash, each server has his/her own transparent tube that spurts out the sweet liquid from a hidden, central drink-machine.

You can also get poutine here, as well as hot dogs, hot pretzels, and more. For an extra kick, indulge in the milk-shake, the same orange velvety goodness—but thicker.

On Wednesday nights especially, the parking lot becomes a see-and-be-seen hangout when hot rod drivers park their cars here for the ultimate show and tell. The Julep's open 24 hours a day starting in late May through September.♦
www.orangejulep.com

Enjoy a Feast Fit for a Village

How do you make chowder for 1,000 and turn it into C$35,000 raised to help feed the needy—both locally and around the world? It's easy. Just book a renowned chef, bring a crew of volunteers to Souris, Prince Edward Island, book the local hockey rink, and before you know it you'll have a Village Feast.

Television celebrity and author, Chef Michael Smith, along with almost 100 volunteers (among them professional chefs and a contingent of military cooks from Canadian Forces Base Gagetown), cooks, barbecues, and bakes. Chowder, as well as steak, potatoes, bread, and strawberry shortcake, are served along with a great opportunity to meet and mingle with local residents and "come from awayers." All money raised from the Village Feast is donated to local charities such as the Souris Foodbank and Coats for Kids, as well as Farmers Helping Farmers, who raise funds to build cookhouses for schools in Kenya.

Chowder, as well as steak, potatoes, bread, and strawberry shortcake, are served.

Besides being a good feast, it's also a raucous party with local entertainment and a popular one—tickets (about C$35) must be purchased ahead of time (details on the website), even though the town consists of only 1,300. These folks clearly understand the meaning of "global village" and "feast," as the Village Feast is truly a celebration of sharing and abundance. ❧

www.ekpei.ca/VF.html

Canadian *moments*

Montréal Moving Day

When many Canadians are lighting their barbecues and attending Canada Day celebrations, the statutory holiday sees a unique chaos descend on Québec, especially Montréal. For thousands of households, July 1 is moving day—*la fête du déménagement.*

Until 1974, all leases in Québec were mandated to end on April 30. As the date interrupted the school year, lawmakers opted to move the date ahead—to June 30.

In July 2004, Hydro-Québec switched over about 120,000 accounts to new addresses, reported the CBC.

During Moving Day, professional movers and residents wobble down three-story spiral staircases with stoves, refrigerators, and dryers. Companies are often booked months in advance. With the rush of business, movers increase rates because of the long days they put in, while rates for van rentals can double and grocery stores are relieved of all empty cardboard boxes.

One inventive moving company even uses bicycle trailers to transport everything, from couches, to washers and dryers, to box springs— sometimes all in the same load.

Montréalers say the mandated lease-end date can make searching for a new home easier.

For those not moving themselves or helping someone else move, the piles of discarded treasures can be a trove of furniture, appliances, and household items. Or for those who prefer to opt for fireworks and barbecuing, the crowds tend to be a bit thinner at Canada Day celebrations.

Join the Party at the Calgary Stampede

An event as big as a western sky

They don't call it "The Greatest Outdoor Show on Earth" for nothing.

Attending the 10-day Stampede is not so much joining a party as entering a state of mind. It touches everything—from the moment you slide out of bed, put on your stetson, and wander down to the nearest Stampede breakfast, through the wee hours when you're line dancing with 100 of your closest (new) friends. Calgarians are known for their friendliness and hospitality for 51 weeks a year. But this week it's more like you're part of the family.

The crown jewel of the event is, of course, the rodeo, where the world's top cowboys compete for more than C$1 million in prizes in bull riding, steer wrestling, chuckwagon races, and other adrenaline-filled events. The most coveted tickets are directly behind the holding pen, but they're not for the meek—it's where two tonnes of pent-up bull are waiting to be released, and the animal's rage is as palpable as the fear of the cowboy perched on its back. Wherever you sit, the one guarantee is entertainment as these cowboys routinely demonstrate extraordinary feats of athleticism. Bareback riders must keep themselves from being flung from their mount using only one hand; in steer wrestling, the cowboy flings himself to the ground from his mount and wrestles a one-tonne animal to the dirt. The crowd roars in support and emotions run high. On the line? Bragging rights, and the biggest cash prizes on the rodeo circuit. In the sprawling Stampede Park, sensory overload continues wherever you go, with whirling amusement rides, cacophonous livestock shows, food fairs, fireworks, lectures—even a casino. You may not get a quiet moment while you're at the Stampede, but there will be too much else going on for you to notice.

That said, there's much to discover when you do explore beyond the grounds. Stampede breakfasts—served daily, early and free!—can easily be found throughout the city. This is where you get the lowdown on the day's can't-miss events while savouring the ubiquitous flapjacks and sausage and guzzling a cuppa joe at a communal table. You may be able to repay the favour later that

night at one of the dozens of bars that are packed all week . . . it's not uncommon for locals to vacate the office by noon in order to indulge in a full day of hootin' and hollerin' at their preferred watering hole.

But perhaps the greatest thing about the Stampede is that there really is something for everyone. Concerts range from traditional country to the latest pop icons. Past headliners have included Katy Perry, Alan Jackson, Taylor Swift, George Strait, and Kid Rock. The event is also hugely popular with kids. Between the midway, petting zoo, and near-constant stimulation, this is a party for all ages. Letting the little ones dress up as a cowboy or cowgirl will not only seem normal, but you may be the one who gets funny looks if you're not wearing a checkered shirt and a worn pair of jeans at the very least. It's the rare person who doesn't get into the spirit of things.

With this much to see and do, crowds—boisterous, enthusiastic, and generally full of civic pride—are a fact of Stampede life. The event regularly draws more than

1.2 million visitors to a city of roughly one million inhabitants, so it's best to simply embrace the widespread excitement and give yourself plenty of time to get from A to B.

The vast majority of events are affordable (rodeo tickets start at around C$36) but reservations are essential—some local watering holes even accept bookings for a place at the bar. To snag the event tickets and a room at your hotel of choice, be sure to make your picks many months in advance. Another great way to really get involved is to volunteer, making it easier to mix with the locals, make new friends, and see another side of this mammoth festival. With 46 volunteer committees (ranging from parade, blacksmith competition, and "miniature donkey" assistance) and a need for more than 2,000 people to help, there are many ways you can make a contribution that will be both rewarding and deeply appreciated.✤

Find out more at:
www.calgarystampede.com

ADVENTURE

Go Sea Kayaking in Serene Clayoquot Sound ▶

Out on Clayoquot Sound, you feel as if you're on the edge of the world—and it's pure peacefulness. Here, you're kayaking alongside shores laden with lush, temperate rainforest and sandy beaches, listening to the ocean breeze, the lapping waves, and the little splash of your paddle. Even if rain comes down amidst July's warmth, it just offers a different view of this 350,000-hectare (860,000-acre) area on Vancouver Island's west coast—an area revered by experienced paddlers that was designated as a UNESCO Biosphere Reserve in 2000.

Many guided sea-kayaking tours launch out of Tofino, a small town known for its luxurious accommodations, Aboriginal artwork, and surfing. Sign up with a reputable operator like Majestic Ocean Kayaking or Pacific Northwest Expeditions. As you paddle around Flores, Vargas, and Meares islands—the latter sparked the famous logging protests of the 1980s—watch

Orcas, minke whales, and grey whales frequent these waters.

out for marine creatures and wildlife. Orcas, minke whales, and grey whales frequent these waters, as do porpoises and seals. Overhead, bald eagles soar. And the sharp-eyed may spot a black bear or deer onshore. Check out Vargas Island's sprawling Ahous Beach, or hike well-camouflaged rainforest trails on other islands. If you're not returning to Tofino nightly, both tent- and lodge-based tours are available.❦
**www.oceankayaking.com,
www.seakayakbc.com**

◀ Relive Dawson City's Gold Rush Days

From the swinging doors at the Sourdough Saloon to the Gold Rush architecture and wooden sidewalks, Dawson City is where the Trail of '98 Klondike Gold Rush ended for thousands of stampeders. Early July is an ideal time to go—take in the birthday celebrations of acclaimed author Pierre Berton, who captured the spirit of the era in his book *Klondike*, while enjoying nearly 24 hours of daylight.

The home where Berton lived for 11 years as a child, now a writers' retreat, is not open to the public. But you can visit the place where writer Jack London lived for about eight months and see an actor read the poetry of Robert Service at the log cabin where he spent three years. Take a Parks Canada walking tour of Dawson City and learn about the town's colourful characters from the past. Stop by the Dawson City Museum to take in the interactive theatre of a miners' meeting and gold-pouring demonstrations.

Enjoy some Gold Rush history at Dredge #4 National Historic Site. Pan for gold at Claim #6. For some Klondike-era entertainment, watch the "Gaslight Follies" at the Palace Grand Theatre and enjoy an evening at Diamond Tooth Gertie's Gambling Hall. Join the Sourtoe Cocktail Club at the Sourdough Saloon after drinking the infamous cocktail featuring a human toe—and letting the severed appendage touch your lips. Then sleep it all off at Bombay Peggy's, a former brothel.❦
www.dawsoncity.ca

Ride the Polar Bear Express Train to James Bay

Don't be fooled by the name—you have as much chance of seeing a polar bear as you do a zebra—but this northern wilderness excursion, from Cochrane to the saltwater shores of James Bay, is more about the pleasures of train travel than the destination (especially if you're starting from faraway Toronto, in which case the train journey to Cochrane is 11 hours, making this a multi-day affair). Reservations for both rail and lodging are essential.

The domed observation car offers incredible views of the rolling forest, while the entertainment car features live music throughout the journey. While parents admire the scenery, one floor below is a family space where kids can watch films, play games, and learn crafts under the watchful eye of staff. The full-on dining car is a treat—offering breakfast, lunch, and dinner (the pan-fried pickerel is a highlight). Given that rail is the only land connection to Moosonee, Ontario, the train remains one of the few flag-stop services on the continent: don't be surprised if the train stops in the middle of nowhere to pick up canoers and kayakers en route.

In summer, the train departs Cochrane at 9:00 a.m. six days a week for the 300-kilometre (186-mile) chug to Moosonee's only saltwater port, a journey of little more than five hours. Arriving at 2:20 p.m., you can choose to stay in Moosonee or the nearby Cree Village Ecolodge, or return to Cochrane the same day (departing at 5:00 p.m. and arriving at 10:20 p.m.), allowing views of the protracted northern latitude sunset. (The train from Cochrane back to Toronto leaves at 8:00 a.m.) As for polar bears, during the layover in Cochrane be sure to visit the residents of the Cochrane Polar Bear Habitat, the only captive polar bear facility in the world.❦
www.ontarionorthland.ca

2nd week of JUL

EVENTS & FESTIVALS

QUIRKY CANADA

▲

Yuk It Up at the Just for Laughs Festival

This international event is the laughingstock of the year. Montréal welcomes both big names and up-and-coming acts, so whether you've come to see a particular comedian at a ticketed indoor venue (in English or French), or simply want to wander the streets for a good laugh on the house, there's no funnier way to spend the summer.

Shows vary from multi-artist galas at Théâtre St-Denis to big marquee names like Bill Cosby at Place des Arts' Salle Wilfrid-Pelletier, but it's not entirely a stand-up comedy affair. There are also street concerts presenting on outdoor stages and performance artists mingling with the crowds for up-close interactive entertainment.

Many famous comedians are known to have jump-started their careers here at this festival. Heavy hitters such as Jerry Seinfeld, Tim Allen, and Dave Chappelle, as well as homegrown acts like Montréal's own Sugar Sammy, fill the city's venues with their hilarious talent.

After the city's acclaimed International Jazz Festival (see p. 150), this is Montréal's second-biggest festival, attracting crowds, talent, and bigwig scouts from all over the world. If you haven't been to Montréal in a while, you'll have to check out the new Place des Festivals where much of the action—and laughs— can be found.✤

www.hahaha.com

Get Comfortable at Wreck Beach Day

Nude, but not lewd, rude, or crude. That's the guiding principle at Wreck Beach, Canada's largest clothing-optional beach. Nestled beneath forested cliffs at the western edge of the University of British Columbia (UBC) campus, this 7.8-kilometre (4.8-mile) stretch of white sand interspersed with tidal rocks and logs is a mecca for sun-hungry naturists. Dare to bare in Vancouver? There's no better opportunity than Wreck Beach Day in the July heat.

Thousands clamber down Trail 6's 470+ steps to doff their duds and enjoy naked activities such as volleyball, kite-flying, sandcastle-making, body-painting, and such. Wreck Beach Day also promotes body acceptance, which seems astute, as many of the beach's most faithful visitors have been coming here since the popularity of nudism exploded in the 1970s.

Whenever you come, an ambience of carefree commerce prevails. You can purchase handmade jewellery, sarongs, or tie-dyed T-shirts. Getting a massage is always an option. Some vendors dish up organic fruit juices and buffalo burgers. Others stroll the beach with flip-flops and satchels, selling drinks (not necessarily alcohol-free) and other substances. If tempted to fully re-enact Haight-Ashbury's Summer of Love, be aware that police do patrol Wreck Beach periodically.✤

www.wreckbeach.org

Golf amidst the Rugged Beauty of the Canadian Shield

Golf, they say, is a good way to ruin a nice walk. But you'd have to shoot a few pretty terrible rounds not to enjoy walking the courses of the Muskoka region, Ontario's original playground of the rich and famous. The courses, some designed by the likes of Nick Faldo and Thomas McBroom, play with the rugged contours of the dramatic Canadian Shield. Forget sand traps; the hazards here are huge chunks of granite.

Courses in the region create a golfer's trail stretching from Gravenhurst to Huntsville.

Muskoka Bay was judged 2007 Best New Canadian golf course by no less an authority than *Golf Digest*; it features a 520.3-metre (569-yard) 12th hole that tees up between massive boulders. Deerhurst Highlands, credited with putting Muskoka on the golf world's radar, features a number of multi-level greens. Taboo Resort's 18 holes, dubbed the home course of Canadian champion Mike Weir, were designed by renowned golf course architect Ron Garl. Courses in the region create a golfer's trail stretching from Gravenhurst to Huntsville that encourages players to follow a linked series of courses.

Green fees for each course are in the range of C$150 for 18 holes. Tour provider Ultimate Golf Vacations offers multi-night packages that take in up to four resorts. ❖

www.muskokagolfcourses.com

It happened
THIS WEEK:

Stratford Festival Opens

"Now is the winter of our discontent/Made glorious by this sun of York," says Richard, Duke of Gloucester, who later becomes the title character of Shakespeare's *Richard III*.

The performance opened at the Stratford Festival on July 13, 1953. Sir Alec Guinness, the English-trained actor who went on to play Ben Obi-Wan Kenobi in the movie *Star Wars: Episode IV*, held the title role.

A comedy, *All's Well that Ends Well*, opened the following evening.

In the 1950s, journalist Tom Patterson championed establishing the theatre festival. Now, with more than 600 productions staged, the festival is a hallmark of Canadian theatre. Stratford operates an acting academy, training Canadian actors in classical techniques and holding nationwide auditions.

"The festival brings a much-needed boost to the profile of the Canadian dramatic scene," wrote the CBC about the festival opening.

Stratford shares its name with Stratford-upon-Avon, England—the birthplace of Shakespeare and where the Royal Shakespeare Company performs.

But a shared name and theatre traditions are not Stratford's only love affair with the bard. Once known as the "Little Thames," the town's tributary was renamed the Avon River in the 1830s.

The city's Shakespeare Hotel opened around the same time as the first sawmill and gristmill were built. The Stratford swans arrived in 1918, and the Shakespearean Gardens opened in 1936.

Paddle the Nahanni River

Run rapids and drift through breathtaking canyons on one of the world's greatest river trips

It's late July and the days are long in the Nahanni National Park Reserve. The sun takes a short snooze, disappearing in the wee hours of the morning. Then it's up again, casting a warm glow over paddlers on the fabled Nahanni River. At Virginia Falls, about twice the height of Niagara Falls, a rainbow slides down the frothing waters. From rugged mountain ranges and deep river canyons to rapids and spectacular plateaus, this UNESCO World Heritage Site has jaw-dropping scenery to keep you enthralled. Although Nahanni attracts fewer than 1,000 visitors a year, it's one of the most breathtaking river trips in the world. It has attracted everyone from paddling legend Bill Mason (who famously called this "the greatest river trip in the world") to Prince Andrew.

Paddling trips start from the gateway community of Fort Simpson. This Dene village of about 1,200 people is where Pope John Paul II made an historic visit in 1987. (The chair he sat in is still on display at the village's visitor centre.) Before climbing aboard a bush plane to get to where you'll start your downriver trip, get your camera ready. You'll need it to record some of the amazing views of the majestic Mackenzie mountain range and the stunning Ram Plateau as you fly over the park.

Anyone can do the trip down the Nahanni by whitewater raft, while moderately skilled paddlers can tackle it by canoe. River trips usually begin at one of two designated landing areas in the park. A paddling trip from Virginia Falls takes seven to 10 days; from Rabbitkettle Lake further upriver it takes 10 to 14 days. The section of the river from Rabbitkettle Lake to Virginia Falls is 118 kilometres (73 miles) long and does not have rapids. Paddlers then reach the roar of majestic Virginia Falls, punctuated by the striking Mason's Rock. Here, the river begins its passage through four stunningly deep canyons that dwarf you on both sides. Get used to it—these canyons stretch from eight kilometres (five miles) to as long as 40 kilometres (25 miles).

After the long portage around Virginia Falls, paddle through Fourth Canyon to Third Canyon and its 1,200-metre (3,937-foot) high walls. Enter the Second Canyon and travel past Headless Creek. Camp in the area of Deadmen Valley, where the bodies of Métis brothers and prospectors Willie and Frank McLeod were found in 1908 after they died mysteriously. The spectacular First Canyon boasts the highest canyon walls in the park. While large parts of the river are a comfortable Class I or Class II rapids, a number of Class III rapids await along the 147-kilometre (91-mile) stretch from Virginia Falls through Canyon Rapids, Figure 8 Rapids, and George's Riffle, to the sulphureous Kraus Hotsprings. These natural hot springs have a very comfortable temperature of

37 degrees Celsius (98.6 degrees Fahrenheit). Down-stream, the river branches off into a number of channels and the rushing whitewater is replaced with a series of placid channels.

The river winds its way through the Mackenzie Mountains, home to moose, woodland caribou, Dall sheep, wolves, mountain goats, grizzlies, and black bears. Ancestors of the Dene First Nation have lived and hunted in the area for thousands of years. Legends have long been told about the area, including the mysterious deaths of brothers Willie and Frank McLeod around 1908. In the late 1920s, gold prospector Albert Faille and adventurer R.M. Patterson travelled along the river, resulting in Patterson's bestselling *Dangerous River.* Then-Prime Minister Pierre Elliott Trudeau visited the Nahanni in 1970. He was so taken with it that Nahanni National Park Reserve was created in 1972, protecting it from possible hydroelectric development. In 1978, it became the first place in the world to be named a UNESCO World Heritage Site. In 1987, the South Nahanni River, well known as one of the top paddling destinations, was named a Canadian Heritage River. The park was expanded to six times its original size by federal legislation passed in 2009, to about 30,000 square kilometres (11,583 square miles), almost the size of Vancouver Island—making it the third-largest park in Canada.

Nahanni's recent expansion means there are opportunities to explore the park beyond paddling the river. The Cirque of the Unclimbables is located in the Ragged Range near Glacier Lake. In 1955, legendary mountaineer Arnold Wexler was frustrated by the sheer jagged, granite walls and named them the Cirque of the Unclimbables. The Lotus Flower Tower, which can only be tackled by serious climbers, was featured in the 1979 classic climbing book *Fifty Classic Climbs of North America.* This is a multi-day trip that only the most experienced trekkers can tackle. The spectacular Ram Plateau offers easier hiking for multi-day trips. This flat-topped dome rises from the Mackenzie Mountains and is covered with wildflowers. It also has dramatic canyons, caves, and clear springs to explore.

Nahanni has three licensed commercial outfitters operating in the park. Nahanni River Adventures (www.nahanni.com) offers canoeing, whitewater, and rafting trips for different skill levels. They also offer trips to Cirque of the Unclimbables and the Ram Plateau. Black Feather (www.blackfeather.com and www.nahanniriver.ca) has canoe trips for different skill levels and trips geared specifically to families or women only. They also offer hiking trips on the Ram Plateau. Nahanni Wilderness Adventures (www.nahanniwild.com) focuses on rafting and canoeing trips.

Find out more at:
www.pc.gc.ca/nahanni

ADVENTURE

Hike Up to an Alpine Club of Canada Backcountry Hut

For experienced and well-equipped backcountry enthusiasts, 28 huts scattered throughout the Canadian Rockies and adjacent mountain ranges are a wonderful alternative to basic, boring motel rooms. By the third week of July, even the loftiest of the huts is snow-free and open for business.

Many huts are very popular and book up well in advance.

Although the huts vary greatly in accessibility and facilities, they do share one common trait—an outdoor-loving clientele looking for adventures beyond the norm. Some make the huts their final destination, while mountaineers use them as a base for more serious expeditions. The easily accessible Arthur O. Wheeler Hut, in Glacier National Park, comes equipped with luxuries like propane cooking and heating, while the Elizabeth Parker Hut, in Yoho National Park, is so popular that beds are assigned annually by lottery. Also in Yoho, the comfortable Stanley Mitchell Hut is remote, but accessible in a day of relatively easy walking along the Takakkaw Falls–Little Yoho Valley. At the other end of the comfort scale, Sapphire Col Hut is a metal shelter perched on a rocky ridge high above the highway through Glacier National Park.

Many huts are very popular and book up well in advance, especially in summer. Plan ahead and make reservations as far ahead as possible through the Alpine Club of Canada.🍁

www.alpineclubofcanada.ca

◀ Relive Traditional Métis Life at Batoche National Historic Site

At the height of summer, with the fun and laughter of Back to Batoche Days in full swing, flowers blooming, and a warm afternoon breeze, it's hard to imagine the intensity of the conflict that took place at Batoche in 1885 when Métis leader Louis Riel led an ill-fated uprising against the Canadian government in protest of a loss of land and rights.

While Riel was eventually hanged for his role in the Northwest Rebellion, the village of Batoche escaped remarkably unscathed, and in 1923 the government stepped in to protect it as a national historic site. Today, the site is anchored by the whitewashed Saint-Antoine-de-Padoue Church, built one year before the rebellion.

Scattered around the church are restored homes and buildings, all staffed with costumed interpreters. Walking trails lead down to the river, past working farms.

Celebrated since 1970, Back to Batoche Days is a chance for the Métis Nation to celebrate its traditions, but also provides an opportunity for others to learn about Métis history and culture. Traditional music, a bannock-baking competition, and events such as log carries and slingshot provide a window to the past, while child-friendly exhibits such as a petting zoo and arts and crafts tables ensure all ages are kept busy.✦
www.pc.gc.ca/batoche

NATURE'S GRANDEUR

Take a Boat Tour of Western Brook Pond ▶

Summer is short but sweet in Gros Morne National Park on Newfoundland's west coast, where the ancient world heaved—forming richly diverse landscapes, including landlocked, glacially carved fiords charmingly known locally as "ponds." Of all the ponds, none is more spectacular than Western Brook—whose rugged beauty is best appreciated by scenic cruise.

Most park visitors base themselves at Rocky Harbour. From there it's a 15-minute drive along a scenic stretch of coast-hugging highway to a nondescript parking lot. Rather than simply jumping aboard a boat, the adventure begins with a three-kilometre (1.8-mile) hike through a delicate coastal plain, crossing boardwalks and passing over low ridges to a dock. (Watch for moose along the way!) After a few minutes of cruising, an unbelievable geological panorama opens up in front of you, with sheer cliffs of billion-year-old rock rising 700 metres (2,300 feet) to the flattened summits of the Long Range Mountains.

Adding to the spectacle are the towering waterfalls that plummet from far above.

The boat cruises are operated by Bontours; the ticket office is at the Ocean View Motel in Rocky Harbour. In July, tours fill up well in advance, so don't head out to the dock without a reservation.✦
www.pc.gc.ca/grosmorne, www.bontours.ca

EVENTS & FESTIVALS

QUIRKY CANADA

Kick Up Your Heels at the Craven Country Jamboree

A short drive from Regina, the picturesque Qu'Appelle Valley comes alive each July for the Craven Country Jamboree, which has a well-earned reputation for attracting some of the biggest names in country music—along with more than 20,000 fans each day.

Since the first Saskatchewan festival kicked off in the mid-1980s with Roy Orbison strutting onto the outdoor stage, fans have been treated to performances by the biggest superstars of the day—John Denver, Willie Nelson, Garth Brooks, Kenny Rogers, Reba McEntire, and George Strait, while in recent years, the stage has been graced by the likes of Tim McGraw, Brad Paisley, Kenny Chesney, Big and Rich, Sugarland, and Rascal Flatts.

Away from the main stage is Main Street, a temporary arrangement set up as a western town. There's a stage for up-and-coming acts, bull-riding demonstrations, a beer garden with a large dance floor, plenty of food vendors, and a place for cowboy church services. For families the jamboree's surprisingly appealing, with a number of children's activities, karaoke, and even songwriting lessons. Most festival-goers set themselves up in the sprawling campground across the Qu'Appelle River from the Main Stage, choosing from among 8,000 sites that provide a mix of reserved, family, and free camping. ❧
www.cravencountryjamboree.com

Gape at Sand Sculpture Masterpieces in Parksville

Hockey fanatics know Parksville as the retirement home of gravel-voiced former hockey TV commentator Howie Meeker. It's also a year-round golf mecca. But each July, a very different sport steals the spotlight in this idyllic beachfront community on Vancouver Island's east coast. The Canadian Open Sand Sculpting Competition & Exhibition attracts tens of thousands of onlookers over one month—close to 100,000 in 2010. Entry is by donation. The best time to come to scenic Community Beach is at the competition's start, when Canadian and American competitors are actually completing their whimsical creations.

Turret-laden castles, sleeping bears, giant poppies … seemingly these sculptures are only limited by the imaginations of the solo artists and teams, and the ticking clock. Competitors get 24 hours of work time over three days, and a diluted glue is sprayed over the finished product to avert potential wind or rain damage. Leave your dogs at home—runaway bowsers are deemed likely to bash into sculptures—but do bring your camera. After all, spectacular snapshots and memories of your kids frolicking on the beach will probably mean more to you afterwards than, say, who advances to the World Championship of Sand Sculpting in Federal Way, Washington. ❧
www.parksvillebeachfest.ca

Enjoy a Beautiful Picnic Lunch alongside a Lighthouse with Ocean Views

Exactly as the name suggests, Lighthouse Picnics supplies picnic-filled baskets from a lighthouse—but the experience is much more than that. Set on a lofty headland beyond the historic Newfoundland village of Ferryland, the setting, food, scenery, and warm sea breeze of late July combine to make this a meal like no other.

The setting, food, scenery, and warm sea breeze of late July combine to make this a meal like no other.

From charming Ferryland, an hour's drive south along the coast from St. John's, walk past the excavations of a 1620s settlement, then follow a well-worn path leading towards the ocean. The 15-minute trail passes along an isthmus and then climbs to a postcard-perfect 1870 red-and-white lighthouse. Here you can order food as simple as freshly baked muffins, or a full picnic lunch that may include specialty cheeses, fish cakes, pepper and mint salad, freshly baked oatmeal bread smothered in molasses, or a sandwich stacked high with locally harvested coldwater shrimp. To round out your lunch, add a generous slab of rhubarb upside-down cake to your order. Picnic baskets—and blankets—are supplied. After placing your order, find a grassy spot on the headland (or request a flag, find a picnic spot, and staff will deliver your order). There, enjoy your gourmet goodies while taking in ocean views that may, if you're lucky, include whales. 🍁

www.lighthousepicnics.ca

Tanya Tagaq's _favourite_ PLACE

Although it's a long journey, throat singer Tanya Tagaq urges others to experience Pond Inlet, a hamlet on the northern edge of Baffin Island, Nunavut.

"[It's] mountainous and stark in that way only Nunavut can be," says the Inuit throat singer and artist. "It's not just one of my favourite places in Canada, it's one of my favourite places in the world."

Tagaq visited Sirmilik National Park as part of a project to express wild places sonically.

"I went in late May, early June and it was astounding. But apparently in July and August . . . after the sea ice leaves, it's the most scenic."

They camped, hiked, and hunted in the region, which is above the treeline. The locals, she says, eat a marine-based diet and hunt bears, narwhals, caribou, and seals.

Hoodoos in the park are stunning formations. Whipped by wind and water, the sandstone pillars tower in a region of the park called the Borden Peninsula. Calling them huge and stories-high, Tagaq recalls a fellow visitor saying the erosion-formed spires were old buildings. She laughs warmly at the thought of an ancient civilization building the hoodoos.

"It's okay to credit nature sometimes," says the artist.

And nature is the true delight of a visit to Pond Inlet, where the tundra and a treeless horizon are characteristic of the North.

"It reminded me of how I felt at home," Tagaq says, speaking of Cambridge Bay, Nunavut, where she grew up. "You draw strength from the land, draw strength from the light."

Play amidst the World's Highest Tides

There's no limit to how you can explore this extraordinary natural wonder

Imagine a coastal area where tidewaters rise and fall the height of a four-story building every six hours and 13 minutes. It happens in New Brunswick, and it's why the Bay of Fundy was named a finalist in a worldwide contest to determine the "New Seven Wonders of Nature."

Constantly changing, the bay and its coastal regions provide huge opportunities for discovery and adventure—especially at the height of summer when interpretive sites, museums, adventure tour companies, and attractions are all in full swing.

Tides here are five to 10 times higher than anywhere else in the world because of the funnel-like narrowing of the bay. This tidal power allows one to kayak around tiny islands in the morning, then walk around the base of these same pillars of rock, 50 feet below—on the ocean floor— just hours later. This phenomenon creates a playground for adventure-seekers, inspiration for artists and photographers, a laboratory for the scientifically minded, discovery for fossil or semi-precious stone hunters, and a window to marine life for nature lovers.

The bay's shoreline starts at Campobello Island and goes north, across the New Brunswick-Nova Scotia border, and back south to the tip of Brier Island. This 140-kilometre (87-mile) long body of water, with 1,200 kilometres (745.6 miles) of coastline, has been called the Amazon rainforest of marine biodiversity. It's home to at least 12 species of whales, and a critical feeding ground for millions of migratory shorebirds on their annual trek from the Arctic to South America.

Midsummer visitors may well see flocks of 100,000 shorebirds feeding in the low-tide mud in the upper bay—around Mary's Point and the Hopewell area (on the New Brunswick side), and on Evangeline Beach (near Grand Pré, Nova Scotia). This is also a great time for whale-watching and wildlife tours.

Horizontal tides occur in flat areas where waters spread out, rather than rushing into narrow areas, creating walls of water. As tides recede they reveal vast areas of mud flats and beaches, sea caves, and sculpted cliffs, sea stacks, and flowerpots. One of the most popular places to experience horizontal tides is the easy-to-get-to Hopewell Rocks, N.B. The site is considered one of Canada's top attractions because of the first-rate interpretation programs and infrastructure. The key to enjoying Hopewell to the fullest is to check the low tide times during your visit; some days low tide may occur outside operating hours,

so call or check the Hopewell Rocks website. Admission covers two days, ensuring you get both a high- and low-tide experience.

The tides provide a myriad of adventure and recreation opportunities all around the Bay of Fundy. Sea kayaking is available at a number of spots along the bay (Hopewell, Grand Manan Island, Alma, St. Martins, Saint John, Deer Island, or Cape Chignecto Provincial Park, N.S.). Exploring the dramatic coastline as the current gently pulls or pushes your kayak is a great way to get up close to the abundant aquatic and bird life. At low tide you'll see boats tipped to one side as they lie in the mud, fishing weirs revealed (wharves high above)—all reminders of the might of the tides.

Thrill-seekers jet boat the Reversing Rapids, a set of whirlpools, waves, and whitewater rapids created as high tides collide with the St. John River in a rocky gorge in Saint John, N.B. Across the Bay in Shubenacadie, N.S., river rafters get their adrenaline fix by using powered Zodiacs to ride the tidal bore (a wall of water) and ensuing tidal rapids. At Cape Enrage, N.B., you can rappel down 40-metre (140- foot) natural cliffs (see p. 146). Or, if you prefer to keep your feet on the ground, hike to sea caves for an intriguing exploration through the chambers left by receding waters near Hillsborough or St. Martins, N.B.

Hikers from all over the world come for the Fundy Trail and Fundy National Park, Cape Chignecto Provincial Park, and Cape D'Or. There are hundreds of walking trails around the bay. Avid hikers gravitate towards the Fundy Circuit in Fundy National Park, a 45-kilometre (28-mile) network of linked trails that takes several days to complete. The less ambitious will enjoy the Digby Admiral Walk around the waterfront of the historic town or roaming the boardwalks at the Sackville Waterfowl Park.

On Grand Manan Island, campers have the option of tent camping along a stretch of rock cliff that descends to the wild ocean below. Incredible sunsets lead to nights filled with whale songs, brilliant stars, and constellations.

Seeking something less physical? Tour lighthouse sites such as Cape Forchu Lightstation (Yarmouth, N.S.) or Southwest Head (Grand Manan, N.B.), eat at lightkeepers' homes at Cape Enrage, N.B., or Cape D'Or, N.S.; enjoy theatre aboard the dry-docked ferry, the Kipawo, in Parrsboro, N.S., or buy freshly cooked lobster from the markets in Alma, N.B., to eat right on the beach. The key: follow your passions. The list of really-neat-things-to-do here is long.🍁

Find out more at:
www.bayoffundytourism.com

Peer into the Crystal-Clear Waters of Canada's First National Marine Conservation Area

With more than 20 historical and natural features of startling beauty, Canada's first National Marine Conservation Area is considered one of the world's best freshwater dive sites for scuba enthusiasts and amateur snorkellers alike.

The absence of plankton (unusual for the Great Lakes) allows for crystal-clear waters, making it much easier to see the park's underwater treasures—even from a boat. Below the surface, divers have an amazing range of wrecks and terrain to explore: the appropriately named W.L. Wetmore, a 61-metre (200-foot) steamer that sank in 1901, sits in 8.5 metres (28 feet) of water. More advanced divers can see the 39.6-metre (130-foot) Arabia, a barque that went down in 1884 and now rests 33.5 metres (110 feet) down. There are also numerous caves, grottoes, overhangs, and submerged cliffs carved out by the passage of glaciers.

When diving below 30 feet (five fathoms), the water temperature plummets, so a diving suit with hood, gloves, and boots is necessary; the nearby town of Tobermory has several good rental shops.

If you'd rather keep out of the water entirely, a popular option is the two-hour, glass-bottomed boat tour. It takes in several lighthouses and some 20 islands, including the aptly named limestone wonder Flowerpot Island, which boasts excellent hiking trails and caves to explore. ◆
www.parkscanada.ca/fathomfive

5 faves

Set sail on the Bluenose

The Bluenose—the majestic schooner that graces Canadian 10-cent pieces—became Canada's most storied ship because of its exceptional speed. In summer, you can set sail on the Bluenose II replica (the original Bluenose sank in 1942), when it alternates ports between Halifax and Lunenburg, the small Nova Scotia town where it was built.

◀ Learn Traditional Craftwork at the Great Northern Arts Festival

A Métis artist sits at a table and explains how to make a traditional Dene rawhide drum as a group of workshop participants listen intently. Then, they pick up their tools and get to work. Every July since 1989, artists and performers from across the North converge on Inuvik in the Beaufort Delta for the 10-day Great Northern Arts Festival. Inuit, Inuvialuit, Gwich'in, Dene, Métis, and non-Aboriginal artists come to show their work, meet other artists, and learn new skills.

In addition to giving demonstrations of their craft, artists also sell their work. The event also includes performances by northern musicians, a fashion show featuring Arctic clothing, screenings of northern films, storytelling, and a traditional dance.

But a highlight is the workshops artists offer to the public. Lasting from two to eight hours long, they allow participants to try their hand at traditional arts and contemporary crafts, such as willow basket making, throat singing, carving, painting, jewellery making, and beading. It's an opportunity for artists and performers to share a piece of northern culture and pass on their knowledge. At the end of the day, participants leave the festival clutching a piece of northern art they had a chance to make themselves. ❧

www.gnaf.org

Fly Over the Glaciers of Kluane National Park

You don't need to be a hardened Arctic adventurer to see spectacular glaciers. The Yukon's Kluane National Park and Reserve has the largest non-polar icefield in the world and some of the world's longest and most spectacular glaciers. Getting there just requires a ticket.

Kluane became a national park in 1993 and covers 21,980 square kilometres (8,487 square miles) of rugged mountains, wide icefields, and lush valleys. About 4,000 Dall sheep live amidst this landscape of rock, ice, and snow, also a UNESCO World Heritage Site.

Climb aboard a Cessna 205 with three others at the small Haines Junction airport, 150 kilometres (93 miles) west of Whitehorse along the Alaska Highway. Moments later, you're soaring over Kluane's verdant and then icy landscape. The bright blue Alsek River runs amidst the rocky peaks. Ice blankets a bowl-shaped canyon.

You're in luck. The top of Mount Logan—Canada's highest peak, at 5,959 metres (19,551 feet)—is poking out amidst the clouds. Then the small plane heads for the icefields. The 65-kilometre (40-mile) long Lowell Glacier appears, carpeting the ground as it meanders between mountain ranges until it empties into the Alsek.

Tours last from 40 minutes to two hours, depending on how much of the park you want to see, with prices ranging from a little over C$100 to more than C$300. ❧

www.yukonairtours.com
www.ontarionorthland.ca

Cape St. Mary's Ecological Reserve

This exceptional habitat is nirvana for bird lovers, and spectacular even if you're not one. The reserve protects the breeding ground of 24,000 northern gannets, 20,000 common mures, and 20,000 black-legged kittiwakes. There is also a 100-metre (328-foot) high sandstone sea stack separated from the mainland by only a few metres.

Toronto Pride Parade

Celebrating Toronto's gay and lesbian community, Pride Week features events, performances, symposia, and parties. It culminates in an extravagant Sunday parade—one of the biggest in North America—with flamboyant costumes, music, and hundreds of thousands of spectators.

Drive the Cowboy Trail

Alberta's famed Cowboy Trail skirts the eastern edge of the Rockies, through rolling foothills and not much else. But that's its charm . . . hills upon hills, rolling gently towards mountains that seem close enough to touch.

Paddle the north shore of Superior

This is one of the best places for kayakers in all of Ontario, where the wild waters of Lake Superior meet the rugged rocks and limitless forests along the shoreline. Lake Superior Provincial Park is a great starting point, with dramatic rock formations like the Devil's Chair, and landscapes that show up in several paintings by members of the Group of Seven.

EVENTS & FESTIVALS

Marvel at Fireworks in English Bay

From the 1986 World's Fair (EXPO '86) to the 2010 Olympic and Paralympic Winter Games, Vancouver has witnessed many dazzling fireworks displays. But if you want to experience a true summer tradition for locals, head to English Bay—in downtown's West End—spread out a beach blanket, and join the 400,000 other spectators gasping and applauding at the Celebration of Light competition.

The free, annual, multi-night event is usually staged on Wednesdays and Saturdays, pitting international fireworks teams from as far away as China, South Africa, and Spain against one another. Who'll pull off the most impressive mix of exploding Catherine wheels, Roman candles, and waterfalls from a barge moored within eyeshot of the palm trees at the intersection of Denman and Davie streets?

Everything's set to music, from the *Star Wars* theme to Queen's "Bohemian Rhapsody," and many onlookers bring radios playing the simulcast on Classic Rock 101 FM.

Waterfront restaurants with patios do a roaring trade, so reserve your table well in advance.

Waterfront restaurants with patios do a roaring trade, so reserve your table well in advance. A few other things to note: do leave your car behind as the West End's closed to traffic. Police confiscate liquor rigorously. For alternative viewing points, try Vanier Park or Kitsilano Beach across the water.❦

www.vancouverfireworks.ca

Bring Your Blue Suede Shoes to Collingwood's Elvis Festival

Ever since Elvis left us, he's found a new place to dwell . . . would you believe it's in the town of Collingwood at the world's largest Elvis festival?

But you don't have to be an Elvis fan to enjoy this exercise in pagan idolatry. For four days and long nights in this Georgian Bay community, the King comes alive in every incarnation—from jailhouse rocker, to GI Joe, to Blue Hawaii. The standards are very high: preliminary competitions weed out the not-so-great pretenders. Thursday night is the First Hurrah pub crawl, Friday night is the street dance (the main street's closed, making way for a giant stage where both competitors and non-competitors are invited onstage). The local arena is transformed into a concert venue with paid shows throughout the weekend featuring the world's top Elvis impersonators recreating keystone concert experiences. Sunday brings the invitation-only gospel competition.

The immersion in all things Elvis doesn't stop at the gold lamé jumpsuit and quivering falsettos. Local restaurants have signed on to provide the King's favourite soul food—including deep-fried peanut butter and banana sandwiches. If you can feel your hips starting to shake you've got till the end of May to register. Amateurs have been known to find themselves singing "Love Me Tender" at 3:00 a.m. at the local Tim Horton's.🍁
www.collingwoodelvisfestival.com

Play a Round at the Iconic Banff Springs Golf Course ▼

By late July, the hallowed fairways and greens of the Banff Springs Golf Course are in perfect condition. This, one of the world's best-known courses, remains a sanctuary for the privileged few who are members of the local golf club and for travelling golfers fortunate enough to experience the combination of natural beauty and tradition provided at the Banff Springs Golf Course.

When it opened in 1928, the Banff Springs Golf Course was the most expensive ever built, with famed architect Stanley Thompson demonstrating perfectly his appreciation of traditional links golf while emphasizing the subtleties of the mountain landscape. Since then, trees have matured, longer tee boxes have been added, and the rotation has changed, but the layout remains a diligent custodian of the architect's timeless design. No hole is more iconic than the Devil's Cauldron, a short Par 3 over a glacial lake nestled below the impossibly steep face of Mount Rundle that's one of the most famously scenic holes in the golf world. Adding to the appeal is an abundance of wildlife. Most famously, herds of 100 or more elk congregate on the course beginning in mid-summer, while bears, coyotes, deer, and Canada geese are all commonly sighted by golfers.🍁
www.fairmont.com/banffsprings/ Recreation/Golf

Your next STEP

TOP PICKS

ADVENTURE

CULTURE & HISTORY

NATURE'S GRANDEUR

EVENTS & FESTIVALS

QUIRKY CANADA

REJUVENATE

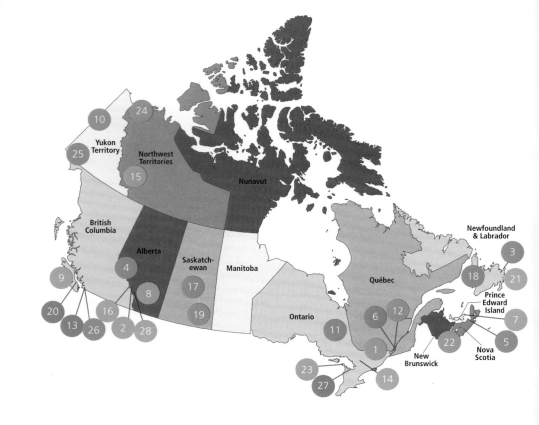

WEEK 1

1 — OTTAWA, ONT.
Canada Day in the capital
www.canadascapital.gc.ca

2 — LAKE LOUISE, ALTA.
Skoki Lodge
www.skoki.com

3 — TRINITY, NFLD.
Newfoundland theatre
www.risingtidetheatre.com

4 — JASPER, ALTA.
Maligne Lake
www.malignelake.com

5 — ANTIGONISH, N.S.
Antigonish Highland Games
www.antigonishhighlandgames.ca

6 — MONTRÉAL, QUE.
Big Orange Julep
www.orangejulep.com

7 — SOURIS, P.E.I.
Village Feast
www.ekpei.ca/VF.html

WEEK 2

8 — CALGARY, ALTA.
Calgary Stampede
www.calgarystampede.com

9 — TOFINO, B.C.
Clayoquot Sound
www.oceankayaking.com

10 — DAWSON CITY, Y.T.
Gold rush history
www.dawsoncity.ca

11 — COCHRANE, ONT.
Train journey to James Bay
www.ontarionorthland.ca

12 — MONTRÉAL, QUE.
Just for Laughs Festival
www.hahaha.com

13 — VANCOUVER, B.C.
Wreck Beach Day nudity
www.wreckbeach.org

14 — LAKE MUSKOKA, ONT.
Canadian shield golfing
www.muskokagolfcourses.com

WEEK 3

15 — NAHANNI NATIONAL PARK,
N.W.T.
Nahanni River paddling
www.pc.gc.ca/nahanni

16 — YOHO NATIONAL PARK, B.C.
Alpine Club of Canada huts
www.alpineclubofcanada.ca

17 — BATOCHE, SASK.
Back to Batoche Days
www.pc.gc.ca/batoche

18 — GROS MORNE NATIONAL PARK,
NFLD.
Boat tour of Western Brook Pond
www.pc.gc.ca/grosmorne

19 — QU'APPELLE, SASK.
Craven Country Jamboree
www.cravencountryjamboree.com

20 — PARKSVILLE, B.C.
Sand sculpting competition
www.parksvillebeachfest.ca

21 — FERRYLAND, NFLD.
Picnicking by a lighthouse
www.lighthousepicnics.ca

WEEK 4

22 — BAY OF FUNDY, N.B.
World's highest tides
www.bayoffundytourism.com

23 — TOBERMORY, ONT.
Great Lakes diving
www.parkscanada.ca/fathomfive

24 — INUVIK, N.W.T.
Great Northern Arts Festival
www.gnaf.org

25 — KLUANE NATIONAL PARK, Y.T.
Glacier tours by airplane
www.yukonairtours.com

26 — VANCOUVER, B.C.
English Bay fireworks
www.vancouverfireworks.ca

27 — COLLINGWOOD, ONT.
Elvis Festival
www.collingwoodelvisfestival.com

28 — BANFF, ALTA.
Banff Springs Golf Course
www.fairmont.com/banffsprings/
Recreation/Golf

AUGUST

Join the Week-Long Party Surrounding the Royal St. John's Regatta

Historic races and a crackling bar scene bring out tens of thousands on Canada's only weather-dependent civic holiday

North America's oldest organized sporting event began in 1816 when visiting ship crews challenged each other to rowing races across St. John's Harbour. Today, the races have grown into the Royal St. John's Regatta—a one-of-a-kind, day-long competition that's the highlight of a bacchanalian week of downtown drinking and dancing best known as the George Street Festival.

Now held east of downtown at Quidi Vidi Lake on the first Wednesday of every August, the rowing contest has morphed into a world-class event drawing competitors from around the world. Attracting up to 40,000 spectators, the regatta's so popular the city long ago declared the day a civic holiday—not to mention one nearly guaranteed to have good weather. If you wake up on the Wednesday and it looks windy or wet outside, turn on the radio or TV: you'll find out whether the city has decided to postpone the holiday (and the regatta) in

It is said St. John's has more pubs, taverns, and bars per capita than anyplace else in Canada.

favour of the following day, when the forecast may be better. Races are also unique in the rarefied world of rowing in that they start and finish at the same point, forcing the seven-person crews to manoeuvre their boats around a series of buoys at the far end of the lake for an exciting sprint to the finish. Adding to the appeal, for competitors, is the fact that boats have been built to the same specifications for more than a century—allowing the tight-knit rowing community to compete not only against the times of other teams but also of the sport's forefathers.

Besides the thrill of competition, spectators at lovely Quidi Vidi Lake will find a country-fair atmosphere with free entertainment, games of chance, food stalls (think homemade Newfoundland ice cream), and even rides for the kids. The lake is just a short drive from downtown, and the crowds spill over to nearby Quidi Vidi Village—a famously photogenic fishing village complete with winding streets and simple century-old residences, some accessible only by water.

It is said St. John's has more pubs, taverns, and bars per capita than anyplace else in Canada, but the capital's reputation

as a party city reaches an entire new level during the George Street Festival. With most of the action focused on a one-block stretch of George Street, watering holes here perform double duty as venues for live music of all kinds—traditional Newfoundland, folk, Irish, country, rock, and jazz. More of a party than a festival, the gathering sees thousands of people descending on the city's main entertainment precinct to listen to bands who hail from across the country—with the action continuing into the wee hours of every morning. No band is more iconic than fan-favourite Great Big Sea, which combines modern rock and traditional Newfoundland folk to create a sound and atmosphere that's unequalled in local popularity. One of George Street's mainstays is Trapper John's Museum N' Pub, usually packed to the rafters throughout the festival. If you manage to squeeze your way through the crowd to the bar, fellow patrons will gladly initiate out-of-town visitors with a traditional "screech-in" ceremony: this is where you have the chance to become an honourary Newfoundlander once you seal your pledge by kissing a fish on the mouth and downing a shot of "screech" (a Newfoundland rum). If you want to escape the frat-house atmosphere of George Street, pull up a barstool at nearby Nautical Nellies or the highly refined Crow's Nest, which opened during World War II as a private retreat for naval officers.

The city itself is wonderful to explore. Although charming, the layout of downtown defies modern logic. The streets follow footpaths laid out 200 years ago, when towns were not planned but simply evolved, with stone staircases climbing grades too steep for paved roads. Contrasts of colour are everywhere— windows may be framed in deep turquoise, red, or bright yellow; window boxes are stuffed to the point of overflowing with bright geraniums and petunias; along the streets, any blank surface serves as an excuse for a pastel-painted mural. Most official attractions revolve around the city's long and vibrant history, highlighted by the spectacular edifice known as The Rooms, combining the provincial museum, art gallery, and archives under one roof. Styled on the simple oceanfront "fishing rooms" where Newfoundlanders would process their catch, this complex is anything but basic, rising high above the historic skyline like a mirage. The best city views are from Signal Hill National Historic Site, with its 360-degree panorama extending across the harbour, downtown, and out across the Atlantic Ocean.❦

Find out more at:
www.stjohns.ca,
www.stjohnsregatta.org

ADVENTURE

Hike the Legendary West Coast Trail

The West Coast Trail is almost too famous for its own good. Between May and September each year, about 6,000 people hike this rugged, amazingly beautiful 75-kilometre (45-mile) route between Bamfield and Port Renfrew on the west coast of Vancouver Island. It's arguably Canada's top multi-day backpacking trip, and one of the best in the world.

Some days, you'll ascend steep wooden trail ladders in dense forests of cedar and spruce—the systems of ladders sometimes reaching 50 stories high—and traverse creaking suspension bridges. Other times, you'll be wading through muddy bogs, clambering over slippery boulders, or checking out the sites of former shipwrecks. This can be treacherous terrain, so you'll move more slowly than you're used to—most people take about seven days to complete the trek. Stop to admire hypnotic waterfalls like Tsusiat Falls, a popular camping and swimming spot. You'll also discover anemones and mussels in tidal pools, and might even catch whales spouting or seals sunning themselves.

Parks Canada limits the number of hikers setting off daily to 52. Pay your trail fee (around C$150), which includes a guaranteed start time, map, and hiking guide; you should book at least three months in advance, by credit card. Attempt the trail only if you're in good shape, travel in a group for safety. It's an adventure in every sense of the word.❧
www.westcoasttrailbc.com

CULTURE & HISTORY

Take a Walk Through Mennonite History

In 1874, 18 Russian Mennonite families arrived in Canada and headed west on ox carts to present-day Manitoba. Here they established a settlement known as Steinbach, named after a village in their homeland. Today, Mennonite traditions live on during Pioneer Days, celebrated throughout Steinbach and at the nearby Mennonite Heritage Village.

Pioneer Days do an exceptional job of bringing Mennonite culture to life, with visitors travelling from afar to join in four action-packed days. Horse shows, threshing and milling demonstrations, live concerts and theatre, and a lively main street parade are the most appealing highlights. While enjoying Pioneer Days, be sure to allot a few hours to fully explore the Mennonite Heritage Village, which sprawls over 15 hectares (38 acres) at the north edge of town. Wander down the recreated Main Street, moving from one era to the next, taking time to chat with interpreters, and stopping by operating businesses such as the General Store.

Feeling hungry? Head to the Livery Barn Restaurant for a hearty meal of traditional Mennonite specialties. Choose between *foarma worscht* (handmade pork sausages) or *vereniki* (boiled dough filled with cream cheese), and try to save room for a slab of melt-in-your-mouth rhubarb pie.❧
www.mennoniteheritagevillage.com

Catch the Big One at the West Coast Fishing Club

Ever dreamed of grinning for the camera with an 18.1 kilogram (40-pound) chinook salmon you just caught on the open Pacific Ocean? That dream can easily become reality at the West Coast Fishing Club, arguably Canada's top fly-in sport fishing option. Its luxurious Clubhouse is located on remote Langara Island in the mystically green-and-blue Haida Gwaii archipelago (formerly the Queen Charlotte Islands), a two-hour trip north of Vancouver by plane and helicopter. August is prime time for trophy anglers.

Exploring pristine waters in Boston Whaler Guardian guide boats to reel in salmon, halibut, and blue shark is only half the story here. You can also spot humpback and orca whales, plus sea lions and deer. Visit an ancient Native village on nearby Graham Island to see Haida totem poles.

From local shellfish to steak, cuisine is a priority here.

Want a taste of modern civilization? In the 3,250-square-metre (35,000-square-foot) Clubhouse, enjoy well-appointed suites with en suite bathrooms and superb rainforest and ocean views. Play poker or watch a 60-inch flatscreen TV in the Aries Lounge, or get a massage at the on-site spa.

From local shellfish to steak, cuisine is a priority here. During the 2010 Winter Games, Clubhouse chef Ryan Stone dished up meals for world leaders at BC Place Stadium—site of the opening and closing ceremonies. Celebrity chefs like David Hawksworth and Jamie Kennedy also occasionally make cameos at the Clubhouse.🍁

www.westcoastfishingclub.com

Chantal Petitclerc's
favourite PLACE

Chantal Petitclerc describes a place with "half-salted water," sea kayaking, and delectable chocolate muffins that's only about five hours from Montréal—it's the region around Québec's Parc national du Bic.

"This is where the St. Lawrence River starts to open wide," says the Paralympic athlete. "I love the fact that it is still in Québec and yet, you really feel like the air smells like the ocean."

The multiple gold-winning medallist enjoys sea kayaking on a lake in the park.

"The waters are not too rough," says Petitclerc, reached between racing events and speaking engagements. "[We] watch the sunrise and, when we are lucky, we get to watch seals and even whales."

Beyond kayaking, the park also has biking routes, campgrounds, and—in winter—snowshoeing trails. Petitclerc, a Companion of the Order of Canada, calls it "nature at its best."

But the region isn't limited to outdoor activities. The Québec-born athlete also recommends the local comforts.

"We always stay at Auberge du Mange Grenouille," she says. "[It's] an old general store turned into a great, luxurious B&B.

"The owners take great care of the gardens, and all the little details. We love to just have a drink there and read a book. The Auberge has one of the best tables of the region with its own sommelier."

En route, Petitclerc recommends dropping by Marché des 3 Fumoirs in L'Isle-Verte. The smokehouse stocks salmon, sturgeon, mackerel, and more.

Her list of treats continues, "We never leave without a stop at the bakery Folles Farines," Petitclerc says. "They have the best bread and most decadent chocolate muffins."

EVENTS & FESTIVALS

Dance in the Streets at Toronto's Caribbean Carnival

The massive influence of Caribbean culture on Toronto is on colourful display at this three-week-long party, formerly known as Caribana, that culminates with the Grand Parade on the Saturday of the August long weekend. Over one million participants—from steel pan bands to soca, calypso, and reggae performers, and miles of elaborately decorated floats—make this the largest event of its kind in North America.

Kicking off at 10:00 a.m., the 4.5-kilometre (2.8-mile) parade along Toronto's Lakeshore Boulevard is a riot of flesh and colour set to the vibrant rhythms of 10,000 masqueraders and their accompanying bands. While most viewers choose to march along with the show, you can also watch from a comfortable seat at Exhibition Place. Given that the whole thing takes between four and six hours to pass, that may be too long to sit without getting up and dancing yourself. More than 30 themed musical events take place just on parade weekend! If you want a sneak peak of Saturday's coming attractions, catch the King & Queen Show at Lamport Stadium the Thursday night before the parade. But once that monster parade starts moving, grab a rum punch—but don't even think about driving.🍁

www.torontocaribbeancarnival.com

Live the Viking Life at the Icelandic Festival of Manitoba ▼

The town of Gimli, 100 kilometres (62 miles) north of Winnipeg, is part of an area known as New Iceland—home to the largest concentration of Icelandic people outside of Iceland. One weekend a year the town goes all out to pay homage to its Icelandic and Viking roots and culture (shields and battle-axes included).

The festival (known as the Islendingadagurinn in Icelandic) is one of the longest-running ethnic festivals in North America, with the current event an incarnation of an 1890 gathering in Winnipeg that began with a small street parade of Icelandic people in traditional costume. The festival is always held on the first weekend of August, coinciding with the date that Iceland accepted a new constitution (also a convenient break for the many local Icelandic farmers, as seeding has been completed, but harvesting has yet to begin). The packed schedule includes a pancake breakfast, arts and crafts, beach volleyball, shot put, a sandcastle competition, a Viking encampment, a demonstration of Viking warfare tactics, a midway, live music, and fireworks over the lake. A longtime festival tradition is the crowning of Fjallkona ("woman of the mountain"), who is chosen as an ideal candidate to represent the community's ties to Iceland. Dressed in a traditional green robe with a gold belt, a white veil, and a crown, the Fjallkona is easily spotted at festival events throughout the town. 🍁
www.icelandicfestival.com

Visit "Canada's Chocolate Town"

If Willy Wonka was Canadian, there's a good chance he'd have taken up residence in St. Stephen, New Brunswick, where they celebrate the world's most popular sweet treat and Canada's oldest candy company—Ganong Bros. Limited. Officially registered as "Canada's Chocolate Town," St. Stephen, a border community on the St. Croix River, has a full week of cacao-inspired activities at its annual Chocolate Festival.

As festival mascots, the Chocolate Mousse, his lovely wife Tiffany, and their adopted baby Teddy help celebrate both the most rich and delicious candy—and the Ganong brothers who began creating chocolates in 1873, a calling continued by their descendants to this day. In the brothers' honour, the first week of August is "choc-full" of concerts, activities, contests, fun, and of course, all things chocolate. Chocolate-influenced meals of all kinds take centre stage and include lunches, brunches, teas, and decadent dinners, followed by chocolate-themed dessert buffets—satisfying even those with the most ardent sweet tooth. Try your hand at dipping candy and nut centres into warm chocolate. (Licking your fingers afterwards is a must!) You can also enter the taste-test contest to find out how well you know your ice cream. And don't forget to bring the rest of the family, as there are competitions and games galore at Chocolate Mania.

The Ganong Bros. old factory is still in use as a shop ("The Chocolatier"). There's also an interactive Chocolate Museum and Discovery Centre where you can take a break from noshing and learn more about all things chocolate. 🍁
www.chocolate-fest.ca

See the Full Majesty of the Night Sky

One of nature's greatest shows is best seen at Canada's world-leading Dark Sky Preserves

One of the most spectacular shows on earth happens almost every night, is free, and is available to anyone who wants to see it. Sadly, the majority of Canadians never do. The show, courtesy of Mother Nature, begins when the sun sets and runs until sun-up the next morning, showcasing the celestial wonder that is the night sky. Constellations, the Milky Way, even satellites passing overhead, create magic that's simply breathtaking.

Urban dwellers miss out because of "sky glow"—residual man-made light from street lights, houses, office buildings, sports fields, and the like, which dramatically reduces the contrast between stars and the night sky. Simply put, if you live in the city and look up at night you'll probably see about 100 stars. What's lost in the glow of city lights is as many as 3,900 more that could be visible with the naked eye.

Happily the Royal Astronomical Society of Canada (RASC) is protecting our nighttime viewing by creating Dark Sky Preserves. Today, Canada leads the world in setting aside these areas of protected land where man-made illumination is extremely limited—or non-existent. Canada now has 13 preserves, sometimes referred to as "astronomy parks," where nearby towns and businesses have agreed to keep or change their lighting so the sky stays black and thousands more stars shine through. Parks Canada is a major player in the preservation of dark skies, along with the RASC (which hosts viewings or events tied to sky events at most preserves). Cooperative efforts are reducing the effect that excess man-made light has on all branches of nature, from aquatic life to mammals, insects to vegetation. Technology, ecology, and local heritage are combining to create places where you can see some of the clearest, darkest skies on earth and learn about the science, legends, and beauty of the universe as it drifts overhead.

The two newest parks in Canada were designated in 2010 and 2011.

Kejimkujik National Park is located in the centre of southwestern Nova Scotia, easily accessible from both nearby coastal towns and the city of Halifax. From space, the communities surrounding the Park look like a pearl necklace of lights at night—with some of the darkest skies on the eastern seaboard.

The many lakes and rivers in "Keji" are excellent viewing points; when you're on the beach, starscapes reflect brilliantly in the water below. Kejimkujik Historic Site was home to the Mi'kmaq people for 2,000 years. Cultural heritage is featured in programs highlighting European astrology as well as Aboriginal sky lore revealed through stories about the skies and visible star patterns. Amphitheatre presentations explain dark sky preserves and what people will see during guided walks. A specially built deck encourages lying down and gazing up at the heavens—year-round.

Across the continent in Alberta, Jasper National Park is world-renowned for its wildlife, fantastic mountain views, ancient glaciers, lakes, and rivers. In early 2011 it added to its list of accolades by becoming the largest Dark Sky Preserve on earth. At 11,228 square kilometres (4,335 square miles), it eclipses the combined total of the rest of the world's dark sky preserves—which add up to only one-fifth of the Jasper total. The star-gazing experience here is accessible to everyone because the year-round Icefields Parkway passes through the darkest skies in all of western Canada and sideroads provide opportunities to leave all artificial light behind. Citizens, the municipality, and the park are working to implement responsible lighting that works both astronomically and ecologically. Two of the best viewing locations in the park are at Pyramid Lake, about 15 kilometres (9.8 miles) outside of town, which boasts 180-degree views to the south from the open shore and some of the darkest skies near the townsite; and the Athabasca Glacier, described as a near-perfect observation site, with some of the darkest skies anywhere. Staff is also helping bring the night sky to life with special programming at the Whistler Campground amphitheatre.

Dark Sky Preserves are creating a new kind of ecotourism, referred to by some as "wilderness astronomy." On a perfect night you may see a shooting star or the creamy brilliance of the Milky Way against the inky blackness of the sky—making for an indescribable, wonderful experience. The only thing that ever delays the show is cloud cover. But the stars are still there, waiting for a clear night. Admission couldn't be easier . . . and all you really need to bring is a blanket to lie on, perhaps binoculars or a telescope, and time to relax and savour it all.

Find out more at:

www.rasc.ca/lpa/darksky.shtml

ADVENTURE

Snorkel with Beluga Whales in Churchill

Churchill may be best known as the "Polar Bear Capital of the World," but watching polar bears from the comfort of a heated bus pales in comparison to snorkelling with beluga whales—reason enough to make the long trek up to Hudson Bay in August.

Each summer, up to 3,000 beluga whales congregate around the mouth of the Churchill River to feed on microscopic plankton. These distinctive white creatures, up to five metres (16 feet) long, are renowned for their gentle and intelligent nature—making them the perfect snorkelling companions. After being outfitted in a thick wetsuit and heading out into the river estuary aboard a Zodiac boat, you'll slide into the water and enter the magical world of the beluga whale. The most curious whales will swim right up to you, while others glide playfully past on their backs. It's an interactive experience not easily forgotten.

Churchill is a long way from anywhere (the only access is by scheduled rail or air service), but there's more to a summer visit than whales. Far beyond the treeline, Churchill is a meeting place of Northern Cree and Inuit culture, with indigenous crafts and caribou burgers vying for your attention in town and the endless tundra and, beyond town limits, the ruins of a fort harkening back to 1732 that beckon.🍁
www.seanorthtours.com

Walk in the Footsteps of the Vikings at L'Anse aux Meadows ▼

The warm, fog-free days of August are the best time of year to visit L'Anse aux Meadows National Historic Site, which protects a village established by the mighty Viking Leif Erikson almost 500 years before Christopher Columbus set eyes on the Americas.

Located on the tip of Newfoundland's Northern Peninsula, the site was only discovered in the 1960s. Long before archaeologists arrived, locals were aware of the odd-shaped, sod-covered ridges across the coastal plain at L'Anse aux Meadows. Subsequent digs uncovered rudimentary houses, workshops with fireplaces, and a trove of artifacts that verified the Norse presence. Today, you can visit the interpretive centre, then wander around the site where panels describe the original uses of buildings now marked by depressions in the grass-covered field.

Within walking distance is Norstead, the recreation of a Viking village overlooking the Atlantic Ocean. You can see a full-size replica of a Viking ship, listen to stories in the dimly lit Chieftain's Hall, watch a blacksmith at work, and sample bread as it comes from the oven in the dining hall. The costumed interpreters completely immerse themselves in character—you can easily spend a few hours listening and watching them at work and play. ❦

www.pc.gc.ca/meadows

Whale-Watching Tours in Grand Manan

The Bay of Fundy is sometimes referred to as a "whale superhighway" with New Brunswick's Grand Manan Island lying right in the middle, making it a great place to venture onto the water for a glimpse of these denizens of the deep. Whale-watchers claim more than 100 individual whales visit each summer, using the bay as a nursery and play area. Among them are more than half the world's population of the North Atlantic right whale, one of the rarest large animals on earth. The most commonly sighted species are the humpback, minke, and finback. Humpbacks and finbacks can be up to 25 metres (82 feet) in length and weigh up to 40,000 kilograms (88,000 pounds). Tours, by boat or yacht, offer whale-watching (weather permitting). There are two main tour operators who go out twice daily for between three and five hours at a cost of C$60–65. Reservations are required. Other sightings while on a tour can include bald eagles, puffins, sea bird colonies, harbour porpoises, Atlantic white-sided dolphins, and seals.

For an immersion in all things whale, start by checking out Whale Camp at www.whalecamp.com. As well as camps for kids, they offer weekend excursions and family programs. The Grand Manan Whale & Seabird Research Station has an interpretive centre, and some spectacular whale skeletons. And if you just want to hear whales and seals sound like underwater, check out www.grandmanannb.com/seals.htm. ❦

www.grandmanannb.com/todo.htm

EVENTS & FESTIVALS

QUIRKY CANADA

Become an Honourary Acadian and March in a Tintamarre

"Tintamarre!" The cry stirs the blood of Acadians celebrating their National Day and is a magical clash of colour and sound, where villagers march through their community, noisemakers and improvised instruments (think pots beaten with spoons) ringing out to announce their whereabouts while demonstrating the joie de vivre of Acadian society. It's all part of the Festival acadien de Clare, held in several villages in Clare, a municipality in southwestern Nova Scotia.

Highlights of the week include the Order of Good Cheer Suppers (replicating a celebratory dinner first held in 1604), a boat parade, a fiddlers' night, and a "Cajun Fais do do en Acadie" (a dance party celebrating links between Maritime Acadians and Louisiana Cajuns that includes musicians from Louisiana). The two-week festival wraps up August 15 with a two-part Tintamarre . . . one part driving, one part walking. Each Tintamarre is loud and colourful, with people and cars decked out in blue, white, and red—the colours of Acadia. Thousands are drawn from around the world by the warm welcome as much as the festivities.

"When you visit here, especially during the Festival, you become an honourary Acadian," says organizer Lisette Gaudet. "We want visitors to experience our culture through our music, food, history, and attractions. Locals are always ready to provide a helping hand, so ask for information or even stories; you'll receive a welcoming greeting."♣
www.festivalacadiendeclare.ca

Join the "Garlic Heads" in Perth

"It's chic to reek" proclaim the organizers of this aromatic celebration of *Allium sativum*. It goes without saying that a hearty appetite and plenty of breath mints are in order.

With more than 50 Ontario garlic growers, promoters, and assorted "garlic heads" on hand, the event begins with a tailgate rib cook-off and continues over two days of this August weekend with innumerable excuses to mash, squeeze, press, and otherwise indulge in the product of the so-called "stinking rose." Cooking demonstrations range from the practical to the folkloric—have you always wondered how they braid garlic?—while lectures on growing, harvest, and preserving garlic will introduce you into the fragrant fraternity. And for good reason: the festival reports that a garlic-rich diet lowers cholesterol and blood pressure, kills intestinal worms, draws out heavy metals (talk about getting the lead out), keeps away colds, and renders a person repellent to mosquitoes. That may not be all it repels but then again you will be among your own pungent kind.

All in all, a fine excuse to visit Perth—a charming Loyalist town a short drive south of Ottawa along the Rideau Canal.♣
www.perthgarlicfestival.com

◀ Sip Okanagan Wines at North America's Only Aboriginal-Owned Winery

Escape the August heat of one of Canada's hottest towns by sipping a glass of award-winning wine at a British Columbia vineyard owned and operated by the Okanagan Indian Band, one of the most progressive in North America.

Overlooking Osoyoos Lake from the south end of the Okanagan Valley, the modern development and expansive vineyards at Nk'Mip Cellars stand in stark contrast to the surrounding desert-like landscape. Join a walking tour to learn about the vineyard, the fermentation room, and cellars, with guides highlighting the success of North America's only Aboriginal-owned winery. The tour ends in the Tasting Room, where visitors gather to sample bottles such as the top-end Qwam Qwmt series. Beyond the Tasting Room is the Patio at Nk'Mip, a grassy terrace overlooking the vineyard and lake. This casual dining area is a fantastic place to enjoy Nk'Mip wines while sampling Pacific Northwest–inspired dishes like venison and cherry meatballs slow-cooked in Pinot Noir and served with crisply roasted potatoes.

The tour ends in the Tasting Room, where visitors gather to sample bottles.

Nk'Mip also encompasses Spirit Ridge Vineyard Resort, an upscale development of adobe-style accommodations, restaurants, and swimming pools overlooking the vineyard; a golf course that winds through the sagebrush; and the Nk'Mip Desert Cultural Centre showcasing First Nations culture and traditions.❧
www.nkmipcellars.com

Canadian *moments*

Acadian National Holiday

Every August 15, the main street in Caraquet, New Brunswick, is overrun with people clanging pots, pans, and spoons. The group makes a tremendous din; some have faces painted with the Acadian flag—the blue, white, and red of the French flag with an added gold star at top left.

Since 1979, Acadians have celebrated their heritage with the colourful, noise-making parade called Tintamarre. Acadians share a history of repression, having been deported from the Maritimes by the British starting in 1755. In a way, the noisy parade says "we are still here."

But Tintamarre is not unique to Caraquet in northern New Brunswick. Parades happen around the Maritimes, be it in Clare, Nova Scotia, or Mont-Carmel, Prince Edward Island. Canada is home to more than 96,000 Acadians, according to the 2006 census, with most living in New Brunswick and Nova Scotia.

At the 1881 National Acadian Convention in Memramcook, New Brunswick, Acadians chose August 15 as their national holiday. The date is shared with Assumption Day, honouring the Virgin Mary. Three years later, a convention in Miscouche, P.E.I., chose the tri-coloured flag.

In the lead up to the Acadian National Holiday in Caraquet, the blue, white, red, and gold of Acadia is everywhere. Locals bedeck their houses with strings of plastic flags, and everything from houses to lobster pots can feature a proud coat of paint— in Acadian colours of course.

Go Camping and Canoeing in the Ontario Wilderness

Spectacular scenery and wildlife abound in these popular parks

Paddling a canoe in Ontario's lake-filled wilderness is simply one of the most memorable things to do in the province. But deciding the right time and place to go can be the difference between remembering beautiful sun-dappled days on the water . . . or racing storms of hungry blackflies. As the old Boy Scouts motto goes: be prepared.

The parks are open year-round, but late August is ideal: the days are warm and sometimes hot at midday, while nights have a crisp edge that foretells the approaching autumn and diminished crowds. Another big bonus: the bugs are mostly gone.

Ontario has 330 provincial parks that together span nine million hectares (22 million acres), attracting about 10 million visitors each year. While many are great, there are a couple of standout places that shouldn't be missed.

Algonquin Park, one of Canada's largest provincial parks, established as a wildlife sanctuary in 1893, is famous for its natural beauty—as well as its profound influence on the Group of Seven artists, who came here frequently to find inspiration. It was here, on

Canoe Lake, that painter Tom Thomson drowned under mysterious circumstances—he was an expert canoeist, so many think foul play was involved.

Nearly a century on (Thomson died in 1917), the spectacular scenery that engaged the Group is still here. Given its easy access from the Toronto area, and its expanse—7,770 square kilometres (3,000 square miles) of wilderness—it's easy to stay for a few days or several weeks. There are more than 1,610 kilometres (1,000 miles) of canoe routes for paddling alone. The park provides sanctuary to moose, beaver, bear, and deer, and sightings are frequent. Hundreds of lakes have native brook trout as well as lake trout. And good news for birders: more than 250 bird species have been recorded in the park, including the rare grey jay, spruce grouse, and many varieties of warbler.

A spectacular route that will steer you away from the crowds is the four-day trip through North Tea, Biggar, Three Mile, and Manitou lakes that winds back to North Tea Lake. Starting just an hour north of Huntsville at access point #1, the scenery is rugged and pristine with the promise of relaxing at long beaches and taking shelter in deep, lush forests. Along the way, there's a good chance of seeing moose in the marshy narrows at the east end of North Tea Lake, before portaging into Biggar Lake and setting up camp. Biggar Lake is a beauty—and there are plenty of deer here to keep you company. Set up camp at Three Mile Lake and refuel before the hefty series of portages (nearly six kilometres, 3.7 miles in total) into Manitou. Once at Manitou, check into one of the pretty campsites—look for one with a firepit protected by a large rock near the portage exit. North Tea Lake offers more campsites than Manitou: the favourites are located along little islands and peninsulas at the far southwestern end of the

Here, you might see moose and caribou, hundreds of bird species, and plenty of black bears.

lake. If you want an easier trip with less portaging, the route can be done in three days if it's limited to North Tea and Manitou lakes.

Lake Superior Provincial Park, a 1,550-square-kilometre (598-square-mile) playground, is one of Ontario's largest parks and stretches along the sometimes rugged, often breathtaking shores of the biggest of the Great Lakes. Here, you might see moose and caribou, hundreds of bird species, and plenty of black bears. There are some 269 camping sites at three campgrounds, eight canoe routes, and 11 hiking trails, from short interpretive hikes to rugged overnight expeditions up to 55 kilometres (34 miles) long.

A great way to arrive is to take the day-long Agawa Canyon Tour Train (see p. 225) to the end of the line from the Algoma Central Railway in Sault Ste. Marie through the wilderness of northern Ontario to Hearst. Once here, you're at the spectacular site of the Agawa

Canyon. The cliffs rise to 175 metres (574 feet) above the river with multiple waterfalls at the site, including Bridal Veil Falls at 68.5 metres (225 feet). At Agawa Bay sits the park's biggest campground. It has a three-kilometre (two-mile) beach. Take the 26-kilometre (16-mile) Towab Trail through the Agawa Valley to the 25-metre (82-feet) Agawa Falls. At Agawa Rock, you can still see traces of the early Ojibway—there are centuries-old paintings depicting animals and scenes from their legends. There's also an unparalleled calm and relaxation here that comes with being far-removed from any bustle—imagine silence broken only by the splash of a fish jumping on a still lake. Like Algonquin, Agawa was famously documented by the Group of Seven.

A thrilling two-day canoe route along the Lower Agawa River begins by taking the train to Canyon Station on the Algoma Central Railway and paddling 29 kilometres (18 miles) with five portages downstream to Highway 17 (where you should arrange to have someone pick you up). It's a route for skilled canoeists with a number of challenges—think sections of rapids and some steep portages—but the rewards are great. The route is really the only way to experience the breathtaking river and the spectacular falls: the river farther upstream above Canyon Station is considered too dangerous for paddling. ❧

Find out more at:
www.algonquinpark.on.ca,
www.lakesuperiorpark.ca

ADVENTURE

Hike the East Coast Trail

Mention hiking in Newfoundland and most people think of Gros Morne National Park, but the East Coast Trail—along the untamed shoreline of the Avalon Peninsula—really gives you a sense of the province, its people, and culture.

The generally uncomplicated route extends from Pouch Cove in the north to Cappahayden more than 200 kilometres (124 miles) to the south. Along the way, it meanders through lush forests, crests rocky cliff tops, crosses fast-flowing rivers, visits eight lighthouses and three national historic sites, and passes through more than 30 fishing villages. The constant is the Atlantic Ocean, rarely out of sight, often delivering the magical view of icebergs and whales.

Although exhilaratingly challenging, few hikers complete the route in one visit. Instead, they take advantage of access points scattered at regular intervals, providing the opportunity for day or overnight hikes. To get a taste for the trail, head to Quidi Vidi Village, within St. John's city limits, and spend a few hours

The constant is the Atlantic Ocean, rarely out of sight, often delivering the magical view of icebergs and whales.

walking north along the rocky coastline to Logy Bay, seemingly a world away from the capital. Farther south, where the trail crosses La Manche Provincial Park, it passes through the site of a fishing village washed away by a winter storm in 1966. ❧

www.eastcoasttrail.ca

◀ Immerse Yourself in the Lore of Anne of Green Gables

It's an amazing thing: every year one small, red-haired orphan draws thousands of visitors to Prince Edward Island. It began more than 100 years ago when author Lucy Maud Montgomery penned *Anne of Green Gables*, starting a love affair with the fictional character that continues—to this day—through books, movies, and television. Legions visit places made famous by the original novel (and the 19 that followed) seeking to experience the gentle seascapes, woodlands, and village life so magically brought to life by the author.

The third week of August is your last chance for some activities at Green Gables in Prince Edward Island National Park and to enjoy the *Anne of Green Gables* Children's Festival. In Charlottetown, *Anne of Green Gables: The Musical* plays at Confederation Centre of the Arts. The story of Anne in love continues in *Anne & Gilbert: The Musical* at Harbourfront Theatre in Summerside. In Cavendish, walk Haunted Woods and Balsam Hollow trails at Green Gables or visit Avonlea Village, where you can step back to 1908 with costumed performers enjoying life as it was in Anne's time. Silver Bush farm, the Anne of Green Gables Museum in Park Corner where the author married, is owned by Montgomery's great-grandchildren, and the facility offers horse-drawn carriage rides around the Lake of Shining Waters. ❧
www.tourismpei.com/anne-of-green-gables

Taste the Salt Plains at Wood Buffalo National Park ▼

Amidst the boreal forest of Wood Buffalo National Park, the salt-encrusted landscape of the Salt Plains is changing colours. The greens of summer are giving way to red and pale orange. The red samphire plant stands out against the white salt. Narrow streams ease their way through the northern boreal plains of Canada's largest national park.

Wood Buffalo is accessible by road from Highway 5 between Hay River and Fort Smith in the Northwest Territories. About 40 minutes from Fort Smith, take a detour down a side road to the Salt Plains Lookout and day-use area. The viewpoint offers a sweeping perspective of the 370-square-kilometre (143-square-mile) Salt Plains. Salt bubbles up in springs to the surface of this flat area and forms salt mounds. This pure table salt was deposited here millions of years ago.

People once used the salt to cure meat and fish. In the 1800s, they began trading it to the Hudson's Bay Company for blankets, pots, knives, and other goods. Now, wildlife is the salt's only consumer. Look through a high-powered telescope to try to spot animals such as bison and bears down below. If you're really lucky, you might see a whooping crane. Take the 500-metre (1,640-foot) switchback trail down the steep escarpment to the Salt Plains. There are no marked trails on this fragile landscape. Keep an eye out for delicate salt mounds, saline springs, and animal tracks. ❧
www.pc.gc.ca/woodbuffalo

EVENTS & FESTIVALS

QUIRKY CANADA

Soak In the Atmosphere at P.E.I. Old Home Week

They're at the post! They're off! With thundering hooves some of the best harness racing horses in Atlantic Canada are flying under a midnight sky in pursuit of the Gold Cup and Saucer. It's the closing race, the grand finale of Old Home Week in Charlottetown, the culmination of 15 racing programs over nine days during the Provincial Exhibition. This is one of the most celebrated harness racing events in eastern Canada and only part of the action. Old Home Week, established in 1888, brings country and town folks together for traditional events and contemporary entertainment. Horse-pulls test the strength of heavy teams. Livestock are judged, as are skills ranging from quilting, to pickling, to photography and art. Agricultural exhibits even include rare breeds of chickens. Many come for the midway, live music, buskers, and children's entertainment and performances, such as canine Fly Ball. As Old Home Week comes into its final days, crowds line downtown streets for the Gold Cup and Saucer Parade. For generations, Old Home Week has drawn back those who moved away while welcoming visitors curious to experience the unique culture that is Island life.✿
www.oldhomeweekpei.com

Place Your Bets at the World Miniature Horse Chuckwagon Championship

On the third weekend of every August a pint-sized spectacle leads to large-scale competition in the pretty southern Alberta town of Cardston. The World Miniature Horse Chuckwagon Championship is a showcase for just how fast horses—ones that aren't much larger than a bicycle—can run.

Miniature horses stand only one metre (three feet) high at the shoulder, and it takes four of them to pull chuckwagons that are half the size of regular wagons. The drivers are the only element of the rigs that are full-sized, but the horse teams generate surprising speed as they gallop around the hockey rink–sized, circular track. Races come complete with a fast-talking announcer (adding a wise-cracking colour commentary) and have all the drama of competitions between full-size equines. Multiple heats decide the qualifiers for a winner-take-all final that determines who is crowned "world champion."

The weekend kicks of with a Friday night Cowboy Social, where spectators can meet the drivers. Between races, there's a pancake breakfast, farmers' market, and live music. You can also visit the Remington Carriage Museum, which organizes the event; it houses the largest on-display collection of horse-drawn vehicles in North America. But invariably, it's the miniature stars who steal the show.✿
www.remingtoncarriagemuseum.com,
www.albertaminichucks.ca

Float in Saskatchewan's Soothing Saltwater Lake

For prairie dwellers, escaping the summer heat of August by swimming in the region's many lakes is a time-honoured tradition. But those who head to Little Manitou Lake, southeast of Saskatoon, enjoy not only a relief from the heat, but a watery experience that can only be enjoyed in two other places in the world.

Little Manitou Lake is notable for its mineral-rich waters, similar only to water found in the Dead Sea and in the Czech Republic. Its unique properties allow bathers unequalled buoyancy—a sensation of almost weightlessness, even if you simply lay on the surface without moving. In fact, swimming is difficult as you really do float atop the water as if supported from below by an inflatable water toy. The lake is fed by an underground spring that gives the lake water unusually high density due to concentrations of mineral salts such as magnesium, sulphate, potassium, sodium, and calcium, as well as iron and silica. The water's

Little Manitou Lake is notable for its mineral-rich waters, similar only to water found in the Dead Sea and in the Czech Republic.

very therapeutic and has been known to cure a variety of skin conditions, as well as relieve stress and pressure from muscles and joints by naturally drawing minerals from within the human body to the skin.🍁
www.watrousmanitou.com

It *happened*
THIS WEEK:

Gold Found in the Yukon

It wasn't until the *Seattle Daily Times* ran a headline saying the steamer Portland "Brought down half a ton of gold" and the *San Francisco Examiner* declared "More than one ton of nuggets" that the Gold Rush to the Klondike truly began.

Those headlines appeared on July 18, 1897— nearly a full year after George Washington Carmack along with Skookum Jim and Tagish Charlie struck gold on August 16, 1896. The group hit it rich on Rabbit Creek, a Klondike River tributary renamed Bonanza as more than 100,000 people trekked to the Klondike in search of riches.

Soon, the Yukon became a colony of Americans. Dawson City was settled where the Klondike tributary joins the wide Yukon River. Those journeying there by ship, rail and trail, or overland were required to procure one tonne of supplies to sustain a year in the desolate region.

But while the gold rush swept in and out with such speed (the population of Dawson rose from 5,000 to 30,000 from 1897 to the following year) it left behind a rich history of writers, entertainers, and miners.

Diamond Tooth Gertie's Casino is Canada's oldest casino, while the works of Robert Service and Jack London live on in the town's heritage sites.

And for those still lured by gold fever, placer mining is one of the region's main economies—aside from tourism, of course.

Search for the Giants of the Deep

Whale-watching here in late summer gives you the chance to glimpse more than a dozen species

Thar' she blows! . . . Few experiences are as thrilling as spotting a whale from the deck of a boat plying the open sea. It's the culmination of a search for one of nature's greatest creatures in their own element, wild and free.

The hunt is exciting. All eyes eagerly search the sea. Everyone tingles with anticipation. Cameras are clutched tightly, finger on shutters. Where will it surface? Will we see a blow, the spray of water that marks its presence, the breech, and the splash of the tail as it dives back into the deep?

"There!" A cry of awe replaces anticipation—the shouts drawn out by the pure majesty of the great beast, and the sheer joy that whales show for playing in their own environment. Although fast-moving and active, they seem to enjoy getting a good look at us, as much as we do of them.

Late August is prime time for whale-watching as the migrations from southern waters are complete. Lured by the ample food supply, 15 species of whales stay until the fall when, like human snowbirds, they again seek the warmth of the south. Finback and minke arrive in the late spring followed by humpback in June. By mid-July, whales—including the rare North Atlantic right whale— have returned.

The Cabot Trail in northern Nova Scotia is world-renowned for whale sightings. Pods of small black Atlantic pilot whales spend summers gorging on squid just offshore. Minke are common, while humpbacks are occasionally seen farther offshore. The threatened fin whales, a species of special concern in Canada, are less common.

The highlands of Cape Breton are one of the few places where you can spot whales from land. From the viewing decks on the headland cliff at the end of the Skyline Trail, you can often see whales spouting in the Gulf of St. Lawrence. Lakies Head Lookoff and Green Cove Trail are also good spots to watch for whales.

Visit a Cape Breton Highlands National Park Information Centre for directions. Pleasant Bay's Whale Interpretive Centre is also a great source of information.

Sightings from land are a teaser. There's no question the ultimate viewing experience is up-close-and-personal from a whale-watching tour vessel. There are numerous tours to choose from, located at communities along the Cabot Trail including Chéticamp, Pleasant Bay, Bay St. Lawrence, and Ingonish.

Each tour is different, unique because of location, length (1.5 to four hours), types of vessels used, and the personalities of those tak-

The highlands of Cape Breton are one of the few places where you can spot whales from land.

ing you to sea. Zodiac operators keep their eyes peeled for blows, then literally chase down whales when they spot them. Exhilarating. Another promises whales pursued with a background of live Celtic music. A great treat. Some operators, such as those at Bay St. Lawrence, in Cape Breton's most isolated coast, use converted fishing boats. They offer a wealth of information about life as lived in coastal communities. An operator out of Pleasant Bay uses a cabin cruiser that doubles as a research boat. It is one of several offering extras, such as hydrophones to hear the whales, and underwater cameras for a look-see below the surface.

With numerous tour choices, it's advisable to investigate options on the web or at a Visitor Information Centre. Most tours include other wildlife or experiences. In Cape Breton, seal, dolphin, porpoise, leatherback turtle, moose, bear, puffin, and eagle sightings are also possible. Some operators include shoreline highlights, such as sea caves, cliffs, and waterfalls, or local history.

Both still and video photographers will revel in the opportunities to capture the adventure on film. Be sure to have fully charged cameras and keep your finger near the shutter button!

The type of boat dictates your experience. Zodiacs place you closer to the water, making an up-close encounter even more thrilling, though the ride can be jarring—but exhilarating—as they speed over swells or waves.

Catamarans and larger vessels offer comforts, such as washrooms, snack bars, and top decks for sightings. First-timers, or anyone a little nervous, will be happier on larger boats. If seasickness is a worry, ask about wristbands or other aids, and choose a calm day. No matter the temperature, dress in warm layers—it's usually much colder on water than on land.

Some tours guarantee a whale sighting. Read the fine print. Remember, these are wild creatures in a huge body of water, affected by the whims of Mother Nature. Regardless, enjoy your grand ocean adventure. In rare cases that a whale is not sighted, most offer refunds— or another trip.❦

Find out more at:
www.cabottrail.travel

ADVENTURE

Take a Road Trip to Remote Northwestern British Columbia

By late August, melting snow has revealed glacier-capped mountains, grizzly bears are feeding on salmon, and the halibut-fishing season is in full swing at the twin towns of Stewart and Hyder, on B.C.'s remote northwest coast.

The trip to Stewart, British Columbia, and Hyder, Alaska, is for adventurous road-trippers only. It's a long drive from anywhere (the nearest airport is five hours away, at Terrace) through the spectacular Coast Mountains, passing glaciers, waterfalls, and northern forests filled with wildlife. At the end of the road, the two gold rush–era towns are sandwiched between towering mountains and one of Canada's longest fiords. The rugged scenery alone makes the trip worthwhile, but watching grizzly bears feast on spawned out salmon in Fish Creek is a wonderful bonus. This is also the time of year when halibut fishing is at its best. Charter operators will lead you to all the local hotspots, chasing one of the most delicious fish you're ever likely to taste.

The trip to Stewart, British Columbia, and Hyder, Alaska, is for adventurous road-trippers only.

At the end of the day, join the tradition and tack a bill to the wall of the Glacier Inn (ensuring you won't return broke), then toss back a shot of 190-proof, pure-grain alcohol in one swallow to qualify for your "I've Been Hyderized" card. **www.stewart-hyder.com**

Explore 18th-Century New France on Cape Breton Island

Visitors to the Fortress of Louisbourg step back to the capital of Île Royale (Cape Breton Island), a thriving seaport in 1744. It was one of the busiest harbours and France's key centre of trade and military strength in the New World; it was also the most extensive (and expensive) European fortifications in North America. Today, it's the largest reconstructed 18th-century French-fortified town in North America, and a national historic site. Ramparts, streets, households, and interpreters help create the look, texture, and mood of another century. Cannons on stone ramparts, a busy waterfront tavern, and the crackling of a kitchen fire immerse visitors into lives lived in a different era. Plan a long visit, as

Louisbourg needs a full day to explore. Special events such as The Feast of St. Louis, held annually in late August to commemorate King Louis IX (1214–1270), a.k.a. Saint Louis of France, require even more time. The recreation of 18th-century celebrations includes cannon salutes, musket firings, dancing, gambling, children's games, and music. Murder mysteries and dinner theatre titillate the imagination, while costumed staff working in period-themed restaurants serves delicious food and beverages based on 18th-century tradition and recipes. Before visiting, check the website as different activities happen on different days.❧
www.fortressoflouisbourg.ca

Gawk at a Quarter-Million Atlantic Puffins

One of the best places in the world to view Atlantic puffins in their natural habitat is Witless Bay Ecological Reserve, where rocky islands attract more than 250,000 breeding pairs each summer through August, when warm weather and generally fog-free conditions make boat tours from Bay Bulls ideal.

The distinctive Atlantic puffin, designated the official bird of Newfoundland and Labrador, borrows the penguin's tuxedo markings but is nicknamed the "sea parrot" for its distinctive triangular red-and-yellow bill. Puffins make Swiss cheese of the islands, as they nest in burrows they've either dug out themselves or inherited from predecessors. The Witless Bay seabird spectacle is not all about puffins. Leach's storm petrels, murres, kittiwakes, herring gulls, Atlantic razorbills, and black guillemots are also regularly spotted, as well as humpback, killer, fin, and minke whales.

Boat tours into the reserve operate from a number of towns along the coastline south of St. John's, but closest

to the capital is O'Brien's Whale and Bird Tours, which depart from Bay Bulls—a 20-minute drive from downtown. It's a well-organized operation, complete with a choice of covered vessels or rigid-hulled Zodiacs. The covered vessels offer more leisurely trips with live Newfoundland music; travelling aboard one of the Zodiacs gets you to the reserve much more quickly.❧
www.obriensboattours.com

EVENTS & FESTIVALS

◀ Squeeze In the Last Bit of Summer Fun at the PNE and CNE

In sports, Vancouver and Toronto are heated rivals, from Olympic bids to major-league hockey and soccer clashes. Yet away from those playing fields, the West Coast metropolis and the Ontario capital agree on one thing: the perfect traditional way to wrap up summer is with a 2.5-week fair loaded with amusement park rides and live entertainment. Both Vancouver's Pacific National Exhibition (PNE) and Toronto's Canadian National Exhibition (CNE) fulfill that mandate.

The settings are slightly different. The PNE, dating back to 1910, graces Hastings Park, east of downtown Vancouver, and next to Pacific Coliseum and a horse-racing track. Bordering Lake Ontario, the 1879-founded CNE boasts more big-heritage buildings on Exhibition Place's 78 hectares (192 acres).

But at both fairs, families love to check out cows, pigs, ostriches, and other farmyard favourites. You can hop on a big Ferris wheel or brave more intense midway rides. The wacky Superdogs show, indoor marketplaces, miniature doughnuts, and international food stalls also grace both fairs. Don't miss free concerts by veteran stars from rockers like Loverboy and Trooper, to divas like Cyndi Lauper and Gloria Gaynor. The only downside for kids in both Toronto and Vancouver? Having to go back to school when the fairs are done.🍁
www.pne.ca, www.theex.com

5 *faves*

Cirque of the Unclimbables

This breathtaking mountain landscape within the boundaries of Nahanni National Park dazzles with tall granite spires surrounding a rolling meadowland. With its criss-crossed gentle hiking trails, the remote Cirque—also known as the "jewel of the Nahanni"—has been compared to such alpine landscapes as Mont Blanc and Patagonia.

Hunt for Spanish Galleons off the Coast of Labrador

Canadians are generally pretty knowledgeable about the country's relatively short history, but there are many episodes in our past that are not well known. One such story is of the Spanish galleons that travelled to Labrador each July and August many hundreds of years ago, four of which sank in a remote Labrador bay—lying undiscovered until the 1970s.

Red Bay, a small settlement off Labrador's coast, was once one of the world's largest whaling ports. It's estimated that between 1540 and 1610 around 2,500 Basque men crossed from Europe each year in up to 30 galleons to harvest right whales, sought after for their whale oil. Archaeologists have done extensive research on the sunken ships that now lie in the cold, shallow water covered with tarpaulins. While you can't view the actual boats, two excellent facilities combine to make up the Red Bay National Historic Site. One is a modern structure centring on a *chalupa*, a wooden whaling boat recovered from the bottom of the bay. You can watch a documentary on the galleon San Juan and have staff point out where each of the galleons is located. Down on the waterfront is another building, this one holding the main collection of artifacts—including pottery and a compass.🍁

www.pc.gc.ca/redbay

Dine at One of the World's Best Restaurants

There are a few truly great restaurants in Canada, but only one has been dubbed one of the top 10 in the world and has international guests who fly in solely for a seat at its exclusive table. For sheer attention to detail and intimacy of contact, Chef Michael Städtlander's Eigensinn Farm is unparalleled—particularly in August, when the farm's bounty is sizzling in the kitchen. But be sure to plan ahead: patrons book months in advance for one of only 12 available seats.

Not only is Städtlander a brilliant chef, he's a working farmer. But the crucial difference is that he raises his livestock from a chef's point of view. His chickens run wild, and feed on oats, barley, hemp, and flax. If trout's on the menu, it's because Städtlander had some luck on the fishing line that morning at the farm's pond.

The C$300 per person cost for his eight-course *prix fixe* menu may seem high. But the difference is that you'll be paying for Städtlander's enthusiasm and insight instead of for overpriced wine. Eigensinn Farm is a bring-your-own-bottle experience, so you'll actually spend far less if you bring a high-end Bordeaux than you would if you selected the same wine off a normal restaurant wine list. Then again, you will be doing yourself a favour by booking into a local B&B: the Eigensinn experience lasts from 7:30 p.m. to 11:00 p.m.🍁

www.eigensinnfarm.com

Peggy's Cove, Nova Scotia

About 42 kilometres (26 miles) southwest of Halifax is the fishing village of Peggy's Cove, which offers postcard-perfect tableaus: an octagonal lighthouse (likely one of the most photographed in the world), tiny fishing shacks, and graceful fishing boats bobbing in the postage stamp-sized harbour.

Nova Scotia's Natal Days

Annapolis Royal Natal Days bring together the past and present as few events do. A military enactment on the grounds of Fort Anne, with Teddy Bear Tea and Doll Carriage Parade for the younger set, dog agility competitions and a motorcycle drive-by add to the fun.

Halifax International Busker Festival

In early August, the 10-day Halifax International Busker Festival brings together talented street performers from around the world, performing in their natural habitat. Best of all, it's free.

Summer fun on Lake Winnipeg

North America's seventh largest lake is 425 kilometres (264 miles) long and its shores shelter some interesting communities and attractive natural areas. At its southeast end, Grand Beach Provincial Park has beautiful white-sand beaches backed by 12-metre (39-foot) high dunes in some places. It's an ideal place to relax on the beach, swim, hike, or camp.

Your next STEP

TOP PICKS
ADVENTURE
CULTURE & HISTORY
NATURE'S GRANDEUR
EVENTS & FESTIVALS
QUIRKY CANADA
REJUVENATE

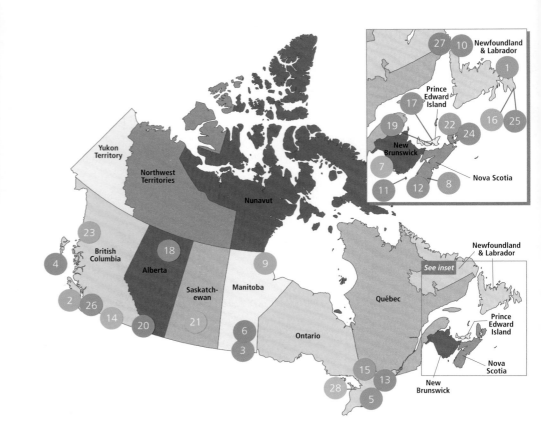

WEEK 1

1 ST. JOHN'S, NFLD.
Royal St. John's Regatta
www.stjohns.ca

2 TOFINO, B.C.
West Coast Trail hiking
www.westcoasttrailbc.com

3 STEINBACH, MAN.
Mennonite heritage
www.mennoniteheritagevillage.com

4 GWAII HAANAS NATIONAL
PARK, B.C.
West Coast Fishing Club
www.westcoastfishingclub.com

5 TORONTO, ONT.
Caribbean Carnival
www.torontocaribbeancarnvial.com

6 GIMLI, MAN.
Manitoba Icelandic Festival
www.icelandicfestival.com

7 ST. STEPHEN, N.B.
St. Stephen Chocolate Festival
www.chocolate-fest.ca

WEEK 2

8 KEJIMKUJIK NATIONAL PARK, N.S.
Night sky–watching
www.rasc.ca/lpa/darksky.shtml

9 CHURCHILL, MAN.
Snorkelling with beluga whales
www.seanorthtours.com

10 L'ANSE AUX MEADOWS, NFLD.
Viking settlement history
www.pc.gc.ca/meadows

11 GRAND MANAN, N.B.
Whale-watching
www.grandmanannb.com/todo.htm

12 LITTLE BROOK, N.S.
Festival acadien de Clare
www.festivalacadiendeclare.ca

13 PERTH, ONT.
Perth Garlic Festival
www.perthgarlicfestival.com

14 OSOYOOS, B.C.
Aboriginal-owned winery
www.nkmipcellars.com

WEEK 3

15 ALGONQUIN PROVINCIAL
PARK, ONT.
Ontario wilderness camping
www.algonquinpark.on.ca

16 BAY BULLS, NFLD.
East Coast Trail hiking
www.eastcoasttrail.ca

17 CAVENDISH, P.E.I.
Anne of Green Gables's home
www.tourismpei.com/anne-
of-green-gables

18 WOOD BUFFALO NATIONAL
PARK, ALTA.
Salt Plains
www.pc.gc.ca/woodbuffalo

19 CHARLOTTETOWN, P.E.I.
Old Home Week horse racing
www.oldhomeweekpei.com

20 CARDSTON, ALTA.
Miniature horse chuckwagon racing
www.remingtoncarriage
museum.com

21 LITTLE MANITOU LAKE, SASK.
Saltwater lake–floating
www.watrousmanitou.com

WEEK 4

22 CAPE BRETON ISLAND, N.S.
Whale-watching on the Cabot Trail
www.cabottrail.travel

23 STEWART, B.C.
Northwest B.C. road-tripping
www.stewart-hyder.com

24 LOUISBOURG, N.S.
18th-century New France history
www.fortressoflouisbourg.ca

25 BAY BULLS, NFLD.
Puffin-watching
www.obriensboattours.com

26 VANCOUVER, B.C.
Pacific National Exhibition
www.pne.ca

27 RED BAY, LABRADOR
Sunken Spanish galleons
www.pc.gc.ca/redbay

28 SINGHAMPTON, ONT.
Dining at world-renowned
Eigensinn Farm
www.eigensinnfarm.com

SEPTEMBER

Immerse Yourself in Hollywood North

Lights, cameras, and action at North America's largest film festival

The Toronto International Film Festival (TIFF) is a must for any serious film lover—and given the infectious buzz around town, is one of the most exciting times of year to visit Toronto (if you don't mind lineups, but more on that later). There's the thrill of being among the first anywhere to see that latest megawatt Hollywood flick—and perhaps a glimpse of its leading stars, too, who come out for evening premieres. Or, the chance to ask a question of a revered film director in a post-movie Q&A. There are also the festival's "fringe benefits," namely, what might be called a festival of parties.

TIFF is widely ranked by industry insiders as the second-most important film festival in the world (after the glamorous spectacle of sunny Cannes in May). There are more than 300 films from 60 countries screened here in only 11 days, with red-carpet galas every night. The festival that began in 1976 as a modest, well-curated collection of films from other festivals—it used to be called the Festival of Festivals—offers something for every movie lover. Galas are glitzy, red-carpet, paparazzi-friendly affairs featuring Hollywood's A-List, decked out to promote their latest flicks: a glimpse of George (Clooney) and Branjelina in the flesh is almost routine in the city at this time of year. But while these premieres hog most of the media attention, the majority of titles are lesser known—ranging from American indies to truly obscure and often rewarding work from far-flung corners of the globe. There's Midnight Madness, for those with a taste for horror and kitsch; Vanguard, for cutting-edge cinema; a wealth of Made-in-Canada features and shorts; Contemporary World Cinema; kids' films; and a plethora of documentaries. For many screenings, the film's cast is in attendance—often meaning that filmmakers are available after the screening for intimate question-and-answer sessions with the audience.

Visiting TIFF requires some advance preparation. If you just show up and hope to get into a screening or two, you'll likely be disappointed. About one-third of all screenings are sold out in advance and many of the more mainstream movies are the first to go. While there are single tickets, anyone planning to really explore the festival should buy a package and plan ahead.

Starting in early July, the festival offers My Choice packages for sale on-line, over the phone, and at the festival box office. In return you get vouchers . . . and the long wait till late August, when the lineup of films,

screening dates and times are confirmed. What to see? The best way to decide is to buy the Advance Order Book at the box office in late August—a preview of the more complete Programme Book. Or, wait for the real deal closer to the opening and be prepared to take a good few hours to read through the program notes. You can also access the film list on-line. There are special rates for seniors and students—though ID must be shown. You're not done yet though. Remember that demand for certain films is very high, so . . . your selections are then entered into a lottery. When the results are finalized, the festival e-mails each buyer a list of confirmed tickets.

Once you're here, don't expect to just sit in the dark. The festival is a scene and all are welcome to get in on the vibe. That often means waiting in long lineups, which can be more pleasant than it sounds—there's a palpable excitement, with gregarious and excited festival-goers buzzing with speculation. The lineups are famous as places to meet, where friendships—even romances—can begin. (Many people return to the festival year after year, which makes for many happy reunions while waiting for films to start.)

Being here also means hanging out in some of the city's trendiest bars and restaurants (new places often time their opening to coincide with festival parties), waiting to catch glimpses of megawatt stars and renowned filmmakers before they disappear into the VIP area. For those with an ambition (and a knack) for getting into private parties, it means schmoozing your way into these invitation-only events, of which there are dozens around town—especially during the festival's first weekend. (This is when many of the most-anticipated premieres take place.) Read the local papers for listings of what's on and turn on the charm, but don't be disappointed if you're stuck out on the sidewalks with the many other party-crashers who get turned away. For some, hunting down movie stars is nearly a full-time occupation: dedicated spotters often wait outside the city's top hotels for hours in hopes of a chance for a quick photo of an A-list star, and will even go so far as to announce the whereabouts of their favourite celeb to other spotters via Twitter.

At the 2010 festival, TIFF debuted its ambitious home base, Bell Lightbox, in the downtown core. It's a multi-purpose venue with five cinemas, two galleries, a library and learning centre, and a handful of studios for seminars, workshops, and lectures. There's also a restaurant and a casual bistro run by the respected Oliver & Bonacini Restaurants chain. But while the King West neighbourhood is now the focal point, the festival continues to operate around downtown at several cinemas. The crowds pack nearby cafés and bars, especially in the tony Yorkville district where many visitors choose to stay. Exploring the festival to its fullest can become an exhausting experience—with screenings starting as early as 9:00 a.m. and many bars holding special permits to stay open until 4:00 a.m. Indeed, sleep may be the last thing on your to-do list!🍁

Find out more at:
www.tiff.net

ADVENTURE

Hike the Fabled Chilkoot Trail

It's early autumn and a group of hikers are coming off the 53-kilometre (32.9-mile) Chilkoot Trail. For five days they were following the footsteps of hardy prospectors who sought their fortunes in these hills in the wake of the 1896 Yukon Klondike gold strike. It was an opportunity for them to relive a part of history and some of its more gruelling challenges.

The Chilkoot Trail starts close to sea level in Dyea, Alaska, and ends at Bennett Lake, B.C. (don't forget your passport—this is an international crossing). Along the way, it climbs more than 900 metres (2,953 feet) through rocky terrain near the summit of the Chilkoot Pass, above the treeline and into alpine tundra. The route's difficulty often means hikers must travel at a snail-like pace of one kilometre (0.6 miles) per hour. Temperatures drop and weather can include wind and hail or snow. (If you're feeling sorry for yourself, remember that 19th-century prospectors climbed the pass carrying one tonne of equipment and supplies.) The trail warms up again as it descends into British Columbia's subalpine boreal forest around Lindeman and Bennett Lakes. As you drink in the views, look for the remains of artifacts that stampeders left along the route.

Only 50 hikers are admitted into Canada each day over the Chilkoot Pass. Reservations and permits, C\$65 for adults, are mandatory and available for the upcoming season beginning in February of each year. Cooler temperatures and fewer bugs make early September an ideal time for a visit. At the end of the trip, climb aboard the White Pass & Yukon Route train to return to Skagway or head to Whitehorse. ❦
www.pc.gc.ca/chilkoot

CULTURE & HISTORY

Understand the Birth of Modern Canada at Charlottetown's Founders' Hall

Hear Ye! Hear Ye! This week in 1864 the first steps towards forming the country of Canada took place in Charlottetown, P.E.I., when 23 enterprising men met with one question on their minds: "shall we unite?" The men, representing four colonies—Prince Edward Island, Nova Scotia, New Brunswick, and the Canadians made up of Canada East and Canada West—met from September 1 to 8. After much debate, and almost as much dining, dancing, and social enjoyment, they determined the answer was "yes" and began the process of forming a nation. The whole affair, now known as the Charlottetown Conference, is celebrated at Founders' Hall: Canada's Birthplace Pavilion, located on the city waterfront in a former CN rail car repair shop. Step into the Time Train Tunnel for a look back through history, beginning in 1864 and concluding with Nunavut joining the country in 1999. Modern technology brings the past to life with holovisuals, games, and state-of-the-art displays. To enhance your exploration of 1864, book a walking tour of the historic area; it begins by meeting costumed "Fathers and Ladies" for games. It's a great way to explore Olde Charlottetown—and a fun experience that sends participants home with a greater appreciation for Canada's story. ❦
www.foundershall.ca

◀ See the Rare White Spirit Bear

It can happen in seconds. A spirit bear's white head appears from the underbrush, and the 181.4-kilogram (400-pound) creature pads across a bubbling stream on Princess Royal Island off B.C.'s central coast. Then he's gone. Was it just a dream?

Only a few intrepid eco-tourists are fortunate enough to spot a spirit bear (a.k.a., a kermode bear) —a rare kind of black bear with a recessive gene for white fur, unique to this region. Your odds increase with a bear-watching enterprise like Spirit Bear Adventures, employing certified guides from the Kitasoo/Xaixais people.

Depart in the morning from the luxurious, longhouse-style Spirit Bear Lodge in the village of Klemtu. A high-speed boat takes you to the island. There, your group of seven or more—enough to prompt bears to keep their distance—follows your

Only a few intrepid eco-tourists are fortunate enough to spot a spirit bear.

guide on foot through lush cedars and ferns, checking for paw prints along trails, seeking that perfect moment.

On your multi-day tour, you'll spot other miracles —both natural and man-made. A grizzly mother and cubs fishing for salmon in a river. Other wildlife, from dolphins to porcupines. Or the sacred, ruined Native site of Dis'ju with its huge logs and deep pit. Savour every second. ❧

www.spiritbear.com

It *happened*
THIS WEEK:

Trans-Canada Highway Opens

It would take about four full days to drive, with not so much as a gas stop or "Timmy's" break. The Trans-Canada is one of the world's longest national highways, connecting St. John's, Newfoundland (in the east) to Victoria, B.C. (in the west).

Though the highway had been open to traffic beginning July 30, Prime Minister John Diefenbaker officially opened the highway at Rogers Pass on September 3.

"May this highway, the longest high-standard highway in all the world, bring Canadians together, bring a renewed determination to all Canadians to do their part to make this nation worthy of its destiny," said the prime minister to a crowd of more than 2,000. Via the Trans-Canada, Rogers Pass lies just 115 kilometres (71 miles) east of Craigellachie, where the Canadian Pacific Railway's Last Spike was hammered in.

Although about half the Trans-Canada was still unpaved at the time of the ceremony, Canadians could drive from the Atlantic to the Pacific on a single 7,821-kilometre (4,860-mile) highway.

Caravans towed by Fords and Chevys headed to the national parks along the route. In Newfoundland, Terra Nova National Park straddles the highway. In the Rockies, Banff, Glacier, and Yoho national parks bring nature to the road. The highway also connects major cities, including Vancouver, Calgary, Regina, Winnipeg, Ottawa, Montréal, Fredericton, and Charlottetown.

In *The Longest Road*, Bob Weber details Canadian experiences on the Trans-Canada Highway— including those of an 11-member family travelling by bus, and university students taking to the road. He writes, "How it opened up the country, how it filled some communities and drained others, and how it freed desires is the people's history of the world's longest road."

EVENTS & FESTIVALS

Watch Cutting-Edge Theatre at the Atlantic Fringe Festival

If accessible, affordable performance theatre is for you, then be prepared for tough decision-making. Over 11 days, the Atlantic Fringe Festival puts on more than 200 performances in five venues across Halifax, encompassing nearly every theatre genre: musicals, dramas, comedies, and even dance. Atlantic Fringe describes itself as "theatre that goes for edges, presses the form, takes risks and is offbeat and fresh." For audiences that means an opportunity to see new works from both emerging and established artists from across Canada, the United States, and the United Kingdom, where the fringe movement originated. Often described as "fun on the cheap," it's an opportunity to present unjuried, uncensored works in an environment that fosters an anyone-can-do-it/ anything-goes attitude, adding an element of adventure for audiences. Ticket prices range from C$3 to $10, encouraging attendance at more than one performance

This is where audiences could get a first look at tomorrow's stars.

an evening. This is where audiences could get a first look at tomorrow's stars, and track down the new and unusual. A big plus: those low-cost admissions help overcome barriers faced by artists by providing venues and funding, while enjoying a theatrical experience like no other in the world. ❧
www.atlanticfringe.ca

◀ Race Your Outhouse along the Streets of Dawson City

A bunch of outhouses were trotting down the street in Dawson City . . . no, this isn't the start of a really bad joke. Every Labour Day weekend since 1977 this very scene takes place, when about a dozen teams participate in the Great Klondike International Outhouse Race.

Teams of five people dress up in costumes and decorate their outhouses using different themes, such as The Elton John, The Royal Flush, The Whizzer of Oz, and The Mad Crapper. Four of them wheel the outhouse along a three-kilometre (1.9-mile) course through the city's streets, while the fifth sits on the pot. One member must be sitting on the outhouse's toilet seat as the others race it down the streets of Dawson City.

Runners often take turns on the toilet. (Not to worry—they keep their pants on for the event.) Crowds line up to cheer on the competing commodes as they use human power to propel themselves to the finish line. The team that completes the race the fastest wins. Prizes are also awarded for the most original outhouse and the best-dressed team. If you want to participate but haven't brought your own outhouse, the visitor centre can rent you one.✹

www.dawsoncity.ca

Tour Niagara's Wine Country by Bicycle ▶

Consider this: the Niagara region has some of Ontario's most beautiful and welcoming bike paths, with many wineries only a short bike ride apart. You begin to see the logic of the Bike Train, a service connecting urban cyclists and the countryside via GO Transit, the province's commuter rail service.

The Greenbelt Express runs between Toronto and Niagara Falls, with stops at stations along the way. Niagara Falls Station is less than a block from the Niagara River Recreation Trail, a 56-kilometre (34.8-mile) paved path that follows alongside the Niagara Parkway to the Niagara-on-the-Lake region—home to more than 30 wineries. Or, get off at St. Catharines and wind your way to Port Dalhousie along the Welland Canal and the vineyards of Twenty Valley. These escarpment vineyards are more plentiful (37 at last count), but the ride's more challenging.

If you don't have your own set of wheels, bike rentals are widely available. If you don't feel like planning

the trip yourself, opt for a guided tour—though operators put the emphasis on *leisurely* when describing their offerings. This isn't necessarily a problem . . . after a few glasses, you'll be in no mood to hurry.✹

www.winesofontario.org

Play Golf's Undiscovered Gem

Enjoy a golf holiday like no other at a stunningly beautiful time of year

Since 1902, when avid enthusiasts placed "holes" in the infield of the horse-racing track at the Charlottetown Exhibition Grounds, golf has been part of summer in Prince Edward Island (P.E.I.). Over the years the locale has changed, but not the enthusiasm for the game.

Today Prince Edward Island lays claim to being Canada's top golf destination, with 10 of the top-100 courses in Canada. In fact, 5 per cent of the top courses in North America are found within the 5,660 square kilometres (2,185 square miles) that make up Canada's smallest province. It has received dozens of accolades over the years, and yet is still relatively unknown. When asked to identify an "undiscovered gem" among the world's golf destinations, members of the International Golf Travel Writers Association named P.E.I. the 2011 Undiscovered Golf Destination of the Year. With more than 30 courses to choose from, there are choices for all levels (and pocketbooks).

Golfers know why September is a great time to hit the fairways in P.E.I.—fewer people, no bugs, and the courses are in great shape. Temperatures are pleasantly cool after the heat of July and August, while the air is clean and invigorating. This is also when P.E.I. is at its most colourful, as the changing season transforms the foliage of woodlands and shorelines to stunning vistas of autumn brilliance.

Labour Day weekend signals a quieter time. Once the kids are back in school and the hustle and bustle of summer winds down, "guy groups" and couples come for golf escapes to take full advantage of the joys of late summer and special deals and lower green fees.

There are as many reasons for P.E.I.'s top ratings as there are courses. When asked what set Prince Edward Island apart one golfer answered, "It's the differences between courses. A lot of places you go, famous places, there's a sameness. Courses may all be spectacular, but they have the same trees, the same feel. Here, in P.E.I., one course differs vastly from another. That adds hugely to the experience."

Indeed, the range of settings is vast: seaside, mature pine, or hardwood forest, river side or inner city, nine to 27 holes, luxurious resort to basic clubhouse. Island courses seem to be part of the landscape, blended in, rather than built upon. Unspoiled countryside, open spaces, sandy beaches, protective sand dunes, and captivating red rock cliffs guarantee inspiring views. When the leaves start to turn, the landscape takes on a special vibrancy.

For most visitors, one taste is not enough: 80 per cent of first-time golfers return to the island. The relaxed atmosphere helps lure many back. When visitors arrive, they're often reminded they need to adjust to "Island Time"—taking the time to relax, slow down, enjoy and create memories. The stresses of busy lives fade away as

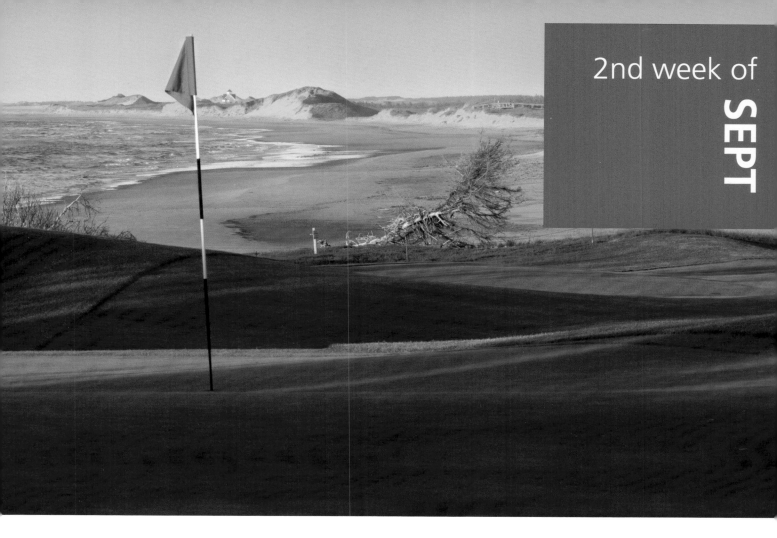

people discover little traffic, short distances to travel, and down-home hospitality.

That such a diverse mix of courses is found in a small area is a real bonus for those who want to squeeze considerable play into a few days. Golfers can play as many as 36 holes in a day, and the reasonable green fees—C$18 to $99—make this more feasible than in many other parts of the world.

The pros have certainly left their mark here too: Mike Weir, Vijay Singh, John Daly, Fred Couples, Jack Nicklaus, and Tom Watson have all played on the island, plus of course the island's own LPGA champion Lori Kane. The island has hosted the popular Golf Channel reality show *Big Break*, and is home to the Canadian Golf Academy, an instruction facility that works with all levels of golfers wanting to polish their skills. Space is almost always available for an hour or two with a pro.

The choice of golf vacations is abundant. Whether planning a stay at a five-star golf resort, a cottage for four, or establishing a base at a hotel or motel, dining and entertainment options are plentiful in September,

When the leaves start to turn, the landscape takes on a special vibrancy.

especially in Charlottetown or Summerside, where evening activities include horse racing, theatre, and an active club scene. Festivals focus on culinary delights, especially local shellfish and the fall harvest.

Golf packages can be tailored to you by Golf PEI, a booking service that can arrange accommodation, tee-off times, and rental cars. They even have special packages that include such goodies as Golf for the Gourmet, and Couples Escape. Or just head on over to P.E.I., and play where the whim takes you.🍁

Find out more at:
www.tourismpei.com/golf

ADVENTURE

CULTURE & HISTORY

Drive the Spectacular Alaska Highway

A driver on the Alaska Highway slows down near Fort Nelson to let an ungainly bear lope across the road. Further along, a mama moose and her two little ones lurk in the trees. Every year, thousands of people witness scenes like this while driving the Alaska Highway, which winds its way for about 2,000 kilometres (1,242.7 miles) through northern British Columbia, up to the Yukon and over to Delta Junction, Alaska.

This historic road began as a one-lane supply route to Alaska in 1942. Today, the scenic route starts at the Mile 0 marker in Dawson Creek, B.C. Before hitting the road, visit the town's Alaska Highway House to learn about how the highway was built and the tremendous impact it has had on local communities. Stop at the museum in Fort Nelson to see a garage crammed with lovingly restored antique cars and go for a soak at the Liard River Hot Springs further north. Other stops include lively Whitehorse and pretty Haines Junction in the shadow of Kluane National Park and Reserve.

Along the way, admire the mountain ranges that watch over the highway. Keep an eye out for bears, moose, caribou, and Dall sheep. Be sure to check out the *Milepost*, an annual publication that details what to see and do along the highway. 🍁

www.themilepost.com

Walk in the Footsteps of History on the Plains of Abraham

It was here, on September 13, 1759, where the French and British armies engaged in bloody battle that ultimately decided the fate of what we know as Canada today. Today, manicured public parks cover old wounds; you can stroll the grounds and partake in many of the cultural activities to commemorate this pivotal day.

The famous conflict led by Generals Louis-Joseph de Montcalm and James Wolfe would only last 15 minutes, but it would forever change the destiny of New France. The events are recounted at the Discovery Pavilion, where a 45-minute multimedia presentation takes you through the 400-year history of Québec, outlining the times of the French and the British, Canada's later creation, and the park's ultimate formation. Also on the Plains of Abraham is the storied Museum of Fine Arts, housed in the former Québec City prison. A lively tour is available, conducted by a guide in the guise of a prison guard.

Otherwise, the Plains' inviting green space is Québec City's answer to New York City's Central Park. At this time of year it's a prime location for in-line skating, jogging, bicycling, soccer, and football. Afterwards, enjoy a quiet picnic while admiring the regal Fairmont Le Château Frontenac hotel towering in the distance. 🍁

www.ccbn-nbc.gc.ca

◀ Visit the Beautiful Glacial Lakes of Banff National Park

In mid-September, the crowds have dispersed but the mountain lakes of Banff National Park remain as beautiful and as appealing as ever. The lakes themselves—namely Louise, Moraine, and Bow—are best-known, and contribute to making the park the scenic beauty it is. Yet, these glacial gems are themselves a memorable highlight for many visitors.

Some lakes are so large the colour changes dramatically from one end to the other.

One of the most obvious signs a lake is glacially fed is the stunning turquoise colour of the water, due to high concentrations of glacial silt. The silt, which has been ground from bedrock by moving glaciers, is so fine that it doesn't sink immediately to the bottom of the lake; instead, it's temporarily suspended in the water. Varying concentrations of silt result in variations in colour between lakes—and even within the same lake—as the rate of air temperature changes, increasing and decreasing glacial melt through the year. Some lakes are so large the colour changes dramatically from one end to the other. At Lake Louise, for example, receding glaciers at the west end fill the lake with a high concentration of silt, creating a brilliant turquoise colour, while at the east end (near the Fairmont Lake Louise) the water is clearer. ❧

www.pc.gc.ca/banff

Canadian *moments*

Labour Day Parades

Asking to work nine hours a day, six days a week seems like a reasonable request by today's labour standards. But in the late 1800s, employers expected a 12-hour workday.

So when Hamilton printers pushed to reduce hours with a strike on March 25, 1872, Toronto workers quickly showed support with a demonstration on April 14. Starting with 2,000 marchers, the Toronto crowd grew to 10,000 by the time it reached Queen's Park.

Today, the annual Labour Day Parade through downtown Toronto is a stream of union acronyms, labour slogans, and families. It's a musical affair with steel drummers, brass marching bands, kilted pipers, and rock bands strumming covers of BTO's "Takin' Care of Business." Attendees now number about 25,000, and the parade works its way from the intersection of Queen Street and University Avenue to the Canadian National Exhibition grounds—where marchers gain free admission.

But back in 1872, laws prohibited striking and union activity. When the organizers of the Toronto demonstration were arrested, Ottawa unions organized a mile-long parade that called in at the house of Canada's first prime minister, Sir John A. Macdonald. The crowd is said to have whisked away the then-prime minister to city hall, where Macdonald spoke against the "barbarous laws" used to jail the strike organizers.

In 1882, U.S. labour leader Peter McGuire attended festivities in Toronto. Inspired, he returned to New York and organized the first American Labor Day on September 5 of that year. But despite the Canadian connection, the U.S. Department of Labor still writes: "There is still some doubt as to who first proposed the holiday for workers."

EVENTS & FESTIVALS

Cheer On Your Favourite Team at the Manitoba Dragon Boat Festival ▶

Originally held to ensure bountiful crops, Chinese dragon boat races are now run throughout the world. The Manitoba event along the Red River (through downtown Winnipeg) attracts competitors from across Canada—not to mention hordes of screaming fans—whose athletic endeavours also raise hundreds of thousands of dollars for the Canadian Cancer Society.

While as many as 140 teams work hard to cross the finish line in first place, the races are a visual spectacle for visitors who line the riverbank shouting encouragement and cheering on the winners. The boats—around 12 metres (39 feet) long and weighing up to 700 kilograms (1,500 pounds)—are similar to dugout canoes, with lavishly painted dragon heads at the bow. Twenty paddlers do their best to keep rowing patterns in sync with one another and a drummer, while listening for commands shouted by the coxswain along a 500-metre (1,640-foot) course—and aiming to cross the finish line in under three minutes.

Festivities spill over from the river to The Forks National Historic Site, at the confluence of the Red and Assiniboine rivers, with food stands, traditional Chinese dance, live music, and the chance to look at a dragon boat up close. Although The Forks has a much shorter history than dragon boat racing, the site's an important part of Canada's own history—and well worth exploring to learn about the indigenous people, explorers, traders, and entrepreneurs who have passed through.🍁
www.facilitymarketing.com

◀ Drink In the Colour at the Atlantic International Balloon Fiesta

Up, up, and away, in a beautiful balloon . . . the chance to silently drift over the beautiful valleys of New Brunswick lures enthusiasts to Sussex for the Atlantic International Balloon Fiesta, held the weekend after Labour Day. No one argues with the organizers' boast that this is Atlantic Canada's most colourful festival. The skies quickly fill with a litany of incredible sights: pink elephants, cows, dragons, Mounties, monster-sized Canadian flags and maple leaves, trucks, tropical fish, tigers, octopus—even a Purple People Eater.

The scene never grows tired, the skyscape so awash in hovering hot air balloons that even locals with front-row seats still get giddy year after year. And the festival isn't just about spectators looking skyward. While the adventurous take to the air to ride a hot air balloon or helicopter, those with their feet firmly on *terra firma* can enjoy a craft fair, "power paragliding" demonstrations, a parade, an antique car show, a horse show, games, amusements, and tasty treats. The highlight? Undoubtedly the twice-daily flights of 30 hot air balloons, and dusk—when the balloons are inflated for the stunningly beautiful "moon/candle glow." Balloonists from all over the world are welcomed with white lights all over town and white sheets on farmer's fields; a visual hello seen from the sky or the highway. Awesome!◆

www.atlanticballoonfiesta.ca

Drink Up Victoria's Beer Scene

Victoria is sometimes dubbed North America's most British city, and for many of its retirees and civil servants, tea is the beverage of choice. Yet recently, the popularity of microbrewed beer has also blossomed in the "Garden City."

For a full-fledged beer bacchanalia, it's hard to beat the Great Canadian Beer Festival. Here, some 45 microbreweries from Canada, the United States, and Europe showcase their suds at Royal Athletic Park one weekend each September. It's Canada's longest-running beer festival, and the grins of satisfaction on the 7,000-odd beer fanatics in attendance say it all.

Victoria also boasts three well-established brewpubs near the downtown core. Great beer and gastronomic excellence intermingle beautifully at Spinnakers. Overlooking the Inner Harbour from the Esquimalt waterfront, Canada's oldest brewpub has perfected its handcrafted ales, lagers, and seasonal brews amidst wood-panelled hominess since 1984. At Swans Brewpub, sip a signature Raspberry Ale inside the heritage hotel's art-laden brick walls, or relax on the glass-enclosed, flower basket–laden patio with a glass of Arctic Ale. The nearby CANOE Brewpub delivers unfiltered, naturally carbonated brews, like the smooth Red Canoe Lager and the award-winning Bavarian Copper Bock.◆

www.gcbf.com, www.spinnakers.com, www.swanshotel.com, www.canoebrewpub.com

Get Inspired at the Terry Fox Run

Canadian run sites across the country pay homage to a hero in the world's largest one-day cancer fundraiser

Few people make an impact on history before reaching their 23rd birthday, but Terry Fox was a rare human being indeed. The curly-haired British Columbia native showed his indomitable spirit when he attempted to run coast to coast across Canada in 1980, striding stubbornly forwards on one good leg and an artificial limb after having lost his right leg to cancer. He was forced to give up his "Marathon of Hope" in support of cancer research as the disease spread to his lungs—taking him in 1981. Today, millions in more than 30 countries worldwide keep Fox's memory alive by participating in various incarnations of The Terry Fox Run each year. Run distances vary, and the goal isn't to win: it's simply to take part, and to add to the more than C$500 million the event has raised for The Terry Fox Foundation—dreaming that someday cancer will be conquered. When you travel and lace up your running shoes in different run locations, you get a heightened appreciation for what this young athlete, running a full marathon every day and inspiring people to care, went through.

St. John's, Newfoundland, is where Fox kicked off his 143-day, 5,373-kilometre (3,339-mile) odyssey, and the capital of Canada's easternmost island province is an ideal place to catch the spirit of the Terry Fox Run. Stop by the harbour where Fox symbolically dipped his artificial limb in the Atlantic Ocean on April 12, 1980, then visit the Terry Fox Mile "0" Memorial Site for a moment of reflection. In 2010, the federal government pledged C$250,000 for the creation of a large bronze sculpture by artist Luben Boykov to commemorate the beginning of Fox's quest, surrounded by memorial gardens. At the

run itself, expect walkers, joggers, parents with strollers, and dog-walkers on the trail stretching alongside Quidi Vidi Lake. Many are there for a family member or friend stricken by cancer, and you'll see banners covered with the names of loved ones. As you breathe in the Atlantic breeze, you'll take stock of being alive.

Two other eastern capital cities also offer distinct settings for the run. You'll find multiple sites in Ottawa, including Carleton University, where wheelchairs and in-line skaters join the celebration. *The Terry Fox Monument*, another bronze depiction of the runner in motion by artist John Hooper (1983), stands on Wellington Street—directly across from the Parliament Buildings. You can also visit the Royal Canadian Mint and purchase a Terry Fox commemorative coin. In Toronto, Ontario's capital, a family feeling pervades some 10 run sites—such as High Park, where clowns, magicians, firemen, and even Toronto Maple Leafs mascot Carleton

JOURNEE TERRY FOX
19 SEPTEMBRE 2010

"I just wish people would realize that anything's possible if you try; dreams are made possible if people try." —Terry Fox

the Bear put in appearances. Notably, Fox's personal favourite moment of the run came in "Hogtown" when he met his hockey idol, former Boston defenceman Bobby Orr. Also noteworthy: although Toronto is Canada's leading corporate centre, no advertising is displayed anywhere at the run, in keeping with Fox's wish to keep his "Marathon of Hope" as pure as possible.

Thunder Bay, Ontario, is known for its fur trading history and hockey players, but if you come here for the Terry Fox Run you'll soon see this small city at the head of Lake Superior also honours Fox's legacy. The Terry Fox Lookout, which surveys the lake from atop cliffs, has a 2.7-metre (nine-foot) statue of the man on a granite base overlooking the Terry Fox Courage Highway, a specially christened 82-kilometre (52-mile) stretch of the Trans-Canada Highway. Sadly, it was in this area that Fox had to abandon his quest—on September 1, 1980. But at St. Ignatius High School, the locally run site organized by the Rotary Club, Fox is warmly remembered as participants show up with the pledge money they've collected. There are no registration fees required to run— but ideally you're contributing something to the cause.

On the West Coast, Fox's spirit burns brightly. Attend the Terry Fox Run at his alma mater, Simon Fraser University, or in his native Port Coquitlam (just outside Vancouver). The PoCo run can draw over 50,000 participants. In downtown Vancouver, admire the new Fox statues outside BC Place Stadium. Or go to Vancouver Island, and you can start your Terry Fox Run at Mile 0 of the Trans-Canada Highway in Victoria, overlooking the ocean, graced by yet another Fox statue. This was his dream destination, one reached in 1985 by another Canada-crossing amputee athlete—Steve Fonyo—after whom a nearby beach is named.

No matter where or how you run, Fox's famous statement will resonate with you afterwards: "I just wish people would realize that anything's possible if you try; dreams are made possible if people try." ❦

Find out more at:
www.terryfox.org

ADVENTURE

Climb the Grouse Grind

Go ahead: change into some Vancouver-based Lululemon workout gear and devour a protein bar. But even that preparation probably won't help you beat the official Grouse Grind course records set by Sebastian Salas (male, 25:01, 2010) and Leslie Johnston (female, 31:04, 2007). Still, who cares? Whether or not you compete in the annual Grouse Grind Mountain Run, anyone who finishes this steep, 2.9-kilometre (1.8-mile) hike up Grouse Mountain deserves a medal. It's a true rite of passage for Vancouverites—and a regular weekly workout for many North Shore residents.

Stretch in the parking lot, and make sure you packed your bottled water, energy snacks, first-aid kit, and other goodies. Then start climbing the trail, sporting high-quality sneakers or hiking shoes—no stiletto heels, please. It's easygoing at first, beneath tall, shady firs and cedars, but your heart will be pumping when you hit the quarter-mark. Scrambles over rugged boulders and wooden bridges lie ahead. Pause periodically to admire the sweeping views back towards Vancouver. Budget a sweaty, thigh burning hours and a half to reach the summit, where restaurants, a wildlife sanctuary, and lumberjack shows await. Afterwards, take the Grouse Mountain Skyride aerial tramway to the bottom. Congratulations!🍁

www.grousemountain.com

◀ Explore the Heart of Toronto's Art Scene

Queen Street West has long been the centre of Toronto's visual arts community. The street's annual Art Crawl is when the neighbourhood invites everyone to come and see the work of some of the city's hottest local artists—and ideally take away some art.

Stretching from Bathurst Street to Roncesvalles Avenue, the event is a wonderful introduction to one of the city's most vibrant, pedestrian-friendly streets. Each year more than 40 "crawl partners," including art galleries, fashion boutiques, restaurants, cafés, and bars, create art-related events and exhibitions. Start your day at Trinity Bellwoods Park, where more than 250 visual artists display (and sell) their works—you can spend as little as C$10 for a memento that may as well be one-of-a-kind. The park has an interactive kids' zone all weekend with presenting artists on hand to show different techniques in ceramics, jewellery-making, and even origami. Each year's event includes a number of different free walking tours inspired by art-oriented themes, usually beginning in a restaurant. Music is integral to the event: the Toronto Blues Society, whose HQ is beside Trinity Bellwoods, offers an art-and-music jam in its backyard, while Saturday evening sees a move further west to the night clubs of neighbouring Parkdale. It's a long stretch of road, so some crawlers opt for a TTC Day Pass and simply jump on and jump off the Queen streetcar.🍁
www.parkdaleliberty.com/show_info. php?page_id=98

Take In Northern Ontario's Fall Colours by Train ▼

Is there a more iconic Canadian image than that of a train chugging across a towering trestle over vast wilderness? If you're hankering for the view from that train's window, the Agawa Canyon tour awaits. This part of Ontario is resplendent with autumnal colours in late September, so be prepared to gape.

This one-day excursion begins in the northern city of Sault Ste. Marie and travels 184 kilometres (114 miles) further north, past rock formations bearing the 10,000-year-old marks of the last glacial retreat. Beyond the extra-wide coach windows lie the rivers, lakes, and forests of the Canadian Shield, the granite vastness that traverses the province like a dividing line. Travellers can track the points of interest via a GPS-activated commentary available in five languages (English, French, Spanish, Japanese, and Mandarin) that outlines the history of the area, from the Aboriginal peoples to the trappers and explorers who opened up the region. Flat-panel monitors provide an engineer's-eye view of the coming attractions via a camera mounted on the locomotive. At the end of the line, in Canyon Park, passengers have a 90-minute break to picnic, explore, and perhaps dip a toe in the pristine, if frigid, waters. Trains depart daily at 8:00 a.m.; fall adult fares are approximately C$100. Reservations are strongly recommended.🍁
www.agawacanyontourtrain.com

EVENTS & FESTIVALS

QUIRKY CANADA

Enjoy a Feast of Activities at the P.E.I. Fall Flavours Festival

The larders are full, so let the feasting begin. The fall harvest in Prince Edward Island triggers a festival that celebrates the bounty of the farm, vineyard, and sea, by showcasing local production, preparation, and flavour through more than 250 different food events, festivals, and activities.

The Fall Flavours Festival brings together chefs, producers, entertainers, and food lovers for feasting, sampling, learning, and experiencing all across the island. Festivities are well underway by mid-September when the Prince Edward Island International Shellfish Festival blends cheering-on competitors in oyster-shucking and chowder-cookoffs, with foot-stomping music at the "Biggest Kitchen Party in Atlantic Canada." Television celebrity chef Michael Smith hosts Chef on Board, a culinary adventure on selected sailings of the Wood Islands Ferry linking P.E.I. with Nova Scotia. Activities continue throughout the month (hands-on experiences, tasting menus, cooking lessons and demos, tours on land or sea, and of markets). Learn to shuck an oyster, make chocolates or cider, dig clams, prepare Mi'kmaq bannock and Indian bread, cook mussels, crack lobsters, or do more things with potatoes than you ever imagined. You can even learn about distilling moonshine and vodka! Some events sell out so check the website and book early. 🍁
www.fallflavors.ca

Shop at Maritime Yard Sales that Go On for Miles

Small bills: check. Comfortable clothes: check. Empty trunk: check. Map: check . . . you're now ready for some profitable adventures, seeking out treasure at Nova Scotia's giant yard sales. Two events stand out, held over consecutive weekends in September—both for their offerings, and the beautiful scenery passed along the way during this yard-sale marathon.

The first full weekend after Labour Day, 80.4 kilometres (50 miles) of the Musquodoboit Valley in Nova Scotia becomes yard sale heaven. A short drive from Halifax, the valley remains deeply tied to the rural way of life. Start at the Visitor Information Centre in Middle Musquodoboit. Besides great deals, there's plenty of great food available throughout the weekend. Vendors offer everything from chili, chowder, and hotdogs, to strawberry shortcake.

In Prince Edward Island a 113-kilometre (70-mile) Coastal Yard Sale boasts more than 150 sites in southeastern P.E.I. Plough the Waves Visitor Information Centre, near the ferry, acts as the hub, with information, vendors, good eats, and a ceilidh on the lawn to wrap things up Sunday afternoon.

At both sales, be prepared to stop at private homes, community halls, churches, tourist attractions, and even small businesses for a mix of private sales and fundraising efforts. Yard sales reflect the Maritime ethic of not throwing away something that has use, but rather passing it along—and hopefully putting a few dollars in the pocket at the same time. Drop in to the local Visitor Information Centres for maps. 🍁
www.musquodoboitvalley.ca,
www.woodislands.ca/yard.html

◀ See the Mountains from the Viewing Car of the Whistler Mountaineer

One stunning way to observe summer yielding to autumn in B.C. is to ride the Whistler Mountaineer, travelling through a vast landscape balanced perfectly between the ocean and mountains. This luxury train makes a 3.5-hour "Sea to Sky Climb" between Vancouver and Whistler, home to most of the events at the 2010 Winter Games. Picture yourself en route.

In a dome coach with enormous glass windows, you relax in a wide seat as the train pulls out of the North Vancouver station. Soon, you're gliding past the multi-million dollar homes of West Vancouver ("West Van"), gazing across Burrard Inlet towards the forested cliffs of Vancouver's Stanley Park. Uniformed servers bring champagne and orange juice, followed by a hot

From local shellfish to steak, cuisine is a priority here.

breakfast with an omelette and fruit plate. Guides reveal the history of sailboat-dotted Howe Sound as you proceed north up the coast.

The journey delivers constant sensory stimulation. The Cheakamus River's churning white water knifing through a deep canyon. The steep 70-metre (230-foot) drop from the top of Brandywine Falls. The breeze ruffling your hair in the open-air Heritage Observation Car, as you try to glimpse a bear or deer. When the train arrives outside Nita Lake Lodge in Whistler, you'll already be anticipating the return trip. ❧
www.whistlermountaineer.com

Johanna Skibsrud's *favourite* PLACE

Johanna Skibsrud, who won the 2010 Giller Prize for her novel *The Sentimentalists*, has memories of clam festivals and high tides near Cape Chignecto, Nova Scotia—an area she recently rediscovered.

"It was a revelation, in a way, because the landscape is so different than other areas of Nova Scotia," says Skibsrud, reached while studying in Paris. "It reminded me of how much there is in Nova Scotia to explore."

Cape Chignecto Provincial Park covers the tip of the peninsula, which juts into the Bay of Fundy between New Brunswick and Nova Scotia.

"They've extended the trail system," she says. "I'm really looking forward to taking a more extended trip there." A 51-kilometre (31.7-mile) trail is the only access to the cape and requires a multi-day hike to visit.

"My family took a trip when I was a kid," she says. She remembers Upper and Lower Economy on the Economy Shore, a string of coastal hamlets between Truro and Parrsboro.

"That's such a beautiful stretch, the drive out there . . . the stunning change of the landscape when the tide is in or out."

Activities depend on the water cycles, whether it's clam digging in the mud flats, sea kayaking, or walking the beaches. One beach, Skibsrud says, is known as the driftwood beach for the tangles of sun-bleached wood that collect there.

On her next trip she hopes to go sea kayaking on the coast.

"[Sea kayaking] is incredible, you are so close to the water, to the rhythms and the patterns," says the young author. "That's the closest I've ever been to feeling the movement of the water."

Hike along Breathtaking Lake O'Hara

Lakes and larch trees are ablaze with fall colours

Quite simply, Lake O'Hara is one of the most special places in the Canadian Rockies, especially in late September when the needles of alpine larch turn a magnificent golden hue amidst the mountain scenery. The namesake lake is surrounded by alpine meadows and dozens of smaller lakes, framed by towering mountains permanently mantled in snow. As if that weren't enough, the entire area is webbed by a network of hiking trails established over the last 90 years by luminaries such as Lawrence Grassi, who was renowned throughout the Canadian Rockies for his trail building. Trails radiate from the lake in all directions; the longest is just 7.5 kilometres (4.7 miles), making Lake O'Hara an especially fine hub for day hiking. What makes this destination all the more special is that a bus access–only quota system limits the number of visitors. After the 20-minute bus ride terminates at the lake, most hikers head for the welcoming sight of Le Relais—a homely log shelter

where trail information is dispensed. From this point, you have enough hiking options to fill a week.

The easiest trail is Lake O'Hara Shoreline, a 40-minute option that encircles the main lake. Although it mainly provides a jumping-off point to other trails, it's an enjoyable walk in its own right, especially in the evening. At the lake's far end is Seven Veil Falls and a short detour to Mary Lake. Beyond O'Hara, one of the easiest lakes to reach is aqua-coloured Lake Oesa, which has the sheer cliffs of Mount Victoria and Mount Lefroy as a backdrop.

If you question O'Hara enthusiasts about their favourite destination, many would opt for the Opabin Plateau. Walking about 90 minutes from the end of the road transports hikers into a dazzling landscape of larch and turquoise lakes framed by towering mountain peaks. Trails criss-cross the plateau, allowing you to spend most of a full day exploring to the end of the valley, where views sweeping back down across the valley take in the full scope of an unforgettable panorama. But it is the golden larch trees that are the late September highlight of Opabin Plateau. The most impressive stands are at the top of the west approach, along and around the approach to Opabin Prospect, a rocky ledge high above Lake O'Hara.

The Opabin Plateau and Lake Oesa are linked by the Alpine Circuit. For experienced hikers not afraid of heights, the circuit is the ultimate Canadian Rockies day hike. More of a route than a trail, it links these two destinations with Schaffer Lake, creating a 12-kilometre (7.5-mile) loop that remains above the treeline almost the entire way. If you've spent the

morning exploring Opabin Plateau, and want to extend the adventure, take the Alpine Circuit route from near Opabin Prospect and you'll soon be climbing into the circuit's most rewarding section, with amazing views down to Lake O'Hara and across to the peaks of the Continental Divide. A possible add-on to the circuit, or a destination in itself, is Lake McArthur, the largest lake in the region. Reached after about an hour's walk, the final section is a short climb onto a ledge—where alpine meadows offer the first views of Lake McArthur. Backed by Mount Biddle and the Biddle Glacier, the deep-blue lake and colourful alpine meadows are an unforgettable panorama.

Cathedral Basin is another worthy destination at Lake O'Hara, but is away from the most popular day-hiking destinations—making it a good place to experience solitude. Reached in under three hours, the basin is dotted with ponds and presents a magnificent panorama of the Lake O'Hara area, with the backdrop of peaks along the Continental Divide laid out to the southeast.

Whether you're staying overnight or just visiting for the day, access to Lake O'Hara is exclusively by bus along a road that's off limits to the general public. Seats on the bus are very limited and highly sought after, especially for the "larch viewing season" of late September. Reservations can be made up to three months in advance, and you really must call the full three months ahead to be assured a spot (for example to book the bus for September 27, you should call at 8:00 a.m. MST on June 27). Two buses run up to the lake each morning, so use the Parks Canada website to find the schedule and have your preferred time in mind before calling; reservations are not required for the afternoon trip back down from the lake. The second consideration is whether you plan to visit Lake O'Hara for just the day, or stay overnight. Lake O'Hara Campground (campground reservations need to be made when booking the bus) is perfect for those equipped for backcountry camping, but by late September overnight temperatures are often below freezing. Another option is a rustic hut operated by the Alpine Club of Canada, with bunk beds and propane heating; reservations can be made through the Alpine Club. The most luxurious option—and one that draws familiar faces year after year—is Lake O'Hara Lodge. The lodge itself has comfortable guest rooms, or splash out on one of 15 lakeside cabins (lodge guests are not required to make their own bus reservations). ❧

Find out more at:
www.pc.gc.ca/yoho,
www.lakeohara.com

ADVENTURE

▲

Try Caving at the Canmore Caverns

Leave the colourful fall foliage of late September behind as you descend into the rarefied world of the Rat's Nest Cave, high on the slopes of Grotto Mountain, near Canmore, Alberta.

The trek up to the cave entrance is a fantastic introduction to the region's geology, with the glacially carved Bow Valley laid out below. Around 1.5 million years ago, meltwater from the same glaciers that flowed through the valley seeped through the soft bedrock of Grotto Mountain, creating a system of caves stretching around four kilometres (2.5 miles). Continuing erosion and flowing water has created a wonderland of underground passages, stalactites, and stalagmites, while

a pool of gin-clear water in the Grotto adds an eerie element to the adventure.

Access to the cave is restricted so, even if you're an experienced caver, join a guided tour offered by Canmore Cave Tours. Wear warm, comfortable clothing, as well as sturdy hiking boots. The guiding company provides other necessities such as coveralls, knee pads, gloves, helmets, and safety ropes. Around two hours are spent exploring underground. With travel time, this standard tour lasts about four hours. Or, upgrade to the six-hour Adventure Tour for the chance to try underground rappelling. ❦

www.canmorecavetours.com

Sneak a Peek at the Cape Dorset Print Collection

Artists comprise more than one-third of Nunavut's population, so touring the region would not be complete without seeing the soapstone carvings, tapestries, and prints that locals create. The centre of the Inuit art scene is the small village of Cape Dorset, on Southern Baffin Island, which put Inuit art on the map more than 60 years ago. While Cape Dorset artists are famous for their carvings and tapestries, the *pièce de résistance* is the Cape Dorset Print Collection, released every year at the end of October. This is the optimal time to visit the studio—both because you can see the latest collection, and meet the artists behind the famous prints.

The prints are characterized by bright colours, abstract shapes, and scenes portraying both the traditional and modern way of life in the Arctic. Images cover everything from seal hunting to snowmobiling to dispensing money from an ATM.

The hub of Dorset's art scene is the West Baffin Eskimo Co-operative, the first Inuit-owned cooperative when it opened in 1959. Today visitors can tour the co-op's two fine-art printmaking studios and, with any luck, can meet the artists in action. Just make sure to call in advance to set up a tour time.✽
www.nunavuttourism.com

Drive the Dempster Highway to the Arctic Circle ▼

It's autumn and the tundra along the Dempster Highway is bathed in colour. Vivid reds, yellows, and golds light the Tombstone, Ogilvie, and Richardson mountain ranges that watch over this 741-kilometre (460-mile) highway from Dawson City, Yukon, to Inuvik, Northwest Territories. This is the only public highway in Canada to cross the Arctic Circle.

The Dempster Highway is a two-lane gravel road that opened in 1979, named after Royal Canadian Mounted Police Inspector William Dempster. As the road slices through the Arctic wilderness, it travels through the Continental Divide, the Mackenzie River, and the Yukon-NWT border. Along the way, the scenery changes from valleys to vast plateaus and open tundra.

Keep an eye out for Dall sheep, mountain goats, moose, caribou, wolves, and bears. Stop to hike and photograph, camp in Tombstone Territorial Park, or overnight at Eagle Plains. Take a picture of yourself at the Arctic Circle and the territorial border. Drive onto the ferry and stop for a visit at Fort McPherson. Bring along spare tires, a jack, extra gas, food, and other supplies. This is a wilderness road where gas stations and restaurants are a rarity. But the isolation is exactly why you're here.✽
www.yukonheritage.com/Sign/northern/ northern.html

◀ Get Literary with The Word on the Street

In an era when many fear traditional reading is lagging behind social media and video games, The Word on the Street festival—held annually—shows just how hungry Canadians are for literary sustenance. Vancouver's Central Library, resembling Rome's Coliseum, provides an exciting setting for the event.

Celebrating Canadian books and magazines, The Word on the Street takes place in multiple cities, including Saskatoon, Halifax, Kitchener, and Toronto, the original site back in 1990. Vancouver's always embraced the event with enthusiasm—unsurprisingly so, with a library system that has 373,000 cardholders and loans out some nine million items each year.

Wander along bustling Homer Street, strewn with exhibitors' tables and white tents, and buy locally published books, or flip through magazines like *YES Mag* and *NUVO*. Budding authors can chat with reps from the Crime Writers of Canada or the Surrey International Writers' Conference. Don't miss the author readings, whether it's Sheri Radford delighting kids with her *Penelope and the Preposterous Birthday Party*, or Jack Whyte reading his latest *King Arthur* blockbuster.

There are also seminars on comic books and graphic novels, Aboriginal storytelling sessions, and chances to meet CBC TV personalities at the neighbouring CBC Plaza. It's a nice, mind-stimulating day out.🍁
www.thewordonthestreet.ca

5 *faves*

Québec City's *The Image Mill* and *Aurora Borealis* light installation

As part of the city's 400th anniversary celebrations, the famous Québec installation artist Robert Lepage created a massive, outdoor multimedia show of photos of city history called *The Image Mill*, projected on industrial grain silos in the Vieux-Port. From dusk until 11:30 p.m., the silos are bathed in a light show called *Aurora Borealis*, inspired by the technicolour of the real northern lights.

Browse Vancouver Island's "Booktown"

Seeking an alternative to September's The Word on the Street festival? Head to the tiny Vancouver Island town of Sidney. It's just a 25-minute drive north of Victoria, near the airport and the Swartz Bay ferry terminal. The seafront buildings are low and quaint, but Sidney lures bibliophiles with towering stacks of books. Boasting more than 10 independent bookstores, it was the first place in Canada designated a "booktown" back in 1996. Sidney shares that distinction with St. Martins, New Brunswick; Hay-on-Wye, England (the original booktown); and about 30 other towns worldwide.

Most of the deliciously musty-scented stores stocking secondhand and vintage titles are clustered along central Beacon Avenue, and knowledgeable booksellers gladly offer guidance. Beacon Books is an ideal venue to discover, say, a century-old edition of the complete works of Charles Dickens. Founded in 1947, nearby The Haunted Bookshop is Vancouver Island's oldest antiquarian bookstore. Here, you might find a leather-backed copy of Sir Walter Scott's *Ivanhoe* or Christopher Milne's *The House at Pooh Corner*. For more contemporary reads, spacious Tanner's Books offers the Island's largest newsstand, with more than 2,000 magazine titles, while Dragon Horse has the latest self-help and spirituality releases.🍁

www.sidneybooktown.ca

Taste the Fruits of "the County"

A booming viticulture (winemaking to you and me) community, an artisanal approach to agriculture, and a plethora of fine restaurants: it's a virtuous circle that has made Ontario's Prince Edward County a Shangri-La for Ontario foodies. Based in the charming town of Picton, the Taste! festival celebrates the harvest of grape and good food on the stalk, the hoof, or the fishing line.

You'll find all manner of fruits and vegetables, locally raised lamb and beef, and pickerel plucked from the nearby Bay of Quinte. This is the palate for the highly regarded chefs who ply their trade in "the County," as locals like to call it. Where else will you find a goat-cheese dairy or a farmer who produces more than 100 varieties of heirloom tomatoes? Each day features a range of events—from cooking demos, to concerts, to barn dances. Waring House Restaurant and Country Inn offers cooking classes. Or sample the product of Huff Estates winery and spend the night. Sandbanks Winery has a kids' grape harvest party where future winos get to squeeze their first grape juice. Buddha Dog in Picton features gourmet hotdogs made with locally processed meat, served with condiments created by chefs from different restaurants in the area.

You can go for the day, but why not stay for a night (or two) and indulge?🍁

www.tastecelebration.ca

Point Pelee butterfly migration
Wonder at the transformation of Point Pelee and Presqu'ile Provincial Park as the monarch butterfly migration sets in and the trees along the shores of Lake Erie literally dip under the weight of millions of these beautiful creatures who alight for a snack en route to Mexico.

Seasonal harvest menus in Vancouver
While the city's fine-dining restaurants are known for using local products year-round, the fruitfulness of late September sees seasonal menus making more use than ever of local bounty. Restaurants like Bishop's, Raincity Grill, and Yaletown's Blue Water Café all feature menus rich in fresh, locally sourced fare.

Hike the Highlands Festival
Hike the Highlands Festival is a 10-day indulgence in guided hikes, nature photography workshops, geo-caching, and Nordic walking for beginners and seasoned trekkers alike. Taking place on Nova Scotia's gorgeous Cape Breton Island, there are two or three guided hikes each day ranging from 2.3 kilometres (1.4 miles) to 18 kilometres (11.2 miles).

Saguenay-St. Lawrence Marine Park
The confluence of waters of the St. Lawrence Estuary with those of the Saguenay Fjord creates a marine environment for more than 15 species of marine mammals, including the protected St. Lawrence beluga whale. The stunning landscapes can be toured by kayak or Zodiac.

Your next STEP

TOP PICKS

ADVENTURE

CULTURE & HISTORY

NATURE'S GRANDEUR

EVENTS & FESTIVALS

QUIRKY CANADA

REJUVENATE

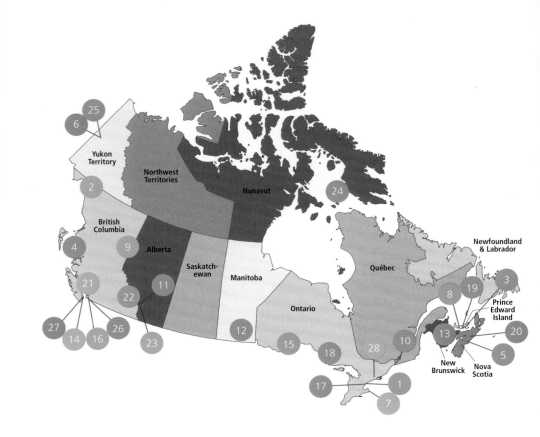

WEEK 1

1 TORONTO, ONT.
Toronto International Film Festival
www.tiff.net

2 BENNETT, B.C.
Chilkoot Trail hiking
www.pc.gc.ca/chilkoot

3 CHARLOTTETOWN, P.E.I.
Canadian history at Founders' Hall
www.foundershall.ca

4 KLEMTU, B.C.
Spirit bear–watching
www.spiritbear.com

5 HALIFAX, N.S.
Atlantic Fringe theatre festival
www.atlanticfringe.ca

6 DAWSON CITY, Y.T.
Outhouse racing
www.dawsoncity.ca

7 NIAGARA FALLS, ONT.
Wine country bike touring
www.winesofontario.org

WEEK 2

8 SUMMERSIDE, P.E.I.
P.E.I. golfing
www.tourismpei.com/golf

9 DAWSON CREEK, B.C.
Alaska Highway
www.themilepost.com

10 QUÉBEC CITY, QUE.
Plains of Abraham
www.ccbn-nbc.gc.ca

11 BANFF, ALTA.
Glacial lakes of Banff
www.pc.gc.ca/banff

12 WINNIPEG, MAN.
Manitoba Dragon Boat Festival
www.facilitymarketing.com

13 SUSSEX, N.B.
Atlantic International Balloon Fiesta
www.atlanticballoonfiesta.ca

14 VICTORIA, B.C.
Victoria beer scene
www.gcbf.com

WEEK 3

15 THUNDER BAY, ONT.
The Terry Fox Run
www.terryfox.org

16 NORTH VANCOUVER, B.C.
The Grouse Grind climb
www.grousemountain.com

17 TORONTO, ONT.
Toronto art scene
www.parkdaleliberty.com/
show_info.php?page_id=98

18 SAULT STE. MARIE, ONT.
Agawa Canyon train tour
www.agawacanyontourtrain.com

19 ARLINGTON, P.E.I.
Fall Flavours Festival
www.fallflavors.ca

20 MIDDLE MUSQUODOBOIT, N.S.
Maritime yard sales
www.musquodoboitvalley.ca

21 WHISTLER, B.C.
Whistler Mountaineer train tour
www.whistlermountaineer.com

WEEK 4

22 LAKE O'HARA, B.C.
Yoho National Park
www.pc.gc.ca/yoho

23 CANMORE, ALTA.
Canmore Caverns caving
www.canmorecavetours.com

24 CAPE DORSET, NUNAVUT
Cape Dorset Print Collection
www.nunavuttourism.com

25 DAWSON CITY, Y.T.
The Dempster Highway
www.yukonheritage.com/Sign/
northern/northern.html

26 VANCOUVER, B.C.
The Word on the Street
www.thewordonthestreet.ca

27 SIDNEY, B.C.
Sidney Booktown
www.sidneybooktown.ca

28 PICTON, ONT.
Taste! regional cuisine festival
www.tastecelebration.ca

OCTOBER

Visit Your Favourite NHL Team on Opening Night

The only way to release four months' worth of pent-up hockey frustration? Make it to the game.

Canada is home to just six of the National Hockey League's 30 franchises, but nowhere do people get more excited about opening day of the NHL season than in this country. Packed arenas. Wall-to-wall media coverage. Colourful jerseys. Canadians crave bone-crunching bodychecks, 161-kilometre (100-mile)-per-hour slapshots, and the passion that erupts when the red lamp lights up behind the opposing goalie. After the Stanley Cup finals end in June, fans are already salivating for the first official puck drop in October. Want a piece of the hottest action

on ice? Head to your favourite team's home arena for opening night.

Take the Vancouver Canucks. British Columbia's NHL team tears it up at downtown's 18,860-capacity Rogers Arena, which hosted Olympic hockey during the 2010 Winter Games. The Canucks have sold out every home game since 2002, and the crowds get pumped up by operatic anthem singer Mark Donnelly, who holds out his microphone and gets the crowd to join him in singing "O Canada." When play starts, you'll marvel at the razzle-dazzle moves of Daniel and Henrik Sedin, identical Swedish twins who always vie for the blue-and-green scoring lead. (In 2009–10, Henrik, Vancouver's captain, topped the NHL with 112 points, the first Canuck to achieve this feat.) The centre-ice video display system—weighing 22,226 kilograms (49,000 pounds) with eight screens featuring 1.2 million pixels—is among North America's best. Can't find tickets? Try the team's on-line Prime Seats Club, where season-ticket holders unload what they can't use. Alternately, head to the Shark Club (180 West Georgia Street), within eyeshot of Rogers Arena, and enjoy opening-day action on more than 40 HDTVs amidst hooting fans, long-legged waitresses, and brews aplenty.

Rexall Place, home of the Edmonton Oilers, was the legendary Wayne Gretzky's old stomping ground during his 1980s heyday. Today, fans in the Alberta capital go wild for talented youngsters like Taylor Hall and Jordan Eberle. The arena has hit an ear-splitting 116 decibels during the playoffs, and often approaches that on opening day. If the opener's against the Calgary Flames, Edmonton's bitter provincial rival, expect some fisticuffs: 250-pound Oilers enforcer Steve MacIntyre knocked out Calgary's Raitis Ivanans in their 2010–11 debut. Big, hard-hitting, red-clad teams are standard fare at Calgary's Scotiabank Saddledome, where the Flames muscled their way to the team's only Stanley Cup in

1989. The Saddledome sits on sacred cowboy turf—the grounds of the Calgary Stampede, which also hosted hockey and figure skating at the XV Olympic Winter Games in 1988. Among Alberta's standout hockey bars, jersey-clad maniacs abound at Edmonton's Elephant & Castle (10314 Whyte Avenue), while Flames Central (219 – 8th Avenue SW), complete with fiery logos and a 9-metre (30-foot) HD projection screen, is Calgary's place to be.

If you're Canadian, you either love or hate the Toronto Maple Leafs—there's no in-between. On opening night, you'll pay the NHL's highest ticket prices to see a club that has won 13 Stanley Cups, but (infamously) none since 1967. The Air Canada Centre, a massive downtown ice palace that opened in 1999, bustles with three restaurants, two bars, and an on-site brewery. Pay a pre-game visit to the Hockey Hall of Fame, just a five-minute walk away and loaded with historic artifacts and interactive exhibits. Wayne Gretzky's restaurant (99 Blue Jays Way) dishes up #99-branded burgers (literally) and displays The Great One's memorabilia, making it an excellent place to watch the game. Even nearby hotels reflect the Ontario capital's passion for the ice gladiators, like the Hotel Le Germain Maple Leaf Square, where puck-shaped armchairs grace rooms and pictures of NHLers hang over beds. Leafs supporters may suffer sleepless nights, but their loyalty's remarkable.

The loyalty of Ottawa Senators fans has been tested recently. The Senators have had their ups and downs since raising their Eastern Conference championship banner in the 2007–08 opening-day ceremony. Fortunately, Scotiabank Place, the team's 19,153-capacity home, is among the NHL's nicer rinks, as you'll discover if you make the half-hour drive from downtown Ottawa to the suburban location for the season opener. Tickets are easier to get in the national capital than elsewhere, and spectators are knowledgeable—such as Canadian prime minister Stephen Harper, who moonlights as a hockey historian. Stock up on cool home-team gear at the Sens Store. If you can't make it to the arena, chow down on signature wings and ribs at Local Heroes (1525 Bank Street) while catching the action on one of their nearly 30 TV screens.

To kick off the NHL season in real style, check out the Montréal Canadiens, the NHL's answer to the New York Yankees. They've won a league-best 24 Stanley Cups! Expect a dazzling pre-game ceremony with the massive "Habs" logos projected on the ice and nods to past greats like Jean Beliveau and Guy Lafleur. While the team's current domicile, the Bell Centre, lacks the hallowed pedigree of the old Montréal Forum, it's one of the liveliest and loudest arenas going. Ecstatic choruses of "Olé, Olé, Olé," an adopted soccer chant, echo through the three-tiered building when the Canadiens score. Grab a traditional smoked meat sandwich from the concessions to round out your experience. This is a taste of Canada's national winter sport you'll never forget.

Find out more at:
www.nhl.com

ADVENTURE

Walk on the Outside of the CN Tower

Here's a chance to take a walk on your wild side. The CN Tower was built as a telecommunications tool, but its EdgeWalk experience is the closest most of us will get to skydiving. Harnessed to steel support rods, you can walk around the perimeter of the observation pod and literally hang out—356 metres (1,168 feet)—above ground. A commemorative video is included in the C$175 fee.

Guinness World Record snobs may quibble it's no longer the world's tallest free-standing structure. But the tower sticks to its Guinness-certified guns: at 553.33 metres (1,815 feet and five inches), the CN Tower remains the world's tallest tower. (A tower being defined as a building where less than 50 per cent of the construction is useable floor space.) Since

October 1, 1975, when it began hoisting visitors upwards via its glass-walled elevators, the tower has contributed to Toronto's branding, and continues to be a homing beacon for pilots of planes, boats, and automobiles—not to mention a handy visual reference for tourists.

If the EdgeWalk is too wild for you, there's always the 24-square-metre (256-square-foot) glass floor where you can gaze past your feet down the tower's sloping flanks. Then head upstairs to the aptly named 360 Restaurant, a rotating dining experience featuring the world's highest wine cellar—the perfect way to spend the C$175 you saved by not walking on the edge.❧
www.cntower.ca

◄ Take a Walking Tour of Historic Old Montréal

Jacques Cartier first set foot in Montréal on October 2, 1535, then called Hochelaga. The famous French explorer climbed the landmass before him, baptizing it Mont Royal. Nearly five centuries later visitors to the island can relive Cartier's autumn days by discovering the historical beauty of Old Montréal.

Once an Amerindian trail, by the early 1700s, Place Jacques-Cartier was occupied by the Marquis de Vaudreuil's residence; then by a boys' college, which was destroyed by a fire in 1803. A marketplace later surfaced and remained until the Marché Bonsecours opened down the street in 1847.

After 1850, hotels opened along intersecting Saint-Paul Street—said to be the oldest street in the city. Just a few blocks away, the Auberge du Vieux-Port on rue de la Commune showcases a small cross-section of the rampart in its basement, from when Montréal was a fortified city.

Today, Place Jacques-Cartier is a lively square bordered by restaurants on either side. The monument at the upper end is, interestingly, not of Cartier, but of one Admiral Horatio Nelson, the subject of much controversy considering it honours a British victory over France in a largely French-speaking city. In 1930, francophone residents responded by erecting a statue nearby commemorating Jean Vauquelin, a French sailor during the Seven Years' War.✤

www.vieux.montreal.qc.ca

Go for a Soak at the Miette Hot Springs ▼

From the Yellowhead Highway through Jasper National Park, Miette Hot Springs Road curves, swerves, rises, and falls many times before ending at the hottest (temperature-wise) hot springs in the Canadian Rockies. This makes Miette Hot Springs the perfect destination when the chill of early October is in the air.

For park visitors of yesteryear, the hot springs were an important attraction; many would travel across the continent to experience their healing powers. The springs were developed more than 100 years ago, though the original hand-hewn log structure was replaced in the 1930s with pools that remained in use until new facilities were built in 1985.

Over all these years, one constant has been the super-hot mineral water flowing out of the ground at 54 degrees Celsius (128 degrees Fahrenheit) and then artificially cooled to a more bearable 39 degrees Celsius (100 degrees Fahrenheit). There are two main outdoor pools, plus a cold-plunge pool, but all three command sublime mountain views across the forested Miette Valley. Before or after your soak, take the short walking trail to the source of the springs. Other trails lead down to the remains of the 1930s "aquacourt" and up to the lofty viewpoint known as Sulphur Skyline.✤

www.pc.gc.ca/jasper

EVENTS & FESTIVALS

QUIRKY CANADA

Be Fabulous at the Vancouver International Film Festival

It may not bring the Hollywood star power of the Sundance, Cannes, or Toronto film festivals, but the Vancouver International Film Festival (VIFF) has carved out an exciting, distinctive niche of its own. This two-week extravaganza shows close to 400 films for 150,000 attendees annually, making it one of North America's five biggest film festivals.

There's a palpable energy, and eager lineups stretching down the block outside the Granville 7 Cinemas in downtown's neon-lit entertainment district. VIFF specializes in presenting East Asian cinema, documentaries, and Canadian films, like 2010's *Incendies*, which received an Oscar nomination for best foreign-language film. Typically, you can also catch the best of what Europe's creating, such as 2006's *The Lives of Others* (Germany).

And star-spotting is possible during VIFF. Watch out for Canadian TV talents like Nancy Robertson (*Corner Gas*), Kristen Kreuk (*Smallville*), or Tricia Helfer (*Battlestar Galactica*). Even some Hollywood veterans like Darryl Hannah or Henry Winkler put in appearances. If you know the right people, you might even score an invitation to Brightlight Pictures' red-carpet gala party at CinCin restaurant, overlooking trendy Robson Street. Lights, camera, action!❧
www.viff.org

Visit Molly's Reach of *The Beachcombers* Fame

If the perky, horns-driven theme music of *The Beachcombers* brings a nostalgic tear to your eye, then there's no better place for you to visit this week than Molly's Reach. The homey café with the distinctive, bright-yellow facade featured prominently in the CBC dramatic series that debuted on October 1, 1972, and ran through 1990—the longest TV run in Canadian history. Located harbourside in the tiny town of Gibsons, dubbed "The Gateway to the Sunshine Coast," Molly's Reach is just a 40-minute ferry ride from West Vancouver and a five-kilometre (three-mile) drive from the Langdale ferry terminal.

Molly's Reach has splendid views of fishing boats moored at Gibsons Landing, and the walls are plastered with photos of the show's characters. Staff happily recall now-deceased stars like Bruno Gerussi (who played coastal, log-salvaging hero Nick Adonidas) and Robert Clothier (who portrayed Nick's rival, Relic). Dig into a scrumptious Pacific Scrambler (eggs, wild salmon, an English muffin, and potato pancakes) for breakfast, or wolf down fish and chips with locally brewed ale batter anytime. Buy a souvenir T-shirt on your way out. Nearby, quaint art galleries, dockside fishing, and picturesquely soaring seagulls offer further diversions.❧
www.mollysreach.ca

Unwind at Luxurious Langdon Hall

Once the country estate of a scion of the aristocratic American Astor clan (think Waldorf-Astoria), this idyllic retreat may be the best place in the country to relax—this week or any other. Langdon Hall does everything exceptionally well, from the eggs Benedict at breakfast, through the petit fours at high tea, to the refined dining that earned its five-diamond rating and its designation as the only Relais & Chateaux establishment in Ontario.

This idyllic retreat may be the best place in the country to relax.

Just over an hour southwest of Toronto, the manor house experience begins the moment you see the imposing mansion at the end of its curving drive. Your chest will puff out like an Astor's as you pull up within the imposing pillars of the portico and the genuinely attentive bellhops (as opposed to ones with their hands outstretched for a tip) whisk your bags to your room. The menu of spa experiences is rivalled only by the restaurant's menu. That said, don't hesitate to order room service and indulge in a private dinner. Guest chambers in the original mansion retain an historic feel, but those in the converted stables have the bonus of walkout access to the gardens—not to mention lower room rates that allow the penny-wise to spend more, perhaps, on some of the offerings on Langdon Hall's vast wine list. Of course, there are always things you could do—there's a croquet lawn, a swimming pool, a snooker table, and four walking trails on the 81-hectare (200-acre) property, including the aptly named Deer Run. But, with food as good as Langdon Hall's you may find yourself simply waiting for your next meal.❦
www.langdonhall.ca

It *happened*
THIS WEEK:

Alexander Keith's Birthday

Green foam antlers, east coast music, and cheers of "Sociable!" overtake Halifax, Nova Scotia, on October 5—all in the name of celebrating Alexander Keith's birthday. Some devotees even place India pale ale bottle caps on the brewmaster's grave at Camp Hill Cemetery.

Though born in Scotland in 1795, Keith made a strong mark on Halifax. He brewed his first India pale ale in 1820, at the age of 25. He went on to become a political figure, serving as Halifax mayor.

"Based on the recipe information we have, today's Keith's IPA is as true to the original as we can make it," writes Graham Kendall, brewmaster emeritus, on the Keith's blog.

The brewery runs tours in its historic Lower Water Street location in Halifax. Costumed guides sing folk songs, tell tales, and serve tastings.

But a few things have changed since Keith fermented his first batch of beer.

Labatt Brewing Company now owns Keith's, and the famous IPA is also brewed in British Columbia, Québec, Ontario, and Newfoundland and Labrador.

Yet Nova Scotians unwaveringly mark the brew as theirs.

The beer's status in Halifax is so entwined with the city's own history that Keith's hosted the 2008 birthday party at Citadel Hill, a national historic site.

Drive the Cabot Trail

One of the world's most breathtaking tours takes you to the heart
of Acadian and Maritime culture

Be sure to drive it clockwise, states one devotee. No, says another, counterclockwise is best. The journey that spurs such debate is Cape Breton's Cabot Trail, a 300-kilometre (186-mile) circle tour of Nova Scotia's northernmost peninsula—considered one of the most scenic drives in the world.

Winding around the protected wilderness of the Cape Breton Highlands National Park, the Cabot Trail is your gateway to adventure, heritage, and the wonders of nature. After crossing the Canso Causeway into Cape Breton, Route 19 takes you through a region that has fostered traditional music for 250 years. You've come at the right time: this is when the Celtic Colours International Festival opens its doors to an extravaganza of all things Celtic. Music-lovers from around the world come to theatres, churches, and fire halls to revel in singing, dancing, and music. The entertainment is very popular, so booking accommodation ahead is a wise move.

At Margaree Harbour join the Cabot Trail for the clockwise drive said (by some) to ensure the greatest views. The journey reveals the magnificent "colours"

being celebrated. Woodlands, tundra, and bogs are a vibrant showcase of autumn reds, golds, yellows, and greens. There are 24 lookouts ahead. Be safe. Pull over. Partake of the visual feast. If you enjoy the quirky, visit Joe's Scarecrow Village at 11852 Cabot Trail in Cap Le Moine to pose and get silly with more than 100 creations.

Chéticamp, a fishing village, personifies French Acadian culture. One of its several museums is devoted to local traditional rug hooking, which has gained world recognition for its unique designs; another focuses on Acadian culture. Flora's award-winning craft shop features the work of local artisans. At the information office at the national park's entrance, ask about recent wildlife sightings and get maps showing hiking trails, beaches, and lookouts.

This jagged coastline has few harbours or beaches. Mountains plunge up to 300 metres (984 feet) into the gulf below. Swells endlessly hammer cliffs, creating headlands and secluded sea stacks. West, across the Gulf of St. Lawrence, you may see Prince Edward Island, misty grey—where sea and sky meet.

Coastal communities offer sea excursions for whale, seabird, seal, and wildlife viewing. At Pleasant Bay a Whale Interpretive Centre answers questions about the magnificent mammals. Headland lookouts on both the Gulf and Atlantic are ideal for spotting fishing boats, sea birds, perhaps a pod of whales, or an eagle fishing.

The park's interior wilderness offers an amazing range of landscapes: magnificent highland plateaus, glacier-carved valleys, river canyons, and Arctic-like barrens. Trails criss-cross the park alongside ocean coast-lines, panoramic peaks, rare taiga forest, and splendid waterfalls; this is a hikers'

heaven. You may spot a moose grazing in the shallow shores of a lake or pond, or even on the roadside—particularly if you venture into the park interior.

As you near the Atlantic Ocean a sideroad to Meat Cove leads to the northernmost community in Nova Scotia, and Cape North's North Highlands Community Museum, where exhibits reveal life experienced by early settlers.

Ingonish, a cluster of five small communities, offers kayaking and golf. Designed in the Scottish tradition, Highland Links is consistently named one of Canada's top-10 courses. Keltic Lodge, perched high on a cliff and surrounded by ocean, provides a stunning view of Cape Smokey rising out of the sea.

St. Ann's Great Hall of the Clans stirs the heart when you attend concerts and visit the "Festival Club" held this week as part of the Celtic Colours International Festival. Free shuttles from Baddeck-area hotels testify to the events held here. The Gaelic College of Celtic Arts and Crafts shop specializes in Celtic jewellery, leather-bound journals, stained glass, and all things Scottish: kilts, clan flags, and the like.

At Baddeck, on the shores of beautiful Bras d'Or Lake,

the Alexander Graham Bell National Historic Site honours inventions—such as the telephone, and Canada's first powered flight—with hands-on activities, artifacts, displays, and a superb view (Bell himself spent many summers here). Mi'kmaq culture can be explored at Wagmatcook Culture and Heritage Centre.

The final leg of the Cabot Trail takes us to the land of sport fishing. Known locally as the Margaree, this inland area boasts 33 pools, six waterfalls, and the Margaree—a designated Canadian Heritage River. Lodges are a base for fly-fishing for trout or Atlantic salmon. Folks here cook up a mean pan-fried trout, and there's even a salmon museum in Margaree Valley.

It's not just the driving that makes the Cabot Trail one of Canada's not-to-be-missed adventures: there are great eats along the way. Acadian and Scottish specialties, wild and local cuisine, and the homemade goodness of traditional down-home meals are as much a part of the trip as the culture and legendary warmth of the people of the Highlands.❀

Find out more at:
www.cabottrail.travel

ADVENTURE

Go Mountain Biking … in a Kilt

Picture a mountain biker hurtling down a steep woodland path, dodging roots, sliding over mud patches, kilt flapping in the wind. Yes, kilt. Here in St. Andrews By-The-Sea, Off-Kilter Biking Kilts has become an integral part of creating fun experiences worth talking about, especially during Bike Fest, held in early October. Cycling in kilts was the brainchild of local mural artist and trail builder Geoff Slater, who formed the biking group Off-Kilter. Slater was inspired by kilts traditionally worn by bellmen at the nearby Algonquin Hotel. Those who get fitted out in a kilt and ride are admitted to the official St. Andrews By-The-Sea Off-Kilter Registry. Take your own bike or use one of the rentals available.

It's advisable to book ahead for Bike Fest weekend rides. The Off-Kilter gang leads easy and moderate rides on rolling terrain, or challenging single-track, depending on your skill level. The rolling New Brunswick landscape is perfect for mountain biking: 80 kilometres (50 miles) of trails (including converted rail lines), beautiful Passamaquoddy Bay, 1,524-metre (5,000-foot) mountains, and freshwater lakes. From sea level at low tide to a volcanic rim that marks the tail end of the Appalachian Mountains, the ride's simply awesome. ❧

www.ripplefitness.ca

Take Out History and Fresh Food at the St. Lawrence Market ▼

St. Lawrence Market is the real thing: a large and bustling food and flower emporium filled with sights and sounds, marvellous aromas, and sensuous bouquets—good enough to be named one of the top-25 markets in the world by the august *FOOD & DRINK* magazine. Wandering the market is a great way to spend a morning, especially at the height of the autumn harvest. And there's no better way to see it than on the St. Lawrence Market History Walking Tour. Reservations are a must.

Offered Tuesday through Saturday beginning at 10:00 a.m., the two-hour tour begins at the main entrance of the South Market (pick up tickets for C$25 at the Market Souvenir Shop on your left as you enter), then moves into the Upper Level—a grand hall divided into areas of specialty, from fish, to fowl, to flowers. The market's 200-year history is fascinating, especially the visit to the jail in the basement—a legacy from when this was Toronto's second City Hall. The tour continues through the Market Gallery with its photos and curios from bygone Toronto. The outdoor component includes the North Market, the original site of the market, as well as Toronto's first Post Office, St. James Cathedral, and St. Lawrence Hall. Afterwards, while away some time by grazing, enjoying a coffee, and people-watching. ❦
www.stlawrencemarket.com

Watch Migrating Snow Geese by the Hundreds

Birds of a feather flock together. And in the case of the snow geese, at this time of year these feathered friends land, en masse, at Cap Tourmente National Wildlife Area. Escape the tourist milieu of Québec City for a day to visit this wondrous micro-climate about 50 kilometres (31 miles) east of the hustle and bustle, a scenic 45-minute drive, and sneak in a viewing of these beautiful birds before they fly south for the winter.

The area's unique plants and wildlife are due to the land's specific geography, intertwining a Laurentian plateau, a coastal plain, and tidal and intertidal marshes just north of the St. Lawrence River. (It goes without saying, but dress warmly.) First and foremost, this is bird paradise, with some 307 species to seek out. As the main migration habitat for snow geese, know that they come here by the hundreds. So bring your binoculars!

The region of Cap Tourmente is an outdoor wonderland that will please nature and history buffs as much as bird lovers. In the fall, this special corner of the world becomes a brilliant tapestry of autumn leaves, packaged in the crisp air of a pre-winter sky. Hikers can explore more than 20 kilometres (12.4 miles) of trails, where animals—such as white-tailed deer—also roam, in what used to be the stomping ground of the famous navigator Samuel de Champlain. ❦
www.captourmente.com

EVENTS & FESTIVALS

QUIRKY CANADA

Party with Purpose at the Black & Blue Festival

Imagine a week packed with high-energy activities held across Montréal, the highlight being a huge dance party that goes non-stop until noon the next day. This is the Black & Blue Festival, an AIDS fundraiser that welcomes gay and straight men and women to live it up in support of a good cause.

What started in 1991 as a small group of Montréalers and 800 of their closest friends has turned into an international event attracting tens of thousands of partiers from all over Canada, as well as the United States, Europe, South America, Australia, and New Zealand. The festival takes over Montréal's Gay Village and surrounding areas for the week, and seemingly ordinary things like brunch become major social occasions. It all begins with the opening cocktail party, and includes the Jock Ball, the Leather Ball, the Military Ball, the Recovery Party, and more than 60 other cultural, artistic, and sports activities. Come dressed to impress. And don't leave your open mind at home.

VIP passes go on sale as early as March, giving you early-bird rates on a package deal. But you can also pick and choose the places you wish to let loose. It's also a wise idea to book your hotels (and any restaurants you might want to visit) at this time, since rooms (and tables) can be hard to come by last-minute.✳
www.bbcm.org

Watch Sailors Race across a Nova Scotia Lake—in Giant Pumpkins (really)

Howard Dill, a farmer near Windsor, Nova Scotia, has been infatuated with pumpkins for years. Big pumpkins. Big enough to be boats! In fact, this four-time Guinness World Records–holder and developer of giant-pumpkin seeds was the catalyst for an international craze for growing giant pumpkins. There are now more than 50 official weigh-off sites in North America, with Windsor hosting one of the best known on the first Saturday in October.

Of course, with all these giant pumpkins, the question became what to do with them? Howard's son Danny thought it might be fun to race them across Lake Pezaquid. It's been more than a decade since the first skeptical spectators turned out to watch five brave participants attempt to manoeuvre hollowed-out giant pumpkins (big enough to hold two paddlers) across the lake. Before the seeds and pulp are removed, the pumpkins can weigh in excess of 544 kilograms (1,200 pounds)—and they save the really big ones for the weigh-in!

Now the second Sunday of October draws thousands to the world's first Pumpkin Regatta. A Children's Wish Parade of Pumpkin Paddlers kicks things off. Races include paddling, motorized, and "experimental" classes. All the fervour over pumpkins evolved into a Windsor–West Hants Pumpkin Festival and the Dill Farm, one of the region's main tourist attractions.✳
www.pumpkinregatta.com

Sample Apple Cider amidst Monastery Orchards

Autumn is the perfect time to take a scenic drive into Québec's Eastern Townships. About an hour south of Montréal, the picturesque Saint-Benoît-du-Lac Monastery is an enchanting hideaway that overlooks Lac Memphrémagog. This time of year is also apple-picking season, during which the Benedictine monks who live and work at the century-old abbey allow the public to visit their orchard—from which they harvest the fruits to make apple cider.

This is a rare opportunity to hear the haunting Gregorian chants performed live.

Bottled in fancy champagne-like bottles with metallic foil wrapping, the cider (C$10) is sold alongside other apple-based products, such as applesauce and apple cider vinegar. The abbey's on-site boutique also sells its popular monk-made artisanal cheeses and other foods, as well as devotional souvenirs such as Christian crosses, medallions and its very own Gregorian chant CD. The boutique, is open from 9:00 a.m. to 4:30 p.m. Monday to Saturday, and Sunday from 12:15 p.m. to 4:30 p.m. The store, however, is always closed for mass (between 10:45 a.m. and 11:50 a.m.), which is also open to the public. This is a rare opportunity to hear the haunting Gregorian chants performed live.🍁
www.st-benoit-du-lac.com

It happened THIS WEEK:

First Canadian in Space

Marc Garneau got the job that more than 4,000 Canadians applied for—the honour of being the first Canadian in space. A 35-year-old electrical engineer from Québec City, Québec, Garneau trained with the navy and then the federal Department of National Defence before making his trip.

On October 5, 1984, Garneau flew as payload specialist with the U.S. space shuttle Challenger, on Mission 41-G. During a mid-mission press interview, Garneau called the view of Earth the most moving aspect of the journey.

"When you look out at your own planet and see absolutely out-of-this-world incredible views of entire subcontinents, you begin to appreciate what the world is really like," said Garneau, while floating in the weightless environment.

While in space, the Québec City–born astronaut used the Canadarm, a Canadian invention, to release a satellite from the shuttle. The engineer also conducted space science, space technology, and life sciences experiments. He returned to Earth on October 13.

Garneau made two further trips to space, in 1996 and 2000—totalling more than 677 hours in space.

On January 22, 1992, Dr. Roberta Bondar—who was also one of the finalists competing for the job Garneau won—became the first Canadian woman in space. She has logged more than eight days in reduced gravity.

Meet Your Favourite Author at the Country's Top Literary Event

Some of the world's top writers descend on Toronto for readings, galas, and signings

I t's one of the most important literary events anywhere: the International Festival of Authors (IFOA), a place to meet your favourite author at a book-signing or heady debate; to listen to thoughtful readings; and discover the latest talents from Canada and abroad. There are interviews conducted by top literary journalists, gala events, and parties. Ironically, the one thing there's little time for is reading—that's for later.

In an age where publishing is undergoing historic change, IFOA continues to prove itself as a top talent draw—and relevant as ever—with an average of 150 participants and more than 50 events. The 11-day festival attracts writers of all stripes, including the likes of Alice Munro and Michael Ondaatje, Ian McEwan and Zadie Smith, Paolo Giordano and Marc Levy, Jonathan Franzen and David Mitchell, David Rakoff and Linda Barry. There are poets, playwrights, novelists, short story writers, and biographers—many of them award-winners. Recent recipients of the Booker Prize are often in

Venues range from darkened theatres to sunny, casual terrace-side rooms.

attendance, as well as the most recent crop of Giller Prize and Governor-General's Literary Awards nominees. Since the launch of IFOA in 1974, more than 7,500 authors from an astonishing 100+ countries have presented their works here—one reason the festival now attracts more than 80,000.

Part of IFOA's continued success can be attributed to the range of curated events and discussions around such issues as childhood literacy, graphic novels, digital books, and the future of publishing. This ties in to the festival's mission, which is, in part, to help audiences, young and old, discover new talent while profiling Canada's best—and offering a platform for international writers.

The festival's opening night is always a splashy event. In 2010, for example, the fundraiser for PEN Canada (a not-for-profit organization in support of freedom of expression) brought together Pulitzer Prize–winning novelist Richard Ford in conversation with the popular journalist and broadcaster Eleanor Wachtel, hosted by bestselling author Mark Kingwell.

Roundtables bring together three or more writers to discuss

and debate an issue, a perspective, a shared theme, or thoughts on literary trends. Fiction authors focus on the voices of their characters, a writer's techniques, and shaping arcs. A session, for instance, might be dedicated to contemplating the role of time and place in story-telling. Insightful events offer up-close glimpses into a writer's mind and way of thinking.

The main events are the often-riveting live readings. Don't conjure up a cardigan-cozy, stifled reading at a local library, but instead a top-notch display of talent. A must-do reading for the hottest Canadian talent is the celebration of the authors shortlisted for the Governor General's Literary Awards, with an evening of readings from the year's nominated works.

Interviews are hour-long events that pair journalists, thinkers, or trendsetters with authors—who discuss their latest works. In 2010, one of the top draws was John Waters, interviewed by Richard Crouse.

There are events for the whole family as well. YoungIFOA is a series of programs that engages and profiles young writers who come together to read, learn about new technologies, play, and party. Some events are led by schoolchildren. All are priced to be family friendly.

There are parties, authors' dinners, and signings around town. Some are part of the festival's official programming (especially the signings) and can be tracked down on-line or in print. But the parties and dinners are harder to find as they're often private, invitation-only events. If you're keen to try to wrestle an entry to, say, a cocktail reception at a downtown bistro, it's best to read the local newspapers for daily tips and listings.

The event's focal point is Harbourfront Centre, on the waterfront. A year-round cultural and performing-arts centre with regular concerts, exhibits, and events for all ages, the setting offers visitors a water-side view of the city. Venues range from darkened theatres to sunny, casual terrace-side rooms.

Many IFOA events sell out, so it's best to book ahead. Tickets generally go on sale in mid-September (on-line) and by phone (or in person) through the Harbourfront box office. Most events cost C$15 to $18, with special rates for students and youth.

IFOA's popularity has expanded to include year-round readings and IFOA Ontario, a touring program that takes authors on the road to more than a dozen locations around the province. If you're prepared to travel outside Toronto, it can be a rewarding way to see a bit more of the province. 🍁

Find out more at:
www.readings.org

ADVENTURE

Run the Toronto Waterfront Marathon ▶

Runners in the know consider the Scotiabank Toronto Waterfront Marathon a good qualifier for the famed Boston Marathon. It's fast and flat (a good way to set a personal best) and well-organized, with bands and neighbourhood entertainment every two kilometres (1.2 miles) to boost flagging spirits, if not aching muscles. The 2010 event saw a men's marathon time of 2:07:58, making it the fastest men's time on Canadian soil. It's an equal opportunity race: the same race also saw the fastest woman's marathon on Canadian soil with a time of 2:22:43.

The run starts amidst the office towers of University Avenue and Adelaide Street and traces west along Lakeshore Boulevard, with energizing breezes from—and some stunning views of—Lake Ontario, then back east to the Beach District before returning to the concrete canyons and echoing mob of well-wishers, to finish at City Hall's Nathan Phillips Square. Register in advance and you can receive a participant's bib with your first name on it . . . it will help the cheerful volunteers along the less crowded stretches shout words of personal encouragement.

You'll be in good company or, better put, just enough company: the participation cap is 4,500, with runners starting in small groups so that it's not overcrowded. Power walkers and slower runners appreciate the luxuriously long time limit of six hours and 30 minutes.

Then again, if you simply want the chance to stroll along major boulevards—now strangely car-free—you can opt for the five-kilometre (3.1-mile) walk.🍁
www.torontowaterfrontmarathon.com

◄ Visit the Church of Canada's Newest Saint

Brother André (1845–1937) is one of Québec's most beloved religious figures. Famous for healing the people who came to him for physical and spiritual healing, he was canonized on October 17, 2010. Roman Catholics, or worshippers of any other religion, can participate in the anniversary of this day at his celebrated Saint-Joseph's Oratory.

Built in Italian Renaissance style, the impressive structure high on the slope of Mount Royal is easily the highest point in the city. There are 283 steps, 99 of them wooden. Worshippers are known to climb these steps on their knees to share in the suffering of Jesus Christ.

Open from 6:30 a.m. to 9:00 p.m. daily, masses are offered in English and French. Recently renovated, the many interior levels are now more easily accessible. There's also a small museum honouring Brother André's legacy.

Visitors to the structure will see it's quite austere (especially when compared to the Notre-Dame Basilica in Old Montréal), but will nevertheless find it impressive thanks to its modern design and imposing size. Now known as Saint Brother André, his tomb—and his enshrined heart—are located inside the oratory. You can also visit the original house of worship on the same grounds, an example of the Montréal saint's humble beginnings when it was erected in 1904. The inside walls are lined with antique crutches left behind by those who have been healed.🍁
www.saint-joseph.org

Spot Seals and Migrating Birds at The Irving Nature Park

Late October is a time of transition at The Irving Nature Park in Saint John, New Brunswick. Keep your eyes seaward to spot seals that begin returning after a summer away; soon, the full colony of harbour and grey seals will be in residence, basking on the rocks at low tide and easily observed from the Seal Observation Deck. The last of the shorebirds migrating from the Arctic to South America are landing at this traditional staging area, fuelling up on shrimp and other goodies in the mud flats. With the summer crowds now departed, the park is the perfect place for solitude and quiet appreciation.

The park—all 600 acres—is maintained by J.D. Irving Limited, and located just minutes from downtown. Best known for its distinctive gas stations, the Irvings (as they're known locally) preserved this dramatic piece of coast as a sanctuary for wildlife and nature lovers. Varied ecosystems define the peninsula of volcanic rock and forest, with a salt marsh along one side and a long sandy cobble beach on the other. The park's rugged beauty is best revealed on trails and lookout points. Year-round activities, like moonlight snowshoeing and meteor shower–viewing, are free, as is admission to the park.🍁
www.jdirving.com

EVENTS & FESTIVALS

QUIRKY CANADA

Book Time at the Vancouver International Writers Festival

What do Margaret Atwood, Michael Ondaatje, and Yann Martel have in common? Not only have all of these Canadian authors won the Booker Prize for the best English-language novel in the Commonwealth, but they've also all appeared at the Vancouver International Writers Festival (VIWF).

You don't have to be a literary fiction fanatic to appreciate the live readings and Q&A sessions at this annual event, held at Granville Island's cozy theatre stages—just across from downtown, under the Granville Street Bridge. Do words like "Muggles," "Quidditch," and "Hogwarts" mean anything to you? J.K. Rowling, creator of the ultra-popular Harry Potter series, did a reading at the 2000 festival. (So many young fans wanted tickets that she appeared across town at the Pacific Coliseum, which holds 16,000.) Vancouver sci-fi writer William Gibson, who defined cyberpunk with his award-winning 1984 novel *Neuromancer*, has graced VIWF several times.

What really gives VIWF its flavour, however, is its charming setting. You can head out with fellow book lovers after a panel discussion or poetry jam and browse through galleries, shop at the Granville Island Public Market, quaff microbrew beer, or simply gaze at sailboats. Ah, the literary life is good!❦
www.writersfest.bc.ca

Stand in the Shadow of the Big Nickel

It's certainly big. At nine metres (30 feet) high and 61 centimetres (two feet) thick, this giant replica of a 1951 Canadian five-cent piece is listed by Guinness World Records as the world's largest coin. In case you want to flip all 13 tonnes: heads is King George VI (Canada's monarch at the time), tails is a nickel refinery. It's all a bit of a scam really: the Big Nickel was built in 1964.

More than a terrific photo op for travellers heading into northern Ontario cottage country, Sudbury's Big Nickel is the centrepiece of Dynamic Earth, an interactive earth sciences museum that taps the city's mining heritage. The permanent exhibits are terrific: in the Earth Gallery visitors can watch an animated representation of the meteorite strike that created the Sudbury Basin, while the aptly named Rockhound Lab offers kids a chance to get their hands on some chunks of the region's finest rocks. Sudbury also makes a great base camp for day trips to the fabulous wilderness beyond: from the pink granite islands and shorelines of Georgian Bay or the spectacular trails near High Falls, to Manitoulin Island—world's largest freshwater island. Several provincial parks are within easy driving distance and some 330 lakes are situated within Greater Sudbury's boundaries.❦
www.dynamicearth.ca

◄ Take a Bite out of Montréal's Bagel Wars

The bagel debate in Montréal is always a heated one. Are you Fairmount or St-Viateur? Each bakery is backed by a devoted following. Most agree, however, that the city's local dough is the tastiest anywhere—especially when compared to New York City's doughy delights. Both places are open 24 hours a day, only walking-distance apart. Why not go to each and taste the difference for yourself?

St-Viateur Bagel and Fairmount Bagel Bakery have been hand-rolling their bread in their current locations since 1957 and 1949, respectively. Dipped in honey water (said to be the secret) and cooked in a wood-fired oven, little has changed over the years.

Most agree that the city's local dough is the tastiest anywhere.

St-Viateur has expanded, adding two cafés (on Monkland and Mont-Royal) where you can order bagels in a restaurant setting. You can also go to Beauty's (at Saint-Urbain and Mont-Royal), a landmark diner since 1942. These brands are also available at most grocery stores and *dépanneurs* (convenience stores) or at MBCo (Montréal Bread Company) at the Montréal–Pierre Elliott Trudeau International Airport—but don't rely on that location only as bagels frequently sell out.

Still, nothing beats dropping by the bakery in person and getting them hot out of the oven. If you happen to find yourself in the Mile End neighbourhood at 3:00 a.m. and needing a little nibble, you might be surprised to see how many people have the same idea—and craving —as you. ❦

**www.stviateurbagel.com,
www.fairmountbagel.com**

Fred Penner's
favourite PLACE

A 42-hour train journey introduces a slower way to travel for children's entertainer Fred Penner, who recommends "the experience of seeing Hudson Bay from the Churchill point of view.

"It's a very rustic, old kind of community," says Penner. "I've been to the mouth of Hudson Bay and seen beluga whales, otters, and seals playing together in the bay."

In 1975 Penner took the train from Winnipeg to Churchill—a route nick-named the Muskeg Express for the terrain it traverses. Over the more than 1,700 kilometres (1,056 miles) the slow journey crosses an empty Manitoba landscape where utility wires are supported by tripods of poles.

"It's well beyond the treeline so there are no trees. It's like a lunar site," says Penner, from his home in Winnipeg. "Someone will just get off, seemingly in the middle of nowhere, and wave to the conductor and trek off into the bush."

As the train edges further north through The Pas, Wabowden, and Gillam, passengers will likely see the northern lights.

"To talk about colours dancing across the sky, it's a spectacular image," says Penner, a Member of the Order of Canada.

Once in Churchill, the small town blends history and remoteness.

"Historically, there is the Prince of Wales Fort, which is a Canadian fort where Samuel Hearne, until the 1780s, was stationed.

"Imagine being up in Churchill, in the middle of winter in this little fort," says Penner. He recounts how a French ship arrived, but Hearne saw it as pointless to fight in the middle of nowhere.

"So Hearne said to his people…let's have them come in for a nice dinner or something."

As the train shuttles between Winnipeg and Churchill on tracks that run past mossy quagmires, Penner says travellers are "committed on a trip like this."

"You can't get off, you don't want to get off, until you reach your destination."

See Dozens of Polar Bears Up-Close

Photo-ops abound from the comfort of "tundra buggies"

Churchill has no road links to the rest of Canada, but that doesn't stop visitors from around the world descending on the "polar bear capital of the world" for the almost-guaranteed opportunity to view these awesome creatures from the safety of specially designed "tundra buggies." The first bear-viewing buggies were developed by a local mechanic in the 1970s, and have evolved greatly. The vehicles are safe and comfortable, have oversized wheels for travelling over the tundra, and outdoor decks that make viewing and photography easy for the twenty-something passengers onboard. The bears are completely unafraid of the vehicles, occasionally standing on their hind legs to get a better view of the human interlopers. Other wildlife frequently sighted includes Arctic hares, snowy owls, and red foxes.

Viewing polar bears in their natural habitat is a thrilling experience, mostly due to their sheer size. They are the world's largest land-based carnivore, with males growing up to 680 kilograms (1,500 pounds). Polar bears are perfectly adapted to cold Arctic temperatures, moving easily across both tundra and sea ice. And, unlike the tired-looking polar bears held captive in zoos, the coats of bears in the wild remain a glistening white, while their playful antics invariably surprise considering their lumbering gait. The bears spend summers ashore, spread across the tundra surrounding Hudson Bay. In late fall, they begin congregating in Churchill—the first place where the sea ice forms—waiting for the ocean to freeze so they can head out to hunt seals. The first bears begin to arrive at Churchill in mid-October, and by the end of the month hundreds of these awesome white animals gather along the shoreline. As they congregate east of town, around Cape Churchill (protected by the Churchill Wildlife Management Area and Wapusk National Park), they're followed by strange-looking buses filled with wildlife enthusiasts.

Although bear-viewing trips will fill your days—and this is realistically the main focus of the long journey north—Churchill itself is an intriguing place to spend some time. But for both cold weather (usually well below freezing, even during the middle of the day) and the chance of bumping into a polar bear, it's not a good time of year for wandering around town—though the town is patrolled and wayward bears are driven out as quickly as they appear. That said, there are a couple of sights worth noting. The downtown Eskimo Museum has a small exhibit on the blending of local Cree, Inuit, Dene, and European cultures, and a collection of Inuit carvings and artifacts. Along the northern edge of town, the waterfront's dominated by towering grain terminals, where grain transported from the prairies is loaded onto massive ships bound for European markets.

Visiting Churchill in late fall requires advance planning, as transportation options and motel rooms are limited. Most visitors arrive as part of a package that includes transportation from Winnipeg, accommodations in Churchill, and day tours out to view the polar bears.

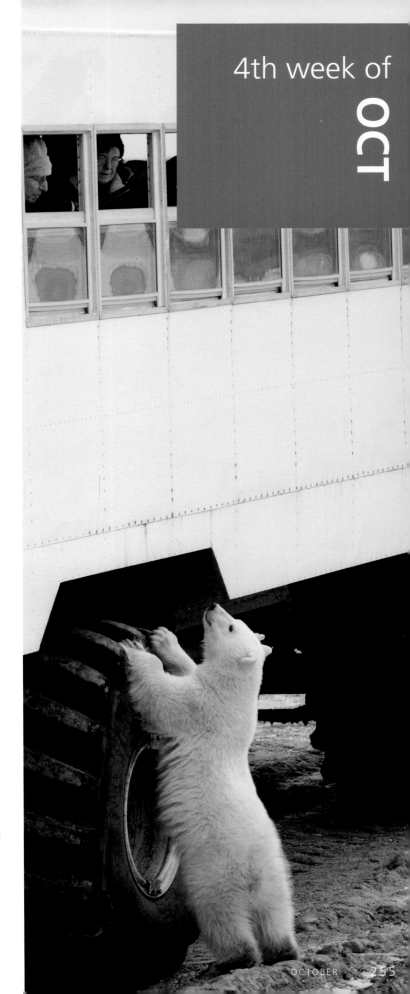

Most packages include two or three day trips out to view the bears, which is plenty (a day trip really does mean a full day out in the bus). One tour company with an excellent reputation is Natural Habitat Adventures, providing packages that include airfares from Winnipeg and a variety of accommodation options. For a truly unique lodging, upgrade to the Tundra Lodge, comprised of mobile platforms parked within the Churchill Wildlife Management Area. Facilities are simple (bathrooms are shared and beds are bunk-style), but the opportunity to stay overnight—out among the polar bears—is unequalled. With entertainment options limited, the dining and lounge rooms become meeting points for like-minded travellers —a hub of social life out on the barren tundra.

By the end of the month hundreds of these awesome white animals gather along the shoreline.

A cheaper option is to travel independently, but as most spots on the day trips are taken by tour companies be sure to have tour bus reservations before leaving for Churchill. Daily scheduled flights link Winnipeg and Churchill, but are expensive. The alternative offers the opportunity to save money, but takes longer—much longer. The Hudson Bay train, operated by VIA Rail, makes the 1,700-kilometre (1,100-mile), 40-hour trip between Winnipeg and Churchill twice weekly. Although the journey is long, it's an opportunity to experience a part of Canada few see up-close. The dense boreal forest gives way to open tundra as the train travels north, and by late October snow often covers the ground—but passengers get to sit back and enjoy the wintery panorama from the warmth and comfort of the train. Prices for a regular seat are one-third the flight cost, but upgrade to a private cabin and the differential is minimal. Before leaving, contact Lazy Bear Lodge for motel-style accommodations and Great White Bear Tours for day trips out to the polar bears. 🍁

Find out more at:
www.churchill.ca, www.nathab.com

ADVENTURE

▲

Cycle the Scenic Kettle Valley Rail Trail

About a century ago, gold and copper mining brought the Kettle Valley Railway into existence in southern British Columbia. Today, those industries have fallen by the wayside, but the old rail line's been converted into a spectacular cycling trail that runs 455 kilometres (283 miles) from Grand Forks in the West Kootenays to Brodie, just off the Coquihalla Highway. Riding through a mix of sub-alpine meadows, evergreen forests, and desert-like conditions is a superb way to immerse yourself in these breathtaking landscapes. The gravel-laden terrain is classified as easy-to-moderate. Even families with kids can handle it.

What truly sets the Kettle Valley Rail Trail apart is its trestles—high, wooden bridges spanning dramatic gullies, sometimes hundreds of feet above ground. A 2003 forest fire destroyed two-thirds of the 18 trestles in renowned Myra Canyon, but the B.C. government had them rebuilt. Now you can pedal your way across, savouring the remarkable views as your heart pounds. You'll also admire the lush orchards and vineyards around Okanagan Lake. You'll see why *Bicycling* magazine has named this one of the world's top-50 cycling routes. Numerous stop-offs enable camping or B&B stays. 🍁
www.kettlevalleyrailway.ca

Enjoy the Work of the Group of Seven amidst Stunning Landscapes ▼

Canada's best-known visual arts collective is the Group of Seven. And there's no better place to interact with their work than the McMichael Gallery. A short drive from Toronto in the historic village of Kleinburg, the gallery is justly admired for its organic relationship with nature; these renowned Canadian landscape artists could not have imagined a better home for their art.

Founded by Robert and Signe McMichael, who began collecting paintings by the Group of Seven and their contemporaries in 1955, the McMichael's 13 exhibition galleries are devoted exclusively to Canadian art. Its permanent collection features nearly 6,000 pieces by Tom Thomson, the Group of Seven, and their peers, as well as work by Aboriginal artists. Surrounded by 40 hectares (100 acres) of conservation land, the gallery is built of fieldstone and hand-hewn logs, and its floor-to-ceiling windows provide stunning views of the thickly treed Humber River Valley, vivid in tones of yellow, orange, and red at this time of year—mirroring the vibrancy of the works on the walls. If you venture out onto the grounds, you can visit a recreation of Tom Thomson's shack and the graves of six of the Group's seven. A.J. Casson, Lawren Harris, A.Y. Jackson, Frank Johnston, Arthur Lismer, and Frederik Varley are buried in a small cemetery, along with gallery co-founders the McMichaels. The fourth week of October marks the birth of Harris and the death of Franklin Carmichael, the only group member not buried on the grounds. ❧
www.mcmichael.ca

Investigate Some Fishy Business at the Capilano Salmon Hatchery

If you think of salmon as something that comes out of a can, it's time to visit the Capilano Salmon Hatchery. This free attraction in North Vancouver, operated by the federal government, delivers an up-close-and-personal look at the life cycle of British Columbia's signature fish. Visiting in October is an ideal time to see big chinook and coho salmon wriggling towards the joys of reproduction.

The hatchery was built on the Capilano River in 1971 since the nearby Cleveland Dam, which contains Vancouver's main water reservoir, had blocked a key migration route (taking away valuable salmon spawning habitat). Here, near Capilano Mountain, the adult salmon are diverted through a concrete river weir, while the younger fish are reared and later released below the dam. You can watch the salmon through Plexiglas windows in the fish ladder as they push their way upstream. Then, check out an adult holding pond where staff sort the salmon by species, dividing them up to ensure appropriate genetic diversity is achieved during spawning.

Interpretive displays about incubation, fishing, and watershed locations—plus a cozy gift shop—enhance an exciting day-trip for all ages. The hatchery's just north of the Capilano Suspension Bridge. ❧
www.pac.dfo-mpo.gc.ca

Shop till You Drop at La Grande Braderie de la Mode Québecoise

In English it's called the Big Fashion Sale by Québec Designers, but everybody knows it by its French name, *La braderie de mode québécoise*. Local style hounds mark their calendars with this biannual event at the Marché Bonsecours where, for four days every April and October, designers sell off last season's stock and knock down prices anywhere from 50 to 80 per cent. Let the shopping frenzy begin!

Not so much a sale as an event, La braderie brings together more than 100 different brands covering everything from ladies and menswear, to accessories, kids' clothing, and lingerie. Doors generally open at 10:00 a.m., but don't underestimate the power of arriving early and being first in line. Bring cash and wear flat shoes.

Some sought-after lines include the high-end Barilà line, trendy streetwear from Bodybag by Jude Clothing and Eve Gravel, as well as denim by Second Clothing or Guido and Mary. Don't miss the winter coats by cold weather experts Mackage, Rudsak, and Soïa & Kyo, as well as recycled fur lines HARRICANA par Mariouche and Rachel F.

There aren't any dressing rooms, so feel free to try on clothing overtop whatever you're wearing. And, remember, if you think you like something don't think twice about it. It might disappear if you look away.✦
www.braderiedemodequebecoise.com

5 faves

Tofino Cold Water Surf Classic

Tofino has become one of the best surfing towns in North America, and many of the sport's biggest names descend on the former fishing village this month for the Canadian stop of the Coldwater Classic series. The water may only be 10 degrees Celsius (50 degrees Fahrenheit), but the winter waves are huge—making for some epic demonstrations of surfing skill.

Spend a Night behind Bars in Ottawa

Most cheap hotels feel like prisons—this one comes by it honestly. The Ottawa Jail Hostel is the only one of its kind in North America, a former prison now converted into a popular Hostelling International location where you can spend the night in the same cells as past inmates.

For 100 years, the Carleton County Gaol was home to all manner of miscreants and also saw the final departure for a number of more serious offenders. Guests don't necessarily have to sleep in former cells—the infirmary is cozy and the prison governor's quarters are positively palatial in comparison—but when else will you have a chance to sleep behind bars? The top floor has been left as it was so current "inmates" can compare and contrast. Speaking of current inmates, rumour has it the place is haunted. At daybreak, you may want to check out in a hurry.

Once you've done your time, Parliament Hill and the ByWard Market are a short walk away. It's a bit more of a stroll to the Museum of Civilization, the National Gallery, and the Canadian War Museum, and (if you're feeling faintly felonious) the Royal Canadian Mint. If you visit the mint, be sure to visit the gift shop with its 12.7-kilogram (28-pound) bar of pure gold. It's worth half a million bucks—and they let you pick it up (though you can't take it with you).

www.carletoncountyjail.com

Sample Whisky at Canada's Only Single-Malt Distillery

If a wee tipple of whisky enjoyed in a Scottish pub (sheltered in a beautiful glen) holds appeal, there's good news. You don't need to cross the Atlantic to find a taste of the highlands. Nestled into the picturesque Inverness hills of Cape Breton, The Glenora Inn & Distillery, in Glenville, Nova Scotia, is everything you need.

Glenora has the distinction of being Canada's only distiller of single-malt whisky, Glen Breton. In addition to fine whisky, they blend rum and produce the world's first Ice Wine-finished single-malt whisky. A guided tour reveals the complexity of making Glen Breton in magnificent copper stills. (You even get a sample!) Aficionados can purchase Glenora's "whisky expressions," only available on-site, or their own single cask bottling from an oak cask. The on-site Glenora Pub offers a wide selection of single-malt whisky and local entertainment. The highly rated restaurant's unique menu items feature Glen Breton, along with local ingredients.

An overnight stay will round out a Scottish-style get-away. Stay in a guest room beside a babbling brook or a hillside chalet boasting an incredible view of the glens—magnificent at a time when fall colours blanket the hillsides. Set in an apple orchard among a natural stand of maple trees, the inn and distillery were constructed in a traditional post-and-beam style. You can't go wrong!

www.glenoradistillery.com

David Dunlap Observatory

Just north of Canada's largest city sits Canada's largest telescope. A research centre of the University of Toronto's Department of Astronomy and Astrophysics by day, on Saturday nights the David Dunlap hosts Observing Nights, where telescopes are set-up on the lawn of the observatory. You may see everything from craters on the moon to Saturn's rings, to galaxies, nebula, and comets.

Whistler Mountain Bike Park

Mountain biking is nearly as popular as skiing at Whistler, and the facilities also compare favourably, with world-class trails, skill centres, and jump parks. The 48 kilometres (30 miles) of marked trails can accommodate almost all ages and experience levels.

Art Across the Marsh

This studio tour encompasses more than 20 artist and artisan studios around New Brunswick's Tantramar Marshes. Studios open to the public for a weekend, providing you with the chance to meet the artists, learn about technique, and see works in progress.

Vancouver Police Museum

If you're fascinated with crime (or Vancouver history), you can spend an enjoyable hour here. The confiscated illegal-weapons display is hair-raising, along with the morgue, a simulated autopsy room (with pieces of damaged body parts in specimen bottles), and forensics lab.

Your next STEP

TOP PICKS
ADVENTURE
CULTURE & HISTORY
NATURE'S GRANDEUR
EVENTS & FESTIVALS
QUIRKY CANADA
REJUVENATE

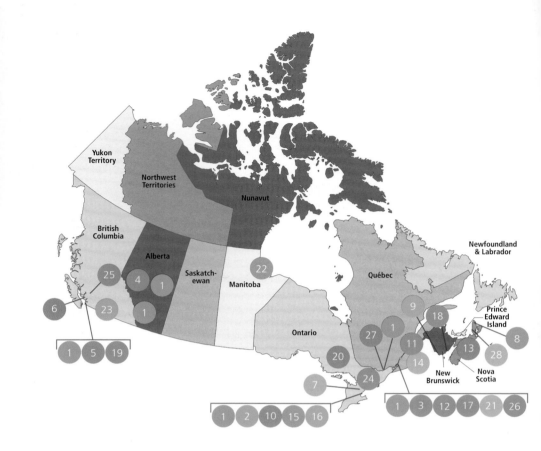

WEEK 1

1 VANCOUVER, CALGARY, EDMONTON, TORONTO, OTTAWA, AND MONTRÉAL
NHL hockey opening night
www.nhl.com

2 TORONTO, ONT.
The CN Tower
www.cntower.ca

3 MONTRÉAL, QUE.
Old Montréal
www.vieux.montreal.qc.ca/

4 JASPER NATIONAL PARK, ALTA.
Miette Hot Springs
www.pc.gc.ca/jasper

5 VANCOUVER, B.C.
Vancouver International Film Festival
www.viff.org

6 GIBSONS, B.C.
Molly's Reach from *The Beachcombers*
www.mollysreach.ca

7 CAMBRIDGE, ONT.
Langdon Hall
www.langdonhall.ca

WEEK 2

8 CAPE BRETON HIGHLANDS NATIONAL PARK, N.S.
Cabot Trail car touring
www.cabottrail.travel

9 ST. ANDREWS, N.B.
Mountain biking in kilts
www.ripplefitness.ca

10 TORONTO, ONT.
St. Lawrence Market
www.stlawrencemarket.com

11 CAP-TOURMENTE, QUE.
Cap Tourmente National Wildlife Area
www.captourmente.com

12 MONTRÉAL, QUE.
Black & Blue Festival and AIDS fundraiser
www.bbcm.org

13 WINDSOR, N.S.
Pumpkin Regatta
www.pumpkinregatta.com

14 SAINT-BENOÎT-DU-LAC, QUE.
Monastery-made apple cider
www.st-benoit-du-lac.com

WEEK 3

15 TORONTO, ONT.
International Festival of Authors
www.readings.org

16 TORONTO, ONT.
Toronto Waterfront Marathon
www.torontowaterfront marathon.com

17 MONTRÉAL, QUE.
Saint Brother André's church
www.saint-joseph.org

18 ST. JOHN, N.B.
The Irving Nature Park
www.jdirving.com

19 VANCOUVER, B.C.
Vancouver Writers Festival
www.writersfest.bc.ca

20 SUDBURY, ONT.
The Big Nickel
www.dynamicearth.ca

21 MONTRÉAL, QUE.
Bagel bakeries
www.stviateurbagel.com

WEEK 4

22 CHURCHILL, MAN.
Polar bear–watching
www.churchill.ca

23 GRAND FORKS, B.C.
Rail trail cycling
www.kettlevalleyrailway.ca

24 KLEINBURG, ONT.
Group of Seven paintings
www.mcmichael.ca

25 VANCOUVER, B.C.
Capilano Salmon Hatchery
www.pac.dfo-mpo.gc.ca

26 MONTRÉAL, QUE.
Local designer fashion sale
www.braderiedemodequebecoise.com

27 OTTAWA, ONT.
Ottawa Jail Hostel
www.carletoncountyjail.com

28 MABOU, N.S.
Single-malt distillery
www.glenoradistillery.com

NOVEMBER

Stay in One of Canada's Historic Railway Hotels

Built in pre-war times to promote tourism from coast to coast, these hotels still set the standard for luxury

Across Canada, railway hotels give a glimpse into our history while delivering a taste of luxury—often in some of the country's most breathtaking settings. The heritage value of these unique hotels has resulted in national historic site designations for some, while others are major tourist attractions. Almost without exception, these iconic hotels have elegant lobbies, handsomely historic dining rooms and lounges, and grandiose ballrooms. Though their popularity hasn't waned in more than a century, off-season periods like early November are the best time visit if you're looking to avoid the crowds—and stay at rates well below what you'd pay in high season.

Soon after the last spike was driven in Canada's transcontinental railway in 1885 (see p. 264), the

Canadian Pacific Railway (CPR) decided the best way to encourage customers to travel on its trains was to build the grandest of hotels along its line. Competing railway companies such as the Grand Trunk Railway and Canadian National followed suit. The result: a string of luxurious hotels stretching from coast to coast that, to this day, attract guests from around the world. Today, though inextricably linked to the railway, the hotels are no longer owned by the railway companies. Many are part of the Fairmont family of hotels, though a few are part of other major chains—such as Halifax's The Westin Nova Scotian and Regina's Hotel Saskatchewan (Radisson). Regardless, they have evolved with the country and are part of Canada's national identity.

While a couple dozen of these properties remain in operation, the following selection reflects the grandeur and history of the golden era of railway hotels.

Sitting on a high bluff overlooking the St. Lawrence River, Québec City's Fairmont Le Château Frontenac is one of Canada's most beloved hotels. Completed in 1893 and expanded many times since, it typifies CPR hotels of the era with its castle-like appearance. The property currently offers 618 guest rooms, each with a distinct European decor, and a number of regally decorated, upscale restaurants. In Toronto, perfectly situated across from Union Station, the Fairmont Royal York (completed in 1929) was the flagship CPR city hotel. Upon opening, the 28-story property boasted more than 1,000 rooms, plus fine-dining restaurants, a concert hall, library—even its own small hospital. Through regular revamps, the Royal York has lost none of its opulence or charm and now offers 1,365 guest rooms.

Across the prairies, The Fort Garry Hotel has been Winnipeg's premier accommodation since opening in 1913 and, like the Fairmont Le Château Frontenac, was built in a classic château style. An overnight rail trip to the west from Winnipeg is another prairie masterpiece, the

Hotel Saskatchewan. With its limestone façade and grandiose public spaces, this imposing 1927 building wouldn't look out of place in a European capital. Even if you don't have reservations, stop by for high tea in the Victoria Tea Room to enjoy a taste of this hotel's storied past.

In the Canadian Rockies, three opulent hotels were built by the railway companies. Each has become legendary in its own right for awe-inspiring mountain settings. On a terrace above a bend in the Bow River is The Fairmont Banff Springs, the world's largest hotel when it opened in 1888 with more than 250 rooms. It was replaced in 1911 with a new hotel and now boasts more than 750 rooms—built in a style reminiscent of a Scottish castle mixed with a French country château. A short drive from Banff, The Fairmont Chateau Lake Louise is a 500-room hotel on the shore of picturesque Lake Louise. It offers views equal to any mountain resort in the world. Originally a row of lakeside tents operated by the Grand Trunk Railway, The Fairmont Jasper Park Lodge is now an upscale resort where guests can rent canoes, take horseback rides through the surrounding wilderness, play golf on one of North America's best courses, canoe across turquoise Lac Beauvert, or simply relax on the sprawling grounds. Though standard rooms are anything but, for the ultimate splurge upgrade to the character-filled 1928, five-bedroom Point Cabin. Oozing old-world charm, it will set you back nearly C$2,000 per night!

The western terminus of the CPR line is Vancouver, where the copper-roofed Fairmont Hotel Vancouver is a downtown landmark. Vancouver's first railway hotel was built in 1887 and half its 200 guest rooms had private bathrooms—something unheard of in the day. It burned to the ground in 1932 and was replaced by the hotel that stands today, which reflects the heritage of CPR-built hotels across the country with its distinctive château-style design.

Beyond the mainland, the westernmost railway hotel is The Fairmont Empress, overlooking Victoria's Inner Harbour. This grandly ostentatious, ivy-covered, 1908 Edwardian hotel is Victoria's most recognizable landmark. Its architect was the well-known Francis Rattenbury, who also designed the local parliament buildings. Even if you don't have reservations, it's worth walking through the hotel lobby to gaze (head back, mouth agape) at the interior razzle-dazzle, and to watch people partake in the traditional afternoon tea. ❦

Find out more at:
www.fairmont.com

ADVENTURE

CULTURE & HISTORY

Teeter across Suspension Bridges on Vancouver's North Shore

Film critic Roger Ebert once noted, "Almost every suspension bridge in the history of the movies has failed while the heroes were trying to cross it." Fortunately, you won't encounter that scenario at the Capilano or Lynn Canyon suspension bridges in North Vancouver. However, you will get a one-two punch of thrills and education at both sites. November rains often create wild water below the North Shore Mountains, amping up the experience.

Feel your heart pounding as you step out on the Capilano Suspension Bridge. Originally built in 1889, its 137-metre (450-foot) span teeters 70 metres (230 feet) above the surging Capilano River. Fear not: 13-tonne concrete blocks anchor it securely. And there's much more to explore. Roam on smaller bridges between giant Douglas firs in Treetop Adventures, view Aboriginal totem poles and interpretive nature exhibits, and chow down at the Canyon Cafe. Don't miss the Cliffwalk attraction (completed in 2011), featuring glass-bottomed decks and narrow walkways along Capilano Canyon's cliffs.

Though narrower and lower, the bouncy Lynn Canyon Suspension Bridge has one big advantage: free admission. Striking views of pools, waterfalls, and second-growth forest abound on nearby trails. Kids also love learning about black bears, mushrooms, and slugs at the Lynn Canyon Ecology Centre.✤
www.capbridge.com, www.lynncanyon.ca

Celebrate the Anniversary of The Last Spike

At Craigellachie, British Columbia, on November 7, 1885, a plain iron spike joined the last two sections of Canadian Pacific's transcontinental rail line, finally connecting Canada from coast to coast. Railway buffs travel across the country to Craigellachie, but the importance of the site is appreciated by all Canadians who visit.

Off the Trans-Canada Highway, signs point to a cairn explaining the story behind the Last Spike and there's a short stretch of track where you can try your hand at hammering in your own Last Spike. Meanwhile, the adjacent Craigellachie railway station stocks a thorough collection of railway books and souvenirs.

The Last Spike is the key site along this section of track, but not the only attraction. Head east from Craigellachie to the Revelstoke Railway Museum, which features an admirable recreation of a Canadian Pacific Railway station, a powerful 1948 steam locomotive, and Business Car No. 4, the ultimate in early rail-travel luxury. An hour's drive further east is Rogers Pass, where workers toiled for three summers to complete the railbed. Interpretive panels at the summit tell of construction hardships, deadly avalanches, and the eventual underground re-routing of the rail line.✤
www.railwaymuseum.com/last_spike.htm

Watch Grizzly Bears Feed at Close Range in the Yukon

More than 30 Yukon grizzly bears head to the 170-square-kilometre (65.6-square-mile) Ni'iinlii Njik (Fishing Branch) Ecological Reserve in northern Yukon each year, just before winter arrives, to fatten themselves up on salmon. This is their destination of choice because this section of the river is one of the few that doesn't freeze this late in the season.

You'll take a nearly two-hour flight from Dawson City to the edge of the Arctic Circle just to get here. Once you arrive, you'll stay in rustic cabins that minimize the camp's ecological footprint.

Just a handful of visitors are taken out each day to watch the grizzlies stuff themselves with chum salmon from the comfort of nearby viewing sites; you can spend up to four hours each day gawking and taking photos of the powerful creatures. There are also moose, wolves, and wolverines to see, and the chance to hike in the mountains—or try your hand at underwater photography.

You'll take a nearly two-hour flight from Dawson City to the edge of the Arctic Circle just to get here.

Bear Cave Mountain Eco-Adventures, led by bear specialist and wildlife photographer Phil Timpany, teamed up with the Vuntut Development Corporation of the community of Old Crow to offer these tours, which can be booked for four, seven, or 10 days. The park is protected as a cultural and historical area for the Vuntut Gwich'in First Nation. Bear Cave Mountain is also aptly named; it has some 20 caves where grizzlies snooze the winter away after feasting on salmon.🍁
www.bearcavemountain.com

It happened THIS WEEK:

The Last Spike

Wearing a high hat, the oldest Canadian Pacific Railway executive took the honour of driving in the last spike of Canada's national railway at Craigellachie, B.C. But as Donald Smith—later known as Lord Strathcona—hammered the spike, the peg bent.

It was quickly replaced with another, ceremoniously finishing one of the world's longest railways on November 7, 1885.

The national railway had been promised when British Columbia joined Canada in 1871. But completing the track had been a financial stretch—and one many sacrificed their lives for.

Employing Chinese labourers was the easiest way to staff the work crews that would create a path through the Rockies. Providing more than two-thirds of the labour in B.C., Chinese railway workers received lower wages—an inequality that saved the project millions. The dangers of the job, including landslides, explosions, and lack of medical care, killed hundreds—if not thousands—of workers. An accurate count was never kept.

Following the last spike ceremony, railway baron Sir William Van Horne wrote to Prime Minister John A. MacDonald to inform him of the news:

"Thanks to your far seeing policy and unwavering support the Canadian Pacific Railway is completed. The last rail was laid this (Saturday) morning at 9.22."

The telegram was transmitted by the telegraph lines that twinned the railway track.

EVENTS & FESTIVALS

Banff Mountain Film & Book Festival ▶

Each November, the town of Banff swells with the arrival of enthusiastic outdoor lovers for a week of cinematic immersion at the famed campus of The Banff Centre. Thousands of attendees ignore the spectacular mountains at their doorstep to happily spend the entire weekend in darkened theatres watching the world's best cinematic collection of adventure-themed films from around the world.

Although the festival began in the 1970s as a competition rewarding the world's best mountain films, it has evolved into much more. Screenings now run the gamut of outdoor adventure sports and themes, while a popular recent addition has been Radical Reels (dedicated to sport-oriented, high-adrenaline films). Adding to the appeal for many are the top climbers and mountaineers invited as guest speakers—including Sir Edmund Hillary, Reinhold Messner, and Catherine Destivelle, all past attendees.

Many devotees attend the event religiously year after year, not just for the films but to catch up with old friends; view the latest in outdoor equipment; engage in mountain-sized discussions about the future of their chosen sports; and admire award-winning books and photographs from those respective competitions.🍁
www.banffcentre.ca/mountainfestival

◀ Pop into Old Montréal's Art Hotel

When Beverly Hills–based fashion designer Georges Marciano moved to Montréal, he did it with style, bringing truckloads of his private collection of Pop Art and displaying it—not in a gallery, but in a chic boutique hotel he purchased in Old Montréal.

Just when you think you've hit all the major museums and galleries in the city, you should look again. LHotel Montreal is that beautiful ornate building on Rue Saint-Jacques with Robert Indiana's *LOVE* sculpture and Botera's *Man on Horse* out front. Inside there are original works from Andy Warhol, Roy Lichtenstein, and Damien Hirst, just to name a few.

Even if you haven't booked a room here (and if you're an art lover, why didn't you?) you can still politely ask the staff if you can roam the halls of the upstairs floors. It's rumoured some rooms will be dedicated or themed with works of individual artists; enquire at the front desk if there are any particular ones with whom you wish to spend the night.

The name of the hotel is another example of Marciano's (who lives in the hotel) tongue-in-cheek sense of humour. You remember his Guess label? It was intended as a kind of Three Stooges joke. As in "What's the name of your collection?"—Guess. In this case, it's: "What hotel are you staying at?"—LHotel. ❧
www.lhotelmontreal.com

Enjoy a Spa Treatment inside an Egyptian Temple

Nordic spas are de rigueur in Québec, where people go to kick back in hot tubs and stir their circulation in cold water pools. But Tyst Trädgård spa takes it one—kooky—step further by adding eclectic massage cabins, each with a fun theme.

A Disney-esque theme spa in the woods? Why not? Situated at Duchesnay, in lac Saint-Joseph, in sprawling countryside about 30 minute's drive from Québec City, you can relax in soothing Scandinavian-inspired hydrotherapy (hot and cold waters, or dry sauna) before checking in to one of four individual huts. The choice depends on your current state of mind . . . or sense of humour.

Experience a "Pharaonic" body treatment in the Egyptian temple, amidst walls adorned with hieroglyphics and mummy tombs. The African temple envelopes you with bamboo and wooden tribal carvings, while the Grotto mimics the feel of an ancient cave. Finally, the Temple of Lights offers chromotherapy, where certain hues boost particular moods.

To dip into the waters, prices start at C$32 during the week (C$37 on weekends) for one hour. Massages start at close to C$100 for 30 minutes. (Make sure to enquire about the unusual bamboo or hot shell treatments.) The combos are great deals, starting at C$100 for 60 minutes of each, hydrotherapy and massage. There are also Romance and Golf packages. ❧
www.tysttradgard.com

Pay Homage to the Fallen in the Nation's Capital

Reflect on our soldiers' sacrifice at moving memorials and thought-provoking museums

It's a revered day in Canada: Remembrance Day, November 11—a solemn, moving time to properly commemorate all Canadian soldiers and their bravery. Buy a poppy from a veteran to pin on your lapel and join the pilgrimage to the nation's capital to honour the country's veterans.

The day originated in 1919 to pay tribute to those who fought in World War I—11:00 a.m. on the 11th day of the 11th month is still the marker for two minutes of silence at schools and institutions from coast to coast to coast. More recently, Remembrance Day has also become a time to pay homage to those who have served in conflicts around the world, from Korea to Afghanistan.

Ottawa and the National War Memorial is ground zero for the nation's tribute, and tens of thousands come to the city for the sombre ceremonies. It's best to get a room at the Fairmont Château Laurier, near Parliament Hill, so you can awake early on the 11th and readily join the crowds in time for the nearby ceremony—which begins promptly at 11:00 a.m. It includes a Canadian Forces 21-gun salute and fly-past. Before the ceremony begins, there's a parade of pipers and war veterans who march from Cartier Square Drill Hall to the War Memorial. Wreaths are laid by dignitaries, including the governor general and the prime minister, alongside those left by veterans and members of the military.

In addition to the politicians, children read poems before the crowds, remembering their ancestors, and tears are shed. Often, the young widows of recently fallen soldiers and their young families are in attendance, and it's not uncommon to see as many as four generations (or more) of Canadians gathered to pay tribute to the dead and their valiant sacrifices. Defending freedom and civil rights, and the heroic acts of individuals who risk their lives to help in battle are the themes.

Once the ceremonies have concluded, other nearby places worth visiting include the Tomb of the Unknown Soldier and the somewhat controversial Canadian War Museum.

The Tomb of the Unknown Soldier opened in 2000 and is the burial site for the (transported) remains of an unidentified Canadian soldier who died in World War I at Vimy Ridge, placed in a special tomb in front of the National War Memorial. The War Memorial was established to honour the more than 116,000 Canadians who sacrificed their lives in WWI, but now represents all Canadians who have died for their country in conflict. A graceful stone archway graced with two statues at the top representing peace and freedom, the memorial is also adorned with figures representing the nation's many fallen soldiers.

[It] is a solemn, moving time to properly commemorate all Canadian soldiers and their bravery.

More divisive is the Canadian War Museum, a fascinating site that both honours the victims of war and offers an unblinking eye on the ravages of conflict. The latter approach has rankled some veterans, who feel their work, colleagues, and fallen friends are being criticized by the museum's exhibits.

Opened in 2005, the museum explores Canada's military past and how it has shaped the nation. The extensive collections expose the brutality of the battlefield at home and abroad through personal accounts, documents, photographs and historic artifacts, military vehicles, artillery, and more. There are some 13,000 pieces in the art collection alone, and the impressive permanent exhibition highlights historic events in Canada's military history. The story is told through interactive exhibits, all set within an impressive and modern building located on the LeBreton Flats just west of downtown. All in all, the museum presents a truly contemporary take on the tolls of human conflict. Each year, on Remembrance Day, the lone artifact in the museum's stunning Memorial Hall—the headstone of the Unknown Soldier from WWI—is illuminated by natural light at precisely 11:00 a.m.

In the week leading up to Remembrance Day, known as Veterans' Week, there are other activities—many organized by the government's Veterans Affairs Canada department. A highlight is the Annual Veteran's Feast, where friends and families of First Nations, Métis, and Inuit veterans gather for supper, music, and stories. The theme is sharing and friendship while paying tribute to veterans at the Odawa Native Friendship Centre.

While Remembrance Day is not a national holiday, many retailers in Ottawa are closed in the morning until the ceremonies have concluded, at 12:30 p.m. ❦

Find out more at:
www.veterans.gc.ca

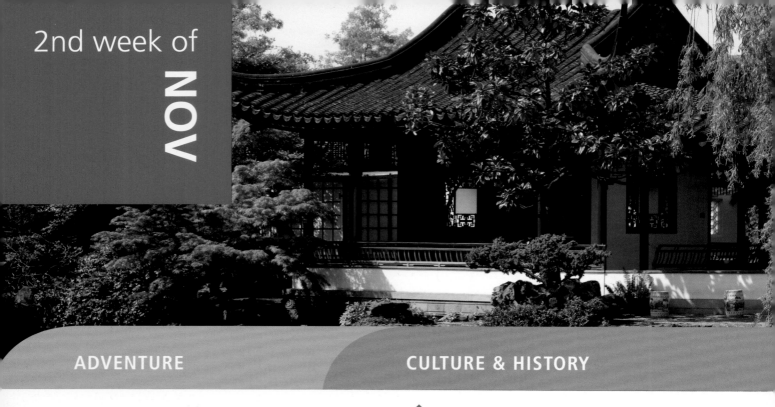

2nd week of NOV

ADVENTURE

CULTURE & HISTORY

Experience Freefall in a Vertical Wind Tunnel

Seek Reflection in the Dr. Sun Yat-Sen Garden

The hardest part of skydiving is stepping out of the plane, especially in November (just try to find a plane). Niagara Freefall removes that worry by keeping the plane on the ground and still throwing you into the sky. How? A giant prop generates a wind column that moves vertically up to 225 kilometres per hour (140 miles) through a heavily padded chamber, 3.7 metres (12 feet) across and six metres (20 feet) high. Step off the padded ledge and the supplied flight suit acts like a kite or sail, essentially converting you into a flying squirrel that never touches down. The wind's not only fast, but climate-controlled—so no nasty blasts of November cold.

This kind of flying ain't cheap: C$75 buys you three minutes in the chamber. But it's a far cry from the sky-high prices of parachuting, where a solo jump course will easily cost you C$300. (Many skydivers use this facility in the off-season to practise their moves.) The price includes a 20-minute training session and all necessary equipment: goggles, helmet, knee and elbow pads, gloves, and earplugs (it's very noisy). Flyers aged seven and older are welcome (those under 18 require an adult be present) and there's a weight limit of 118 kilograms (260 pounds). ❧
www.niagarafreefall.com

In the waning days of the year, when sun yields to shadow, Vancouver's Dr. Sun Yat-Sen Classical Chinese Garden is a haven of reflection and tranquility. Nestled inside Chinatown behind stone walls, steps away from the towering, ornate Millennium Gate, it became the first true Ming Dynasty–style garden outside China when it was completed, just before Expo '86 (the 1986 World's Fair) by artisans from Suzhou. The garden is named after the political activist who is considered the "father of modern China," but a visit today—even a brief one— conjures up ancient, philosophical values.

Stroll through the free, outer public park, which segues into the paid-admission garden. At this time of year, orange-tinged maple and gingko leaves create a sense of reverie. Admire the "three friends of winter"— bamboo, pine, and winter-flowering plum. Weathered limestone rocks harmonize beautifully with jade-green ponds, populated by fish and turtles, surrounded by stone lanterns and elegant wooden pavilions. If rain begins to fall, seek refuge beneath the covered walkways. It's all designed to reflect the balance between yin and yang. You'll understand why Taoist scholars visit such gardens to hone their keenest insights. ❧
www.vancouverchinesegarden.com

Learn to Harvest Malpeque Oysters off the Coast of P.E.I.

Malpeque oysters, judged the world's tastiest at a Paris exhibition in 1900, continue to be recognized as some of the world's finest. Known for their unique taste, they grow only in the bays of Prince Edward Island, and the way oysters are fished has not changed substantially over the years. Fishermen still set out in small boats the way their fathers and grandfathers did—and you can join them.

Fishermen still set out in small boats the way their fathers and grandfathers did.

To join the harvest, sign up for a Tong and Shuck Experience at Experience PEI. Bundle up, put on your grubbin' duds, and get ready for an adventure. Oyster fisher Brian Lewis or his brother Erskin will supply rubber boots, load you into their boat, and take you out into Salutation Cove for a hands-on lesson. Participants use tongs (similar to garden rakes) to grab oysters from the bottom. The brothers, who have been in the oyster business all their lives, show you how to shuck and enjoy them as the locals do: on the half shell. You'll never have a fresher oyster, as these are at their prime in November.

Back at the packing plant you'll learn how oysters are cleaned, graded, and prepared for shipment, then participate in a shucking session where you can enjoy more samples before leaving with a box to take with you. The half-day adventure (C$85/person) must be booked ahead.🍁

www.experiencepei.ca

Alisa Smith and J.B. MacKinnon's

favourite PLACE

An escape into remote British Columbia also means exploring the local offerings for *The 100 Mile Diet* authors Alisa Smith and J. B. MacKinnon. They say a trip along Highway 16 from Prince George to Prince Rupert visits a rich region of central B.C.

"It's one of the great but little-known road trips in Canada," write the authors, praising the spectacular scenery and local delicacies.

Be it shopping at the Smithers farmers' market or fishing for Dolly Varden trout, the pair can source plenty for a local dinner. For dessert, they recommend the "good homemade pie" that's readily available in the fall.

Other local foods include fermented oolichan grease, a "unique traditional food that is like a cross between olive oil and Icelandic hákarl."

Northern B.C. also holds a special meaning to them, as the place that inspired their local-based diet.

"We also like to pause and remember that the 100-Mile Diet was first inspired by a wild-foraged meal in a train-access-only town in the Skeena Valley," they say, while on the road away from their home in Vancouver.

Smith and MacKinnon suggest visitors "spend some time in deep backcountry." The region is known for its spirit bears—or black bears with white fur.

But it's always a balance between keeping special places protected and secret, or sharing them, say the writers.

"So much of rural Canada is threatened by shortsighted mining, logging, and power schemes. Our country needs more defenders, and you won't defend things that you don't know and love."

EVENTS & FESTIVALS

Get a Taste of Farm Life at the Royal Agricultural Winter Fair

The smell of fresh straw mixes with a whiff of the animal stall in this annual salute to Canada's colonial past and the vanishing art of animal husbandry. Once you've seen a cow milked by an automated milker, you'll walk away amazed anyone ever did it by hand.

Historically a bastion of Upper Canada royalists—hence the name—this annual show, just west of downtown Toronto, is long past its heyday as a coming-out ball for horse-fancying debutantes. But it remains a marvellous excuse to escape the first days of winter amidst miles of bunting, silky ribbons of blue, red, and gold, and the endless patter of an auctioneer dispensing heads of cattle. The butter sculpting competition has to be seen to be believed: competitors have one day to realize their vision on a 25-kilogram (55-pound) block of butter. Kids will love the petting area where they can get their mitts on four-legged juniors—including kids of the goat variety. The keynote Royal Horse Show features competitions in show-jumping, dressage, and bull riding—a competitive nod to Calgary's Stampede. For more sedate viewing, the fair celebrates the cornucopia of autumn's final harvests, including the finalists of the My Giant Vegetable Challenge. The competition gets surprisingly intense, as befits the world's largest indoor agricultural and equestrian competition. If you've ever wondered what a 454-kilogram (1,000-pound) pumpkin looks like, this is your chance.🍁

www.royalfair.org

Return to *Hell's Kitchen* with Araxi's Heavenly Cuisine ▼

Does your favourite word start with "F?" No, no . . . not THAT one. More like "fine," "food," or "feast?" Whatever you were thinking, if you love foul-mouthed celebrity chef Gordon Ramsay, then treat yourself to a meal at Araxi—perhaps on Ramsay's birthday (November 8). The flagship Whistler property of restaurateur Jack Evrensel's Top Table Group, Araxi made headlines in 2009 when Dave Levey, the sixth-season winner of Ramsay's reality TV show *Hell's Kitchen*, was awarded a cooking job there. The New Jersey native got to work in Whistler during the 2010 Olympic Winter Games.

Beyond the glitz and glamour of TV, Araxi simply makes great food. At this intimately lit Village Square institution, don't miss the fresh seafood dishes, from Qualicum Bay scallops to Nova Scotia lobster plucked live from the tank. Many ingredients are locally sourced by executive chef James Walt, like Fraser Valley chicken and Pemberton root vegetables. The international wine collection, including more than 11,000 bottles, perennially earns *Wine Spectator's* Best of Award of Excellence. Unsurprisingly, Araxi's not cheap. Still, Ramsay could have been speaking for this elite restaurant when he once proclaimed, "I maintain standards and I strive for perfection."❧
www.araxi.com

Rock the Commodore Ballroom

When the Commodore Ballroom reopened after extensive renovations in November 1999, savvy music fans across Canada lit their Bic lighters—ahem, cellphones—in salute. Celebrate that anniversary and sample the rockin' lineup that normally graces November. This legendary, 1,000-capacity club remains the kingpin of Vancouver's neon-lit entertainment district on Granville Street.

It's not just about the high-calibre acts, though Coldplay, Tom Waits, and Roger Daltrey—plus hometown heroes Nickelback and Michael Bublé—are among the names that have performed here since '99. It's the 1929-built venue's rich atmosphere.

The Commodore's famous spring-loaded dance floor enables joyful boinging beneath gleaming brass chandeliers. Sound and sightlines throughout the house are stunning. Big video screens stage-side and in the upstairs balcony bar enhance the experience. It's general admission with limited seating, so arrive early if you want a table. Free Wi-Fi and a high-end menu ranging from albacore tuna to potato gnocchi are nice additional touches. You can shimmy through the crowds right up to the stage five minutes before showtime if you yearn to feel the lead guitarist's sweat dripping on you. Artists often appear at the merchandise table afterwards to autograph swag. Rock on!❧
www.livenation.com/Commodore-Ballroom-tickets-Vancouver/venue/139274

Hunt Down Unique Holiday Gifts (and squeeze in some time for pampering)

Shop till you're ready to drop . . . into a revitalizing spa

It's the holiday season and Toronto is in full festive swing, lights a-twinkling and shops a-hopping. As a bonus for the intrepid buyer dedicated to finding unique gifts for loved ones, the city offers spa treatments as distinctive as the retail goods for sale: souvenirs of a kind that will keep the city warm-at-heart in these dark days of winter. So, plan a day or two (or more), and expect to shop till you drop . . . into a retreat for plenty of pampering.

Start your day at the Canadian National Exhibition grounds—making time for a brief tour of the pretty Princess Gates at the entrance—for a solid morning of retail rummaging. Exploring the artisan creations at the One of a Kind craft exhibit is a reward in itself, but the real goal—finding the perfect gift—is guaranteed. Originally launched in Toronto, this show features some truly exceptional items, such as stunning woven scarves that double as jewellery by Marie-Pierre Daigle, adorable owl pillows made by Hilary Cosgrove, or elegant bowls

crafted from paper by the Montréal-based Pas À Papier. There are hand-crafted, hand-painted wooden puzzles for tots that are like little works of art from Sleepy Hollow. Designers bring their unique touches to blown-glass chandeliers, ornate jewellery, fashions made with natural fibres, wooden furniture, beautiful birdhouses, and just about any decorative touch you can imagine. More than 400 artists from across Canada display their unique wares at this show.

After a few intense hours of exploring the best of Canadian crafts, it's time to take a break.

Ever had a Canadian wrap? It's not something you eat, but a luxurious and soothing spa treatment made with seaweed from British Columbia—available at the top-notch, centrally located Stillwater Spa. Water is the theme here, with plenty of aqua therapies, including whirlpools and saunas. To kick back, there are private cabana-like nooks with recliners and personal TV screens equipped with headsets. Treatments include the inventive and patriotic, like the Canadian grain facial (with grain from Alberta).

Feeling rejuvenated, you're ready for some more shopping. The Stillwater is steps away from the tony Mink Mile, which runs along Bloor Street West from Yonge Street to Avenue Road. Now sexier than ever after an extensive revamp, with widened sidewalks and shiny new shops, everything's all dressed up with decorations for the holiday season. Browse the couture stores from Gucci to Chanel and top labels such as MaxMara, but don't miss the MO851, a Canadian-owned leather store selling classic-yet-cool

jackets. Another particular find nearby is The Cookbook Store, a neighbourhood gem that stands out for its fine selection of cookbooks, food memoirs, and the best in food writing. If you're lucky enough to be in town for one of their many book launches, book the date. (Also know that Julia Child was here.) Not to be missed on the strip is Holt Renfrew, Canada's answer to Saks Fifth Avenue in the United States. Here, you'll find all the top designers and latest fashions. Plus, the store makes a point of stocking Canadian designers you won't find elsewhere. Names to look for include Jeremy Laing, Greta Constantine, Dean Davidson, and Karen McClintock, among others. Just ask any of the very helpful staff for tips.

It's easy to while away hours at Holt's. If it's a little pick-me-up you need, check out the luxe in-store spa. Decorated in modern-chic blonde wood and glass, the spa provides a good range of cosmetic services from manicures to massage. After a day of hitting the pavement, treat your toes to a Peppermint Sea Salt Pedicure—a treatment that combines peppermint sea salts and oils, calling candy canes to mind.

If you have a second day to spare and are looking to get something special for an art-lover, the shop at the city's major art space, the Art Gallery of Ontario (AGO), offers quality prints, trinkets, calendars, and other memorabilia related to major exhibits. A rare find just around the corner is Onsite, the tiny gallery connected to the Ontario College of Art & Design (OCAD). It's a much edgier offering, with modern works, and new artists and designers. If you're looking to collect contemporary Canadian art, the Bau-Xi Gallery, across from the AGO, features contemporary works by artists from across the country.

Nearby is Elmwood Spa, one of the city's top spas. Convenient to Yonge and Dundas, it's a favourite day spa where you can spend many serene hours being pampered. They really have it all: massages and facials, a range of water therapies centred around a lovely pool, steam rooms, a whirlpool, and a poolside lounge. The brand is so highly respected it has its own line of beauty products, lotions, and potions. So drop in for yourself and leave with a gift. Cross another name off your gift list . . . or maybe leave with a little something for yourself. You deserve it!

Find out more at:
www.toronto.com/shopping

ADVENTURE

Speed Down Grouse Mountain on a Zipline

You don't have to travel far from downtown Vancouver to experience the thrills of ziplining—and spring's a gorgeous time for it. Just 15 minutes away on the North Shore is Grouse Mountain, which opened its series of ziplines in 2008. Take the Skyride aerial tramway with its panoramic Vancouver view, fork out about C$100 for your two-hour tour, get your ziplining harness, helmet, and safety instructions. And away you go!

Although you might have the "Gonna Fly Now" theme from Rocky running through your head as you prepare to tackle the lines, the feeling of zooming along a wire at speeds of up to 80 kilometres (50 miles) per hour is surprisingly Zen-like. Gaze down at the shimmering waters of Blue Grouse Lake or relish the infinite green of old-growth forest as you race towards the next wooden platform. Between launch points, you'll hike along wilderness trails while guides point out local birds and critters and describe how Aboriginal people of the West Coast traditionally used plants and berries. When you take a chairlift higher up the mountain, watch for the grizzly bears in the enclosed Refuge for Endangered Wildlife. By the time your final run from the peak of Grouse to nearby Dam Mountain arrives, your spirits will be soaring.❦
www.grousemountain.com

◀ Visit Fort Langley— Where B.C. was Born

A bronze statue of Sir James Douglas stands outside the stockade walls of Fort Langley. Yet it barely hints at the importance of the longtime Hudson's Bay Company fur trader who ruled as B.C.'s first governor for eight years. Enter this former trading post, a national historic site located 40 minutes outside Vancouver, and celebrate Douglas Day to get a vivid taste of 19th-century life.

It was on November 19, 1858, that Douglas signed a proclamation officially making British Columbia a Crown Colony of Great Britain. (Note that Douglas Day festivities are sometimes held on weekend dates such as the 18th or 20th for convenience; it's not strictly the 19th.) Park admission is free for Douglas Day. Watch a re-enactment of the historic signing, with gallant soldiers firing a black-powder salute and raising the flag. Other costumed interpreters will be happy to teach you about blacksmithing, barrel-making, and other trades of the era. Explore historic structures, including an 1840-built storehouse— believed to be B.C.'s oldest building, and stroke beaver skins and HBC blankets.

You can even pan for gold, evoking memories of the 1858 Fraser Valley Gold Rush when thousands of prospectors swelled the nearby village, also called Fort Langley. It's a rich history here indeed.❧
www.fortlangley.com

Make a Splash at the Vancouver Aquarium ▼

Maybe your kids know all the words to Raffi's "Baby Beluga." Or maybe the sight of sea creatures simply soothes your soul. Either way, you owe yourself a visit to the Vancouver Aquarium, beautifully tucked away amidst the mighty trees of Stanley Park. It's open year-round with more than 70,000 animals. It was Canada's first aquarium when it debuted in 1956, and remains one of the five largest in North America.

Gape in delight at ghostly white beluga whales swimming in their habitat, like torpedoes performing underwater ballet. A backlit display of pink jellyfish proves as captivatingly psychedelic as a Pink Floyd video. Thrill to the jumps of Pacific white-sided dolphins, which devour herring from their trainers with saucy abandon. Paddling around on their backs, the sea otters are as cute as they come. That contrasts with the lethal piranhas and freshwater stingrays you'll discover in the Graham Amazon Gallery.

Dedicated to conserving aquatic life, the aquarium manages to entertain while educating. Don't miss the 4-D Experience, where actual sprays of water and gusts of wind accompany a 15-minute, three-dimensional movie that vividly depicts humpback whales and sea lions all over our blue planet.❧
www.vanaqua.org

3rd week of NOV

EVENTS & FESTIVALS

QUIRKY CANADA

Shucking and Slurping at the Clayoquot Oyster Festival

Tofino, a tiny resort town on Vancouver Island's west coast, is best-known for its beach-strolling, surfing, and storm-watching opportunities. However, facing unspoiled, open Pacific Ocean waters has other advantages—like an amazing oyster harvest. In the third week of November, the community puts to good use some of the 50,000 gallons of oysters reaped from Clayoquot Sound each year.

The weekend-long Clayoquot Oyster Festival offers many ways to enjoy these mouth-watering marine molluscs. Tour a working oyster farm, chat with oyster experts, or hobnob with visiting foodies and cookbook authors. Show off your mastery of half-shell gluttony at the outrageous slurping contest. You can even try to meet the love of your life at the Mermaid's Ball costume party at the Tofino Community Centre, where revellers dressed up as pirates and princesses sample more aphrodisiacal seafood snacks. The Oyster Gala, dishing up dozens of oyster recipes from local restaurants and pairing them with B.C.-made wines and beers, provides the grand finale for the Clayoquot Oyster Festival. Events are individually ticketed and sell quickly, so buy yours well in advance. Book accommodations early too.❦
www.oystergala.com

See the World at the West Edmonton Mall

It's late November in Canada and winter's closing in, but at West Edmonton Mall it's still possible to head to the beach for sunbathing and surfing, to play volleyball on a sandy court, eat at an outdoor Parisian café, then retreat to your hotel room and sink into a hot tub surrounded by lush tropical forest.

Calgary's stampede may be billed as the greatest *outdoor* show on earth, but Edmonton has what can surely be billed as the greatest *indoor* show on earth— North America's largest shopping and amusement complex. The statistics are simply staggering: covering an area of more than 464,515 square metres (five million square feet), it has 20,000 parking stalls, 23,000 employees, the same power consumption as a city with a population of 50,000, and 325,000 light bulbs. The mall boasts the world's largest indoor amusement park, the world's largest indoor water park (where the temperature is a balmy 30 degrees Celsius, 85 degrees Fahrenheit), the world's largest indoor lake, and the world's highest indoor bungee jump. Much more than an oversized shopping mall, Edmonton's top tourist attraction is a shop-and-play, four-season wonderland, where many visitors check into the 355-room luxury Fantasyland Hotel, stay a weekend, and never set foot outside the mall's 58 entrances. Just don't forget to start your holiday shopping while you're here.❦
www.wem.ca

Taste the Work of Canada's Top Student Chefs

The next big stars of fine dining are being groomed at Charlottetown's Culinary Institute of Canada, and you can sample their mouthwatering work at the institute's Lucy Maud Dining Room. Students here compete on the international stage, often bringing home the gold from competitions at the Culinary Olympics and the World Culinary Grand Prix level.

The dining room boasts a menu attuned to chefs training in the preparation of seasonal cuisine. In November, for example, local P.E.I. shellfish—particularly mussels and oysters—are at their peak. Regional seafood is the heart of the institute's most popular dishes: Atlantic seafood chowder, walnut-crusted salmon, and pistachio-and-chive crusted South Shore "Victorian" baby halibut. The best deal is invariably the International Table d'Hôte, a three-course menu that changes daily for a very reasonable C$30. For both lunch and dinner, second-year students staff the kitchens—under the supervision of world-class instructors. The institute's wine program ensures an interesting list drawing from Australia, France, Italy, and California, along with a strong presence of Canadian wines.

The most exciting meals are those presented as practise sessions before students head off to compete internationally. When calling for reservations ask about any special dinners or events on the horizon. The exceptional dining experience is enhanced by the equally beautiful view. Situated right on the harbour looking towards Northumberland Strait, it's a spectacular vista with red cliffs, passing ships, and crashing waves. The ambience of the dining room is warm and elegant—perfect for an intimate supper on a frosty winter's evening. ✤
www.hollandcollege.com/culinary_
institute_of_canada/lucy_maud_
dining_room.php

Canadian moments

The Grey Cup

Despite Canada's legendary love of hockey, it is the Canadian Football League's late-November Grey Cup that draws more than six million viewers. That's nearly one-fifth of the population—and more than any other Canadian television event.

The Grey Cup refers to both the championship game and the trophy. A silver chalice, the Grey Cup was donated in 1909 by then-Governor General of Canada, the 4th Earl Grey (the tea was named for the second Earl Grey).

At the 1948 Grey Cup, Calgary Stampeders fans brought 12 horses to Toronto by train. Going beyond flapjack breakfasts and cowboy hats, one Calgarian rode a horse through the lobby of the Royal York Hotel (today The Fairmont Royal York). Not only did the Stampeders ride out a perfect season, defeating the Ottawa Rough Riders to win the cup, but it started a tradition of pre-game festivities that tends to overrun the host city each year.

In 1962, the game got a further boost when Parliament legislated the game must be broadcast in all regions, citing the issue as a matter of national unity. It was that same year the game was played over two days in Toronto—the first day cut short by dense fog.

The competition went international in 1993 when the league expanded to include the Sacramento Gold Miners. More U.S. teams were added, including a Baltimore team that snatched the trophy in 1995. All U.S. teams eventually folded or moved north (the Baltimore team became the Montréal Alouettes), and the football league now has eight Canadian teams.

Hit the Slopes for the Opening of Ski Season on Vancouver's North Shore

Powder hounds can choose from three nearby resorts and be back to the city for dinnertime

There's nothing like soft white flakes, swift chair-lifts, and the swooshing sounds of skis and snowboards at the start of the snow season. Canada enjoys some of the world's best ski resorts, from the 3,300 hectares (8,000 acres) of terrain in Alberta's Banff/Lake Louise ski area to Québec's super-scenic Mont-Tremblant, about an hour from Montréal. Yet for easy access from a major urban centre, you can't beat the three dynamic resorts on Vancouver's North Shore: Cypress, Grouse, and Seymour mountains. All are half an hour or less from downtown —in fact, any Vancouverite will tell you that if you get lost while walking or driving around, just look for the mountains and you'll know which way is north. When fresh powder adorns those peaks circa late November, it signals the true onset of winter . . . and the adrenalin rush that awaits on the slopes.

It's always a race for resorts to get their runs open, but Mount Seymour makes a point of celebrating its kickoff by hosting the ROME Premature Jibulation.

Snowboarders flock to this annual free, open-park jam, which graces multiple hills around North America. The local shred community loves to pull tricks at four different terrain parks. Mount Seymour also caters to budget-conscious skiers and families, offering the most affordable day passes on the North Shore (think under C$50 per adult, under C$40 for students and seniors, and under C$30 for kids). More than 20 downhill runs, mostly intermediate-level, provide enough variety to keep everyone amused. With tobogganing and tubing for the young 'uns, there's something for everyone. For a change of pace, go snowshoeing amidst lakes and old-growth forest on the Discovery Snowshoe Trails. You can go solo, or splurge on a guided evening tour that includes chocolate fondue in a hand-carved snow lounge.

Travelling to Grouse Mountain is simple. The 1,250-metre (4,100-foot) peak, which originally opened for skiing in 1929, can be reached by public transit as well as by car. The Skyride aerial tram shuttling skiers to the summit is an experience in itself, giving a tremendous panorama of the North Shore and the downtown skyline across Burrard Inlet. Grouse has four quad chairs—two high-speed—that serve 26 runs, including eight black diamonds. Want to get your downhill buzz on after dark? Half the runs are illuminated at night till 10:00 p.m. In addition to skiing, snowboarding (two terrain parks), and snowshoeing (four groomed trails), dozens of other activities complement your Grouse experience. Go for a sleigh ride, try ziplining, fly around in a heli-jet, or tour the "Eye of the Wind" turbine, which generates wind power. Check out the enclosed Refuge for Endangered Wildlife; though the grizzly bears are likely hibernating, you could spot timber wolves on the prowl. With the holidays approaching, you can see real reindeer at Santa's Workshop, or catch classic Christmas flicks with the kids in the Theatre in the Sky. Hungry? Head into the Peak Chalet and choose from

several restaurants, ranging from Lupins Café's soups and sandwiches to The Observatory's Fraser Valley duck breast and Hecate Straight sablefish. You may recognize the chalet's spacious atrium, which NBC's *TODAY* show used as its set during the 2010 Olympic Winter Games.

When fresh powder adorns those peaks circa late November, it signals the true onset of winter.

Cypress Mountain has even more Olympic history. In 2010, this big West Vancouver ski area hosted Olympic snowboarding (half-pipe, parallel giant slalom, and snowboard cross) and freestyle skiing (moguls, aerials, and ski-cross). Hometown heroine Maëlle Ricker became the first Canadian woman to win gold that year, triumphing in snowboard cross. Today, little remains physically from the Games. Yet two-plankers will appreciate the excellent quantity and variety of downhill runs—close to 50, spread out over neighbouring Mount Strachan and Black Mountain, served by six chairlifts. Cypress boasts the largest vertical drop on the North Shore at 610 metres (2,001 feet). If you prefer Nordic skiing, try out the 19 kilometres (11.8 miles) of groomed cross-country trails, 7.5 kilometres (4.7 miles) of which are lit for night use. Snowshoeing, with 10 kilometres (6.2 miles) of trails, and snowtubing, including a tow lift, are also on the menu. When you crave a break, the Crazy Raven Bar & Grill and a 600-seat cafeteria dish up casual plates in the Cypress Creek Day Lodge.

The nicest part about skiing on the North Shore? You can return to Vancouver and, after a full day on the slopes, still be able to enjoy a seafood dinner in Yaletown or catch a play at the Queen Elizabeth Theatre before climbing into bed. The combination of skiing adventure and urban civilization is hard to match anywhere else in the world.

Find out more at:
www.mountseymour.com,
www.grousemountain.com,
www.cypressmountain.com

Explore the Vancouver Island Coast via Cargo Ship

Want to revisit a time before life unfolded at the speed of Twitter? Take a one-day, round-trip on the M.V. Frances Barkley, chugging along Vancouver Island's west coast from the logging town of Port Alberni to the fishing village of Bamfield. Built in 1958 and named after the first European woman to reach these shores, the 200-passenger freighter doesn't just offer scenic views of Pacific Rim National Park, but also delivers food, logging equipment, and other cargo to small communities along the way. Travelling in late November offers a true feel of edge-of-the-world tranquility.

As you progress down the Alberni Inlet, check out venerable lumber mills in the shadow of imposing coastal mountains covered with fir and spruce trees. With luck, you might spot deer or swans at the inlet's narrowest point. Picturesque coves, former gold-panning sites, and rocky islands dot the route, like the Broken Group Islands in the middle of Barkley Sound. Pore over the ship's charts after downing hearty bacon-and-egg sandwiches. When you hit Bamfield, visit the general store or cappuccino bar off the boardwalk, or take a quick peek at the Bamfield Marine Science Centre, before boarding the freighter again. Windproof attire is recommended for the open decks. Depending on routing, the trip takes nine or 10 hours. 🍁
www.ladyrosemarine.com

5 faves

Canadian Museum of Civilization
Life-size renderings of the social, cultural, and material history of Canada since the landings of the first Europeans in A.D. 1000 will captivate even the most reluctant museum-goer. The majestic Grand Hall displays more than 40 gigantic totem poles from the Pacific Northwest and looks out on to Ottawa River from its perch in Gatineau, Québec.

◀ Canadian Aboriginal Festival

For one week in November, Copps Coliseum in Hamilton is filled with the sights and sounds of the oldest civilizations in North America. Cree, Ojibway, Cherokee, Cheyenne, Métis: representatives from more than 100 nations from every region of Canada and the United States come together to demonstrate their talents in dance, music, cuisine, and arts and crafts. As the event's organizers say, "You don't have to be an Aboriginal to enjoy."

Interest in Aboriginal peoples is enjoying a renaissance. The threat of climate change, combined with a growing awareness that humanity is inextricably connected with nature, has created an interest in a culture so closely tied to the natural world. The event shows off the talents of First Nations people across a wide range of fields. Festivities begin on the Friday evening with the gala Canadian Aboriginal Music Awards show. Saturday's main event is the Pow Wow Dance Circle, an opportunity for participants to show their colours. Workshops are available in such crafts as soapstone carving, birchbark canoe–making, and traditional healing, while the exhibition space features more than 200 booths offering an array of handicrafts and samples of traditional cuisine. A lacrosse skills competition pits the best amateur players against each other in lightning-fact action. It's one-stop shopping for an immersion in Aboriginal traditions and talents —all brought to your doorstep in an urban setting.❈
www.canab.com

Explore Unspoiled Nature and Ancient Haida Culture in Gwaii Haanas

In 2010, some 5,000 square kilometres (1,930 square miles) of land and water in the Haida Gwaii archipelago off the northern coast of British Columbia was designated as the Gwaii Haanas National Park Reserve and Haida Heritage Site. Gwaii Haanas, in what was formerly known as the Queen Charlotte Islands, means "Islands of Beauty." Deep evergreen forests overlook an ocean teeming with salmon, halibut, and octopus. With such natural bounty, it's little wonder the Haida Native people have lived here for millennia. The advantage of visiting this remote destination in November is that you'll enjoy even more reflective solitude than usual (most visitors come between May and September).

SGaang Gwaay, a UNESCO World Heritage Site, is a must-see. Walk along the beach past ruined longhouses from this 19th-century Haida village, near 32 proud totemic and mortuary poles—weather-beaten but erect. Soak up the solemn splendour.

Beneath the nearby trees, you may spot black bears, pine martens, or weasels—many differing genetically from their mainland cousins, one reason the area's sometimes dubbed "Canada's Galapagos."

To keep Gwaii Haanas pristine, the government restricts the number of visitors, and fees apply. Various tour companies offer boat-based trips with wildlife-watching, Haida wood-carving demos, and traditional feasts. The park can only be accessed by boat or float plane.❈
www.pc.gc.ca/gwaiihaanas

Casa Loma

The century-old castle just north of downtown Toronto has all the makings of a great tale—opulent suites, secret passageways, and an underground tunnel. It's built like a medieval palace, with an 18-metre (59-foot) Great Hall, two towers, and sections modelled after Windsor Castle— plenty of material to send your imagination.

Silver Wave Film Festival

This Fredericton festival screens New Brunswick's best feature films, documentaries, and short films that were shot in the province and produced by local filmmakers, along with selections from around the world. Besides the screenings, there are parties, receptions, workshops, and the esteemed Silver Wave Awards.

Rendezvous with Madness

This unique festival, organized by the Toronto-based Centre for Addiction and Mental Health, screens features, short films, and videos that address issues of mental health and addiction, in formats including documentaries and animated films. Dubbing itself "a film festival with many personalities," it screens edgy, thought-provoking films.

Granville Island

You can really do it all here: wander the busy public market jammed with food stalls, browse the dozen artist studios along Railspur Alley, see the works of students and grads of the Emily Carr University of Art + Design, or paddle into the sunset by taking a kayak lesson from Ecomarine Ocean Kayak Centre.

1960

1990

EVENTS & FESTIVALS

Listen to Women in the House of Blues

Much of the blues consists of men singing about their troubles with the fairer sex—which makes it only fair that the other half get a chance to have their say. A little bit country, a little bit jazz, a little bit of anything goes, the Women's Blues Revue delivers what you'd expect: accomplished musicians and slightly-more-brilliant high notes, along with some thrilling sounds from new voices across the register. And, yes—men are welcome. They just can't play.

The revue began as a grassroots project of the Toronto Blues Society—itself a grassroots project to keep the blues flame alive—to shine a light on female performers, particularly musicians who often struggle to grow an audience (of either sex). From its beginning in small clubs throughout the city, the festival's popularity has grown to fill Massey Hall—the city's best concert stage. Each event is anchored by an all-star band (needless to say, the band consists of all women) joined by an eclectic mix of female vocalists and musicians from across the bluesy spectrum. Performers past and present include Alana Bridgewater, Kellylee Evans, Little Miss Higgins, Robin Banks, Rita Chiarelli, and Alejandra Ribera. Expect to pay between C$35 and C$50 per ticket. ♣
www.torontobluessociety.com

◄ See One of the World's Largest Shoe Collections

Museums normally pay homage to man's greatest achievements, and the Bata Shoe Museum makes a credible argument that humble footwear deserves to be celebrated in the same style. Imelda Marcos would love this museum, but anyone from the foot fanatic to the phobic will find something interesting here—from prehistoric footwear to Justin Bieber's latest designer runners.

Even the building, designed by Raymond Moriyama and located at the edge of the University of Toronto's downtown campus, looks like a whimsical shoebox—perfect for storing the Bata family's 10,000-item collection. (The family also owns the shoe store chain.) The museum's main gallery, "All About Shoes," traces the history of footwear, beginning with a plaster cast of some of the earliest known human footprints—dating back to 4 million B.C. You'll come across such specialty shoes as spiked clogs (used to crush chestnuts in 17th-century France), Elton John's 12-inch-plus platforms, and Prime Minister Pierre Elliott Trudeau's well-worn sandals. One display focuses on Canadian footwear fashioned by the Inuit, while another highlights 19th-century ladies' footwear. The second-story galleries house ever-changing exhibits, which have taken on some serious topics such as the history of foot-binding in China. The museum strikes a compelling balance between the educational and the entertaining, such that it's likely to be the source of a dinner-party anecdote or two.❧
www.batashoemuseum.ca

Warm Up with Québec's Best Microbrews ▼

Québec is well-known for her microbreweries. On a chilly November evening in Montréal, there's nothing quite like a good beer—well, maybe a good beer and a hockey game. Around this time of year, local breweries start busting out their winter ales, so it's a fine time to check out their latest offerings.

Dieu du Ciel!, in the so-hip-it's-painful Mile End neighbourhood, displays its latest concoctions on a large blackboard near the entrance. As the "city" outpost of their Saint-Jerôme brewery, this is the place to go for serious artisanal beer. Only brewed once a year, with the aim of keeping you warm through the Canadian winter, Blanche Neige ("Snow White")—with a whopping 9.5 per cent alcohol content—has a unique flavour of cinnamon and clove.

Another pub to try out is the McAuslan Brewery, a proudly Scottish label founded by namesake and native son Peter McAuslan. The brasserie is a casual spot with a charming patio overlooking the canal. At this time of the year, you might still be able to enjoy their popular Pumpkin Ale brewed only in autumn.

For a beer-influenced menu, add Fourquet Fourchette to your list. A New France–themed restaurant with costumed servers, it brings together food and beer brewed by Unibroue (another Québec brewing institution)—either through suggested pairings or by including beer as a main ingredient in the dish (or both). So, bon appétit—and bottoms up!❧
www.dieuduciel.com, mcauslan.com/en, www.fourquet-fourchette.com

Your next STEP

TOP PICKS

ADVENTURE

CULTURE & HISTORY

NATURE'S GRANDEUR

EVENTS & FESTIVALS

QUIRKY CANADA

REJUVENATE

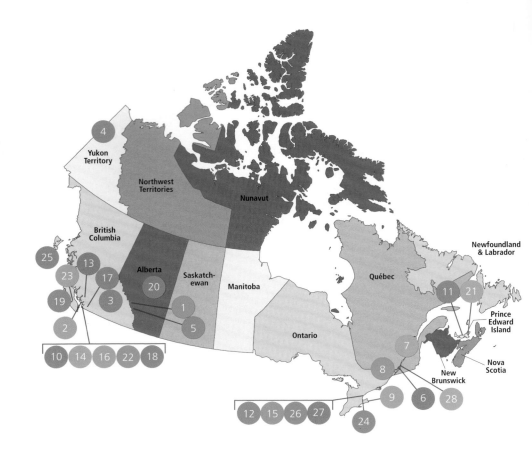

WEEK 1

1 LAKE LOUISE, ALTA.
Fairmont Chateau Lake Louise
www.fairmont.com

2 NORTH VANCOUVER, B.C.
Capilano Suspension Bridge
www.capbridge.com

3 CRAIGELLACHIE, B.C.
Site of The Last Spike
www.railwaymuseum.com/
last_spike.htm

4 NI'IINLII NJIK ECOLOGICAL
RESERVE, Y.T.
Grizzly bear–watching
www.bearcavemountain.com

5 BANFF, ALTA.
Banff Mountain Film and Book
Festival
www.banffcentre.ca/mountain
festival

6 MONTRÉAL, QUE.
Old Montréal's art hotel
www.lhotelmontreal.com

7 SAINTE-CATHERINE-DE-LA-
JACQUES-CARTIER, QUE.
Tyst Trädgårdv spa
www.tysttradgard.com

WEEK 2

8 OTTAWA, ONT.
Remembrance Day in the nation's
capital
www.veterans.gc.ca

9 NIAGARA FALLS, ONT.
Niagara Freefall
www.niagarafreefall.com

10 VANCOUVER, B.C.
Dr. Sun Yat-Sen Chinese Garden
www.vancouverchinesegarden.com

11 MALPEQUE, P.E.I.
Malpeque oyster harvesting
www.experiencepei.ca

12 TORONTO, ONT.
Royal Agricultural Winter Fair
www.royalfair.org

13 WHISTLER, B.C.
Hell's Kitchen restaurant
www.araxi.com

14 VANCOUVER, B.C.
Commodore Ballroom
www.livenation.com/Commodore-
Ballroom-tickets-Vancouver/
venue/139274

WEEK 3

15 TORONTO, ONT.
Toronto holiday shopping
www.toronto.com/shopping

16 NORTH VANCOUVER, B.C.
Grouse Mountain ziplining
www.grousemountain.com

17 FORT LANGLEY, B.C.
B.C.'s birthplace
www.fortlangley.com

18 VANCOUVER, B.C.
Vancouver Aquarium
www.vanaqua.org

19 TOFINO, B.C.
Clayoquot Oyster Festival
www.oystergala.com

20 EDMONTON, ALTA.
West Edmonton Mall
www.wem.ca

21 CHARLOTTETOWN, P.E.I.
Culinary Institute of Canada
www.hollandcollege.com/
culinary_institute_of_canada/
lucy_maud_dining_room.php

WEEK 4

22 VANCOUVER, B.C.
North Shore skiing
www.mountseymour.com

23 PORT ALBERNI, B.C.
Tour on the M.V. Frances Barkley
www.ladyrosemarine.com

24 HAMILTON, ONT.
Canadian Aboriginal Festival
www.canab.com

25 GWAII HAANAS, B.C.
National Park and Haida
Heritage Site
www.pc.gc.ca/gwaiihaanas

26 TORONTO, ONT.
Women's Blues Revue
www.torontobluessociety.com

27 TORONTO, ONT.
Bata Shoe Museum
www.batashoemuseum.ca

28 CHAMBLY, QUE.
Québec's best microbrews
www.dieuduciel.com

DECEMBER

Take In Two of Canada's Top Cultural Showcases

The AGO and ROM feature some of the best collections on the continent

With the holiday season just around the corner, escape the cold outside and take advantage of minimal crowds while (at your own speed) relishing all that Toronto's top cultural institutions have to offer. There's plenty! The AGO (Art Gallery of Ontario) and the ROM (Royal Ontario Museum) are two of Canada's finest centres of art, history, enlightenment, and exploration. Allow a day for each destination—more, if you can. And with top-notch dining at both, a fine meal helps round out the experience.

Enter the AGO from the main door on Dundas Street into Walker Court and take in Frank Gehry's stunning renovation, completed in 2008. The "starchitect" is a local boy—in fact, he grew up in the neighbourhood—and his passion for this C$276 million project is in evidence throughout, with fine work in wood and glass. Ride the elevator to the top floor and walk down the sculpted circular staircase that offers quaint, urban views of the neighbourhood and across—to Toronto's down-town core. Then amble through the Galleria Italia, a Gehry signature masterpiece of wood and glass anchored by a local artist's towering cedar trunk that's puzzlingly carved from the inside to expose interior branches.

The "O" in the gallery's name is for Ontario, but it might well be called the Art Gallery of Canada for its impressive collection of national masters past and present. Famous for its Group of Seven canvases, the AGO boasts the singular Thomson collection, the passion of late media baron Ken Thomson. Alone, this collection spans 20 rooms, each one rich in Canadian paintings and featuring greats such as the incomparable David Milne. The Aboriginal collections are another highlight, from a breathtaking collection of carved miniatures dating back to 9000 BC to the contemporary vivid paintings of Norval Morrisseau.

With a collection numbering nearly 80,000 pieces, the AGO delivers a stunning selection of Henry Moore sculptures, European masterworks, and a photography gallery. There are notable international exhibits as well, including a private permanent collection of African art and touring shows such as the populist *Maharaja*, an exhibit of abstract expressionist New York from that city's Museum of Modern Art, or visiting works from Paris's Centre Pompidou.

If art appreciation stirs your appetite, you're in luck. At the fine-dining room FRANK (the name is a nod to Gehry), dishes range from elegant to homey, from magret of duck to grilled cheese sandwiches. The excellent wine list is all-Canadian. For a quick bite, there's a café and espresso bar.

The ROM—Canada's largest museum and North America's fifth-largest—is rich in exhibits exploring natural history and world cultures. There are more than six million objects in-store.

The massive and controversial renovation designed by Daniel Libeskind, another starchitect, divides locals and visitors alike: some love it, others decry its design. The new crystal, housing six galleries, hangs out over Bloor Street—hiding the main entrance. From the crystal's interior there are peekaboo views to the street below. But unlike the AGO redesign, the ROM's content and building are often out of sync. For example, some of the impressive displays of dinosaur bones on the second floor—a main attraction for all ages that includes the largest mounted dinosaur in Canada at 27.4-metres (90-feet) long—are pushed into awkward corners. Nonetheless, the collections are so stunning, it's easy to ignore the idiosyncrasies of the reno and carry on with the real event.

Don't miss the Chinese galleries, which feature an intact Ming tomb, as well as the Bishop White Gallery of Chinese Temple Art—one of the best-preserved examples of its kind. There are wonderful galleries exploring the ancient world (Egypt, Greece, Cyprus, and Bronze Age Aegean showcases are standouts) that could easily take up a few hours perusing tablets and statues, art, and artifacts.

For kids, the immersive Bat Cave is a very popular draw, as are galleries devoted to wildlife, with displays exploring Canada's iconic birds and mammals—including polar and grizzly bears—as well as exotica from sharks to the goby, the tiniest of fish. (In fact, the museum's Centre for Biodiversity and Conservation Biology is a world leader in preservation.) Also for children are hands-on galleries that invite little ones to play educational games, such as the CIBC Discovery Gallery's "dinosaur dig" (a hit with would-be paleontologists).

The four towering totem poles, carved by the Nisga'a and Haida peoples of Canada's Pacific Northwest Coast, form a stunning display that's part of the ROM's Iconic Objects collection. Other essentials are a piece of the Tagish Lake Meteorite (a rock that plummeted to earth carrying organic material dating back 4.5 billion years) and, in the Galleries of Africa, a bust that's likely that of Cleopatra, as well as one of the world's three known Ptolemaic sculptures in the world today.

You can easily take a full day to explore the museum in its entirety, especially if that includes a meal at either the refined c5 (one of Toronto's top restaurants) or at the humble cafeteria, Food Studio (located in the museum's basement).❁

Find out more at:
www.ago.net, www.rom.on.ca

ADVENTURE

CULTURE & HISTORY

Learn to Dogsled in Whitehorse

It's the first day of musher school at Muktuk Adventures just outside Whitehorse and the weather is warming up. The yard is enveloped in a cacophony of dogs barking: "Pick me! Pick me!" as teams get ready to hit the trail. These working dogs are genetically programmed to run. Silence descends as the rookie mushers and their dog teams head down to the Takhini River.

Former Yukon Quest champion Frank Turner and his wife Anne Taylor have more than 100 Alaskan huskies at their kennel. Wannabe mushers can learn to care for and run dog teams during a multi-day stay. Participants help feed the dogs, learn how to harness them, put on little booties to protect their paws, drive a dog team, and bond with their canine teammates.

This mode of transportation is more whimsical than travelling by car. Mushers stand on wooden runners on the back of the sled and hold onto a horizontal bar. They shift their weight to control the sled's direction as they round corners along the trail. A rubber plate between the runners serves as a brake. Forget about calling out "mush, mush" to get going. A cheerful "Let's go!" is enough to hit the gas pedal on these canines.🍁
www.muktuk.com

Ice Skate in Front of Toronto's City Hall

One of the great pleasures of winter in Canada is ice-skating, and whether you can cut figure eights or have never worn skates, Nathan Phillips Square at Toronto City Hall is one of the most festive seasonal sights in the nation, especially during the Cavalcade of Lights.

More than 30,000 people turn out for this official lighting of Toronto's Christmas tree and the luminous decorations of the city's showcase plaza, accompanied by live music and capped off with a fireworks display and then a giant skating party. The rink is open from first light until 10:00 p.m. seven days a week and skate rentals are C$10 for two hours. Late afternoon and early evening find the rink at its busiest. But even after its official closure, many head out on to the dark surface to play shinny (a casual version of hockey) by the light of the office towers. After you've finished your skating—or perhaps to warm your toes—roam the square and admire the curved edifices of City Hall. Or, you can get a start on your Christmas shopping in the city's largest mall, the Toronto Eaton Centre, just a block away.🍁
www.toronto.ca

See the Best of Canada's Great Outdoors from the Comfort of Indoors

Canada is a big country teeming with natural wonders, but they become harder to explore when covered by an early winter snowfall. So, head indoors—to the Canadian Museum of Nature, which has been celebrating and explaining Canada's natural history to Canadians since it opened in 1912. Displays are impressive and comprehensive, particularly the dinosaur exhibits, which tell the story of the great beasts' extinction while showcasing western Canada's role in the field of paleontology.

Displays are impressive and comprehensive, particularly the dinosaur exhibits.

The museum, properly known as the Victoria Memorial Building, reopened in 2010 following a massive rebuild that upgraded everything, refurbished the museum's heritage interiors, and—most significantly—added a spectacular glass "lantern" to the entrance hall, a symbolic restoration of the original tower that was removed in 1916 due to ground instability. The second floor features one of only two blue whales on display in Canada, while the third floor is dominated by the Earth Gallery and its 800 specimens of rocks and minerals. A high-definition digital globe visually demonstrates the Earth's evolution from space junk to home planet. The fourth floor offers a stunning collection of Canadian birds, touch-screen displays, and a wild-bird play area for younger visitors.

Entrance is about C$10, with family rates and free admission for children under the age of three. Nature documentaries are shown daily in English and French in the high-definition screening room. ❧
www.nature.ca

It *happened* THIS WEEK:

Halifax Explosion

As the burning SS Mont-Blanc drifted towards Pier 6, no warning flag told of the explosives aboard. Children heading to school gathered to watch the ship that had collided with the SS Imo in the narrows of Halifax Harbour. Onlookers stood at their windows watching the blaze.

When the 200 tonnes of TNT, 2,300 tonnes of picric acid, 35 tonnes of benzol, 10 tonnes of gun cotton, and rounds of ammunition lit, it caused the biggest man-made explosion in history prior to the testing of nuclear weapons. (Robert Oppenheimer used data from the Halifax blast to calculate the power of the nuclear bombs that Americans dropped on Hiroshima and Nagasaki, nearly three decades later.)

Windows shattered and buildings collapsed. The explosion killed nearly 2,000 immediately, injured 9,000, and levelled much of downtown Halifax's north end. Parts of the Mont-Blanc were found more than five kilometres (3.5 miles) away.

The following day—as trains raced from points west with doctors and supplies aboard—a blizzard smothered the broken city in 40 centimetres (16 inches) of snow.

Part of the rebuilt city, today's trendy Hydrostone district, owes its history to the explosion. And Massachusetts, which quickly sent help, sees a tall evergreen placed in the Boston Common at Christmas as an annual thank-you gift.

EVENTS & FESTIVALS

Commemorate the Halifax Explosion

The Halifax Explosion Memorial Concert pays homage to lives lost on one of the darkest days in Canadian history. On December 6, 1917, during World War I, almost 2,000 men, women, and children were killed and more than 9,000 injured when one of the biggest man-made explosions in the world (prior to the atomic bomb) devastated more than 132 hectares (325 acres) of Halifax and Dartmouth. A collision in the harbour resulted in 12,000 buildings laid flat or made uninhabitable when, at 9:04:35 a.m., a munitions ship bound for Europe exploded. In minutes the thriving city, which was heavily involved in the war effort, resembled the worst battleground.

The Memorial Concert, organized by the Maritime Museum of the Atlantic, in Halifax, invites people in for a free evening of entertainment. Donations are accepted for a designated charity. Described as a real community event, it draws on local entertainers for music

On the waterfront, the museum's vessels are festooned with white lights in their rigging— a wonderful photo-op.

and storytelling, as well as exhibits to commemorate lives lost, acts of heroism, and the changes to life in the city brought about by the explosion. On the waterfront, the museum's vessels are festooned with white lights in their rigging—a wonderful photo-op.✦
www.halifaxexplosion.org

◀ # Marvel at Exotic Birds and Plants at the Bloedel Floral Conservatory

Venturing into the Bloedel Floral Conservatory, with its flamboyant abundance of tropical flora and fauna, is a bit like experiencing Arthur Conan Doyle's sci-fi adventure *The Lost World*. Actually, this geodesic Plexiglas dome at the summit of Queen Elizabeth Park nearly became a "lost world" itself, facing closure due to flagging attendance before the Vancouver Board of Parks and Recreation voted, in 2010, to keep it open. Today, numbers are rebounding. Pay a visit to celebrate the facility's debut, dating back to December 6, 1969.

Outside, view an adjacent plaza laden with fountains and an abstract Henry Moore sculpture entitled *Knife Edge—Two Piece*. At Christmas, seasonal lights often grace the conservatory's exterior. Next, pay a modest admission fee and explore the greenery-shrouded paths inside.

Some 100 species of birds fly free beneath the dome, ranging from parrots and canaries to Sierra Leone turacos and Napoleon weavers. Admire colourful koi fish in ponds and inhale the sweet scent of hibiscus and lilies as you wander through simulated climate zones, from rainforest to desert. Overall, the conservatory offers more than 500 plant species. Its soothing effect on your mood, though, is what you'll take away. ❦

www.vancouver.ca/parks/parks/bloedel/ index.htm

Get Your Christmas Shopping Done at B.C.'s Biggest Mall ▼

Some people embrace the madness of Christmas shopping, while others put it off to the last minute. Whatever your approach, Metropolis at Metrotown is the place to be for Vancouver-area shoppers.

Located in the suburb of Burnaby, just a 15-minute drive or SkyTrain transit ride from downtown Vancouver, Metropolis at Metrotown is as enormous as the 1927 sci-fi flick by Fritz Lang whose name it shares. It's easy to spot off Kingsway with its towering, gaudy, neon-lit facade. B.C.'s biggest shopping mall contains some 450 stores spread out over 160,000 square metres (1.7 million square feet). Pretty much everything is for sale here.

To the strains of "Silver Bells" and "White Christmas," browse through three bustling levels of shopping concourses lit by huge skylights. Moms on a mission and chattering Asian teenagers clutch bulging bags from American Apparel, The Bay, Chapters, and other brand-name retailers. Check about extended holiday shopping hours.

Tired of indulging in the shopping bonanza? Take a break at the 10-screen movie theatre, indoor rock-climbing wall, or Canada's biggest mall food court. Better yet, visit the on-site Burnaby Christmas Bureau to donate cash, toys, or food to seniors or families in need. ❦

www.metropolisatmetrotown.com

Celebrate the Perfect Small-Town Christmas

This picturesque wonderland pulls out all the stops to embrace the spirit of the season

Do dreams of an old-fashioned Christmas prance through your head? Your wish can come true with a holiday season visit to St. Andrews By-The-Sea, a small town with a big heart. This New Brunswick seaside town decks its halls, strings Christmas lights, and tunes up carollers like no other, keeping the traditions of the Yule season alive. Sumptuous food and the spirit of the season welcome residents and visitors alike.

Preparations start early. As the calendar turns to December, Christmas lights and garlands adorn the 18th-century light stands of Water Street, part of the Heritage District, with buildings that date from the early 1800s. Shopkeepers decorate windows with festive white lights, stars, angels, snow, and spots of whimsy to entice people to browse for perfect gifts for those special someones . . .

Local churches schedule Christmas entertainments and bazaars. The Ross Memorial Museum decks its halls for an annual Christmas Open House and volunteers bake delicious cookies and morsels for all to enjoy as they take a step back in time to enjoy the Christmases of yesteryear.

The first Friday of December sees the official lighting of the Town Tree in Market Square, with a local choir carolling and encouraging everyone to take part. Guests are invited to enjoy hot apple cider while sharing a story or two.

The adjacent Town Wharf displays a sparkle of the lights in Passamaquoddy Bay that's quite magical. Many homes in the "Historic Town Plat" (a decorative map), trimmed with lights and greenery, give the impression you've stepped back in time—to 1860 or so.

The St. Andrews Fire Department hosts the Annual Santa Claus Parade around this time. It's small as parades go, but the intimacy draws warmly dressed folk who line the streets to enjoy the evening's small-town magic. Following the parade, Santa and Mrs. Claus move to the local fire hall, where Santa patiently listens to each child's wish list before joining the family skate at the nearby arena.

The magic of Christmas is alive throughout the town, and especially at the spectacular Algonquin Hotel, where staff make time for a decorating party to adorn this historic property like a fairy castle, putting up trees, wreaths, and garland while enjoying hot chocolate, coffee, and cookies. Each tree is decorated in a different style—the elegant silver and blue tree in The Library is a beautiful backdrop for an evening meal, while the more homey tree in the Right Whale Pub is decorated with traditional red and greens, reminiscent of trees found in homes.

And there are more trees. In the true spirit of Christmas giving, the Festival of Trees is sponsored by town businesses. All trees are part of a silent auction to benefit the Volunteer Centre of

This New Brunswick seaside town decks its halls, strings Christmas lights, and tunes up carollers like no other.

Charlotte County and the food bank. Arranged throughout the lobbies of the Algonquin Hotel, trees are available 24 hours a day for visitors to see and bid on. Part of the fun comes with "Dine Around" the Festival of Trees. The Algonquin is just one of the stops along the six-course culinary tour that includes the likes of the Rossmount Inn, Savour the Restaurant, and the Europa Inn & Restaurant.

Whether you're a guest for a meal or overnight, there's nothing quite like relaxing in front of a wood fire with a glass of wine or mug of hot chocolate, enjoying the company of others. Hearing the laugh of children or the soft notes of Christmas carols echoing through the lobby,

as singers in period costumes regale onlookers, brightens the hearts of everyone.

The hotel also hosts Gingerbread Dreams—a gingerbread house–decorating event and competition involving children from all over the county. Carolling on Christmas Eve, Christmas Fireside Storytelling for children, and hotel tours (front and back of house) ensure the Christmas spirit is kindled throughout the holiday season. The Algonquin also offers a Christmas lunch buffet and Christmas dinner, as well as a New Year's Day brunch to wind down the season.

Whether walking picturesque snow-lined streets, being greeted with cheerful and welcoming smiles at local shops, or enjoying an exquisite dinner, the spirit of Christmas surrounds everyone as they celebrate the season in this seaside town.

Accommodations for visitors range from the luxurious Algonquin to bed and breakfasts. The actual calendar for Christmas events changes from year to year. To find out what magic is happening on a given day, contact the Town of Saint Andrews or the Algonquin Hotel.🍁

Find out more at:
www.townofstandrews.ca

ADVENTURE

Shoot and Ski with Whistler's Discover Biathlon Program

Whether you're a firm advocate of gun control or a card-carrying NRA member, you can still get your kicks—and a nice cardio workout—by signing up for the Discover Biathlon program at Whistler Olympic Park, which boasts 55 kilometres (34 miles) of groomed cross-country ski trails. Located in the Callaghan Valley just outside Whistler, the host mountain resort of the Vancouver 2010 Winter Games, the park offers visitors the chance to learn the ins and outs of this classic Nordic sport—which became part of the Olympic Winter Games sport program in 1960—in a fun, safe, controlled environment.

Lessons, lasting 90 minutes amidst snow-encrusted cedar and pine trees, cost less than C$80, including equipment rental. Your instructor teaches you the skate-skiing method that marks the sport's modern incarnation, as you

It's a genuine adrenaline kick.

figure out how to build a steady rhythm with your legs (*sans* poles) while keeping your chin up. Then you head over to the shooting range and lie down on a mat, prop your rifle up on a wooden block, and aim at targets 50 metres (164 feet) away. It's a genuine adrenaline kick.

While you may not be ready to challenge 2010 Olympic gold medallist Emil Hegle Svendsen of Norway in the 20-kilometre individual pursuit anytime soon, you're guaranteed to have fun!❧
www.whistlerolympicpark.com

Explore the Haunting Art of Emily Carr ▼

Emily Carr is an inspiration for late bloomers. The Victoria-born painter of shadowy landscapes and Native totem poles didn't create her most famous works until hitting her late fifties. She remains arguably Canada's best-known female artist. You can commemorate her birth, on December 13, 1871, by visiting Carr landmarks around Victoria and Vancouver.

In Victoria's Inner Harbour, photograph the quirky bronze statue of Carr with her pet monkey Woo, next to the Empress Hotel. Then stroll south along Government Street past the Parliament Buildings to Emily Carr House, a national historic site, where Carr lived until being orphaned at age 16. (The 19th-century house with Carr's books and letters is closed after September 30, but enthusiasts can book a private tour.) About four kilometres (2.5 miles) away, the Art Gallery of Greater Victoria holds a fine, small Carr collection: the 1929 oil painting *Odds and Ends* characteristically depicts murky stumps and mountains. You can also visit Carr's grave in nearby Ross Bay Cemetery.

Carr entrusted most of her finest pieces (more than 200) to the Vancouver Art Gallery. View masterworks like the moody, psychedelic *Big Raven* here, and you'll appreciate how she took influences like the Group of Seven and the post-impressionists and created something unique for British Columbia.❧
www.emilycarr.ca

◄ Ride Whistler's Dizzying Peak 2 Peak Gondola

It's an experience so magnificently intense it can bring tears to your eyes. That might sound like hype—until you actually ride Whistler's Peak 2 Peak Gondola, the world's biggest. Connecting Whistler and Blackcomb Mountains at Canada's top ski resort, it provides a panorama of snowy trees, icy lakes, and deep valleys surrounded by coastal peaks that's almost beyond description. Selected cars have glass floors, upping the visual delights.

Those into engineering find this iconic attraction just as compelling as nature-lovers do. The product of advanced Swiss engineering, Peak 2 Peak opened in December 2009 at a cost of C$52 million. It has the world's longest unsupported lift span at 3.03 kilometres (1.88 miles), but the crossing takes just 11 minutes. That's remarkable, as the total distance —4.4 kilometres (2.73 miles)—is three times longer than San Francisco's Golden Gate Bridge.

The biggest beneficiaries are skiers seeking an ultra-varied experience at the home of former 2010 Olympic Winter Games alpine events. With a lift ticket, riding on the Peak 2 Peak is free. Grab lunch at Whistler Mountain's Roundhouse Lodge, then Peak 2 Peak it over to Blackcomb for popular runs like Jersey Cream or Ross's Gold. Or, pull tricks at the terrain parks on both mountains. The options are endless.❧
www.whistlerblackcomb.com

EVENTS & FESTIVALS

QUIRKY CANADA

Shop for One-of-a-Kind Holiday Treasures

Just in time for the holiday gift-giving season, Québec's Salon des Artisans shows off its fine ceramics, local beauty products, handmade home decor accessories, and one-of-a-kind jewellery. There's a selection process for those who'd like to exhibit their wares here, and many people consider this the best place to discover fresh, up-and-coming talents.

There are more than 200 artisans attending, so you'll not only get original, handmade gifts, but in many cases you'll be able to meet the artists behind them. Some are full-time creators, while others are just talented hobbyists. Besides the typical things you might expect at a fair like this—such as organic soaps, stylish necklaces, paintings, sculptures, and furniture—you'll also find more obscure offerings such as interesting textiles, blown glass, and stringed instruments. Increasingly popular are repurposed goods; ever think you'd see a purse made from retired seatbelts or bicycle tires?

Not too far from the Hippodrome de Québec, the Pepsi Coliseum, and the Place Fleur de Lys shopping centre, the site for this haute arts and crafts fair is less than 10 minutes away by car in the sleek Centre de foires exposition space. Entry is free.✤
www.salondesartisans.com

Take a Peek at Miniature World in Victoria

Looking for a nice, warm escape from the madness of Christmas preparations? Victoria's Miniature World definitely enables you to rise above your surroundings.

This quaint attraction, tucked away inside The Fairmont Empress Hotel just off the Inner Harbour, is loaded with elaborate, glassed-in exhibits depicting history and folklore in clever, teeny-tiny ways. The most memorable is the Great Canadian Railway, which sends model trains chugging through turn-of-the-century Canadian cities from Vancouver to the Maritimes. Squint in amazement at miniature frontier saloons, grain elevators, sailing ships, and bridges.

Other must-see models include the sprawling midway and parade of Circus World, scenes from World War II and the American War of Independence, the over-the-top Titania's Palace, and a fabulous collection of dollhouses. Specially commissioned animated dioramas with trains and carousels are set up to celebrate Christmas. It's no surprise, then, that kids delight in hunting down the six Santas hidden throughout Miniature World for the season.

Exhibit captions can be a little corny, but the artistry makes it all worthwhile. Budget an hour or two to wander through and soak up the nuances. You'll come out feeling like you've written the alternative ending to *Gulliver's Travels*—where Gulliver wins.✤
www.miniatureworld.com

Dine at One of Canada's Most Unusual Restaurants

Halfway between eclectic and eccentric, the Grizzly House has been one of Banff's most popular restaurants for over four decades. In fact, it remains so busy—both because of its distinctive menu and unique decor—that no reservations are taken through summer. In mid-December, though, when the crowds of tourists are at a minimum, you should be able to take your pick of tables.

Each table comes equipped with a telephone for cross-table conversation.

Opened in 1967 as Western Canada's first disco, the Grizzly House was originally known as Banff's premier venue for touring bands and go-go dancers. Over time, it has morphed into a restaurant with signature fondues reflecting owner Peter Steiner's Swiss heritage. For the true Grizzly House experience, order the very non-traditional dipping meats—shark, rattlesnake, ostrich, or alligator. For the less adventurous, there's a variety of wild game—elk, venison, and Alberta beef—as well as seafood. Aside from the menu, the decor can be described simply as "unique," with twisted wood, a motorbike hanging from the ceiling, and a melted telephone on the wall. Each table comes equipped with a telephone for cross-table conversation. You can also put a call through to your server, a cab, diners in the private booth, or even those who spend too long in the bathroom. Save room for a fruity chocolate fondue to round out one of Canada's most unique dining experiences. ❖

www.banffgrizzlyhouse.com

Roch Voisine's
favourite PLACE

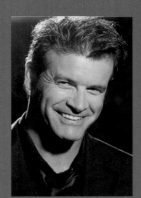

The highs and lows of British Columbia's Gulf Islands lure award-winning musician Roch Voisine from his home in the east.

"I like the mountains and the ocean," says Voisine from his base in Montréal. "I'd love to have one of those big cottages, on the Channel Islands."

The combination of mountains and ocean means Voisine can pursue some of his favourite activities. The New Brunswick–born musician loves to ski and go boating.

"The West Coast has culture and nature," he says. "And it's laid back."

But Voisine, an Officer of the Order of Canada, holds a love for many Canadian destinations. Charlevoix, Québec, is a spectacular ski area on the St. Lawrence River, he says. The Prairies are breathtaking for their vastness.

"You understand why they call it big-sky country."

While travel certainly inspires "songs about being lonely on the road," the West Coast gets a special mention in his 1996 hit "Kissing Rain."

"We wandered through a hundred days, and watched the stars on Halfmoon Bay," sings Voisine in the song. The British Columbia community is on the Sunshine Coast.

While his music takes him many places, Voisine can still list many more he'd like to visit.

"When you're on tour, you don't get much time to do the tourist thing," he says. "You look at [the scenery] from the backseat of a car, or in-between sound checks."

Watch the Northern Lights

The long nights of winter are the best time to watch nature's dance

t's the winter solstice, the longest night of the year. The sky is clear. Suddenly, the northern lights appear. They're faint at first, then brighter. They start to shimmy across Mother Nature's dance floor, two green bands separating and coming together like lovers in a warm embrace. Welcome to the aurora borealis, the best natural light show that you can find.

At this time of year, there's daylight for up to five hours closer to the 60th parallel and Yellowknife. But should you venture north of the Arctic Circle, the sun goes down around this time of year and doesn't return until early January. Residents of Inuvik celebrate the moment with the annual Sunrise Festival. With too little sun and so many hours of uninterrupted darkness, it's a good time of year to see the aurora borealis. All you need is a clear sky away from trees and city lights, warm clothes—and for Mother Nature to hit an imaginary switch that makes the northern lights magically appear.

The aurora borealis is an unpredictable natural phenomenon that occurs when oxygen, nitrogen, solar wind, and magnetic fields come together to produce dancing waves of coloured bands of light. It's named after Aurora, the Roman goddess of dawn, and Boreas, the Greek name for north wind. It is most easily seen near the poles because of the longer darkness and the magnetic fields. Most of the Northwest Territories is located under the aurora oval, a ring of geomagnetic activity, which increases the chance of seeing the magic lights. When a package of charged particles comes from the sun, you could say that it lands in the aurora oval. The communities sitting beneath it get the best view of the colourful lightshow.

Yellowknife has 240 nights where it's dark enough to see the aurora if she decides to come out and dance. The northern lights are expected to be at the peak of their 11-year cycle in 2012 and 2013. Yellowknife organization Astronomy North (http://astronomynorth.com/aurora-forecast) has a website that offers an Aurora Forecast for the coming days. It tells you the likelihood of spotting the northern lights and whether your chances are better early in the evening or after midnight.

Once you've checked the forecast, find a hill well away from city lights and a good vantage point from which to see the vastness of the sky. Then be patient and get ready to wait. They could show up

anytime, but they're more likely between about 10 p.m. and 2 a.m. Bundle up in layered clothing before you head out—long johns, a parka, insulated snow pants, warm mitts, a hat, and scarf. Don't forget to grab a thermos of hot chocolate, as staying toasty is part of the experience.

Sitting on a hill waiting for the northern lights to show up isn't the only way to experience them. Aurora Village, (www.auroravillage.com) an operator near Yellowknife, sets up heated Aurora viewing chairs on a huge deck. The staff also keeps visitors entertained until Mother Nature turns on the lights. Hop onto a snowmobile and let Yellowknife Outdoor Adventures (www.yellowknifeoutdooradventures.com) drive you out to a cozy cabin with a viewing deck. If you're feeling particularly daring, put on your bathing suit and sit in the hot tub at Blachford Lake Lodge (www.blachfordlakelodge.com) with your head tilted towards the heavens. You'll be nice and warm—until you climb out of the tub.

If getting there via unusual forms of transportation is half the fun, take one of those old eight-passenger Bombardier snowmobiles from Hay River to Great Slave Lake with Great Slave Tours (http://www.spectacularnwt.com/node/225). Or, drive off in a Hagglunds BV206 with Enodah Wilderness Travel (www.enodah.com). These versatile, all-terrain, amphibious vehicles were developed to allow the Swedish Army to transport troops and equipment through the snow and bog of northern Sweden. If you're looking for a quiet ride, try dogsledding to a cabin or camp with Arctic Adventure Tours (www.whitehuskies.com) in Inuvik or Beck's Kennels (www.beckskennels.com) in Yellowknife. The dogs will be excited before you head out, but then silence will descend once their paws hit the trail.

You can also see the unpredictable aurora on your own. If you want to enjoy the hospitality and added experience of an operator, most aurora-viewing trips in the Northwest Territories depart from Yellowknife. Whether it's soaking in a hot tub, travelling in unusual vehicles, or being pulled by a dog team, choose the experience that makes your heart sing . . . before the aurora descends. It doesn't matter what way you choose to see the aurora. If she comes out to dance on the longest night of the year, it will be the best light show you've ever seen. ❦

Find out more at:
www.spectacularnwt.com

ADVENTURE

Go Snowshoeing in Kouchibouguac National Park

As the holidays approach, New Brunswick's outdoors enthusiasts dream of a white Christmas—particularly the pristine snow, which means they can strap on snow-shoes for the season's inaugural adventure. The first stop is Kouchibouguac National Park, usually one of the first spots in the area to get a good snowfall. Here, salt marshes, tidal rivers, sheltered lagoons, abandoned fields, and tall forests all beg to be explored anew. The park's name (pronounced *Kou-she-boo-gwack*) comes from the Mi'kmaq language and means "river of the long tides." The 238-square-kilometre (92-square-mile) national park has 60 kilometres (37 miles) of summer cycling paths that are perfect for snowshoeing, with easy access to wilderness trails. An easy sport for folks of all ages, snow-shoeing is also inexpensive and low-risk (as far as injury)—not to mention being a superior calorie-burner that lets you explore out-of-the-way places.

Snowshoes are available for rent at the Pijeboogwek wax hut, located across the road from the Park Information Centre. Keep a lookout for birds: the annual Christmas Bird Count, sponsored by the National Audubon Society, records sightings from mid-December to early January. It has been going on in the park for more than 40 years. Walk quietly and you might spot deer, small animals—even moose—as you watch for your feathered friends. ❧
www.pc.gc.ca/eng/pn-np/nb/ kouchibouguac/activ/hiver-winter.aspx

CULTURE & HISTORY

Celebrate Christmas Mass at Montréal's Notre-Dame Basilica

Both an architectural and archaeological jewel dating to 1829, the Notre-Dame Basilica is a grand symbol of Montréal's Roman Catholic heritage. Although Christmas Eve here is a largely religious ceremony, anyone and everyone who wishes to attend the special December 24 mass to honour of the birth of Jesus Christ in exquisite surroundings is welcome.

Tickets, however, must be purchased ahead of time —at the Basilica. They go on sale at the beginning of September and tend to sell out quickly. Recent prices were C$5 for adults and C$2 for children 17 years of age and younger. If you don't mind sitting in the second balcony, seats there are free.

There are actually three services: at 7:00 p.m., 9:30 p.m., and the midnight Mass (the first two times are most popular for young families with children). The traditional Christmas service includes beautiful choir and organ performances, as well as a sermon explaining this second-most holy day on the Christian calendar (after Easter).

Part of the evening's magic is the beauty of the setting. Each December, the Gothic Revival exterior is decorated with three white-light angels hovering over the entrance, set against a glowing cobalt blue backdrop. Inside, an ornately carved wood interior graced with antique sculptures is also backlit with a celestial blue hue. The ceiling, also blue—and dotted with golden stars—is a glorious nod to the heavens. ❧
www.notredamebasilica.ca/en

Grow Your Holiday Spirit at Montréal's Botanical Garden

'Tis the season to be jolly. If you're a Christmas romantic, you can get your holiday fill at the Montréal Botanical Garden. Besides the winter wonderland that is the garden itself, the Main Exhibition Greenhouse offers inspirational displays and festive activities to put you in the mood—a tradition since 1956.

There will be hundreds of poinsettias and other holiday florals on show in the greenhouse, as well as fun displays such as the choir of cacti with Christmas hats. While you're there why not partake in carolling old classics, or craft sessions where you can learn to make your own decorations?

Admission includes entry into the nearby Insectarium. Don't leave the grounds without a stroll to the fragrant evergreens on-site, free if you don't

There will be hundreds of poinsettias and other holiday florals on show in the greenhouse.

enter the buildings. Bird feeders around the park also ensure you'll meet some fine-feathered friends along the way. If you're up to it and the snow conditions are optimal, the grounds are also open for cross-country skiing (also free if you don't count the C$10 parking fee). Bring your own skis and poles, and venture into nearby Maisonneuve Park if you wish—which has ice-skating to boot.❀
www.ville.montreal.qc.ca/jardin

Canadian moments

Mummers

Each Christmas in Newfoundland outports— isolated by the ocean, the weather, and the rugged coastline—groups of disguised locals have traditionally wandered among the wooden houses.

"Any Mummers allowed in?" someone asks, knocking at a door. The mummers enter: pillowcases, fishing overalls, and crocheted doilies hiding their identities.

Mummering—also called jannying, jennying, or mumming—is adapted from an old English Christmas custom. The Mummers arrive on one of the 12 days of Christmas to entertain with jokes, songs, and foolery. They change their voices by talking while inhaling and share drinks with the hosts. Although the tradition was legally abolished in the province in 1861, it continued in more remote Newfoundland.

In 1983 "The Mummer's Song," recorded by Newfoundland folk duet Simani, largely revived the practice throughout the province.

"There's big ones 'n' small ones 'n' tall ones 'n' thin, boys dressed as women and girls dressed as men," goes the storytelling song, fused with Newfoundland humour and character.

If the host guesses someone's identity, the janny must unmask. Be it stoking the fire, locking the door, or offering a drink of "the strong stuff," Newfoundlanders employ various tactics to unmask their visitors.

"Is he wearin' his mother's big forty-two bra?" goes the song. "I knows but I'm not gonna say."

EVENTS & FESTIVALS

Revel in the Glory of Handel's *Messiah*

One of the staples of the Christmas season is the Toronto Symphony Orchestra (TSO) presentation of Handel's *Messiah*. "Messiah" means anointed one, which pretty much describes this work's place in the repertoire of symphonies around the world.

This *Messiah* makes for one crowded house: apart from the soloists and choral voices, there are more than 60 instruments onstage, including muted-trumpets and a marimba. Originally performed at Easter and continuously enjoyed in one variation or another since its debut in Dublin in 1741, the three-part telling of the story of Jesus Christ concludes with the ringing refrains of the "Hallelujah Chorus." In 2010, TSO conductor laureate Sir Andrew Davis re-orchestrated the piece to critical acclaim, removing some of the Victorian "cobwebs," as one critic put it. This new version, dubbed Toronto's Favourite Messiah, is likely to become the standard for TSO revivals to come. Book early though, as the TSO only does five or six shows a season. If you miss out, the symphony also offers *Christmas Holiday Pops* and

Apart from the soloists and choral voices, there are more than 60 instruments onstage, including muted-trumpets and a marimba.

one performance of *The Twelve Days of Christmas*, including a partridge in a pear tree and the requisite number of lords a-leaping and maids a-milking.❦
www.tso.ca

Grab the Spirit of Christmas in Mahone Bay ▼

Immerse yourself in the Christmas spirit with a trip to find each and every of the one-of-a-kind Father Christmas figures put up in the picturesque Nova Scotia town of Mahone Bay. Warning: this may dramatically increase your feelings of Christmas cheer.

Creative folks in this seaside town create as many as 65 larger-than-life Father Christmas figures to line the streets, stand outside churches, watch over doorsteps, survey shoppers, and even adorn evergreen trees around town. Each of the "old world" Victorian Father Christmas figures is unique, its personality shining through the detailed faces, elaborate robes, and exquisite costumes. The figures appear in time for the Christmas Festival, held to usher in December, and remain until after St. Nick has performed his annual duties.

The figures are created to build a warm and inviting atmosphere. It works! Known for its artisans, gourmet food, and craft and decor shops, the town's homes and businesses are transformed by the statues into a magical Christmas scene. It all began in 2006, with a successful Scarecrow Festival that sparked a creative spirit in many locals. That afterglow was subsequently transformed into countless hours creating Father Christmas figures expressing joy, peace, and cheer. Each is more unique than the last, helping make the spirit of the holiday season come alive in Mahone Bay like nowhere else. ❦

www.mahonebay.com

◀ Experience a European-Style Christmas Market at the Distillery District

An ideal event for anyone who has a little Virginia (or Virgil) who believes there is a Santa Claus, the Toronto Christmas Market beckons with festive sounds and sights and tastes. The 19th-century buildings and cobblestones of Toronto's Distillery District add that touch of Christmases past.

A rite of Christmas in central Europe dating back to the Middle Ages, street markets are usually held in town commons where people gather to buy gifts, gossip about who's wearing what, and otherwise prepare for a day of feast. This modern version features traditional elements such as carollers, children's choirs, a German brass band, heart-warming grog—and, guaranteed, many crafty gift ideas. There are some anachronisms—such as the presence of giant characters from *Grimm's Fairy Tales* and Santa's elves running around snapping photographs of your loved ones (you can buy copies on-line the next day), but a reindeer zoo adds a degree of verisimilitude. The Distillery District has several fine food stores so there's plenty of good chow to wash down with the craft beers and mulled wine (sorry Glühwein). The tree, typically 12 metres (40 feet) high and swathed in thousands of lights, is always a spectacle. ❦

www.torontochristmasmarket.com

Bring In the New Year at Montréal's Biggest Party Spots

Celebrate in first-class style with some of the city's legendary nightlife

Montréal is known for her *bon vivant* culinary landscape, unapologetic nightlife, and overall hedonistic state of mind. With both Gallic French-Canadian and hearty Scottish roots, it's no surprise that revellers from near and far make pilgrimages to this party town. If you're looking for a way to ring in the new year with a bang, there's no need to look any further.

Let's start with the F-word, that being "free." Le Grand Bal du Nouvel An is held each year at scenic Place Jacques-Cartier, an open square in the Old Port that, yes, is surrounded by touristy restaurants and shops, but boasts a stellar view of the Quays—a perfect setting for the fireworks display at midnight. (Kiddies are welcome, if they can stay awake.) The courtyard "ball," as it's dubbed, invites partygoers of all ages onto its huge outdoor dance floor and entertains all night with traditional French-Canadian folk music acts. Get down and spin your partner round and round to the tune of fiddlers, spoon clappers, and jovial harmonica players.

For straight-up bars, there's always a happy gang at English pub Burgundy Lion in the up-and-coming neighbourhood Little Burgundy, near the Atwater Market. The spiffied-up staff hands out bubbly and noisemakers just before midnight. Downtown, there's Hurley's Irish Pub on Crescent Street. If you're more martini than pitchers of beer, head uptown to the decidedly French Baldwin Barmacie. None of these establishments charge admittance, but spots are generally first-come, first-served.

Moving indoors and into deeper pockets, Montréal's vibrant supperclub scene offers all-inclusive deals where you and your better half (or band of BFFs) can bask in the triad of merriment: that is, drinks, dinner, and dancing. Tickets are generally in the C$100-range per person, and usually include party favours and sparkling wine at midnight. The cost of your trendy new outfit is totally up to you, but do come dressed to impress. There are the see-and-be-seen affairs on Saint-Laurent Boulevard (a.k.a. the Main) such as Buonanotte and Globe, or the francophone hotspot Macaroni Bar, a little more north. More savvy urbanites gravitate towards Old Montréal to places such as cozy nooks Barroco or L'Auberge Saint-Gabriel restaurants. The latter provides a particularly historic context, built in the 17th century by a French soldier—the first inn in North America, and the first establishment under British rule to legally serve alcohol. Executive chef Eric Gonzalez presides over the mainly French menu outfitted by local terroir ingredients. If, after dessert, you seek a little more dining and dancing, basement nightclub Velvet awaits.

Another trendy—and deliciously convenient— option is reserving a table at one of Montréal's celebrated boutique hotels that also offer similar all-in-one arrangements. Plus, you'll have the added bonus of being able to forego the hunt for a taxi and retiring straight to your room via elevator. Beautiful locals and their visiting entourages can be found at the dark den of

St. Paul Hotel's Le Vauvert restaurant, the Place d'Armes Hotel & Suites' new ballroom, DJ-equipped Suite 701 bar and lounge, or the W Hotel's designer chic Otto restaurant, where afterwards you can catwalk down to the after party at Wunderbar lounge on the opposite

If you're looking for a way to ring in the new year with a bang, there's no need to look any further.

side of the lobby. For a more old-school vibe, the storied Le Beaver Club Restaurant at mega-hotel Fairmont Queen Elizabeth traditionally holds an upscale jazz-orchestra affair with hats, balloons, and a big bottle of bubbly per couple. A more intimate night of live music unravels at Upstairs Jazz Bar & Grill. For those looking for a calmer kind of decadence, albeit one with gastronomic pleasures, foodies will surely delight at Le Club Chasse et Pêche, a romantic, dimly lit dining room, or within the elegant all-white walls of Nuances at the Montréal Casino. (Quick tip: there's a great view of the fireworks display from here.)

If stamina isn't an issue, hardcore partiers can sweat the old year at Resolution (the location varies, but recently it was at the Bell Centre), a 15-hour dance party with tech, trance, and house music, brought to you by the same people that organize the yearly Bal en Blanc around Easter. The gay community also holds their annual Bal des Boys, which occupies several venues and includes four days of dance parties, live entertainment, and even a morning-after brunch. Extreme extroverts will feel at home at Carnavalesque, a freakish, fetish, carnival, burlesque event held by Cirque De Boudoir.

Finally, if after a night of gallivanting you're looking to chase your champagne with a cherry cola, Schwartz's famous smoked meat delicatessen is open well past Cinderella's curfew (the munchies can affect anyone). Indulge in the full-fat option and join the staff in celebrating their original New Year's Eve opening back in 1928. Cheers to that!🍁

Find out more at:
www.lesfeeriesduvieuxmontreal.info

Cross-Country Ski from Hut to Hut in Charlevoix

La Traversée de Charlevoix is a challenging seven-day, six-night trek over 105 kilometres (65.2 miles) of Québec's backcountry. Recommended only for advanced Nordic skiers, this excursion brings you up-close-and-personal with the wonders of winter.

Day One begins in the town of Saint-Urbain. Over the week, spend your nights in cabins spaced about 20 kilometres (12.4 miles) apart. Around Day Four, you'll arrive at the Hautes-Gorges-de-la-Rivière-Malbaie national park where you'll see the highest cliffs east of the Rockies. Finally, your journey ends at Mont-Grand-Fonds.

Although there are no set tracks or an official guide, paths are indicated with clear signage. Accommodations are basic and chalet-style. The main floor has a big communal table and a kitchen equipped with two propane burners, a wood stove, and a cupboard for pots, utensils, and the like. There's no running water or electricity, but, yes, there's an outhouse. Upstairs is a co-ed style dorm that can accommodate up to 15.

Beyond that, there are two main packages: the Autonomous or the Deluxe. *MacGyver* wannabes will spring for the first option, which, as the name suggests, has you travelling on your own—though a minimum of three is recommended as you carry everything you need. The second option adds a little luxury to the experience: a snowmobile drops off your gear and food at each stop along the way. Option #2 also includes a provision that has your car waiting for you at your point of arrival.🍁

www.traverseedecharlevoix.qc.ca

Take a Tour of the Old Montréal Forum

The Montréal Forum opened in 1924. After seven decades as the sporting and entertainment venue of the city, the indoor arena at the corner of Sainte-Catherine and Atwater *a accroché ses patins*—or, has hung up his/her skates, as they say. It was a sad time for hockey fans who considered the Forum a shrine to the city's beloved Montréal Canadiens hockey club (in 1996 the team moved to more state-of-the-art facilities at the Bell Centre). Though the building was completely gutted and reinvented as a retail and service complex called the Pepsi Forum, the Montréal Forum legend lives on.

The arena has welcomed such artists as the Beatles and Frank Sinatra, as well as boxing events and symphonic orchestras. On December 31, 1975, it hosted a game between the Canadiens and the former U.S.S.R.'s Central Red Army team. It resulted in a 3–3 tie that many consider the greatest hockey game ever played. But the address is best known as the home where 24 Stanley Cups were won—22 by the Canadiens, and two by the Maroons (who played from 1924 to 1938) for whom the arena was originally built.

The facility's current incarnation as a four-story funhouse connected by escalators and a central glass elevator offers a 22-screen cinema, restaurants, shops, a comedy bar, and bowling alley. To honour its past, original stadium seats are scattered throughout and a "centre ice" was recreated, complete with a small cross-section of the grandstand and all-purpose gift shop with much on offer. The main entrance also features a Québec Walk of Fame where, among others, hockey hero Maurice Richard and songstress Céline Dion are immortalized with bronze stars.

www.forumpepsi.com

Snowshoe through the Rich Wilderness of Riding Mountain National Park ▶

By late December, Riding Mountain National Park—a three-hour drive northwest from the Manitoba capital of Winnipeg—is a wonderland of snow-covered forests and frozen lakes, perfect for exploring on snowshoes.

Snowshoeing is easy and inexpensive, and an incredibly healthy pastime. Unlike cross-country skiing, which is mostly restricted to existing trails, snowshoeing is almost bereft of limitations, allowing you to walk across frozen lakes and ponds or to follow animal tracks wherever they lead. The natural beauty of Riding Mountain National Park in winter is unforgettable. Even in the depths of winter, birds and animals are both abundant and widespread. Bison, elk, coyotes, and red fox all call the park home and are seen often, while wolves are present but harder to spot. Although most owls are nocturnal, head out on snowshoes during daylight hours and you may see great grey owls and northern hawk owls. Head out after dark, with only the moon to light your way, and you may spy great horned owls.

Based just outside Riding Mountain National Park, Earth Rhythms offers small group tours into the park year-round, including customized snowshoe tours lasting anywhere from one hour to a full day, with an option for starlight nighttime treks.

www.earthrhythms.ca

4th week of

DEC

EVENTS & FESTIVALS

Be the First in North America to Ring in the New Year

With wicked snow storms and cold winds whipped up across the Atlantic Ocean, the long winters experienced in Newfoundland can be harsh. But these hardships are quickly forgotten by residents of St. John's on the last day of December, when they become the first people in North America to usher in the new year.

For downtown St. John's restaurants, December 31 is one of the busiest nights of the year—so make advance dinner reservations at a local favourite, such as AQUA Kitchen and Bar. A far cry from the city's traditional pubs, this sleek dining room offers up an exceptional menu of local and sustainable dishes ranging from a caribou burger topped with crabapple ketchup to seared cod served with a pile of traditional pork scrunchions. Although the streets will be busy by the time you emerge from AQUA, the pubs will be busier. Follow the crowds to George Street and choose Trapper John's or Green Sleeves for a pint or two of locally brewed ale from the Quidi Vidi Brewery. Before you know it, it's almost midnight and time to head outside for a fireworks display that lights up St. John's Harbour and the snow-covered city. For most revellers, the fireworks don't signal the end of the celebrations, but are a sparkling outdoor interlude in a long night of drinking and dancing in the raucous confines of local pubs. ❧

www.stjohns.ca/visitors/index.jsp

5 faves

Victoria Bug Zoo

In the heart of downtown Victoria, enter an amazing world of international insects: walking sticks, praying mantises, tarantulas, and scorpions, to name a few. Although all the creepy-crawlies are behind glass, an entomologist (bug scientist) is on hand to answer questions and show you how to handle some of the multi-legged creatures.

Slurp Down Some of Montréal's Best Poutine at La Banquise

Poutine rules in the province of Québec. The oddly named fast food is as ubiquitous in Montréal as the Canadiens hockey logo—in other words, everywhere. One of the best places to try this favourite is La Banquise. While the 24-hour diner serves poutine every day and all year, it seems nothing else hits the spot with more oomph on a frosty winter day.

Poutine may look like a mound of mess on your plate, but once you've had a taste it's nothing but bliss. The comforting fast food (and instant hangover remedy) is basically french fries, gravy, and cheese curds . . . the best poutine is a poutine with curds that squeak as you chew them.

La Banquise curiously means "iceberg," referring to the restaurant's 1968 origins as an ice-cream parlour. Over the years, the business still belongs to the same family but the reins have shifted to a new generation.

There are about 25 variations of poutine at La Banquise, including La mexicane (hot peppers, tomatoes, and black olives) or the Hawaii 5.0 (ham and pineapple). Go all out and wash it down with a local microbrewed beer. On weekend evenings, patrons can enjoy their poutine accompanied by the sound of trendy music in a festive atmosphere. Thanks to its steady flow of club kids, the popular after-hours hangout is also likely the only diner to employ a doorman for crowd control.🍁

www.restolabanquise.com

◀ Dine on Rappie Pie for the Holidays

Rappie pie is to an Acadian as turkey is to an Englishman—comfort food and a huge part of Christmas and New Year traditions. Mention it in certain areas of Nova Scotia and eyes light up in anticipation. Grated potatoes or *patates râpées* (hence the name "rappie" pie), meat, broth, and onions are baked to a golden crust. Whether it's the flavour, the tradition of a dish shared with family, or the satisfaction of preserving heritage, the rappie pie experience is one that's rooted in Acadian culture.

Rappie pie is most easily enjoyed in southwestern Nova Scotia, particularly in the Pubnico, Yarmouth, Clare, and Wedgeport areas. Restaurants like the Red Cap in West Pubnico always have rappie pie on the menu, serving it in the old way with butter or molasses. West Pubnico is also home to today's kings of rappie pie. D'Eon's Rappie Pie grew out of a family bakery business and now supplies supermarkets and other clientele in the Halifax area, all the way to Truro, Amherst, and along the Annapolis Valley. What's more, taste for rappie pie has been reborn, now that D'Eon's has taken the labour out of its preparation. Christmastime is their single busiest time of year . . . but even then, you can still take your own dish in for them to fill!🍁

www.deonsrappiepie.com

The Art Gallery of Alberta

The stunning new facility is the home of revolving world-class exhibits: on any given day you could take in Degas, Picasso, and Emily Carr. It's also a champion of First Nations contemporary art, and a permanent home for Alberta's top artists.

TELUS World of Science—Calgary

A sleek new modern location opened in fall 2011 near the Calgary Zoo, the first new science centre in Canada in more than 25 years. Built with ecologically inspired architecture and design, the centre's permanent exhibits cover topics from the human body to Earth and space.

Montréal's Musée des beaux–arts

Canada's first museum devoted exclusively to the visual arts opened in 1912. Temporary exhibits are dazzling and have focused in recent years on musician Miles Davis, fashion designer Yves Saint Laurent, and Cuban art.

Marble Mountain

Atlantic Canada's biggest and best winter resort has 37 ski runs on hills that rise steeply from the Humber River just north of Corner Brook, Newfoundland. Trails cater to both skiers and snowboarders of all abilities, and there are lessons and daycare available for kids. At day's end, the whole family can retire to the magnificent post-and-beam day lodge.

Your next STEP

TOP PICKS
ADVENTURE
CULTURE & HISTORY
NATURE'S GRANDEUR
EVENTS & FESTIVALS
QUIRKY CANADA
REJUVENATE

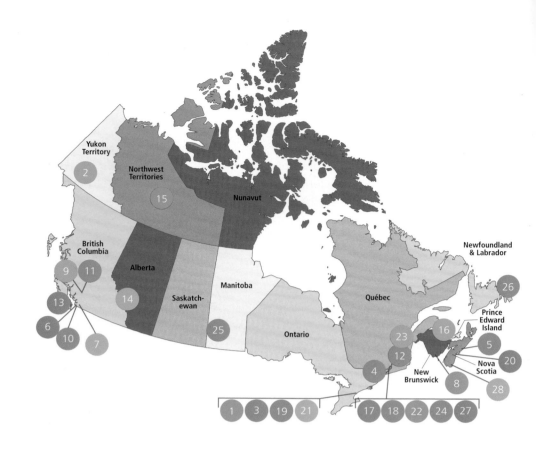

WEEK 1

1. TORONTO, ONT.
AGO and ROM
www.ago.net, www.rom.on.ca

2. WHITEHORSE, Y.T.
Learn to dogsled
www.muktuk.com

3. TORONTO, ONT.
Nathan Philips Square skating
www.toronto.ca

4. OTTAWA, ONT.
The Canadian Museum of Nature
www.nature.ca

5. HALIFAX, N.S.
Halifax Explosion Memorial Concert
www.halifaxexplosion.org

6. VANCOUVER, B.C.
Bloedel Floral Conservatory
www.vancouver.ca/parks/parks/
bloedel/index.htm

7. BURNABY, B.C.
B.C.'s biggest mall
www.metropolisatmetrotown.com

WEEK 2

8. SAINT ANDREWS, N.B.
Small-town Christmas
www.townofstandrews.ca

9. WHISTLER, B.C.
Discover Biathlon program
www.whistlerolympicpark.com

10. VANCOUVER, B.C.
Emily Carr's art
www.emilycarr.ca

11. WHISTLER, B.C.
Peak 2 Peak Gondola
www.whistlerblackcomb.com

12. QUÉBEC CITY, QUE.
Salon des Artisans
www.salondesartisans.com

13. VICTORIA, B.C.
Miniature World
www.miniatureworld.com

14. BANFF, ALTA.
The Grizzly House restaurant
www.banffgrizzlyhouse.com

WEEK 3

15. YELLOWKNIFE, N.W.T.
Northern lights–watching
www.spectacularnwt.com

16. KOUCHIBOUGUAC NATIONAL
PARK, N.B.
Snowshoeing
www.pc.gc.ca/eng/pn-np/nb
/kouchibouguac/activ/hiver-
winter.aspx

17. MONTRÉAL, QUE.
Christmas Mass at Notre-Dame
Basilica
www.notredamebasilica.ca/en

18. MONTRÉAL, QUE.
Montréal Botanical Garden
www.ville.montreal.qc.ca/jardin

19. TORONTO, ONT.
Toronto Symphony Orchestra's
Messiah
www.tso.ca

20. MAHONE BAY, N.S.
Father Christmas figures
www.mahonebay.com

21. TORONTO, ONT.
Toronto Christmas Market
www.torontochristmasmarket.com

WEEK 4

22. MONTRÉAL, QUE.
New Year's Eve nightlife
www.lesfeeriesduvieuxmontreal.info

23. CHARLEVOIX, QUE.
Hut-to-hut backcountry skiing
www.traverseedecharlevoix.qc.ca

24. MONTRÉAL, QUE.
Old Montréal Forum
www.forumpepsi.com

25. RIDING MOUNTAIN NATIONAL PARK,
MAN.
Wilderness snowshoeing
www.earthrhythms.ca

26. ST. JOHN'S, NFLD.
Ringing in the new year first
www.stjohns.ca/visitors/index.jsp

27. MONTRÉAL, QUE.
Montréal's best poutine
www.restolabanquise.com

28. WEST PUBNICO, N.S.
Rappie pie
www.deonsrappiepie.com

index

NOTE: The following abbreviations have been used in the index:
NHS: National Historic Site; NP: National Park; PP: Provincial Park.

photo credits

p 1: © Dave Jack; p 2: © Tremblant Resort Association; p 3: © Tremblant Resort Association; p 4: © Cliff Lemire On Site Photos; p 5: © Ryan Creary/All Canada Photos; p 6: © Dave McMahon; p 8: © Wine Country Ontario; p 9: © Wine Country Ontario; p 10: 2011 Adam Cornick (Acorn Art & Photography); p 12: © Miguel Legault; p 13: © Matthew Gates Ross Farm Museum; p 14: © Ottawa Tourism; p 15: © National Capital Commission; p 16: © W.L. McKinnon; p 17: © Ann Cutting; p 18: © Andrew Klaver Photography; p 19: © Ken Ross/Viestiphoto.com; p 20: © Lucidio Studio, Inc./Alamy/All Canada Photos; p 21: © B&Y Photography/ Alamy/All Canada Photos; p 22: © Dave Jack; p 24: © Photo courtesy of the Tunnels of Moose Jaw; p 25: © Keri Coles; p 27: © Wayne Lynch / All Canada Photos; p 28: © Carnaval de Québec; p 29: © Carnaval de Québec ; p 30: © Montreal Biodome; p 31: © Photo courtesy of Michael Kusugak and Annick Press; p 32: © Elimitchell/Dreamstime.com; p 33: © Explore the Bruce; p 34: © Brian Smith/ World Pond Hockey Championships Inc.; p 35: © Brian Smith/World Pond Hockey Championships Inc.; p 36: © Les amis de la montagne; p 38: © Montreal Fashion Week Photo: jimmyhamelin.com; p 39: © Rick Collins (http://www.rickcollinsphotography.com); p 40: © Jon Wick; p 41: © Jon Wick; p 42: © Marty Mascarin/Fort William Historical Park; p 43: © Photo courtesy of Aventurex; p 44: © Baker Creek Chalets & Bistro; p 46: © FestivalMontréalenLumière/Francois Pesant; p 47: © FestivalMontréalenLumière/ Victor Diaz Lamich; p 48: © Winsport Canada; p 49: © steve bly/Alamy/All Canada Photos; p 50: © Yukon Sourdough Rendezvous Festival; p 53: © Henry Georgi/All Canada Photos; p 54: © Lee Thomas/Alamy/All Canada Photos; p 55: © Photo courtesy of James Malone; p 56: © Photo courtesy of Ionut Popa/www.travelue.com; p 58: © Scandinave Spa Mont-Tremblant; p 59: © Xavier Dachez (Xdachez.com); p 60: © Wickaninnish Inn; p 61: © Wickaninnish Inn; p 62: © Mike Gere Photography/Robson Helimagic, Valemount British Columbia; p 64: © Geoff S. Brooks; p 65: © Jason Simpson; p 66: © Derek Lepper/www.dereklepper.com; p 67: © Derek Lepper/ www.dereklepper.com; p 68: © Drew Hadley/Alamy/All Canada Photos; p 69: © Meeno; p 70: © balazsgardi.com/Red Bull Content Pool; p 71: © Red Stag Tavern, Halifax, NS; p 72: © icpix_can/Alamy/All Canada Photos; p 73: © Roderick Chen/All Canada Photos; p 74: © The Butchart Gardens Ltd.; p 75: © Peter Magil; p 76: © Photo courtesy of David Niddrie; p 79: © jeremykoreski.com; p 80: © AP Photo/The Canadian Press, Paul Chiasson; p 81: © AP Photo/The Canadian Press, Paul Chiasson; p 82: © Legislative Assembly of Nunavut; p 84: © Train Station Inn; p 85: © Sarah Caufield; p 86: © Fred Lemire; p 87: © Wolfgang Kaehler; p 88: © jeremykoreski.com; p 90: © Henry Georgi/All Canada Photos; p 91: © Daniel Jolly; p 92: © Rick Horne (Flickr - RR Horne); p 93: © The Vancouver Sun; p 94: © K. Teed/Nitobe Memorial Garden; p 95: © Jordan Manley, Great Canadian Heli-Skiing; p 96: © Town of Nackawic; p 97: © Photo courtesy of Canadian Broadcasting Corporation; p 98: © Dan Hudson photo; p 99: © Dan Hudson photo; p 100: Robert Cocquyt/Dreamstime.com; p 101: © Sylvain Pineault/Dreamstime.com; p 102: © Tibor Bognar/Alamy/ All Canada Photos; p 105: © www.oceanadventures.bc.ca; p 106: © Rolf Hicker/All Canada Photos; p 107: © Don Weixl/All Canada Photos; p 108: © Myriadstars/Dreamstime.com; p 109: © Photo courtesy of Laurent Lecordier; p 110: © Dolores Breau MPA; p 112: © Geraint Wyn Davies as King Arthur in Camelot. Photography by David Hou.; p 113: © Tom Patterson Island, Avon River, Photo by Andy Foster, 2005.; p 114: © Derek Lepper/www.dereklepper.com; p 115: © Photo courtesy of Jeff Nash - Hockey Canada; p 116: © Ron Hay; p 117: © Rocky Mountaineer; p 118: © Courtesy of Salt Spring Island Parks and Recreation; p 119: © Josh McCulloch/ All Canada Photos; p 120: © VanHorn.co/Jazmin Million; p 121: © www.oceanadventures.bc.ca; p 122: © Miguel Legault; p 123: © John E Marriott/All Canada Photos; p 124: © Brewster Travel Canada; p 126: © Fairmont Hotels & Resorts; p 127: © Maid of the Mist; p 128: © Alan Norsworthy - Photographer; p 131: © Shelter Lee; p 132: © Andrew Hempstead; p 133: © Fremte/http://commons.wikimedia.org/wiki/File:Grewowls_cabin_ajawaan_lake.jpg; p 134: © Chilliwack River Rafting Adventures (via Kevin Kimmett); p 135: © Cappi Thompson; p 136: © Gaétan Fontaine; p 138: © Photo courtesy of destinationlabrador.com; p 139: © Rolf Hicker/All Canada Photos; p 140: © Chris Harris/All Canada Photos; p 142: © Clayoquot Wilderness Resort Ltd.; p 143: © Luminato; p 144: © Photo courtesy of BC Provincial Capital Commission; p 145: © Photo courtesy of BC Provincial Capital Commission; p 146: © Claire Jullien as Candida Morell in Candida. Photo by Emily Cooper; p 147: © www.trail-rides.ca; p 148: © Arthur D. Chapman; p 149: © Jeremy Adshade; p 150: © Steve Mandamadiotis/Dreamstime.com; p 151: © Festival International de Jazz de Montréal/Jean-François Leblanc; p 152: © Yuan Dong; p 154: © danharperphotography.com; p 155: © Kevin Wolfe; p 157: © John E Marriott/All Canada Photos; p 158: © National Capital Commission; p 159: © National Capital Commission; p 160: © Robert Ciavarro; p 161: © Fallsview/Dreamstime.com; p 162: © Hussein Abdallah; p 164: © Mike Ridewood;

p 165: © Chris Bolin; p 166: © canadabrian/ Alamy/All Canada Photos; p 167: © Clayoquot Wilderness Resort Ltd.;
p 168: © Eric Myre/(Juste Pour Rire 2010); p 170: © Terry A. Parker/All Canada Photos; p 171: © Gierszep/http://commons.wikimedia.org/
wiki/File:Nahanni_-_VirginiaFalls.jpg; p 172: © Nayan Sthankiya; p 173: © Stefan Reicheneder/http://commons.wikimedia.org/
wiki/File:Gros_Morne_NP_westernbrookpond3.jpg; p 174: © Paul Horsley/All Canada Photos; p 175: © Sarah Race;
p 176: © bayoffundytourism.com; p 177: © bayoffundytourism.com; p 178: © Terry Halifax - woman pictured is Margarat Vittrekura;
p 180: © Laura Stöber; p 181: © Fairmont Hotels & Resorts; p 183: © J.A. Kraulis/All Canada Photos; p 184: © HP Canada/Alamy/All
Canada Photos; p 185: © Darek Nakonieczny, NL sportphoto.com; p 186: © Chris Cheadle/All Canada Photos; p 187: © Serena Ovens;
p 188: © David Craig/http://commons.wikimedia.org/wiki/File:Caribana2.jpg; p 189: © Photo: Linda M. Goodman, Gimli, Manitoba;
p 190: © Robert Postma/All Canada Photos; p 191: © Robert Postma/All Canada Photos; p 192: © Mike Macri/Sea North Tours;
p 193: © Scott Baltjes; p 194: © Courtesy Nk'Mip Cellars. 'Keepsake Photography'; p 196: © Km2008/Dreamstime.com;
p 197: © Paul Madden/All Canada Photos; p 198: © Ully Bliel/ullybleil.ca; p 199: © J.A. Kraulis/All Canada Photos; p 200: © Remington
Carriage Museum; p 202: © Rolf Hicker/All Canada Photos; p 203: © Naturfoto-Online/Alamy/All Canada Photos; p 204: © Rolf Hicker/
All Canada Photos; p 205: © O'Brien's Boat Tours, Bay Bulls, NL; p 206: © Photo courtesy of the Pacific National Exhibition;
p 209: © Photo courtesy of the Wine Country Ontario; p 210: © George Pimentel/WireImage for TIFF; p 211: © Vito Amati/WireImage
for TIFF; p 212: © Spirit Bear Lodge/Doug Neasloss; p 214: © dawsoncity.ca; p 215: © Photo courtesy of the Wine Country Ontario;
p 216: © Golf PEI; p 217: © Golf PEI; p 218: © All Canada Photos; p 220: © Atlantic Balloon Fiesta, www.AtlanticBalloonFiesta.ca;
p 221: © Facility Marketing Group Inc./Manitoba Dragon Boat Festival. Photo: www.davemcknight.com; p 222: © The Terry Fox
Foundation; p 223: © Josh Vine/Dreamstime.com; p 224: © Image Courtesy of Queen West Art Crawl; p 225: © Photo courtesy of CN/
Algoma Central Railway; p 226: © Ken Paul/All Canada Photos; p 227: © Kristin Skibsrud Ross; p 228: © John Sylvester/All Canada
Photos; p 229: © Photawa/Dreamstime.com; p 230: © The Grotto by Adam Walker; p 231: © John Sylvester/All Canada Photos;
p 232: © Drew Stewart; p 235: © Sergey Uryadnikov/Dreamstime.com; p 236: © Francois Lacasse/Getty Images; p 237: © Jeff
Vinnick/Getty Images; p 238: © Photo: Denis Tremblay, Source: www.old.montreal.qc.ca; p 239: © Brenda Falvey/Parks Canada;
p 240: © Paul Mckinnon/Dreamstime.com; p 242: © novascotia.com; p 243: © novascotia.com; p 244: © Madpix, www.ripplefitness.ca;
p 245: © City of Toronto; p 246: © Kelly Mercer; p 248: © readings.org; p 249: © readings.org; p 250: © Alain Carpentier;
p 251: © www.STWM.ca; p 252: © Tawfik Mohammed; p 253: © Photo courtesy of Fred Penner; p 254: © Sergey Uryadnikov/
Dreamstime.com; p 255: © Rolf Hicker/All Canada Photos; p 256: © Don Weixl/All Canada Photos;p 257: © Greig Reekie Photography;
p 258: © John Sylvester/All Canada Photos; p 261: © Noel Hendrikson/Vancouver Aquarium; p 262: © Fairmont Hotels & Resorts;
p 263: © Fairmont Hotels & Resorts; p 264: © Photograph by Jaden Nyberg; p 266: © Photo courtesy of LHotel Montreal;
p 267: © The Banff Centre; p 268: © Patrick Cardinal; p 269: © Shawn Taylor/Alamy/All Canada Photos; p 270: © Vismax/Dreamstime.com;
p 271: © Paul Joseph; p 272: © Michelle Dunn; p 273: © Steve Li; p 274: © Richard Picton; p 275: © Retina2020/Dreamstime.com;
p 276: © Parks Canada; p 277: © NoelHendrikson/Vancouver Aquarium; p 278: © West Edmonton Mall; p 280: © Grouse Mountain
Resort; p 281: © Photo: J. J. Koeman, Location: Cypress Mountain; p 282: © Nikola Bilic/Alamy/All Canada Photos; p 284: © 2011
Bata Shoe Museum, Toronto, Canada (photo: Philip Castleton); p 285: © Photo courtesy of Fourquet Fourchette Restaurants;
p 287: © Steve Shuey/Alamy/All Canada Photos; p 288: © Royal Ontario Museum, 2011; p 289: © Kathy deWitt/Alamy/All Canada
Photos; p 290: © Barrett & MacKay/All Canada Photos; p 292: © Alex Downie; p 293: © A Christmas display at Metropolis
at Metrotown, British Columbia's largest shopping centre; p 294: © Cindy Kohler; p 295: © Photo courtesy of Cindy Kohler;
p 296: © Paul Morrison; p 297: © Emily Carr, Kwakiutl House, 1912, oil on card, Collection of the Vancouver Art Gallery, Emily Carr
Trust; p 298: © Photo courtesy of Tom Carmony; p 299: © S. Corsi, RV International; p 300: © Robert Postma/All Canada Photos;
p 301: © Aurora Village; p 302: © Sonicyan/Dreamstime.com; p 304: © Mclellan Group; p 305: © Gilbert van Ryckevorsel of Sub
Sea Deco Arts; p 306: © dbimages/Alamy/All Canada Photos; p 307: © VanHorn.co/Jazmin Million; p 308: © Tourisme Charlevoix,
Jean-Fancois Bergeron; p 309: © Celes Davar; p 310: © Photo courtesy of Le Village historique acadien de la Nouvelle-Écosse

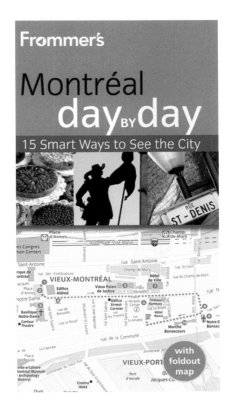
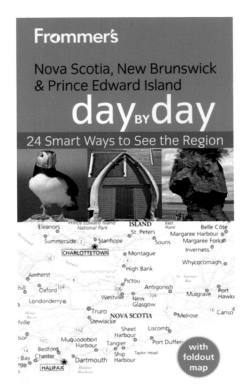
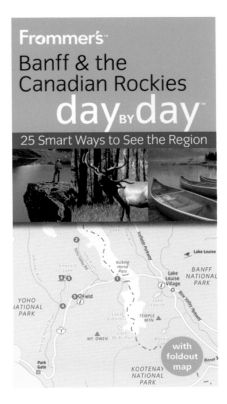
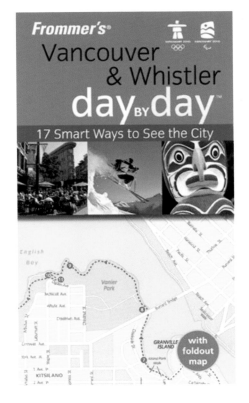

Also available from Frommer's™

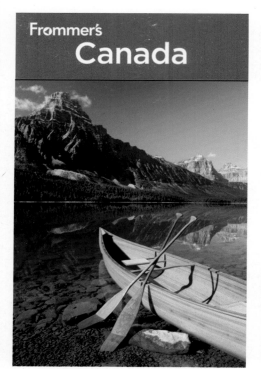

Frommer's
Canada

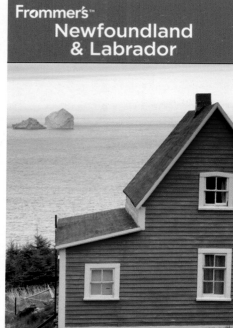

Frommer's™
Newfoundland
& Labrador

Frommer's
Ottawa

Frommer's
Alberta

Frommer's™
Niagara Region

Frommer's
Vancouver & Victoria 2011

Free Pocket MAP